AF793067

Workplace Investigations

OXFORD LABOUR LAW

General Editors: Alan Bogg, Professor of Labour Law at University of Bristol Law School; A. C. L. Davies, Dean of the Oxford Law Faculty; Keith Ewing, Professor of Public Law at King's College London; and Mark Freedland, Emeritus Research Fellow in Law at St John's College and Emeritus Professor of Employment Law in the University of Oxford.

The *Oxford Labour Law* series (formerly known as the *Oxford Monographs on Labour Law* series) has come to represent a significant contribution to the literature of British, European, and international labour law. The series recognizes the arrival not only of a renewed interest in labour law generally, but also the need for fresh approaches to the study of labour law following a period of momentous change in the UK and Europe. The series is concerned with all aspects of labour law, including traditional subjects of study such as collective labour law and individual employment law. It also includes works that concentrate on the growing role of human rights and the combating of discrimination in employment, and others that examine the law and economics of the labour market and the impact of social security law and of national and supranational employment policies upon patterns of employment and the employment contract. Two of the contributing authors to the series, Lucy Vickers and Diamond Ashiagbor, have received awards from the Society of Legal Scholars in respect of their books.

Also Available in the Series

Shaping Contracts for Work
The Normative Influence of Terms Implied by Law
GABRIELLE GOLDING

Human Rights Due Diligence and Labour Governance
INGRID LANDAU

Catholic Social Teaching and Labour Law
An Ethical Perspective on Work
MARK BELL

Structural Injustice and Workers' Rights
VIRGINIA MANTOUVALOU

Reforming Age Discrimination Law
Beyond Individual Enforcement
ALYSIA BLACKHAM

Putting Human Rights to Work
Labour Law, the ECHR, and the Employment Relation
PHILIPPA COLLINS

Strike Ballots, Democracy, and Law
BREEN CREIGHTON, CATRINA DENVIR, RICHARD JOHNSTONE, SHAE MCCRYSTAL, ALICE ORCHISTON

Living Wage
Regulatory Solutions to Informal and Precarious Work in Global Supply Chains
SHELLEY MARSHALL

A Purposive Approach to Labour Law
GUY DAVIDOV

Workplace Investigations

Justice and the Legal Regulation of Employer Conduct

ADRIANA ORIFICI

Senior Lecturer, Department of Business Law and Taxation, Monash University, Melbourne, Australia

OXFORD
UNIVERSITY PRESS

OXFORD
UNIVERSITY PRESS

Great Clarendon Street, Oxford, OX2 6DP,
United Kingdom

Oxford University Press is a department of the University of Oxford.
It furthers the University's objective of excellence in research, scholarship,
and education by publishing worldwide. Oxford is a registered trade mark of
Oxford University Press in the UK and in certain other countries.

© Adriana Orifici 2026

The moral rights of the author have been asserted.

All rights reserved. No part of this publication may be reproduced, stored in a retrieval system, transmitted, used for text and data mining, or used for training artificial intelligence, in any form or by any means, without the prior permission in writing of Oxford University Press, or as expressly permitted by law, by licence or under terms agreed with the appropriate reprographics rights organization. Enquiries concerning reproduction outside the scope of the above should be sent to the Rights Department, Oxford University Press, at the address above.

You must not circulate this work in any other form
and you must impose this same condition on any acquirer.

Public sector information reproduced under Open Government Licence v3.0
(https://www.nationalarchives.gov.uk/doc/open-government-licence/)

Published in the United States of America by Oxford University Press
198 Madison Avenue, New York, NY 10016, United States of America.

British Library Cataloguing in Publication Data
Data available

Library of Congress Control Number: 2026936042

ISBN 9780198969990

DOI: 10.1093/9780198970019.001.0001

Printed and bound by
CPI Group (UK) Ltd., Croydon, CR0 4YY

The manufacturer's authorized representative in the EU for product safety is
Oxford University Press España S.A. of Parque Empresarial San Fernando de Henares,
Avenida de Castilla, 2 – 28830 Madrid (www.oup.es/en or product.safety@oup.com).
OUP España S.A. also acts as importer into Spain of products made by the manufacturer.

MIX
Paper | Supporting
responsible forestry
FSC® C013604
FSC
www.fsc.org

For Adrian

General Editors' Preface

For many workers, the 'employer' is not a person but a complex organizational entity involving a web of relationships with co-workers, supervisors, external contractors, customers, and service users. It is also not merely the place where we go to work. Employing organizations sometimes operate like mini-states. They wield significant coercive powers over workers with finely tuned mechanisms of disciplinary control. As collectivism has declined in many countries, the regulatory gap has been filled by a new cadre of specialists in Human Resource Management (HRM). While HRM partners are often charged with the stewardship of employee well-being, they are indisputably an instrument of management. In terms of the workplace constitution, HRM often blends functions of the executive, judiciary, and the formulation and enactment of workplace rules. This belies any notion that there might be a separation of powers in the post-collectivist workplace.

In this important new monograph, Dr Adriana Orifici examines the role and functions of the workplace investigation in the governance of modern firms. The workplace investigation performs a multiplicity of goals. It ensures that the employer complies with its workplace duties in ensuring a safe and healthy working environment. It is both a disciplinary mechanism for addressing wrongdoing and a way of ensuring due process for workers accused of serious misconduct. It also provides a tool for ensuring managerial supervision and control, exercised rationally in the interests of the firm and its shareholders. The adjustment of these sometimes-conflicting goals is mediated by HRM. Dr Orifici explores the interactions between statute law, judicial decisions, and the localized 'law' of the workplace in the development of workplace investigations.

This is an ambitious and original work. Dr Orifici blends normative and doctrinal methods to provide a compelling reconstructive critique of the law of workplace investigations. This is based around the ideal of citizenship at work. Citizenship demands a measure of respect for dignity and autonomy. This requires justice in the regulation of workplace investigations, just as citizens in the polity are entitled to basic requirements of due process. It is a vital topic, and Dr Orifici offers a compelling vision. We are very pleased to welcome this monograph into the series.

ALB/ACLD/KDE/MRF

Acknowledgements

This book draws on my doctoral research, and I gratefully acknowledge that it was supported by a Melbourne Research Scholarship and an Australian Government Research Training Scholarship.

This research benefited immensely from the generous support and feedback provided by my doctoral supervisors, Beth Gaze and Anna Chapman, and comments on draft chapters provided by Ingrid Landau and Jill Murray. I gratefully acknowledge the invaluable advice and assistance provided by Helen Anderson, Chris Arup, Richard Mitchell, and Tim Lindsey during this project. I am also grateful to my two doctoral examiners for their helpful feedback.

I acknowledge John Tobin who taught me, many years ago, how legal research can achieve real-world impact, and the mentorship of Ross Jackson, Bruce Moore, and Lindy Richardson, who each supported the start of my career in the field of labour law.

I am also forever grateful to my friend and mentor Kobi Liens for her support and advice during this project, and to Michael McIver for helpful discussions about the subject of workplace investigations and the law.

Thank you to my colleagues and friends in the Department of Business Law and Taxation at Monash University. I would like to particularly thank John Bevacqua, Carolyn Sutherland, and Michelle Welsh, as I could not have completed this work without their support, and Catrina Denvir and Andrew Moshirnia for timely encouragement and advice. I also acknowledge excellent referencing support provided by research assistant Brandon Pergolini.

Aspects of chapters 4 and 5 build on my articles 'Unsystematic and Unsettled: A Map of the Legal Dimensions of Workplace Investigations in Australia', which was published in (2019) 42(3) University of New South Wales Law Journal 1075, and 'Reframing *Addis*: A Clarification of the Law of Damages for Psychiatric Injury in Dismissal in *Elisha v Vision Australia Ltd*', which was published in (2025) 38(3) Australian Journal of Labour Law 1, and I am grateful to the editors of these journals and anonymous referees for their helpful feedback on these papers.

I would also like to express my sincere gratitude to the OUP Series Editors Alan Bogg, Anne Davies, Keith Ewing, and Mark Freedland for supporting the publication of my work in the series. I am also grateful to the two anonymous referees who provided comments on the draft manuscript and proposal. I benefitted greatly from their feedback.

Over many years, friends and family have sustained me while I have worked on this project. To my friends Claire Bongiorno, Romina Calabro, Sharron Clark, Ashli Ellis, Alessandra Giacomello, Vera Lund, Antoinette Marshall, Susanna Moore, Kate O'Connor, Sara Summerbell, Maria Azzurra Tranfaglia, and Marija Vukovic, I am forever grateful.

I was buoyed by the love of my grandmother, Olga Abate, while I worked on this research, and I regret that she did not live to see it published. I could not have completed this book without the kindness and support of my parents, Umberto and Yvonne Abate, or my family, Luca and Emma Abate, Loretta and Tania Black, and Cirino and Rita Orifici.

To Adrian, Rafael, and Claudia, thank you for your unwavering support, positivity, and love. Adrian, thank you for everything. Rafael and Claudia, thank you for being so patient and enthusiastic while I worked on this project. I hope that you read this book one day, and it encourages you to approach the world of work with curiosity and ask questions about fairness and justice.

Contents

Table of Cases

AUSTRALIA

UNITED KINGDOM

Table of Legislation

COMMONWEALTH

Statutes

Statutory Instruments

Other Rules

AUSTRALIAN CAPITAL TERRITORY

Statutes

Other Rules

NEW SOUTH WALES

Statutes

Statutory Instruments

NORTHERN TERRITORY

Statutes

Statutory Instruments

QUEENSLAND

Statutes

Abbreviations

AHRC	Australian Human Rights Commission
AIER	Australian Institute of Employment Rights
FCA	Federal Court of Australia
FW Act	Fair Work Act 2009 (Cth)
FWC	Fair Work Commission
HCA	High Court of Australia
NES	National Employment Standards under the *FW Act*
PCBU	Person conducting a business or undertaking
WHS	Work health and safety

1
Introduction
The Emerging Legal Challenge of Employer Conduct in Workplace Investigations

I Introduction

Workplace investigations are significant and widespread processes in Australian workplaces.[1] Employers are increasingly deploying these processes as part of responding to potential misconduct by employees (called 'respondents' in this monograph). Employers use workplace investigations to inquire into a wide range of matters from suspected bullying and sexual harassment,[2] to potential breaches of internal policies and codes of conduct.[3] Media reports discuss how employers use workplace investigations to respond to suspicions of worker misconduct,[4] and parliamentary reports recognize that workplace investigations are an important tool that employers use to respond to concerning workplace behaviours.[5]

In this study, I examine the law in Australia that applies to employer conduct towards respondents in workplace investigations and normatively evaluate how the law should be reformed to promote justice for respondents. I employ doctrinal and empirical legal research methods to conduct this examination. I draw on philosophical scholarship about work law to conceptualize a framework of justice for respondents that builds on the *Charter* and includes nine elements.[6] I reflect on the legal,

[1] Leonie Green, 'The Who, What and How of Workplace Investigations' (2018) Australasian Law Management Journal 1, 1; Melinda Rollinson, 'Call in the Experts' *The Sydney Morning Herald* (27 September 2018) <https://www.smh.com.au/business/workplace/call-in-the-experts-20180927-p506hp.html> accessed 9 July 2025.

[2] See, eg, Jordan Baker and Calum Jaspan, 'Nine Investigates Complaints as Staff Voice Anger at Response to Workplace Report' *The Age* (18 October 2024) <https://www.theage.com.au/national/nine-staff-furious-at-response-to-gut-wrenching-devastating-report-20241018-p5kjgk.html> accessed 9 July 2025.

[3] See, eg, Phillip Thomson, 'Public Servant's Joke Gone Wrong: Code of Conduct Investigation after Staff Member Pulls a Knife' *The Age* (26 February 2016) <https://www.theage.com.au/public-service/public-servants-joke-gone-wrong-code-of-conduct-investigation-after-staff-member-pulls-a-knife-20160223-gn1cjl.html> accessed 9 July 2025.

[4] See, eg, Angus Thomson, '"It Was Hell": Former Sydney Hospital Doctor Speaks Out' *The Sydney Morning Herald* (5 July 2023) <https://www.smh.com.au/national/nsw/it-was-hell-former-sydney-hospital-doctor-speaks-out-20230704-p5dll4.html> accessed 9 July 2025.

[5] House of Representatives Standing Committee on Education and Employment, Parliament of Australia, 'Workplace Bullying: We Just Want It to Stop' (Final Report 2012) 80–96; AHRC, 'Respect@Work: Sexual Harassment National Inquiry Report' (Final Report 2020) 35, 704–05.

[6] Mordy Bromberg and Mark Irving (eds), *Australian Charter of Employment Rights* (Hardie Grant Books 2007).

Workplace Investigations. Adriana Orifici, Oxford University Press. © Adriana Orifici 2026.
DOI: 10.1093/9780198970019.003.0001

philosophical, and empirical strands of analysis and put forward an agenda of law reform to further justice for respondents in workplace investigations.

This chapter introduces the monograph. I explain how workplace investigations have emerged as a prominent HRM tool. I canvass why it is important to scrutinize these underexamined processes from a legal perspective, and how and why the case study of Australia is instructive for comparable jurisdictions, such as the United Kingdom and Canada. I put forward the theoretical framework and method, and provide an overview of the chapters.

II The Rise of the HRM Phenomenon of Workplace Investigations

There is much at stake for all parties involved in workplace investigations into suspected employee misconduct. The employer must navigate legal risks that arise from undertaking (or deciding not to undertake) a workplace investigation,[7] reputational risk and potential criticism by a court or regulator where a workplace investigation process is conducted poorly (or not at all),[8] organizational risks such as that an investigation will destroy workplace morale, harmony, and productivity,[9] and commercial risks including that a workplace investigation could be costly and/or time consuming,[10] or that a worker is highly valued and will resign if the employer raises allegations of misconduct.

The stakes are no less significant for workers who make complaints or provide witness accounts during workplace investigations. Complainants and witnesses may fear victimization for speaking out, or retaliation from the worker accused of misconduct.[11] Recounting traumatic incidents to managers or investigators can be distressing and confronting.[12] There is a risk that a workplace investigation will result in mental harm to these workers.[13]

Much is also at risk for the worker accused of misconduct who is known as the respondent.[14] A respondent faces losing their job at the end of an investigation. Respondents in workplace investigations must also deal with the risk that their

[7] See, eg, Grevis Beard and Rose Bryant-Smith, 'Delay Workplace Investigations at Your Peril' (2008) 82 Law Institute Journal 40, 40; Katie Gardiner and Elaine Acaro, 'Overview of Workplace Investigations in Australia' (2021) 164 Precedent 22, 22–24.

[8] See, eg, Charlotte Grieve, 'AMP Reels from Scandal amid Calls for Scrutiny of Workplace Investigations' *The Age* (25 August 2020) <https://www.theage.com.au/business/banking-and-finance/amp-reels-from-scandal-amid-calls-for-scrutiny-of-workplace-investigations-20200825-p55p6d.html> accessed 9 July 2025.

[9] See, eg, House of Representatives Standing Committee on Education and Employment, Parliament of Australia (n 5) 85.

[10] See, eg, Green (n 1) 1; James Mattson and Mark Paul, 'Workplace Investigations: Time to Reform Our Thinking?' (Australian Labour Law Association Conference, Melbourne, Australia, 4 November 2016) 2.

[11] Gardiner and Acaro (n 7) 23.

[12] See, eg, AHRC (n 5) 686–87.

[13] See, eg, Nicholas Ellery and others, 'Mental Health and Workplace Investigations: What Are Your Obligations?' (2018) 70 Governance Directions 82, 82.

[14] See, eg, Patrick Turner, 'Workplace Investigations: Being the Respondent in a Workplace Complaint' (*Maurice Blackburn*) <https://www.mauriceblackburn.com.au/blog/employment-issues/being-respondent-in-a-workplace-complaint/> accessed 9 July 2025.

professional standing and reputation will be damaged during the investigation process.[15] The time, effort, and emotional strain required to respond to allegations can detrimentally affect respondents' productivity, work performance, and lives outside of work.[16] Like complainants and witnesses, respondents in workplace investigations can experience stress and harm to their mental health.[17]

Despite the widespread use of workplace investigations and the high stakes for all parties, legal scholars rarely discuss how employers conduct workplace investigations, nor do they consider matters that commonly cause conflict or controversy. Legal scholarship fails to problematize the legal regulation of workplace investigations or consider employer practices from the perspective of the law.

Academic literature lacks a sustained and in-depth examination of the legal regulation of workplace investigations.[18] Few scholars have critically or normatively analysed the legal regulation of employer conduct during these processes,[19] and the field is barely recognized in legal scholarship. Texts that examine workplace investigations written by legal scholars tend to focus on specific court decisions,[20] or on how employers use workplace investigations to address complaints of bullying or sexual harassment,[21]

[15] AHRC (n 5) 279.

[16] Giri Sivaraman, 'Poor Workplace Investigations Can Leave Path of Destruction' *Brisbane Times* (7 February 2017) <https://www.brisbanetimes.com.au/business/workplace/poor-workplace-investigations-can-leave-path-of-destruction-20170207-gu7kmo.html> accessed 9 July 2025; AHRC (n 5) 279.

[17] Ellery and others (n 13) 82.

[18] Both in Australia and the United Kingdom, some scholarship about work regulation discusses workplace investigations but considers the subject as part of examining disciplinary action or broader issues about the contract of employment. See, eg, Douglas Brodie and Joellen Riley, 'A Duty of Good Management? Protected Interests and the Employment Contract' (2019) 50 Victoria University of Wellington Law Review 303; Peter Holland, 'Drug Testing in the Australian Workplace: Still a Contested Terrain' (2016) 58 Journal of Industrial Relations 688; Hugh Collins, 'Constructive Dismissal and the West Lothian Question: Aberdeen City Council v McNeill' (2011) 40 Industrial Law Journal 439; Lizzie Barmes, 'The Continuing Conceptual Crisis in the Common Law of the Contract of Employment' (2004) 67 Modern Law Review 435. Scholarship about regulation and compliance also considers workplace investigations as a tool of corporate compliance, see further Klaus J Hopt, 'Internal Investigations, Whistleblowing and External Monitoring, Comparative Experiences, Economic Insights, Findings from Corporate Practice' (2021) Law Working Paper N° 574/2021 <https://www.ssrn.com/abstract=3812497> accessed 9 July 2025.

[19] For a preliminary map, see Adriana Orifici, 'Unsystematic and Unsettled: A Map of the Legal Dimensions of Workplace Investigations in Australia' (2019) 42 University of New South Wales Law Journal 1075. For scholarship that addresses specific issues, see further eg, Andrew Eastwood and Mark Smyth, 'Internal Investigations and Privilege: A Response to Recent Challenges' (2018) 33 Australian Journal of Corporate Law 3; Allison Ballard and Patricia Easteal, 'Procedural Fairness in Workplace Investigations: Potential Flaws and Proposals for Change' (2018) 43 Alternative Law Journal 177; Richard Naughton, 'Termination of Employment and Workplace Investigations' (2016) 22 Employment Law Bulletin 186; Natalie Williams, '*Bartlett v Australia & New Zealand Banking Group Ltd* [2016] NSWCA 30 (7 March 2016)' (2016) 37 Adelaide Law Review 571.

[20] Naughton (n 19); Williams (n 19); Michael Byrnes and Julian Arndt, 'Major Court and Tribunal Decisions in Australia in 2013' (2014) 56 Journal of Industrial Relations 365, 374–75. On conflicts of interest, see, eg, Chris Molnar, 'Apprehended Conflicts of Interest in Employment Investigations and Decision-Making' (2015) 21 Employment Law Bulletin 91. See also shorter examinations of case law in Ellery and others (n 13); Michael Baldwin and Claudia Lewin, 'High Court to Determine Employer's Duties During Workplace Investigations' (2017) 21 Inhouse Counsel 222. Textbooks on work regulation also briefly refer to relevant cases see, eg, Carolyn Sappideen, Paul O'Grady, and Joellen Riley, *Macken's Law of Employment* (9th edn, Thomson Reuters 2022) [5.240], [6.200], [8.120].

[21] Allison Ballard, 'In the Shadow of the Law: The Silence of Workplace Abuse' (PhD thesis, University of Canberra 2019); Therese MacDermott, 'Managing Individual Workplace Grievances and Disciplinary Procedures' (2002) Australian Centre for Industrial Relations Research and Training Working Paper 80;

or on misconduct within the public sector.[22] Instead, most interest in workplace investigations arises in HRM scholarship.[23]

The absence of critical legal scholarship on workplace investigations is not only apparent in Australia, but in the United Kingdom, New Zealand, and Canada. The lack of academic interest in workplace investigations, particularly among legal scholars, is surprising given that they are commonplace in the public and private sectors in these locations.[24] Two key reasons might account for why these processes have been overlooked in legal scholarship.

The first reason is that the professions, including lawyers, have legitimized workplace investigation processes over time, as organizational responses to the law.[25] The law prescribes a wide range of obligations with which an employee must comply. However, in locations such as Australia, the United Kingdom, New Zealand, and Canada, the law does not often mandate the processes that firms must adopt to determine if an employee has breached a legal obligation.[26] The theory of 'legal endogeneity' suggests that workplace investigations may have become a standard organizational response because these processes have developed an aura of legitimacy.[27] This is reflected in views expressed by Australian courts and tribunals that support organizations' use of workplace investigations in response to suspected employee misconduct.[28] It is also mirrored in ways that professions, including lawyers, propagate the legitimacy of workplace investigations as a tool to respond to suspected misconduct in a manner that minimizes the risk of legal claims.[29]

The legalistic character of many workplace investigations, and the enmeshment of lawyers as advisors and investigators in these processes, is also likely to have contributed to perceptions of legitimacy.[30] However, as Edelman et al note, although professions will 'construct stories about what forms of compliance will minimize interference by legal institutions', the firms that adopt these structures will 'often inject managerial goals into the legal form to make it better fit their objectives'.[31] This

Sam Eichenbaum, 'Employment Policy and Breach of Contract: The Conundrum Continues' (2015) 21 Employment Law Bulletin 14.

[22] See, eg, Max Spry, 'Natural Justice and Public Sector Misconduct Investigations' (2007) 54 Australian Institute of Administrative Law Forum 117; Louise Floyd and others, *Employment, Labour and Industrial Law in Australia* (Cambridge University Press 2018) 276–84.

[23] See, eg, Catherine Burr and Anne Wyatt, 'Investigation of Workplace Bullying and Harassment Complaints' in Premilla D'Cruz and others (eds), *Dignity and Inclusion at Work* (Springer 2021); Moira Jenkins, Helen Winefield, and Aspa Sarris, 'Consequences of Being Accused of Workplace Bullying: An Exploratory Study' (2011) 4 International Journal of Workplace Health Management 33; Glennis M Hanley and Anne O'Rourke, 'The Race without a Finishing Line: Legislative Means for Confronting Bullying in the Australian Workplace' (2016) 54 Asia Pacific Journal of Human Resources 352. See further chapter 2.

[24] See chapter 2.

[25] Lauren B Edelman, Christopher Uggen, and Howard S Erlanger, 'The Endogeneity of Legal Regulation: Grievance Procedures as Rational Myth' (1999) 105 American Journal of Sociology 406.

[26] See chapter 2.

[27] Lauren B Edelman, *Working Law: Courts, Corporations, and Symbolic Civil Rights* (University of Chicago Press 2016) 26.

[28] See, eg, FWC, 'Unfair Dismissals Benchbook' (2025) 112 <https://www.fwc.gov.au/benchbook/unfair-dismissals-benchbook> accessed 15 July 2025.

[29] See, eg, Gardiner and Acaro (n 7) 24. See further chapter 2.

[30] See chapter 2.

[31] Edelman, Uggen, and Erlanger (n 25) 445–46.

perspective explains why workplace investigations have been uncritically regarded by the professions, including lawyers, and why legal scrutiny of these processes is needed. In this monograph, I interrogate the aims and behaviours of employers that conduct workplace investigations and propose reforms to the law that are informed by the empirical context.[32]

The second reason is that workplace investigations are internalized and individualized processes beyond direct legal regulation and so have eluded the scrutiny of labour lawyers. Specifically, workplace investigations emerged as a common tool of HRM at a time when organizations changed significantly, but the focus of work regulation principally remained on the 'unitary' concept of the employer.[33] As Judy Fudge succinctly observed, this conceptual distortion has meant that the 'complex multilateral relationship between people within a work organization is thus equated with a simple bilateral relationship between two individuals', the employer and employee.[34] Experts have recognized that this conceptualization poses a range of problems in the context of the development of more complex employment relationships,[35] but it also distorts understanding of internal processes and relations of power within organizations.[36]

Workplace investigations might appear to be bilateral interactions between the employer as a unitary entity, and a respondent. However, they draw in a variety of employees and agents who exercise power and perform functions on behalf of the employer, including as managers.[37] The employer as a legal person is also a party in the workplace investigation.[38] The conceptualization of the employer as a unitary entity in labour law, and the idea of the employment relationship as personal and bilateral, obscures the complex dimensions and hierarchies of employer power and control that underpin these internal processes. In this monograph, I unveil these tensions and complexities as part of problematizing workplace investigations from a legal perspective.

The rise of workplace investigations as a common tool of HRM has also been enabled by a central shift in labour law from collectivism towards individualization.[39]

32 See chapter 3.

33 Paul Davies and Mark Freedland, 'The Complexities of the Employing Enterprise' in Guy Davidov and Brian A Langille (eds), *Boundaries and Frontiers of Labour Law: Goals and Means in the Regulation of Work* (Bloomsbury 2006) 274.

34 Judy Fudge, 'Fragmenting Work and Fragmenting Organizations: The Contract of Employment and the Scope of Labour Regulation' (2006) 44 Osgoode Hall Law Journal 609, 623.

35 ibid 616.

36 Davies and Freedland (n 33) 280–83.

37 Hugh Collins terms this ongoing control by the employer an exercise of 'bureaucratic power', see Hugh Collins, 'Market Power, Bureaucratic Power, and the Contract of Employment' (1986) 15 Industrial Law Journal 1.

38 See chapter 2.

39 See, eg, Richard Mitchell and Joel Fetter, 'Human Resource Management and Individualisation in Australian Labour Law' (2003) 45 Journal of Industrial Relations 292, 292; Alan Bogg, '"Individualism" and "Collectivism" in Collective Labour Law' (2017) 46 Industrial Law Journal 72; Gordon Anderson, 'Employment Rights in an Era of Individualised Employment' (2007) 38 Victoria University of Wellington Law Review 417, 424–25; Fudge (n 34) 623. For a discussion in the context of workplace investigations in Norway, see Tereza Østbø Kuldova and Bitten Nordrik, 'Workplace Investigations, the Epistemic Power of Managerialism and the Hollowing out of the Norwegian Model of Co-Determination' (2023) 48 Capital & Class 463.

Specifically, the decline in unionization and collective industrial relations over time has directed power to the common law contract of employment as an 'individualist body of norms',[40] and afforded primacy to the individual contract between an employer and employee.[41] This change aligned with the rise of HRM in firms, which embodied a cooperative and '"high trust" agenda for enterprise strategy and governance',[42] and promoted divestment of responsibility for employment relations to the employer and employee at the workplace level.[43] Workplace investigations were facilitated by the individualization of workplace governance; these processes were depicted as 'neutral' but employers could use them to exercise power and control via individualized employment relations.[44]

The individualization of employment relations was also mirrored in the expansion of individual codified labour and equality rights over time, and this broader development has also enabled the development of workplace investigations as a common HRM tool in organizations.[45] As Lizzie Barmes observed in the context of the United Kingdom, political, social, and economic forces contributed to the rise of liberal individualist approaches to workplace regulation and relations and, overall, this has marginalized 'more plural, collective workplace ways of being'.[46] This monograph examines how workplace investigations intersect with individual labour and equality rights under statute and exposes the limitations of these rights in providing meaningful protections to respondents in these processes. It illuminates how employees who are wronged by employer conduct during workplace investigations mostly rely on unhelpful or ill-suited individual labour and equality rights to seek legal redress on their own.[47]

While the geographic focus of this monograph is Australia, researchers, practitioners and policymakers in other systems where workplace investigations are a common tool of HRM will find the doctrinal, theoretical, and empirical account of workplace investigations instructive. The shift from collective to individualized employment relations is reflected in the rise of workplace investigations, and the themes of individualization in the legal regulation of work and in working lives that underpin the emergence of these processes have broad relevance and resonance. I provide an account of justice in workplace investigations,[48] which identifies the ongoing relevance of collective values in empowering workers in these processes and informs law reform proposals that integrate individual and collective dimensions.

40 Bogg (n 39) 84.
41 Anderson (n 39) 420.
42 Mitchell and Fetter (n 39) 294.
43 ibid 296.
44 See chapter 2.
45 Lizzie Barmes, *Bullying and Behavioural Conflict at Work: The Duality of Individual Rights* (OUP 2016) 1. See also Lizzie Barmes, 'Silencing at Work: Sexual Harassment, Workplace Misconduct and NDAs' (2023) 52 Industrial Law Journal 68.
46 Barmes, *Bullying and Behavioural Conflict at Work* (n 45) 1.
47 See, eg, cases examined in chapter 4, and the statutory analysis in chapter 5.
48 See chapter 3.

III The Focus on Respondents

Scholars and commentators who discuss workplace investigations primarily focus on the interests and concerns of two parties to the workplace investigation: complainants and employers. For example, scholarship and parliamentary reports mostly consider the impacts on workers who have suffered from bullying or sexual harassment at work and have made complaints to their employers in detail.[49] Commentaries by advisors to employers explore the risks that employers face when they conduct investigations.[50] In contrast, the position of respondents is far less theorized or studied,[51] even though they also encounter substantial risks and potentially great harm during a workplace investigation process.

For these reasons, in this monograph, I focus on issues of legal regulation with the respondent as the subject of the law. The impacts of workplace investigations on respondents are little understood or examined in scholarship but are discernible from other texts that discuss workplace investigations. For example, advocates who represent respondents in workplace investigations have begun to raise concerns about how respondents are treated during these processes,[52] and media articles include reports about intimidating and unprofessional employer conduct.[53] Legal claims pursued by respondents against their employers also include allegations by respondents that their employers acted incompetently or negligently towards them, or prejudged the outcome of the investigation.[54]

Respondents may have engaged in misconduct that warrants disciplinary action in their employment. Yet, the way an employer arrives at a finding of misconduct has profound consequences for that respondent. Respondents depend on an employer's process to tell their side of the story and to have their account treated as being provided in good faith. The possibility for allegations of misconduct to be based on vexatious complaints amplifies the need to consider respondents as subjects of the law.[55] As Jeremy Waldron has observed, '*everyone's* maltreatment . . . can be regarded as a sacrilege, a violation of human dignity, which (in the words of Edmund Burke) ten thousand swords must leap from their scabbards to avenge.'[56]

There are few insights in the scholarship about respondents' own views and experiences of workplace investigations.[57] Employers usually conduct workplace

[49] See, eg, Ballard and Easteal (n 19); Ballard (n 21) 231–60; AHRC (n 5) 257–75.
[50] See further chapter 2 III.
[51] AHRC (n 5) 279.
[52] See, eg, Sivaraman (n 16).
[53] See, eg, Mathew Dunckley, 'Westpac Worker Subjected to Five Hour "Star Chamber" Wins Back Job' *The Age* (2 December 2018) <https://www.theage.com.au/business/banking-and-finance/westpac-worker-subjected-to-five-hour-star-chamber-wins-back-job-20181202-p50jpg.html> accessed 9 July 2025; Adam Carey, 'No Water, No Loo for Yarra Trams Staff Grilled over Napoleon Poster, Court Hears' *The Age* (10 May 2016) <http://www.theage.com.au/victoria/no-water-no-loo-for-yarra-trams-staff-grilled-over-napoleon-poster-court-hears-20160510-gorspx.html> accessed 9 July 2025.
[54] See, eg, *Elisha v Vision Australia Ltd* [2022] VSC 754.
[55] See, eg, *Re SB* (2014) IR 127, [105], [109] (Commissioner Pearce).
[56] Jeremy Waldron, 'Law, Dignity and Self-Control' in Jeremy Waldron and Meir Dan-Cohen (eds), *Dignity, Rank, and Rights* (OUP 2012) 69–70 (original emphasis).
[57] A small number of empirical studies exist in Australia, see, eg, Burr and Wyatt (n 23); Jenkins, Winefield, and Sarris (n 23). For a study in Norway, see Kuldova and Nordrik (n 39).

investigations confidentially and often claim legal professional privilege over the communications and documents that are produced.[58] Legal disputes between employers and respondents regarding workplace investigations tend to be settled prior to hearing,[59] and reports produced by workplace investigators are rarely made available to the complainant or respondent,[60] or discussed outside the organization.[61] The confidential nature of workplace investigations means that respondents' views and experiences of workplace investigations are little understood and require further investigation.

IV Conceptualizing Justice for Respondents in Workplace Investigations

Given the importance of workplace investigations as a tool of organizational management, the fragmented state of legal regulation, and the lack of academic attention within law to the topic, it is necessary to develop a theoretical basis on which to consider the possibility of law reform. Each of these factors amplifies the vulnerability of the respondent during workplace investigations. As this monograph explores, the law is unsettled and unclear, and the pathways of legal redress that are available to respondents are complex to navigate and uncertain.

The absence of clear legal standards in statute for workplace investigations means that the vulnerability of respondents may translate into detriment, injury, and harm. A theory of justice is required to help explain the need to reform the law so that it specifically regulates workplace investigations and sets out the rights and obligations of all parties who are involved in these processes, including respondents.

I argue that the law governing work is a body of law that is primarily intended to protect vulnerable workers from the unmitigated power of the employer.[62] Respondents are vulnerable to the power of the employer during a workplace investigation.[63] It is the employer that decides crucial matters such as whether a workplace investigation is needed, the process used, the person who will conduct the investigation, the scope and terms of reference for the investigation, whether the respondent is directed not to

[58] See, eg, Green (n 1) 1; Nick Ruskin, 'Role of Lawyers in Workplace Investigations' (2014) 18 Inhouse Counsel 62, 62.

[59] See, eg, Michael King, 'Pathways and Partnerships: A Study of Private Policing Economic Crime in Australia' (PhD thesis, Queensland University of Technology 2021) 86; Alex Crockett, Isabella Armao, and Justine Sammut, 'Piercing the Secrecy Veil and Restricting NDA Use in Sexual Harassment Claims in Australia: Victoria Leads the Way' (2022) 27 Employment Law Bulletin 78, 78.

[60] See, eg, Charlotte Grieve, 'AMP's Behaviour "unacceptable" Says Lawyer for Former Employee' *The Sydney Morning Herald* (21 August 2020) <https://www.smh.com.au/business/banking-and-finance/amp-s-behaviour-unacceptable-says-lawyer-for-former-employee-20200821-p55nzz.html> accessed 31 July 2025; Charlotte Grieve, 'Lawyers for Former AMP Employee Demand Documents Ahead of Harassment Report Release' *The Sydney Morning Herald* (19 August 2020) <https://www.smh.com.au/business/banking-and-finance/amp-to-release-sexual-harassment-report-stands-by-execs-20200819-p55n3q.html> accessed 26 July 2025.

[61] Paul Bonny, Sigi Goode, and David Lacey, 'Revisiting Employee Fraud: Gender, Investigation Outcomes and Offender Motivation' (2015) 22 Journal of Financial Crime 447, 448.

[62] Otto Kahn-Freund, *Labour and the Law* (Stevens for the Hamlyn Trust 1972) 6.

[63] This issue is briefly considered in Brodie and Riley (n 18) 313.

perform work during the investigation, and what (if any) management action will be taken following the investigation.

The concept of justice for workers is a complex notion, and academic discourse includes vigorous debate regarding what values need to be promoted through the law of work to ensure justice for workers.[64] Drawing on the ideas of Harry Arthurs, I suggest that different values are of relevance depending on the issue or subject in question.[65] I recognize the idea of citizenship at work as a value that is apposite when considering justice for respondents in workplace investigations.

I suggest that the idea of citizenship at work is useful because respondents in workplace investigations are rarely seen as requiring the protection of work law to mitigate their vulnerability to employer power. The concept of citizenship at work presents a lens through which all workers are equally entitled to legal protection, including with respect to dismissal and WHS.[66] The concept also promotes the need for all workers to be given an opportunity to provide input into the processes that employers use to make decisions that affect them and to seek representation.[67]

While the idea of citizenship at work is broad, I argue that it has distinctly developed the law of work within the Australian context, and that the authors of the *Charter* have produced a template of rights for Australian workers that is underpinned by the concept of citizenship at work.[68] The template in the *Charter* is both aspirational and descriptive. Each right reflects a dimension of collective or individual citizenship within the workplace. This spans from the right to bargain collectively and be represented by a union in the workplace[69] to the right to work with dignity.[70]

I draw on and modify the template of rights under the *Charter* to establish a framework of justice in workplace investigations for respondents that includes nine elements. I use this framework to evaluate the legal regulation of workplace investigations and propose an agenda for law reform. In this way, this study predominantly draws on philosophical scholarship about work law that adopts a purposive approach and conceives of work regulation as a mechanism by which to achieve social goals or promote universal values.[71]

[64] See, eg, Hugh Collins, Gillian Lester, and Virginia Mantouvalou (eds), *Philosophical Foundations of Labour Law* (OUP 2019); Guy Davidov, *A Purposive Approach to Labour Law* (OUP 2016); Guy Davidov and Brian A Langille (eds), *The Idea of Labour Law* (OUP 2011). See further, chapter 3.

[65] Harry Arthurs, 'Foreword: Mining the Philosophers' Stone: Sixteen Tons and What Do You Get? Another Day Older and Deeper in Doubt' in Hugh Collins, Gillian Lester, and Virginia Mantouvalou (eds), *Philosophical Foundations of Labour Law* (OUP 2018) vi.

[66] Ronald C McCallum, 'Citizenship at Work: An Australian Perspective' (2011) Sydney Law School Research Paper No 11/17 <https://papers.ssrn.com/abstract=1769271> accessed 28 July 2025; Hugh Collins, *Employment Law* (2nd edn, OUP 2010) 24.

[67] McCallum (n 66).

[68] Mordy Bromberg, 'Introduction' in Mordy Bromberg and Mark Irving (eds), *Australian Charter of Employment Rights* (Hardie Grant Books 2007) 1–8. This is one of three rationales provided by the authors for the *Charter.*

[69] Mark Irving, 'Union Membership and Representation' in Mordy Bromberg and Mark Irving (eds), *Australian Charter of Employment Rights* (Hardie Grant Books 2007).

[70] Greg Bamber and Bob Russell, 'Work with Dignity' in Mordy Bromberg and Mark Irving (eds), *Australian Charter of Employment Rights* (Hardie Grant Books 2007).

[71] See, eg, Davidov (n 64); Simon Deakin, 'Labor Law: The Pragmatist's Guide—Comments on *A Purposive Approach to Labor Law*' (2017) 16 Jerusalem Review of Legal Studies 28; Guy Mundlak, 'The Power of Purpose: Comments on *A Purposive Approach to Labour Law*' (2017) 16 Jerusalem Review of Legal Studies 40; Ruth Dukes, 'Identifying the Purposes of Labor Law: Discussion of Guy Davidov's *A*

Respondents have potentially engaged in theft, fraud, bullying, or sexual harassment, and it may be for this reason that they are given less attention in the analysis of the legal regulation of individual workplace behaviours in protective work statutes. By viewing the employer as an entity that bears obligations to citizens at work (similar to the way a nation-state has obligations to its citizens), the concept of citizenship at work promotes the right of workers to a fair process, irrespective of the outcome (in a similar way to the nation-state owing citizens the right to natural justice in criminal and civil procedure).[72] In this way, the idea of citizenship at work provides a compelling template for conceptualizing justice for respondents in workplace investigations.

V Method

This study uses several research methods to understand employer practices during workplace investigations, to investigate the practices of employers and the views and experiences of respondents about workplace investigations, to scrutinize and critique the legal regulation of employer conduct towards respondents in workplace investigations, and to propose how the law should be reformed to promote justice for respondents.

I conduct a traditional literature review that synthesizes and critiques an extensive body of HRM literature.[73] This analysis fills a gap in knowledge about how employers conduct workplace investigations and how these practices affect respondents as subjects of the law.[74] I use this review to problematize the concept of a workplace investigation and to consider employer practices, and common conflicts and controversies, from a legal perspective.

I also use qualitative content analysis to derive information about how respondents experience workplace investigations from the text of a sample of decisions of the FWC under the unfair dismissal provisions in pt 3-2 of the *FW Act*.[75] Qualitative content analysis involves coding and analysis of themes in texts.[76] I use this method to make findings about the views and experiences of respondents in the sample of decisions and to identify themes from those findings. This improves understanding of the perspectives of respondents regarding workplace investigations.

I combine these methods with doctrinal legal analysis to deepen understanding of employer practices during workplace investigations and the experiences of

Purposive Approach to Labour Law' (2017) 16 Jerusalem Review of Legal Studies 52. For a critique of this approach see, eg, Zoe Adams, *Labour and the Wage: A Critical Perspective* (OUP 2020) 1–4.

[72] Guy Mundlak, 'Industrial Citizenship, Social Citizenship, Corporate Citizenship: I Just Want My Wages' (2007) 8 Theoretical Inquiries in Law 719, 746.

[73] On the recognition that the literature review is a distinct research method see, eg, Jill Jesson, Lydia Matheson, and Fiona M Lacey, *Doing Your Literature Review: Traditional and Systematic Techniques* (SAGE 2011) 73; Chris Hart, *Doing a Literature Review: Releasing the Social Science Research Imagination* (SAGE 2002) 27.

[74] See further chapter 2.

[75] *Fair Work Act 2009 (Cth)* pt 3-2. This part provides a protection against unfair dismissal to eligible employees. See further chapter 5 III(B).

[76] Klaus Krippendorff, *Content Analysis: An Introduction to Its Methodology* (4th edn, SAGE 2019).

respondents. I do so to provide a picture of the internal world of employer practices in which the law operates that is lacking in the literature,[77] and to consider these practices from a legal perspective. I use the information about the practice of workplace investigations and respondents' views and experiences to inform novel proposals about how legal mechanisms can be improved.[78]

Doctrinal research involves identifying and critically examining the 'essential features' of statute and case law (and other relevant materials) to create a 'combined or synthesized' account of the legal rules that apply to a specific legal issue or problem.[79] This method is often described as a 'two-part process' where relevant legal texts are, firstly, identified and, secondly, interpreted and analysed.[80] The broad aim is to interpret relevant legal concepts, rules, and principles to create an 'arguably correct and complete statement of the law' on a matter.[81]

As noted, legal scholarship lacks a sustained and critical examination of the legal regulation of workplace investigations.[82] The law that applies to employer conduct towards respondents during workplace investigations is disparate and encompasses both judge-made and statute law. Perhaps surprisingly, there is no overarching or comprehensive statutory code that directly governs workplace investigations despite their prevalence and centrality as an HRM tool. Instead, employers rely on express and implied terms under the contract of employment to conduct workplace investigations and to direct respondents to participate and answer questions.[83] The contract of employment gives employers broad managerial power during these processes.[84] Various statutory provisions might apply to aspects of employer conduct towards respondents, depending on the circumstances.

This monograph uses the method of doctrinal legal research to systematically identify and thoroughly examine judge-made and statute law that regulates the conduct of employers towards respondents during these processes. I first use doctrinal analysis to examine judge-made law. I analyse key decisions of superior and appellate courts in Australia decided between 1 January 2000 and 1 June 2025 in the areas of contract and tort law that develop principles that apply to employer conduct towards respondents during workplace investigations. I identify principles that have been developed by courts as well as central gaps in the law. I argue that key principles are unsettled and underdeveloped and that some courts have expressed reluctance to develop the law in ways that would further constrain employer conduct during workplace investigations.

[77] Hazel Genn, Martin Partington, and Sally Wheeler, 'Law in the Real World: Improving Our Understanding of How Law Works' (Nuffield Foundation, 2006) 5–6.

[78] Mark A Hall and Ronald F Wright, 'Systematic Content Analysis of Judicial Opinions' (2008) 96 California Law Review 63, 66; Alysia Blackham, 'Why Do Employment Age Discrimination Cases Fail? An Analysis of Australian Case Law' (2020) 42 Sydney Law Review 1, 3–5.

[79] Terry Hutchinson, 'Doctrinal Research: Researching the Jury' in Dawn Watkins and Mandy Burton (eds), *Research Methods in Law* (2nd edn, Routledge 2017) 13. Other relevant materials might include aids of statutory interpretation (such as explanatory memoranda), non-binding authoritative determinations, and legal scholarship.

[80] ibid 18.

[81] ibid 13.

[82] A preliminary map is set out in Orifici (n 19).

[83] On express and implied terms under contracts of employment in Australia, see further Mark Irving, *The Contract of Employment* (2nd edn, LexisNexis Butterworths 2019) 390–427.

[84] Brodie and Riley (n 18).

I next use doctrinal legal analysis to collate and scrutinize seven key areas of statute that apply to employer conduct towards respondents during workplace investigations. I consolidate applicable statutory provisions and consider how courts and tribunals have interpreted them in disputes pursued by respondents about employer conduct during workplace investigations. I analyse provisions under four areas of the *FW Act* that apply to employer conduct towards respondents during workplace investigations. These areas are the general protections against adverse action,[85] the protection against unfair dismissal,[86] protections against bullying at work,[87] and the framework for making and enforcing enterprise agreements.[88]

I also examine provisions that apply to employer conduct during workplace investigations in six other key areas of legislation in Australia. These areas are anti-discrimination laws, WHS laws, workers' compensation laws, laws that apply to employees in the public service, whistleblowing laws, and evidence laws. I synthesize the statutory analysis and critically consider central gaps, issues, and inconsistencies in the law. I argue that the statutory regulation of workplace investigations is also inadequate because it is fragmented and unduly complex, and Parliament should consider reforming the law.

VI Defining the Scope of a Workplace Investigation into Suspected Employee Misconduct

The term 'workplace investigation' can have different meanings in different contexts,[89] and legal scholarship lacks a comprehensive identification of the features of a workplace investigation into employee misconduct. To ensure clarity, it is therefore important to define the concept of a workplace investigation in this study. A workplace investigation into employee misconduct can be articulated by reference to two key features.[90] These features emerge from the literature written by lawyers and workplace investigators who advise employers.[91]

The first feature is that workplace investigations involve a range of parties, including employer representatives (such as a case manager and other HRM personnel) and decision-makers,[92] one or more workers (who participate as complainants, respondents, or witnesses) and their support persons and representatives, and an investigator

[85] *FW Act pt 3-1.*
[86] ibid pt 3-2.
[87] ibid pt 6-4B.
[88] ibid pt 2-4.
[89] Eg, the term can be used to refer to investigations by regulators pursuant to statutory powers: Fair Work Ombudsman, 'Workplace Investigations' <https://www.fairwork.gov.au/about-us/compliance-and-enforcement/workplace-investigations> accessed 25 July 2025.
[90] Henceforth, this monograph uses the term 'workplace investigation' to specifically refer to a workplace investigation into employee misconduct.
[91] These texts are examined further in chapter 2.
[92] The essential steps are set out in Paula Hoctor, Michael Robertson, and Kerryn Tredwell, 'Workplace Investigation Overview' in Paula Hoctor and Kerryn Tredwell (eds), *Workplace Investigations: Principles and Practice* (2nd edn, LexisNexis Butterworths 2023).

(who may be an employee or an external agent).[93] Respondents may be workers at any level of seniority within the organization. The skills and practices of persons who conduct workplace investigations vary considerably, and no specific qualification is required to perform this work.[94]

The second feature is that workplace investigations include a series of common steps. According to these steps, an employer identifies (or is informed of) an issue that potentially involves worker misconduct, develops written terms of reference and specific allegations for investigation, engages an investigator (who interviews workers, collects and evaluates evidentiary material, and reports on the findings),[95] uses the investigator's report to make decisions (such as a decision to discipline a worker), and gives 'feedback' to the workers involved about the outcome.[96]

Beyond these features, the actual practices of employers are little theorized or studied in legal scholarship. As there is a broad scope for employers to exercise managerial power during workplace investigations, employer practices vary widely. A detailed examination of workplace investigations that examines employer practices from a legal perspective follows in chapter 2.

VII Chapter Overview

In chapter 2, I critically examine and consolidate what can be known about how Australian employers conduct workplace investigations from existing sources and identify matters of controversy. The field of HRM literature is central to this inquiry and is important to understand, as it describes current employer practices, and new managers learn about workplace investigations from these texts. This examination of HRM texts fills a gap in legal scholarship by problematizing the concept of a workplace investigation and providing a sustained examination of employer practices, conflicts, and controversies that are considered from a legal perspective.

I identify that employer practices are diverse and varied. I discern a range of controversies and conflicts, such as the inherently conflicted role that is played by employers during workplace investigations and uncertainty amongst employers and their advisors regarding whether they must ensure procedural fairness in all workplace investigations. I recognize that the HRM texts indicate that managerial discretion plays a central role in workplace investigations and how these processes can potentially harm

[93] Green (n 1) 2. On the wide-ranging vocational backgrounds of workplace investigators in Australia, see Michael King, 'Out of Obscurity: The Contemporary Private Investigator in Australia' (2020) 22 International Journal of Police Science & Management 285, 290.

[94] Ballard and Easteal (n 19) 179; Rollinson (n 1). See also Michael King, 'What Makes a Successful Corporate Investigator: An Exploration of Private Investigators Attributes' (2020) 27 Journal of Financial Crime 701, 705.

[95] On interview practices see further Michael King, 'Financial Fraud Investigative Interviewing—Corporate Investigators' Beliefs and Practices: A Qualitative Inquiry' (2021) 28 Journal of Financial Crime 345; Katie Sweatman and Nick Ruskin, 'Gone Fishing: When and How to Conduct Workplace Investigations' (2012) 15 Inhouse Counsel 282.

[96] Jodie Fox and others, *Workplace Investigations* (3rd edn, CCH Australia 2020) 395–96; Harriet Stacey and Alison Page, *Investigative Interviewing: A Guide for Workplace Investigators* (WISE Workplace 2012) 2.

or injure respondents. I argue that the controversies, conflicts, and potential harms are amplified by the absence of direct and clear statutory regulation of workplace investigations.

In chapter 3, I develop a framework of justice in workplace investigations, with the respondent as the subject of the law, in six steps. First, I examine the concept of justice at work within legal scholarship. I argue that a concept of justice at work has traditionally been, and continues to be, to protect workers, having regard to the subordination of labour to capital. Second, I analyse the role of work regulation in achieving justice at work. I argue that work regulation continues to be crucial to advancing social goals and/or universal values for employees.[97] Third, I consider debates between scholars regarding the social goals and/or universal values that work law should promote to achieve justice at work. I argue that workplace democracy and citizenship are apposite values when considering justice for respondents in workplace investigations. This is because respondents are rarely seen as requiring the protection of work law to mitigate their vulnerability to employer power, and citizenship at work presents a lens through which all workers are equally entitled to legal protection.

Fourth, I examine how ideas regarding justice through workplace democracy and citizenship at work have evolved in the scholarship. I argue that these values continue to have potential in terms of promoting justice for workers and can be adapted to contemporary work contexts, including in terms of workplace investigations. Fifth, I examine how a specific idea of justice through citizenship at work has developed in the Australian context. I consider how Australian law has developed to feature a tradition of egalitarianism and presumption of social and political rights at work that have led to a distinct concept of citizenship at work. I argue that the *Charter* is underscored by this distinct concept of citizenship at work and presents a cogent vision of justice that is fitting for respondents in workplace investigations.[98] Sixth, I critically analyse the rights under the *Charter* and use it as a basis to develop a framework of justice in workplace investigations for respondents that includes nine key elements.

In chapter 4, I critically examine key decisions of superior and appellate courts decided between 1 January 2000 and 1 June 2025 in the areas of contract and tort law that develop principles that apply to employer conduct towards respondents during workplace investigations. I identify principles that have been developed by courts as well as central gaps in the law.

I argue that key principles are unsettled and underdeveloped and that some courts have expressed reluctance to develop the law in ways that would further constrain employer conduct during workplace investigations. I identify that one justification provided by courts for this approach is that it is more appropriate for the law that interacts with statutory rules about dismissal to be developed by Parliament through legislative reform. I also posit that decisions are underpinned by finely balanced public policy considerations that prioritize the need for employers to conduct workplace investigations efficiently over the risk of mental injury that they pose to respondents.

In chapter 5, I analyse how provisions that span across seven key areas of Australian legislation apply to employer conduct towards respondents during workplace

[97] See, eg, Dukes (n 71).
[98] Bromberg and Irving (n 6).

investigations. I consolidate applicable provisions and consider how courts and tribunals have interpreted them in disputes pursued by respondents about employer conduct during workplace investigations.

Chapter 5 is divided into three main parts. First, I explain the method that I used to collect and analyse the applicable statutory provisions and relevant court and tribunal decisions. Second, I analyse provisions under four areas of the *FW Act* that apply to employer conduct during workplace investigations. Third, I examine provisions that apply to employer conduct during workplace investigations in six other key areas of legislation. I argue that the statutory regulation of workplace investigations is fragmented and inadequate, and Parliament should consider reforming the law.

Chapter 6 responds to the absence of respondents' perspectives on workplace investigations in HRM literature or legal scholarship. I derive information about how respondents experience workplace investigations from a sample of 183 decisions of the FWC made under pt 3-2 of the *FW Act*, which sets out the protection against unfair dismissal. I use the method of qualitative content analysis to examine the decisions.

This chapter is set out in four main parts. First, I explain the context of the data and why I have decided to derive information about the views and experiences of respondents from the text of decisions made under pt 3-2 of the *FW Act*. Second, I outline the method of qualitative content analysis.[99] Third, I describe the findings about the views and experiences of respondents. Fourth, I explain four central themes from the sample of cases, which relate to informational asymmetry between employers and respondents, denial/ minimization by employers of respondents' voices and opportunities for advocacy, denial by employers of respondents' requests for accommodation, and harm to respondents' psychological health. I argue that these themes reflect the lived experiences of the respondents in the sample and support law reform that promotes justice for respondents in workplace investigations.

In chapter 7, I positively and normatively analyse whether the legal regulation of workplace investigations promotes justice for respondents and draw on that analysis to propose an agenda of law reform. I apply the idea of justice in workplace investigations that I developed in chapter 3. I argue that legal regulation is fragmented and inadequate in terms of promoting justice for respondents. I posit that work law should be reformed to give explicit attention to respondents as subjects of the law and include reasonable constraints on employer power during workplace investigations.

I argue that work regulation must explicitly address the need for employers to conduct workplace investigations to address misconduct and also respond to the risk posed to respondents by unacceptable forms of conduct and treatment by employers during these processes. I develop a proposal for law reform that is informed by the preceding positive and normative analysis.

In chapter 8, I consolidate this study's main findings and conclusions and reinforce the need to reform the law to promote justice for respondents in workplace investigations.

[99] Richard Kirkham and Elizabeth O'Loughlin, 'A Content Analysis of Judicial Decision-Making' in Naomi Creutzfeldt, Marc Mason, and Kirsten McConnachie (eds), *Routledge Handbook of Socio-Legal Theory and Methods* (Routledge 2020) 330.

VIII Conclusion

In this work, I offer new and innovative legal and empirical insights into workplace investigations and provide the first theoretically-driven legal examination of this HRM process. The focus of this book is limited to employer conduct towards respondents, and examination of the legal regulation of employer conduct towards complainants, witnesses, or others affected by these processes, is beyond its scope. It therefore offers one piece of the puzzle in analysing the complex and multifaceted dimensions of workplace investigations from a legal perspective.

The analysis in this monograph is instructive to researchers, practitioners, unions, and policymakers in Australia and beyond. The basis for, and implications of, problematizing workplace investigations from a legal perspective have broad resonance in contexts where these processes are common HRM practices. The exploration of philosophical themes about justice, employer power, individual labour and equality rights, and managerial discretion invites reflection on the normative rationale for legal protections that apply at work.

2

Employer Practices, Conflicts, and Controversies in Workplace Investigations

An Examination of HRM Literature

I Introduction

In chapter 1, I examined the rise of the HRM phenomenon of workplace investigations and the broad developments that have led to their prevalence in Australian workplaces and beyond. This chapter builds on this to critically examine what is known about how employers conduct Australian workplace investigations from existing sources and to identify matters of controversy. This examination problematizes the concept of a workplace investigation from a legal perspective and sets out a sustained examination of employer practices, conflicts, and controversies. It is important to understand the field of HRM as it describes current employer practices and new managers learn about workplace investigations from these texts. As Edelman and Mark Suchman identify, the law and organizations can be seen as 'dynamically intertwined'.[1] It is possible to see the law of work as 'endogenous', with employer practices eventually reflected in the content of the law.[2]

The analysis of HRM texts in this chapter reveals that employer practices are diverse and varied. It also reveals a range of controversies and conflicts such as the inherently conflicted role that is played by employers during workplace investigations and uncertainty regarding whether employers must ensure procedural fairness in all workplace investigations. The HRM texts also indicate that managerial discretion plays a central role in workplace investigations and that these processes can potentially harm or injure respondents. I argue that the controversies, conflicts, and potential harms are amplified by the absence of direct and clear legal regulation of workplace investigations.

This chapter is divided into four main parts. Part II explains the context and method that I use to examine HRM texts. Part III adopts this method to map what is known about employer practices during workplace investigations from Australian HRM scholarship, HRM textbooks, practitioner-focused writings (in periodicals, at conferences and in the media), and promotional literature. Part IV then sets out a critical analysis of the HRM texts to identify central sources of controversy and conflict

[1] Lauren B Edelman and Mark C Suchman, 'The Legal Environments of Organizations' (1997) 23 Annual Review of Sociology 479, 480.

[2] ibid 502–03. See also Lauren B Edelman, 'Law at Work: The Endogenous Construction of Civil Rights' in Laura Beth Nielsen and Robert L Nelson (eds), *Handbook of Employment Discrimination Research: Rights and Realities* (Springer 2005) 337–38.

Workplace Investigations. Adriana Orifici, Oxford University Press. © Adriana Orifici 2026.
DOI: 10.1093/9780198970019.003.0002

in workplace investigations. Part V then provides an examination of how HRM texts reflect a confined picture of workplace investigations because they mostly provide an employer's perspective and rarely discuss in detail the views or experiences of parties such as respondents.

II Context and Method

Australian HRM literature began the consideration of workplace investigations for seemingly practical reasons. Over time, three specialized manuals for workplace investigators,[3] and a plethora of shorter texts written by lawyers and workplace investigators, have emerged. These texts are published as practitioner-focused periodicals, practitioner-focused conference papers, media articles, and on promotional websites.

Except for a few sources within the HRM scholarship,[4] HRM texts about workplace investigations are mainly descriptive rather than critically focused. They consider conflicts, controversies, and the legal and compliance issues at surface level. This is perhaps unsurprising given that the central purpose of the texts is to inform and instruct. Authors have predominantly written these texts for an audience of employers and/or other lawyers and workplace investigators. They mainly adopt an granular approach to describing practical and legal dimensions of workplace investigations absent of critical or normative analysis or evaluation of the law.

HRM texts about workplace investigations are rarely discussed in the legal scholarship. Again, this is unsurprising given that this small body of literature mostly consists of doctrinal examinations of court and tribunal decisions.[5] Allison Ballard and Patricia Easteal refer to commentaries by practitioners,[6] but do not do so systematically or critically. For example, Ballard's inquiry uses these texts to investigate the 'risks for employers' that arise from workplace investigations.[7] Their work provides a starting point for examining and evaluating the broader literature from a legal perspective and with attention given to the respondent as the subject of the law.

[3] Jodie Fox and others, *Workplace Investigations* (4th edn, Wolters Kluwer 2023); Paula Hoctor and Kerryn Tredwell (eds), *Workplace Investigations: Principles and Practice* (2nd edn, LexisNexis Butterworths 2023). A third manual focuses specifically on interviews during workplace investigations, Harriet Stacey and Alison Page, *Investigative Interviewing: A Guide for Workplace Investigators* (WISE Workplace 2012).

[4] See, eg, Catherine Burr and Anne Wyatt, 'Investigation of Workplace Bullying and Harassment Complaints' in Premilla D'Cruz and others (eds), *Dignity and Inclusion at Work* (Springer 2021); Moira Jenkins, Helen Winefield, and Aspa Sarris, 'Consequences of Being Accused of Workplace Bullying: An Exploratory Study' (2011) 4 International Journal of Workplace Health Management 33.

[5] See, eg, Richard Naughton, 'Termination of Employment and Workplace Investigations' (2016) 22 Employment Law Bulletin 186; Natalie Williams, '*Bartlett v Australia & New Zealand Banking Group Ltd* [2016] NSWCA 30 (7 March 2016)' (2016) 37 Adelaide Law Review 571. See also Carolyn Sappideen, Paul O'Grady, and Joellen Riley, *Macken's Law of Employment* (9th edn, Thomson Reuters 2022) 194–95. A preliminary map of legal dimensions is set out in Adriana Orifici, 'Unsystematic and Unsettled: A Map of the Legal Dimensions of Workplace Investigations in Australia' (2019) 42 University of New South Wales Law Journal 1075.

[6] Allison Ballard, 'In the Shadow of the Law: The Silence of Workplace Abuse' (PhD thesis, University of Canberra 2019); Allison Ballard and Patricia Easteal, 'Procedural Fairness in Workplace Investigations: Potential Flaws and Proposals for Change' (2018) 43 Alternative Law Journal 177.

[7] Ballard (n 6) 259. Ballard's conclusions are primarily instructional and oriented towards employers and legal compliance: ibid 259–60.

In this chapter, I focus on HRM texts by Australian authors because this study examines the legal regulation of Australian workplace investigations. HRM texts on workplace investigations also exist in countries including the United States and United Kingdom.[8] US workplace investigations are described in textbooks,[9] contributions to HRM and law journals,[10] and practitioner-oriented periodicals, guides, and conference papers.[11] There are also many commentaries about workplace investigations in the United Kingdom in sources such as HRM scholarship,[12] practitioner-oriented periodicals,[13] and practitioner webpages.[14] They describe quite different employer practices and procedures.

I have used a traditional literature review to synthesize and critically analyse HRM texts written by scholars and practitioners between 1980 and 2023 that substantively discuss workplace investigations.[15] A traditional literature review 'usually aim[s] to give either an overview or an introduction to a research field'.[16] This was a fitting method for examining the HRM texts because it enabled the voluminous body of sources to be synthesized, examined, and evaluated to form a coherent interpretation.[17] Using this method, I formulated a review question,[18] identified relevant sources and their accessibility,[19] analysed and evaluated the sources,[20] and synthesized and interpreted the literature.[21]

[8] A small number of contributions to practitioner periodicals in the United States refer to Australian workplace investigations, and these are considered below in chapter 2 III(C).

[9] See, eg, Lisa Guerin, *The Essential Guide to Workplace Investigations* (6th edn, Nolo 2022).

[10] See, eg, Linda B Dwoskin and Melissa Bergman Squire, 'Best Practices in Conducting Internal Workplace Investigations of Discrimination and Harassment Complaints' (2018) 44 Employee Relations Law Journal 20; Kirsten Scheurer Branigan and others, 'Conducting Effective Independent Workplace Investigations in a Post—#Metoo Era' (2019) 74 Dispute Resolution Journal 85.

[11] See, eg, Lynn D Lieber, 'HR and the "High-Level" Workplace Investigation' (2012) 39 Employment Relations Today 85; Teresa L Butler, 'The FCRA and Workplace Investigations' (2020) 15 The Labour Lawyer 391. See also 'AWI Publications—Guiding Principles, AWI Weekly and AWI Journal' <https://www.awi.org/page/publications> accessed 7 July 2025.

[12] See, eg, Chris Woodrow and David E Guest, 'When Good HR Gets Bad Results: Exploring the Challenge of HR Implementation in the Case of Workplace Bullying: Implementation of Workplace Bullying Policy' (2014) 24 Human Resource Management Journal 38.

[13] See, eg, John Baker, 'Investigating Fraud and Bribery by Staff' (2017) 4 Public Finance 46; Tina Elliot, 'Under Investigation' (2016) Employers' Law 18; Ashleigh Webber, 'Duty of Care and the Employee Accused of Wrongdoing' (*Personnel Today*, 31 July 2019) <https://www.personneltoday.com/hr/dismissed-worker-duty-of-care/> accessed 27 July 2025.

[14] See, eg, Michael Crowther, 'Wrigleys' Essential Employment Guide—The Disciplinary Process' (*Wrigleys Solicitors LLP*, 18 November 2021) <https://www.wrigleys.co.uk/news/employment-hr/wrigleys-essential-employment-guide-the-disciplinary-process/> accessed 27 July 2025; Emily Plosker, 'Employers Can Factor into a Disciplinary Investigation Prior Incidents Even If They Went Unpunished at the Time' (*BDBF LLP*, 1 February 2018) <https://www.bdbf.co.uk/employers-can-factor-disciplinary-investigation-prior-incidents-even-went-unpunished-time/> accessed 27 July 2025.

[15] Jill Jesson, Lydia Matheson, and Fiona M Lacey, *Doing Your Literature Review: Traditional and Systematic Techniques* (SAGE 2011) 31–45, 76–80; Maggie Walter, *Social Research Methods* (4th edn, OUP 2019) 53.

[16] Susanne Hempel, *Conducting Your Literature Review* (American Psychological Association 2020) 4.

[17] Jesson, Matheson, and Lacey (n 15) 47–48.

[18] Hempel (n 16) 14–16. The question was: what is known about workplace investigations using HRM texts and what are the key conflicts and controversies?

[19] Jesson, Matheson, and Lacey (n 15) 31–45.

[20] ibid 48; Hempel (n 16) 91–99.

[21] Hempel (n 16) 91–99.

I collated the body of HRM texts through keyword searches of university library catalogues,[22] and databases that included academic scholarship in the field of HRM,[23] written in the time frame between January 1980 and December 2023. In addition, I searched databases using keywords to locate books, practitioner periodicals, practitioner-focused conference papers, media pieces,[24] and promotional writing on the websites of Australian law and workplace investigations firms.[25] Again, the time frame between January 1980 and December 2023 was used for these searches to locate a large body of texts.[26]

Through these searches, I located a small body of HRM scholarship on Australian workplace investigations and three Australian textbooks for practitioners dedicated to workplace investigations.[27] In addition, I identified a smaller body of practitioner periodicals, practitioner-focused conference papers, and media articles about workplace investigations and a larger body of promotional writing on the websites of Australian legal and workplace investigations firms. I sorted these texts chronologically and systematized them in an electronic database.[28]

As the HRM texts were voluminous and diverse, I first categorized the texts based on their purpose and then critically analysed each category with a focus on practices, conflicts, and controversies. I used this analysis to produce a map of key employer practices and a critical examination of central controversies and conflicts with a focus on the respondent as the subject of the law. I also analysed how the views and perspectives about workplace investigations in the HRM texts might be limited by identifying whose perspectives were featured or considered in the texts. This examination is an original contribution to the scholarship because it departs from description and explanation and undertakes a critical and analytical approach to examining HRM texts about workplace investigations.

[22] These databases comprised the University of Melbourne and Monash University library catalogues.

[23] The keywords were: 'workplace investigation*'; 'internal investigation*'; 'disciplinary investigation*'; 'workplace inquir*'; 'complaint investigation*'; and 'disciplinary inquir*'. The following databases were searched: AustLII Journals; EBSCO databases (Academic Search Premier, Index to Legal Periodicals, SocIndex); Google Scholar; HEIN Online databases; INFORMIT databases (including AGIS (law) and APA-FT (public affairs); ProQuest databases (Political Science Database, Social Science Database, Sociology Database); SSRN. The following databases were searched to locate books: TROVE (the catalogue of the National Library); e-book platforms (BRILL, Hart/Bloomsbury, Oxford University Press, Routledge/Taylor & Francis, Springer, EBSCO e-books, and ProQuest e-books).

[24] The media pieces examined were either written by practitioners or included comments based on interviews with practitioners. Media pieces include news articles, opinion pieces, editorials, interviews, radio or television reports, and podcasts.

[25] The same keywords were searched. The following databases were searched: BSCO databases (Academic Search Premier, Index to Legal Periodicals, SocIndex; Emerald Insight); Google; HEIN Online databases; INFORMIT databases (including AGIS (law) and APA-FT (public affairs)); Gale General OneFile.

[26] Websites were examined as current on the date of the search.

[27] Jodie Fox and others, *Workplace Investigations* (3rd edn, CCH Australia 2020); Hoctor and Tredwell (n 3); Stacey and Page (n 3).

[28] The database identifies the following features of the texts: 'author (where specified)', 'title', 'firm', 'date', 'url', 'legal decision/s considered (if applic.)'.

III Varied and Diverse: A Map of Employer Practices in Workplace Investigations

Four categories of HRM literature on workplace investigations were reviewed to develop a map of common employer practices and perspectives. I commence by examining HRM scholarship and then three textbooks dedicated to Australian workplace investigations are reviewed. Next, I analyse relevant practitioner periodicals, contributions to practitioner-focused conferences and media publications, and then promotional writing on the websites of law firms and workplace investigators.

A HRM scholarship

Discussions of workplace investigations are included in HRM scholarship and in scholarship in the related fields of management and organizational psychology. Workplace investigators Catherine Burr and Anne Wyatt set out an 'international literature review' on bullying and harassment investigations, which includes some HRM literature about workplace investigations.[29] Burr and Wyatt noted that references to workplace investigations began to regularly appear in HRM scholarship in the early 2000s.[30] However, workplace investigations are also mentioned in HRM scholarship from the 1990s.[31]

In addition to the sources included in the review by Burr and Wyatt, is a broader body of international HRM scholarship that considers workplace investigations.[32] This body of HRM scholarship is mostly written by authors in the United States, United Kingdom, and European Union and discusses how workplace investigations are conducted in those locations. Much of this scholarship focuses on workplace investigations about complaints of bullying or sexual harassment. It does not discuss Australian workplace investigations although it canvasses problematic issues in workplace investigations that align with the conflicts and controversies discussed below.

Only a small body of HRM scholarship considers Australian workplace investigations and, in each relevant source, the authors discuss the subject as part of examining

[29] Burr and Wyatt (n 4) 149–50.

[30] ibid 150.

[31] See, eg, Kurt Jensen and Brian H Kleiner, 'How to Determine Proper Corrective Action Following Sexual Harassment Investigations' (1999) 18 Equal Opportunities International 23; David B Reynolds and Brian H Kleiner, 'Understanding and Managing Sexual Harassment in Organisations' (1995) 14 Equal Opportunities International 37; Vivienne Walker, 'Confidentiality—The Personnel Dilemma' (1992) 4 Employee Counselling Today 15.

[32] See, eg, in the US: Caren B Goldberg, Shannon L Rawski, and Elissa L Perry, 'The Direct and Indirect Effects of Organizational Tolerance for Sexual Harassment on the Effectiveness of Sexual Harassment Investigation Training for HR Managers' (2019) 30 Human Resource Development Quarterly 81; Benjamin J Thomas and Spencer Harris, 'A New, Established Approach to Managing Misbehavior: System Justification Theory' (2021) 50 Personnel Review 1582. See, eg, in the United Kingdom and European Union: Helge Hoel and Ståle Valvatne Einarsen, 'Investigating Complaints of Bullying and Harassment' in Ståle Valvatne Einarsen and others (eds), *Bullying and Harassment in the Workplace* (2nd edn, Taylor & Francis Group 2010); Hazel Mawdsley and Alison Thirlwall, 'Third-Party Interventions in Workplace Bullying: A Neoliberal Agenda?' (2019) 41 Employee Relations: The International Journal 506.

broader topics such as workplace bullying or sexual harassment. Some texts only briefly mention workplace investigations.[33] However, three articles report on key empirical studies and discuss important dimensions of the phenomenon.[34] In the first, Moira Jenkins et al have set out a thematic analysis of thirty surveys and twenty-four interviews with managers accused of workplace bullying and discussed how these workers experienced 'bullying investigations'.[35] The authors have emphasized that they were not aware of any other literature that examined the effects of being investigated for alleged bullying or harassment.[36] Interpreting the qualitative data from the perspective of organizational psychology, the authors have found that an employer's investigation can potentially lead to negative health consequences for respondents and victims. They have also found that some employers do conduct investigations without providing respondents with appropriate support or counselling.[37] They have found that some of the respondents viewed investigations as lacking in fairness or just treatment and argued that this highlighted the importance of employers adhering to the principles of organizational justice when investigating bullying complaints.[38] This study provides a starting point for understanding the views and experiences of respondents and that workplace investigations can potentially harm or injure respondents.

In the second study, Paula McDonald et al have set out an empirical examination of 632 cases of sexual harassment reported to an Australian community advocacy organization and briefly discussed workplace investigations in this context.[39] The authors have found that employers sometimes unreasonably refuse to initiate workplace investigations into complaints of sexual harassment,[40] delay commencing investigations,[41] or take a long time to investigate.[42] The authors have examined the data from the perspective of management and feminist theory and asserted that deferred or delayed investigations comprised 'unsatisfactory organisational responses' that could be costly and damaging to all parties.[43] This study reinforces that all workers who are parties in workplace investigations face the risk of injury and harm.

In the third study, Nikola Djurkovic et al have examined the roles of HRM professionals (HRPs) and employee representatives (ERs) in workplace investigations as part of reporting on a qualitative study about how HRPs and ERs perceived their roles

[33] See, eg, Glennis M Hanley and Anne O'Rourke, 'The Race without a Finishing Line: Legislative Means for Confronting Bullying in the Australian Workplace' (2016) 54 Asia Pacific Journal of Human Resources 352, 358, 360.

[34] Jenkins, Winefield, and Sarris (n 4); Paula McDonald, Sandra Backstrom, and Kerriann Dear, 'Reporting Sexual Harassment: Claims and Remedies' (2008) 46 Asia Pacific Journal of Human Resources 173; Nikola Djurkovic and others, 'The Role of Human Resource Professionals (HRPs) in Managing Workplace Bullying: Perspectives from HRPs and Employee Representatives in Australia' (2021) 50 Personnel Review 1599.

[35] Jenkins, Winefield, and Sarris (n 4) 33.

[36] ibid 34.

[37] ibid 44.

[38] ibid 34–35.

[39] McDonald, Backstrom, and Dear (n 34).

[40] ibid 182.

[41] ibid.

[42] ibid.

[43] ibid 188.

in 'managing' workplace bullying.[44] The authors interviewed seventeen HRPs and ERs and found that they often described undertaking concurrent roles in response to complaints of bullying, such as by providing advice to workers as well as organizing or conducting workplace investigations.[45] The authors have found that some of the interviewees expressed confusion about their responsibilities to work impartially and neutrally as investigators and to also act as 'conflict mediators' to resolve complaints.[46] The authors have noted that some interviewees stated they were 'compromised' as investigators because their loyalty was to management.[47] Applying an organizational management perspective, the authors argued that internal policies needed to stipulate the role of HRPs and ERs in responding to complaints. This study provides empirical evidence about potential conflicts of interest that arise for employers during workplace investigations as they must concurrently manage the process, provide support to workers, and respond to organizational risks.

While the empirical insights about workplace investigations are helpful, the studies are not specifically focused on workplace investigations but on broader issues. Also, like the legal scholarship examined in chapter 1, the HRM scholarship does not scrutinize employer practices in workplace investigations in detail. The purpose of these texts is not to problematize the concept of a workplace investigation from a legal perspective or to critique the legal regulation of these processes and they do not rely on legal theory.[48] Nevertheless, they provide helpful insights about employer practices and the potential for these practices to lead to harm to parties, including respondents.

B HRM textbooks

While most HRM textbooks about workplace investigations describe practices in the United States, United Kingdom, and European Union,[49] there are three textbooks that focus on Australian workplace investigations.[50] These textbooks are widely read amongst practitioners[51] and are instructional and descriptive in tone. They each

[44] Djurkovic and others (n 34). The study comprised interviews with twelve HRPs and five ERs in Australian organizations.

[45] ibid 1602–03.

[46] ibid 1603.

[47] ibid 1604.

[48] On the distinction between 'organizational justice' theory and theories of justice in law, see further chapter 3 II.

[49] See, eg, in the US: Eugene F Ferraro, *Investigations in the Workplace* (2nd edn, Taylor & Francis 2012); Guerin (n 9); Amy Oppenheimer and Craig Pratt, *Investigating Workplace Harassment: How to Be Fair, Thorough, and Legal* (Society for Human Resource Management 2008). See, eg, in Canada: Christine Thomlinson and Janice Rubin, *Human Resources Guide to Workplace Investigations* (2nd edn, Thomson Reuters 2018). See, eg, in the UK and EU: Derek Eccleston and Kate Goschen, *The Manager's Guide to Discipline* (Taylor & Francis Group 2008); Stefan Heissner, *Managing Business Integrity: Prevent, Detect, and Investigate White-Collar Crime and Corruption* (Springer 2015); John Stredwick, *An Introduction to Human Resource Management* (3rd edn, Taylor & Francis Group 2013).

[50] Fox and others (n 3); Hoctor and Tredwell (n 3); Stacey and Page (n 3). While workplace investigations are also mentioned in some general HRM textbooks, the concept is not described in detail. See, eg, Pieter Nel and others, *Human Resource Management in Australia* (2nd edn, OUP 2016) 424–25.

[51] In his preface to its third edition, Joe Catanzariti, a former Vice President of the FWC, noted that readership extended to 'human resources professionals, employees, employers, trade unions, academics,

discuss case law and statutory rules in detail, but in general the law is not critically or normatively analysed. This is unsurprising as the stated purpose of these textbooks is to provide information and instruction to persons such as legal practitioners and investigators working in the field. Each textbook is a useful source for building understanding of employer practices, the reasons employers conduct workplace investigations, and ideas held by employers and practitioners about pivotal concepts such as 'procedural fairness' and the 'standard of proof' in workplace investigations. Five key insights from the HRM texts are considered further below.

First, beyond the two key features of workplace investigations discussed in chapter 1 VI, the textbooks illuminate that employers' practices are varied and diverse.[52] The authors have recognized that some employers conduct investigations informally and with little documentation, while other employers prepare extensive documentary records and use highly legalistic and forensic approaches.[53] Similarly, the authors have described how many employers use detailed internal policies to govern their workplace investigations, whereas other employers have no written policies on the subject.[54] The authors have also noted that some employers even conduct 'preliminary assessments', 'preliminary investigations', or 'preliminary inquiries' before commencing workplace investigations and this illuminates that employer practices can involve many individual procedural steps.[55] The textbooks reveal that there is broad scope for employers to exercise managerial power during workplace investigations and this means that their processes vary widely and can change between investigations.[56] As observed by Fox et al, subject to 'any mandatory requirements in the organisation's policies and procedures, the choice is [the employer's] as to what process is required'.[57]

Second, the textbooks provide insights into the variety of actors and stakeholders who may be involved in a workplace investigation. As noted in chapter 1 VI, workplace investigations will usually involve employer representatives and decision-makers, workers (who participate as complainants, respondents, or witnesses) and their support persons and representatives, and an investigator (who may be an employee or an external agent). The textbooks reveal that other parties can also be involved 'behind the scenes' and may include legal advisors who act for the employer,[58] 'expert'

lawyers and the public at large': Fox and others (n 27) vii. See also Sarah Ford, 'At Last, a Workplace Investigations Manual' (2019) 39 The Proctor 40.

[52] Justine Turnbull, 'Initial Considerations' in Paula Hoctor and Kerryn Tredwell (eds), *Workplace Investigations: Principles and Practice* (2nd edn, LexisNexis Butterworths 2023) 21–31.

[53] Fox and others (n 3) 31; Amelia Peters, 'Planning the Investigation' in Paula Hoctor and Kerryn Tredwell (eds), *Workplace Investigations: Principles and Practice* (2nd edn, LexisNexis Butterworths 2023) 51; Stacey and Page (n 3) 14.

[54] Fox and others (n 3) 386; Turnbull (n 52) 23–25; Stacey and Page (n 3) 33.

[55] Fox et al state that in a 'preliminary investigation', an employer will examine the 'available information or "evidence" . . . [and] then make "observations" about what appears to have happened in this situation' without making formal findings of fact and without the need to afford the respondent procedural fairness. The authors assert that it is nevertheless 'good practice' to afford procedural fairness in these processes: Fox and others (n 3) 37. See also Turnbull (n 52) 24; Peters (n 53) 40.

[56] Fox and others (n 3) 35–40; Turnbull (n 52) 23; Stacey and Page (n 3) 15–16.

[57] Fox and others (n 3) 33.

[58] Turnbull (n 52) 36; Paula Hoctor, 'Legal Professional Privilege' in Paula Hoctor and Kerryn Tredwell (eds), *Workplace Investigations: Principles and Practice* (2nd edn, LexisNexis Butterworths 2023) 205–22; Fox and others (n 3) 105–06.

advisors such as computer forensic analysts,[59] line managers of workers who are involved,[60] board members,[61] communications advisors,[62] representatives of statutory authorities or ombudspersons,[63] and customers/members of the public.[64] The array of possible actors in workplace investigations reinforces that some employers' processes are intricate and resource-intensive and illuminates potential disparities between employers and workers in terms of resources and power.

Third, the textbooks provide insights regarding the reasons why employers conduct workplace investigations. The textbooks reinforce that workplace investigations are a tool of management that enable employers to respond to potential worker misconduct,[65] establish 'facts' to justify disciplinary action,[66] and mitigate (or avoid further) legal and organizational risks.[67] However, the textbooks also indicate that it is possible for employers to use workplace investigations for illegitimate purposes. For example, Fox et al caution against investigations that are undertaken to pressure employees to resign, undertake de facto performance management, are 'instigated with malice' or to victimize a respondent, where the employer intends to control the outcome or elicit a particular outcome or finding, or where only 'vague, generalised' allegations are available,[68] as well as 'fishing expeditions'.[69] These insights also reinforce the scope of management power in workplace investigations as employers do not (nor are they required to) explain the rationale for deciding to conduct a workplace investigation to affected workers, and the decision to conduct a workplace investigation is a matter of managerial discretion.

Fourth, the textbooks highlight a dualism whereby employers regard workplace investigations as a tool to mitigate legal risk but also recognize that these processes can lead to legal risk for employers. Each textbook notes that an employer's decision to conduct a workplace investigation may be mandated by law or motivated by a concern to mitigate legal risk.[70] In addition, each textbook describes how the process of conducting a workplace investigation can enliven various legal obligations for employers and rights for workers.[71] The textbooks also describe legal mechanisms that

[59] Kerryn Tredwell and Helen Donovan, 'Categories and Sufficiency of Evidence' in Paula Hoctor and Kerryn Tredwell (eds), *Workplace Investigations: Principles and Practice* (2nd edn, LexisNexis Butterworths 2023) 126; Fox and others (n 3) 75; Stacey and Page (n 3) 14.

[60] Corila Roos, Melissa Bostock, and Susan Forder, 'Management of a Successful Workplace Investigation' in Paula Hoctor and Kerryn Tredwell (eds), *Workplace Investigations: Principles and Practice* (2nd edn, LexisNexis Butterworths 2023) 57.

[61] ibid; Fox and others (n 3) 33.

[62] Fox and others (n 3) 361; Peters (n 53) 58.

[63] Peters (n 53) 57; Fox and others (n 3) 33.

[64] Peters (n 53) 57; Rachel Cornes, 'Procedural Fairness in Workplace Investigations' in Paula Hoctor and Kerryn Tredwell (eds), *Workplace Investigations: Principles and Practice* (2nd edn, LexisNexis Butterworths 2023) 105; Fox and others (n 3) 33.

[65] See, eg, Turnbull (n 52) 22.

[66] ibid; Fox and others (n 3) 17–18. Stacey and Page note this is the function of workplace investigations: Stacey and Page (n 3) 3.

[67] Paula Hoctor, 'Workplace Investigations and the Emergence of an Australian Profession' in Paula Hoctor and Kerryn Tredwell (eds), *Workplace Investigations: Principles and Practice* (2nd edn, LexisNexis Butterworths 2023) 2–3; Turnbull (n 52) 22–23; Stacey and Page (n 3) 2; Fox and others (n 3) 8, 10, 16, 388.

[68] The authors describe these purposes as 'abuse[s] of process': Fox and others (n 3) 32.

[69] ibid 272.

[70] ibid 24–32; Hoctor (n 67) 1–9; Stacey and Page (n 3) 2.

[71] Fox and others (n 3) 23–29, 115–16; Hoctor (n 67) 1–9; Stacey and Page (n 3) 20.

employers can use to mitigate risk in workplace investigations, such as directing respondents and witnesses to sign binding 'interview protocols',[72] which can include terms that require them to maintain confidentiality. The textbooks state that key areas of the law that apply during workplace investigations are complex and employers find it challenging to navigate legal rules and risks.[73] Legal complexity and risk are primarily described in these texts from the perspective of the employer,[74] but it is apparent that this issue is relevant to all parties and stakeholders.

Fifth, the textbooks deepen understanding about how employers and practitioners view and conceptualize 'procedural fairness' and the 'standard of proof' in workplace investigations.[75] The term 'procedural fairness' is legally defined in the field of administrative law in Australia and consists of two basic rules, which are the 'hearing rule' and 'bias rule'.[76] The principle requires a decision-maker to apply a fair process when making a decision that substantively and directly affects a person's rights or interests.[77] In summary, the 'hearing rule' generally requires that if a person is going to be detrimentally affected by a decision, they must be given an opportunity to respond at a fair hearing before a decision is made.[78] In addition, the 'bias rule' generally requires that the decision-maker is disinterested and has not pre-judged the outcome.[79] However, judicial decisions have established that the specific content of these rules varies from case to case and depends on the nature of the proceedings and the statutory context.[80] The common law principles do not apply to decisions made during workplace investigations when they are conducted by employers in the private sector,[81] but can apply to various decisions made during workplace investigations by employers in the public sector.[82] This is because employers within the public sector must generally follow administrative law principles when making decisions about employment.[83]

Each textbook states that employers that conduct workplace investigations 'should' or 'must' afford 'procedural fairness' to respondents.[84] Fox et al refer to 'procedural

[72] See, eg, Peters (n 53) 47–52.

[73] See, eg, Paula Hoctor, Michael Robertson, and Kerryn Tredwell, 'Workplace Investigation Overview' in Paula Hoctor and Kerryn Tredwell (eds), *Workplace Investigations: Principles and Practice* (2nd edn, LexisNexis Butterworths 2023) 66; Aoife Sweeney and Rachel Cornes, 'Gathering Evidence' in Paula Hoctor and Kerryn Tredwell (eds), *Workplace Investigations: Principles and Practice* (LexisNexis Butterworths 2023) 145.

[74] See, eg, Hoctor (n 67) 1.

[75] See, eg, Fox and others (n 3) 182–83; Cornes (n 64); Tredwell and Donovan (n 59).

[76] See further *Plaintiff S157/2002 v Commonwealth* (2003) 211 CLR 476 [25] (Gleeson CJ). On the common law duty to afford procedural fairness in administrative decision-making subject in the absence of a clear contrary statutory intention, see *Kioa v West* (1985) 159 CLR 550, 584; *Minister for Immigration and Border Protection v WZARH* (2015) 256 CLR 326, 335.

[77] Mark Robinson (ed), *Judicial Review—The Laws of Australia* (Thomson Reuters 2014) 301.

[78] ibid 304. See also *Minister for Immigration and Border Protection v SZSSJ* (2016) 259 CLR 180, 207.

[79] Robinson (n 77) 305. See also *CNY17 v Minister for Immigration and Border Protection* (2019) 268 CLR 76, 98.

[80] Robinson (n 77) 301.

[81] Administrative law principles apply to decision-makers in the public sector in the context of employment decisions. See further chapter 5 IV(D).

[82] Robinson (n 77) 129–30.

[83] In addition to obligations under judge-made administrative law, specific statutory obligations to afford procedural fairness may also apply to decision-makers in the public sector, see, eg, *Public Service Act 1999 (Cth) s 15(4)(b).*

[84] Fox and others (n 3) 182; Hoctor (n 67) 7–8; Cornes (n 64) 103–04; Stacey and Page (n 3) 14.

fairness' as a 'golden rule' of workplace investigations,[85] and Hoctor states that an 'investigation that is procedurally unfair will be flawed'.[86] Each textbook also refers to the 'hearing rule' and the 'bias rule'.[87] However, the textbooks often illustrate how these rules apply with reference to examples drawn from decisions of the FWC under pt 3-2 of the *FW Act*.[88] Under pt 3-2, the absence of either a 'fair hearing'[89] or an unbiased decision-maker[90] can be a factor that results in a decision by the FWC that the dismissal of an employee was 'harsh, unjust or unreasonable'[91] and in the imposition of remedial orders.[92] The FWC does not apply the principle of procedural fairness in the strict manner of the courts, but as part of broadly considering unfairness to the dismissed worker.[93] Overall, the textbooks reflect a view that employers should ensure procedural fairness in workplace investigations. They highlight how employers and practitioners can construct principles about what procedural fairness in workplace investigations entails from non-binding adjudications of the FWC in the absence of direct legal regulation.[94]

The textbooks also explain that practitioners and employers apply the 'civil standard of proof' in workplace investigations[95] and may also sporadically apply the principle established in the decision of the HCA in *Briginshaw v Briginshaw*.[96] The civil standard of proof is applied in civil proceedings.[97] It requires a finding to be proved 'on the balance of probabilities'.[98] The decision of the court in *Briginshaw* requires that where allegations are more 'serious' in nature and can lead to a more 'serious' outcome, stronger evidence might need to be adduced to meet the civil standard of proof.[99] The textbooks reveal that practitioners and employers consider that it is a matter for investigators to decide whether the *Briginshaw* standard is applied during an investigation. For example, Fox et al, state that if the investigation 'is not an obvious case of dismissal, at the time of writing the investigation report, it can be difficult to know if this rule should be applied or not'.[100] This comment indicates that, while the *Briginshaw* principle has the purpose of protecting respondents where an investigation might result in their dismissal or harm to their reputation, there is no obligation for investigators to consistently apply this principle and they may misunderstand its import.[101]

[85] Fox and others (n 3) 182.
[86] Hoctor (n 67) 7.
[87] See, eg, Fox and others (n 3) 182; Cornes (n 64) 104; Stacey and Page (n 3) 14–22.
[88] Part 3-2 provides eligible employees with a protection against unfair dismissal, see, eg, Cornes (n 64) 107–09; Fox and others (n 3) 183.
[89] *Fair Work Act 2009 (Cth) s 387(c).*
[90] See, eg, *Batchem v Water Corporation* [2016] FWC 9088.
[91] *FW Act s 387.*
[92] ibid ss 385–87.
[93] Robinson (n 77) 130.
[94] See, eg, Cornes (n 64).
[95] See, eg, Tredwell and Donovan (n 59) 133; Fox and others (n 3) 314; Stacey and Page (n 3) 24.
[96] *Briginshaw v Briginshaw* (1938) 60 CLR 336. See Fox and others (n 3) 315; Tredwell and Donovan (n 59) 133–34; Stacey and Page (n 3) 24.
[97] *Evidence Act 1995 (Cth) s 140.*
[98] ibid s 140(1).
[99] *Briginshaw* (n 96) 362.
[100] Fox and others (n 3) 316.
[101] On the misunderstood status of *Briginshaw* more generally see further Stephen Gageler, 'Evidence and Truth' (2017) 13 Judicial Review 1.

Overall, the textbooks provide important information about how employers and practitioners view and conduct workplace investigations. The textbooks reveal the priorities and concerns of employers and point towards a range of tensions, contradictions, and controversies. These sources enable understanding of the diversity of employer practices during workplace investigations, the role of managerial discretion and employer power, how employers conceptualize 'procedural fairness' and the 'standard of proof', and the uneasy coupling of the objective of 'neutrality' and the frequently opposed interests of employers and workers. Understanding is built further by analysis of practitioner publications and promotional material, which are each considered further below.

C Practitioner-focused periodicals, conference papers, and media pieces

Commentaries on Australian workplace investigations written by legal practitioners and workplace investigators are also set out in periodicals written for lawyers, workplace investigators, and/or HRM professionals, as well as in papers presented at practitioner-focused conferences and media pieces. These texts are descriptive, informative, cautionary, or opinionative in tone.[102] They augment understanding of what workplace investigations entail by illuminating the role(s) of lawyers, prevalence of claims of legal professional privilege, application and content of the principle of 'procedural fairness', and divergent interests of employers and workers.

First, contributions to practitioner-oriented periodicals and conferences deepen understanding of the role(s) of lawyers in workplace investigations.[103] Commentators have stated that it is common for employers to engage lawyers as workplace investigators,[104] although some have warned that the practice of engaging lawyers as investigators can compromise the independence of an investigation.[105] In addition, authors have noted that employers might not directly engage workplace investigators who are external agents but may, instead, commission lawyers to do so on their behalf.[106] Employers might also seek legal advice from in-house or external lawyers about matters including procedural steps or the preparation of investigation reports.[107] These

[102] See, eg, Joe Catanzariti and David Birch, 'A Cautionary Tale on Workplace Bullying and Its Investigation: Wood v Rainbow Coast Neighbourhood Centre Inc' 18 Employment Law Bulletin 82; Lachlan Boucaut and Tom Kavanagh, 'A Limitation on Employer Power to Direct Employees to Attend an Interview' (*Allens*, 30 June 2021) <https://www.allens.com.au/insights-news/insights/2021/06/a-limitation-on-employer-power-to-direct-employees-to-attend-an-interview/> accessed 27 July 2025.

[103] See, eg, Nick Ruskin, 'Role of Lawyers in Workplace Investigations' (2014) 18 Inhouse Counsel 62, 63; Katie Sweatman and Nick Ruskin, 'Gone Fishing: When and How to Conduct Workplace Investigations' (2012) 15 Inhouse Counsel 282.

[104] See, eg, James Mattson and Mark Paul, 'Workplace Investigations: Time to Reform Our Thinking?' (Australian Labour Law Association Conference, Melbourne, 4 November 2016) 3; Katie Gardiner and Elaine Acaro, 'Overview of Workplace Investigations in Australia' (2021) 164 Precedent 22, 23.

[105] See, eg, Sarah Tidley, 'Workplace Investigations, Australian Style' (2013) 4 Association of Workplace Investigators Journal 17, 18.

[106] Ruskin (n 103) 62; Catherine Dunlop and Richard Hanson, 'Don't Touch My Stuff: Client Legal Privilege in Employment Law' (2016) 22 Employment Law Bulletin 278, 280.

[107] Tidley also noted that sometimes law firms engaged to provide advice on an investigation also conduct the investigation, which can be perceived as diminishing the impartiality of the investigator: Tidley (n 105) 18. See also Peter RA Gray, 'Fearless or Fraught—The Investigator's Approach' (Australasian Association of Workplace Investigators Conference, Melbourne, 20 October 2017).

texts reinforce that an array of legal actors can be directly and indirectly involved in workplace investigations for different purposes.[108] The descriptions expose a practical reality of layers of legalism in many workplace investigations. For example, lawyers can function as 'intermediaries' between employers and investigators,[109] as well as between employers and respondents and/or their legal and/or union representatives.[110] The texts also illuminate that lawyers representing the interests of employers can be present at every stage of a workplace investigation, but their presence might not be visible to respondents in some cases. The texts mainly discuss the involvement of lawyers with a tone of neutrality, but most adopt the employer's perspective.[111] These texts reveal that employers use lawyers as resources in workplace investigations to mitigate risks to the organization. The investment in legal resources could increase the imbalance of power between employers and respondents in workplace investigations.

Second, these texts explain how employers use claims of legal professional privilege to maintain confidentiality over documents and communications that are produced during workplace investigations.[112] Legal professional privilege is a common law principle, by which communications between lawyers and clients remain confidential in prescribed circumstances. These circumstances are either where the communications are for the dominant purpose of obtaining legal advice or for use in relation to litigation in existence or within reasonable contemplation.[113]

The texts generally describe legal professional privilege as serving a protective function for employers in workplace investigations.[114] For example, authors note that the privilege can enable employers to refuse requests by workers and external parties to access documents.[115] Lawyers Catherine Dunlop and Richard Hanson note that a claim of legal professional privilege enables documents to be 'withheld' from the 'other party' during an investigation.[116] While lawyer Nick Ruskin also recognizes similar 'benefits' to employers, he also notes that this approach can be detrimental to workers. Ruskin observes that:

> there have been comments by plaintiff lawyers [for workers] that the barrier provided by legal professional privilege will create unfairness and will be challenged because the investigation will not be entirely independent. It is said that within the walls of

[108] See, eg, Sweatman and Ruskin (n 103) 282.
[109] Ruskin (n 103) 62.
[110] See, eg, Tidley (n 105) 17; Meryl Remedios, 'Ten Tips for Successful Workplace Investigations' (2017) 69 Governance Directions 234, 235.
[111] See, eg, Sweatman and Ruskin (n 103) 282.
[112] See, eg, Brian C Williamson, 'Disciplinary Investigations: The Need to Be Both Effective and Fair' (14 February 2019) 3 <http://brianwilliamson.com.au/Docs/Investigations%20-%20BCW%20-%20140219.pdf> accessed 25 July 2025.
[113] See further chapter 5 IV(F).
[114] See, eg, Jennifer Wyborn, Charisse Matthews, and Caroline Beasley, 'Workplace Investigations Refresher Part 3: Legal Professional Privilege and Workplace Investigation Reports' (*Clayton Utz*, 1 April 2021) <https://www.claytonutz.com/knowledge/2021/april/workplace-investigations-refresher-part-3-legal-professional-privilege-and-workplace-investigation-reports> accessed 25 July 2025; Leanne Nickels and Kate Hennessy, 'Stop Bully! How the New Anti-Bullying Measures in the Fair Work Act Operate' (2014) 18 Inhouse Counsel 19, 21; Williamson (n 112) 4.
[115] See, eg, Dunlop and Hanson (n 106) 278; Ruskin (n 103) 62.
[116] Dunlop and Hanson (n 106) 278.

> legal professional privilege the external investigators can chat happily with the organisation and get an insight into the true picture as painted by the organisation of the issues. The organisation can encourage the investigator as to the way in which the investigator might reach its conclusions, it can peruse a draft report and provide comment on recommendations that might flow from the report. Therefore, one can expect that in the future, complainants who are legally advised will not be content to allow the investigation to be carried out by an external party without an endeavour to obtain assurances about the true independence of the process.[117]

Two key tensions are apparent from texts that discuss how employers use claims of legal professional privilege during workplace investigations. First, commentators simultaneously endorse the use of legal professional privilege but are equivocal about the scope of its application to the circumstances of a factual inquiry.[118] It is implicit that employers might make claims of legal professional privilege over documents in workplace investigations in circumstances where it is legally uncertain that the privilege applies. A worker who wishes to challenge an employer's claim of legal professional privilege through legal proceedings must weigh up factors such as cost, lost time, and an uncertain outcome. Second, while commentators reiterate that workplace investigations are 'impartial' processes conducted by investigators,[119] they explain ways that employers can use legal professional privilege to protect their interests.[120] These interests may not align with those held by workers such as respondents who are involved in the investigation.

Third, these texts set out diverse views regarding whether it is necessary for employers in the private sector to ensure procedural fairness during workplace investigations and what procedural fairness entails.[121] This stands in contrast with the more consistent view set out in the three HRM textbooks that employers should ensure procedural fairness in workplace investigations. For example, some lawyers unambiguously assert that procedural fairness must be provided in all workplace investigations.[122] Others assert that procedural fairness 'should' be provided, including to avoid legal claims by workers and scrutiny by courts and tribunals, but an employer must balance ensuring procedural fairness against other considerations such as timeliness.[123] In contrast, other lawyers state that procedural fairness is not legally required and so is not a mandatory feature of all workplace investigations. For example,

[117] Ruskin (n 103) 62.

[118] See, eg, Remedios (n 110) 235; Nickels and Hennessy (n 114) 21; Jonathon Ellis and Rani John, 'Protecting Privilege during Internal Investigations: Is Lawyer Work Product at Risk?' (2017) 33 Law Society of NSW Journal 88, 89.

[119] See, eg, Grevis Beard and Rose Bryant-Smith, 'Delay Workplace Investigations at Your Peril' (2008) 82 Law Institute Journal 40, 40; Nicholas Ellery and others, 'Mental Health and Workplace Investigations: What Are Your Obligations?' (2018) 70 Governance Directions 82.

[120] Ruskin (n 103) 62.

[121] See, eg, Corlia Roos and Kerryn Tredwell, 'Perils in the Pursuit of Procedural Fairness' (Australasian Association of Workplace Investigators Conference, Sydney, 23–25 October, 2019).

[122] See, eg, Gardiner and Acaro (n 104) 23; Paul Moorhouse, 'When Does Dishonesty Provide a Valid Reason for Dismissal?' (2021) 80 Law Society Journal 86, 86.

[123] Jennifer Wyborn and others, 'Workplace Investigations Refresher 01: Where to Begin' (*Clayton Utz*, 4 February 2021) <https://www.claytonutz.com/insights/2021/february/workplace-investigations-refresher-part-1-where-to-begin> accessed 31 July 2025.

lawyers James Mattson and Mark Paul asserted that there is no legal requirement for employers to provide respondents with procedural fairness but '[i]t is not hard to find a law firm saying: "employers must conduct workplace investigations . . . in a manner that affords procedural fairness." '[124]

The concept of procedural fairness is also described differently across these sources. Some commentators refer to principles under administrative law to define procedural fairness in workplace investigations.[125] Other lawyers describe procedural fairness by reference to the factors that are used by the FWC to determine whether a dismissal was 'harsh, unjust or unreasonable' under the unfair dismissal protection set out in pt 3-2 of the *FW Act*,[126] while other commentators combine these concepts.[127] These texts reinforce that there is inconsistency amongst employers and their advisors about the requirement to afford procedural fairness in workplace investigations or about how to define the principle in the absence of clear statutory rules.

Fourth, a small body of practitioner periodicals, conference papers, and media articles provides an alternative perspective on workplace investigations. These sources refer to workers such as respondents who have been impacted by workplace investigations that were conducted poorly or for illegitimate purposes by employers[128] or key issues of concern to workers. For example, lawyers have commented on instances where employers have initiated workplace investigations to address suspicions of wrongdoing about which there is little evidence,[129] pressure workers to make admissions about others,[130] induce respondents to resign or otherwise cease employment,[131] inquire against the wishes of complainants,[132] achieve a predetermined outcome,[133] or silence aggrieved workers and deter them from making complaints to external bodies.[134] In addition, commentators describe poor processes that can

[124] Mattson and Paul (n 104) 6. By way of example, see Gardiner and Acaro (n 104) 23.

[125] See, eg, Roos and Tredwell (n 121); Joanna Betteridge, 'Useful Cases for Investigators to Achieve Practical Justice' (Australasian Association of Workplace Investigators Conference, Melbourne, 20 October 2017).

[126] See, eg, Andrew Tobin and Adele Garnett, 'Misconduct Investigations: Our Top Tips' (2015) 67 Governance Directions 306, 310.

[127] Tanya Cirkovic, 'Avoiding Practical Injustice—Observations from the Bench' (Australasian Association of Workplace Investigators Conference, Melbourne, 20 October 2017); Betteridge (n 125).

[128] These sources mainly comprise op-ed articles written by commentators for news media, commentators' expert comments as published in news media or contributions to industry conferences.

[129] Lucy McNally, 'Random Drug Tests Spark Claims of Homophobic Bullying at Newtown Police Station' *ABC News* (9 October 2016) <http://www.abc.net.au/news/2016-10-09/allegations-of-homophobic-bullying-at-newtown-police-station/7916186> accessed 25 July 2025; Emma Starkey, 'What Does Practical Justice Look Like for Complainants and Respondents?' (Australasian Association of Workplace Investigators Conference, Melbourne, 20 October 2017).

[130] Giri Sivaraman, 'Poor Workplace Investigations Can Leave Path of Destruction' *Brisbane Times* (7 February 2017) <https://www.brisbanetimes.com.au/business/workplace/poor-workplace-investigations-can-leave-path-of-destruction-20170207-gu7kmo.html> accessed 9 July 2025.

[131] ibid; Emma Thornton, Giri Sivaraman, and Michelle James, 'EILS Seminar: Workplace Investigations' (16 June 2016) <http://www.slideshare.net/mauriceblackburn/eils-seminar-workplace-investigations-june-2016> accessed 31 July 2025.

[132] See, eg, Starkey (n 129).

[133] See, eg, Josh Bornstein, 'HR Is Not Always Here to Help' *The Age* (15 October 2015) <https://www.theage.com.au/business/workplace/hr-are-not-always-here-to-help-20151013-gk8d9k.html> accessed 31 July 2025; Thornton, Sivaraman, and James (n 131).

[134] See, eg, Charlotte Grieve, 'AMP's Behaviour "unacceptable" Says Lawyer for Former Employee' *The Sydney Morning Herald* (21 August 2020) <https://www.smh.com.au/business/banking-and-finance/amp-s-behaviour-unacceptable-says-lawyer-for-former-employee-20200821-p55nzz.html> accessed 31 July

negatively impact workers, including where employers have conducted interviews with respondents and witnesses in ways that are oppressive or intimidating,[135] have denied respondents a fair process,[136] or have conducted 'forensic inquiries into minor incidents and include interviews with everyone even tangentially relevant to the subject matter of the complaint'.[137] Commentators also discuss how employers' claims of legal professional privilege over documents produced during workplace investigations can impact workers. For example, Josh Bornstein has observed that '[b]ehind this barrier [of legal professional privilege] it is impossible for an employee to know what is going on and whether the integrity of the investigation is being maintained'.[138] These texts illuminate that workplace investigations have the potential to cause harm and injury to workers, including respondents.

These texts also discuss poor conduct by employers who 'suspend' respondents during workplace investigations. Suspensions involve directions by employers for respondents to not perform their duties during a workplace investigation either with or without pay.[139] Employers sometimes rely on express contractual terms to suspend workers or will suspend respondents by giving them lawful and reasonable directions pursuant to the implied duty of obedience owed by employees towards their employers.[140] Commentators note that employers 'often' suspend respondents[141] and might do so without proper justification.[142] Lawyer John Wilson notes that respondents may be suspended without adequate support from the employer.[143] These texts reinforce the scope of management power in determining procedural matters during workplace investigations and point to how this can potentially lead to harm or detriment to respondents.

Overall, these texts reveal that employers engage lawyers in various roles to protect organizational interests. Employers may take protective action by claiming legal professional privilege during workplace investigations. The texts point towards adversarial rather than inquisitorial dynamics between parties during workplace

2025; John Wilson, 'The Most Common Workplace Issues That Never Reach the Courts' (*The Mandarin*, 21 August 2017) <https://www.themandarin.com.au/82592-common-workplace-issues-never-reach-courts/> accessed 31 July 2025.

[135] See, eg, John Wilson, 'Dodging Quagmires in Disciplinary Investigations' *The Age* (31 March 2014) <https://www.theage.com.au/public-service/dodging-quagmires-in-disciplinary-investigations-20140330-35rh5.html> accessed 25 July 2025; Williamson (n 112) 5.

[136] Thornton, Sivaraman, and James (n 131).

[137] John Wilson, 'Investigating Bullying or Bullying by Investigation?' *The Sydney Morning Herald* (28 April 2017) <https://www.smh.com.au/public-service/investigating-bullying-or-bullying-by-investigation-20170428-gvv4mx.html> accessed 25 July 2025.

[138] Workplace Express, 'Bullying Jurisdiction to Put Spotlight on Unregulated Workplace Investigators: Lawyer' *Workplace Express* (9 April 2014).

[139] Sweatman and Ruskin (n 103).

[140] On a direction to suspend comprising a lawful and reasonable direction under the common law of the contract of employment, see *Avenia v Railway & Transport Health Fund Ltd* (2017) 272 IR 151 [164].

[141] Sivaraman (n 130).

[142] See, eg, Henrietta Cook and Timna Jacks, 'La Trobe University Could Face Legal Action over Suspension of Safe Schools Co-Founder Roz Ward' *The Age* (2 June 2016) <https://www.theage.com.au/national/victoria/lawyers-academics-condemn-la-trobe-universitys-suspension-of-safe-schools-cofounder-roz-ward-20160602-gp9nmz.html> accessed 31 July 2025; Sivaraman (n 130).

[143] Wilson, 'Bullying by Investigation?' (n 137).

investigations.[144] They also reveal employers can potentially conduct workplace investigations for illegitimate reasons, although the prevalence of these types of practices is unknown and not encouraged by authors of the texts. A small body of commentaries provides insights into the types of risks and harms that respondents may experience during poorly or illegitimately conducted workplace investigations, but workers' own voices are largely absent from the texts.

D Promotional sources

In addition, a voluminous body of promotional literature that discusses workplace investigations is published on the websites of Australian legal and workplace investigations firms. These texts provide information to current and prospective clients on legislative changes and the outcomes of recent court and tribunal decisions. Most are written by practitioners who advise employers, although a smaller body of texts are written by practitioners who represent workers. These sources enable understanding of employer practices including about managing 'difficult' workers during workplace investigations[145] and of how employers and practitioners draw on decisions of the FWC to develop ideas of 'best practice' workplace investigations.

The promotional material includes insights regarding resistance by respondents to workplace investigations. Commentators note that workers may refuse to participate in workplace investigations, take leave after the investigation has commenced, become reticent or reluctant participants during the process,[146] or pursue a legal claim.[147] They give employers tips on how to deal with uncooperative respondents,[148] such as completing the investigation without the respondent's input.[149] Promotional texts highlight how the interests of parties can conflict and how this can be reflected in worker resistance.[150]

Many promotional texts describe recent decisions made under the unfair dismissal protection in pt 3-2 of the *FW Act* that consider workplace investigations. These decisions do not have precedential value and are largely determined by the facts in dispute. They are nevertheless of importance to employers because a worker who has been

144 Mattson and Paul (n 104).

145 See, eg, 'Difficult People in Workplace Investigations' (*Lander & Rogers*, April 2018) <https://www.landers.com.au/legal-insights-news/how-to-deal-with-difficult-people-in-a-workplace-investigation> accessed 31 July 2025.

146 See, eg, Skye Rose, 'Workplace Investigations Series—Navigating the "Human" Element in HR Investigations (Part 2)' (*Moores*, 17 September 2019) <https://www.moores.com.au/news/workplace-investigations-series-navigating-the-human-element-in-hr-investigations-part-2/> accessed 31 July 2025.

147 See, eg, Justine Turnbull, 'Participants in a Workplace Investigation—The Untouchables?' (*Seyfarth: Workplace Law & Strategy*, 27 March 2015) <https://www.workplacelawandstrategy.com.au/2015/03/participants-in-a-workplace-investigation-the-untouchables/> accessed 31 July 2025.

148 See, eg, Vince Scopelliti, 'How to Deal with an Uncooperative Respondent' (*WISE Workplace*, 29 May 2019) <https://www.wiseworkplace.com.au/2019/05/how-to-deal-with-an-uncooperative-respondent/> accessed 31 July 2025; Rose (n 146).

149 See, eg, Kairen Harris, 'Thorny Issues for Workplace Investigation Processes' (*Worklogic*, 27 March 2018) <https://www.worklogic.com.au/review-of-actions/thorny-issues-for-workplace-investigation-processes/> accessed 31 July 2025; Tidley (n 105).

150 See, eg, Turnbull (n 147).

dismissed following a workplace investigation may be eligible to apply to the FWC for remedial orders on the basis that the dismissal was 'harsh, unjust or unreasonable'. For example, texts include 'lessons' for employers about timeliness,[151] impartiality,[152] and reasonable support for workers,[153] from these decisions. These texts show that employers and practitioners are using FWC decisions to guide their practices in the absence of direct and explicit statutory rules under work law with respect to workplace investigations.

While the promotional texts provide important insights into the practices and perspectives of employers, few provide information about workers' perspectives and experiences. They reinforce the central role of lawyers and external workplace investigators as sources of information and advice for employers. However, the literature lacks a deeper examination of why respondents might be reluctant or unable to participate in workplace investigations, nor does it critically consider the law.

IV Contested and Complex: Controversies and Conflicts in Workplace Investigations as Discerned from HRM Texts

The examination of HRM texts reveals that there is a lack of in-depth critical discussion regarding employer practices in workplace investigations, the legal regulation of these processes, or common controversies and conflicts. In this part, I critically consider nine insights from the HRM texts about employer practices and central controversies and conflicts in workplace investigations.

First, the HRM texts reveal that the processes adopted by employers during workplace investigations vary widely, and an underpinning controversy is that an employer might not explain the process to an affected worker, such as a respondent, or apply a consistent process between investigations.[154] The literature reveals the central role that managerial discretion can play in determining whether and how an employer will conduct a workplace investigation, and how an employer evaluates and uses the information collected. An employer will generally exercise managerial power having regard to any legal and/or organizational risks that might result from its actions.[155] However, there is no indication in the texts that employers generally consult workers regarding whether or how an investigation is to be conducted.

[151] See, eg, Ben Motro and Joe Murphy, 'The Do's and Dont's of Workplace Investigations' (*Piper Alderman*, 13 August 2021) <https://piperalderman.com.au/insight/the-dos-and-donts-of-workplace-investigations/> accessed 31 July 2025.

[152] See, eg, Claire McGee, 'Being a Workplace Investigator Is No Job for a "Wilting Flower"' (*Gilshenan & Luton*, 3 August 2020) <https://www.gnl.com.au/articles/2020/august/workplace-investigations-objectivity/> accessed 31 July 2025; Eden Elliot, 'Within "Spitting Distance" of a Fair Investigation?' (*WISE Workplace Training*, 7 December 2016) <https://www.wiseworkplacetraining.com.au/2016/12/07/within-spitting-distance-of-a-fair-investigation/> accessed 31 July 2025.

[153] See, eg, Vince Scopelliti, 'Supporting Stakeholder Wellbeing During an Investigation' (*WISE Workplace*, 26 March 2021) <https://www.wiseworkplace.com.au/2021/03/supporting-stakeholder-wellbeing-during-an-investigation/> accessed 31 July 2025.

[154] See, eg, Turnbull (n 52) 23; Wyborn and others (n 123).

[155] See, eg, Hoctor (n 67) 4.

Second, the HRM texts illuminate that a wide range of actors can be involved in a workplace investigation, and a key controversy is that many of these actors may be invisible to workers, such as respondents. The texts refer to different actors who potentially work 'behind the scenes', beyond the employer, participating workers, and the investigator. These additional actors include forensic accountants and handwriting experts.[156] Employers are not required to inform workers about the various actors who are involved in the process. The range of actors who may assist employers during workplace investigations potentially amplifies the disparity in power and resources between employers and respondents.

Third, HRM texts broadly conceive of the law as a source of risks and rights (for employers and workers) and illuminate how employers use legal mechanisms during workplace investigations including to protect their interests. Commentators reiterate that an employer may decide it has no option but to conduct a workplace investigation to mitigate legal risk, even though the workplace investigation process can itself be a source of legal risk that must be managed. The texts discuss how employers can use claims of legal professional privilege to protect their interests during workplace investigations. The HRM textbooks reinforce the importance of legal compliance in workplace investigations but generally overlook the protective function of the law of work.[157]

Fourth, the HRM texts reveal ideas about 'best practice' in workplace investigations, and a central controversy is that employers and practitioners express diverse ideas about concepts that are central to 'best practice'.[158] For example, lawyers hold different views about whether it is necessary for employers to afford procedural fairness in all workplace investigations and, if so, what procedural fairness entails. Commentaries that describe procedural fairness as a 'golden rule' stand in stark contrast to other views that it is not required in all inquiries. Similarly, there is uncertainty about whether or when an employer or investigator should consider the principle from *Briginshaw*. These inconsistent views may be explained by the absence of direct and clear statutory regulation about how employers must conduct workplace investigations.[159] They illuminate an instance in which HRM professionals, lawyers, and organizations have developed dissonant constructions of legal compliance.[160]

Fifth, HRM texts reveal a tension between 'best practice' ideals and the necessity for employers to act pragmatically. Commentators observe that employers

[156] See, eg, Tredwell and Donovan (n 59) 162; Vince Scopelliti, 'Document Examiners: When to Make Use of Them' (*WISE Workplace*, 13 September 2017) <https://www.wiseworkplace.com.au/2017/09/document-examiners-when-to-make-use-of-them/> accessed 31 July 2025.

[157] On the protective function of workplace investigations for employers, rather than workers, see, eg, Wilson, 'Dodging Quagmires' (n 135).

[158] See, eg, Jennifer Wyborn, Ashleigh Discipio, and Caroline Beasley, 'Workplace Investigations Refresher Part 11: Weighing Evidence' (*Clayton Utz*, 23 December 2021) <https://www.claytonutz.com/insights/2021/december/workplace-investigations-refresher-part-11-weighing-evidence> accessed 31 July 2025.

[159] John Wilson and Kieran Pender, 'Searching for an Elusive Truth: Briginshaw in the Workplace' (2021) 259 Ethos: Law Society of the ACT Journal 36, 259.

[160] Lauren B Edelman, 'Legal Ambiguity and Symbolic Structures: Organizational Mediation of Civil Rights Law' (1992) 97 American Journal of Sociology 1531, 1532.

often find workplace investigations challenging and complex to conduct,[161] and the range of risks, actors, and priorities of participants explains why this is so. Texts note that workplace investigations must be substantively fair but need not be perfect.[162] Workplace investigators Corila Roos and Kerryn Tredwell encapsulate this view by describing a workplace investigation as involving a 'situational balancing act',[163] and Fox et al explain that workplace investigations require employers to strike a 'delicate balance of a range of competing interests'.[164] The HRM texts show that employers must make choices between conflicting priorities such as timeliness and fairness/thoroughness;[165] confidentiality and transparency;[166] anonymity of complainants and employer accountability,[167] and HRM's impartiality and its role in instructing investigators.[168] Each of these choices is determined by the employer and is likely to affect workers, including respondents.[169]

Sixth, the texts reveal that employers can commence investigations for improper purposes or unreasonably, and this can harm or injure respondents.[170] Practitioners note that most employers will initiate a workplace investigation for legitimate reasons. They warn employers about the risks of commencing workplace investigations for illegitimate purposes, such as to induce a respondent to resign.[171] They also warn employers against acting unreasonably during workplace investigations, such as by imposing an inflexible and arbitrary 'one size fits all' approach.[172] It is unknown whether it is common for employers to commence workplace investigations for unfair or ulterior purposes. However, an underpinning message that arises from these cautionary texts is that it is possible for employers to use workplace investigations in a punitive manner.

[161] See, eg, Vince Scopelliti, 'Outsourcing or In-House Investigations?' (*WISE Workplace*, 3 October 2019) <https://www.wiseworkplace.com.au/2019/10/outsourcing-or-in-house-investigations/> accessed 31 July 2025; Wilson, 'Dodging Quagmires' (n 135).

[162] Cornes (n 64) 106; Fox and others (n 3) 21.

[163] Roos and Tredwell (n 121).

[164] Fox and others (n 3) 183.

[165] See, eg, Ian Freckelton, 'Foreword' in Paula Hoctor and Michael Robertson (eds), *Workplace Investigations: Principles and Practice* (1st edn, LexisNexis Butterworths 2018) vii; Michael Robertson, 'Workplace Investigator Ethics' in Paula Hoctor and Kerryn Tredwell (eds), *Workplace Investigations: Principles and Practice* (2nd edn, LexisNexis Butterworths 2023) 239.

[166] See, eg, Hoctor (n 67) 8; Belinda Copley and Susan Forder, 'Sexual Harassment Investigations' in Paula Hoctor and Kerryn Tredwell (eds), *Workplace Investigations: Principles and Practice* (2nd edn, LexisNexis Butterworths 2023) 291.

[167] See, eg, Kerryn Tredwell, 'Making Findings and Writing the Investigation Report' in Paula Hoctor and Kerryn Tredwell (eds), *Workplace Investigations: Principles and Practice* (2nd edn, LexisNexis Butterworths 2023) 247–48.

[168] See, eg, Rachel Cornes, 'Drafting Allegations' in Paula Hoctor and Kerryn Tredwell (eds), *Workplace Investigations: Principles and Practice* (2nd edn, LexisNexis Butterworths 2023) 93.

[169] Skye Rose, 'Workplace Investigations Series—Getting It Right (Part 1)' (*Moores*, 5 July 2019) <https://www.moores.com.au/news/workplace-investigations-series-getting-it-right-part-1/> accessed 25 July 2025.

[170] See, eg, Peter JA Sams, 'Workplace Investigations—The Good, the Bad and the Ugly' (Australasian Association of Workplace Investigators Conference, 25 October 2019).

[171] Thornton, Sivaraman, and James (n 131).

[172] See, eg, Jarrad McAuliffe and Joe Murphy, '"Exemplary" Investigation Process Still Results in Successful Workers Compensation Claim' (*Piper Alderman*, 18 August 2021) <https://piperalderman.com.au/insight/exemplary-investigation-process-still-results-in-successful-workers-compensation-claim/> accessed 31 July 2025.

Seventh, even if an employer has legitimate reasons for conducting a workplace investigation, it may conduct the investigation incompetently and/or act unreasonably, and this can lead to or exacerbate harm to workers. The texts reinforce that workplace investigations are difficult processes for employers to manage,[173] and that employer representatives and workplace investigators may not always have the skills or experience to conduct them effectively.[174] The literature is replete with the concept of 'good' and 'bad' workplace investigations.[175] Descriptions of 'bad' workplace investigations refer to flawed processes that are inconsistent with an employer's internal policies,[176] involve intimidating conduct towards workers during interviews,[177] conflation of the roles of investigator and decision-maker,[178] or feature unreasonable delays.[179] The texts include concerns that there is a lack of training and legal standards for employers and workplace investigators, and this can add to the incidence of poor practice during workplace investigations.[180]

Eighth, the HRM texts reveal that workplace investigations can have negative impacts on the mental health of employees including respondents, irrespective of the findings of the investigation or whether an employer conducted the investigation competently and reasonably.[181] The texts include comments that workplace investigations are inherently stressful, confronting, and distressing for respondents.[182] The empirical study by Jenkins et al sets out specific examples of the impacts of workplace investigations on the mental health of respondents who participated in the study. Lawyers representing workers observe that, in an 'ideal' workplace investigation, the employer will be committed to protecting the mental health of workers, but the reality can differ.[183] HRM texts refer to the need for employers to consider the mental health of workers, but the inherent risk that workplace investigations can pose to the mental health of respondents is an underexamined controversy in the literature.[184]

Ninth, the sources reveal a conflict between the purported 'independence' of an investigation and the need for employers to actively protect their legal and reputational

[173] See, eg, Ellery and others (n 119).

[174] Williamson (n 112).

[175] See, eg, Sams (n 170); Jodie Fox, 'Four Tips for Conducting Trauma Informed Investigation Interviews' (*Worklogic*, 16 November 2021) <https://www.worklogic.com.au/workplace-investigations/four-tips-in-conducting-trauma-informed-investigations/> accessed 31 July 2025; McAuliffe and Murphy (n 172).

[176] See, eg, Jennifer Beck, 'Importance of Fair Workplace Investigations' (2012) 50 Law Society Journal 46.

[177] Vince Scopelliti, 'Interview Techniques for Workplace Investigations' (*WISE Workplace*, 24 July 2019)<https://www.wiseworkplace.com.au/2019/07/interview-techniques-for-workplace-investigations/> accessed 31 July 2025.

[178] Vince Scopelliti, 'When a Pre-Determined View Leads to an Unfair Investigation' (*WISE Workplace*, 10 October 2019) <https://www.wiseworkplace.com.au/2019/10/when-a-pre-determined-view-leads-to-an-unfair-investigation/> accessed 31 July 2025.

[179] Beard and Bryant-Smith (n 119); Wilson, 'Bullying by Investigation?' (n 137).

[180] Workplace Express (n 138).

[181] Scopelliti, 'Supporting Stakeholder Wellbeing During an Investigation' (n 153); Jill Murphy, 'Alternatives to Workplace Investigations' (*Worklogic*, 13 October 2021) <https://www.worklogic.com.au/workplace-investigations/alternatives-to-workplace-investigations/> accessed 31 July 2025; Ellery and others (n 119).

[182] See, eg, Wilson, 'Dodging Quagmires' (n 135); Remedios (n 110).

[183] Thornton, Sivaraman, and James (n 131); Sivaraman (n 130).

[184] See, eg, Ellery and others (n 119).

interests.[185] It is apparent from the sources that the position of an employer in a workplace investigation is inherently conflicted.[186] Central to this tension is an underpinning conflict of interest that arises from employers running purportedly 'independent' inquiries in which they are fundamentally interested, and then being the recipients of findings that potentially introduce or increase risk or harm to the employer. Some texts suggest that appointing an external investigator resolves this conflict.[187] Yet this does not seem to address concerns raised in some texts about the possibility that employers might still interfere with the investigator's process to mitigate organizational risks. This could comprise the employer unduly interfering in the investigator's activities,[188] conducting a 'parallel internal investigation' to achieve organizational objectives or influence the investigation outcome,[189] altering the investigator's findings (e.g., by having legal advisors comment on 'draft reports'),[190] or failing to act on the findings.[191] The conflicted position of the employer during a workplace investigation is an underexamined controversy that affects all parties in these processes.

This critical examination of employer practices, controversies and conflicts in workplace investigations illuminates what is known about workplace investigations from HRM texts. The sources predominantly provide the perspective of the employer, although some texts do consider other perspectives. It is therefore important to examine the perspectives and interests that are prioritized in HRM texts, and how this might limit how commentators describe or consider the risks and implications of workplace investigations.

V The Eye of the Employer? A Critical Analysis of Perspectives on Workplace Investigations in HRM Texts

There are three central ways that the understanding of Australian workplace investigations in the existing literature alone seems to be limited. Specifically, the views and perspectives of workers including respondents are minimized, adversarial conduct by employers and workers during workplace investigations is hard to discern, and employers' use of workplace investigations to rehearse and prepare for litigation is not explicitly considered.

As noted above, employers' experiences of workplace investigations are visible in the literature, but workers' views and experiences are less often discussed. As a result, the voices and views of workers, including respondents, are minimized. Respondents are primarily described as the subjects of workplace investigations, as sources of

[185] See, eg, Chris Molnar, 'Apprehended Conflicts of Interest in Employment Investigations and Decision-Making' (2015) 21 Employment Law Bulletin 91.

[186] This view is supported by a finding from the empirical study of workplace investigators conducted by Ballard who refers to the possibility for 'conflicts of interest and possible collusion or conspiracy': Ballard (n 6) 257.

[187] See, eg, Sweatman and Ruskin (n 103); Cornes (n 64) 106; Williamson (n 112) 3.

[188] See, eg, Roos and Tredwell (n 121); Thornton, Sivaraman, and James (n 131); Sweatman and Ruskin (n 103).

[189] Fox and others (n 3) 193.

[190] See, eg, Thornton, Sivaraman, and James (n 131); Workplace Express (n 138).

[191] Remedios (n 110).

information, and as the actors who may resist or challenge the investigation process or outcome, including by pursuing a legal claim.[192] The texts do not systematically or critically consider legal decisions to better understand workers' perspectives or concerns and instead approach decisions as sources of 'lessons' for employers and investigators, including on how to conduct investigations, respond to grievances or legal claims by respondents. Except for the qualitative study by Jenkins et al, which reports on interviews with a small sample of managers who faced allegations of bullying,[193] there is a lack of attention given to understanding the experiences of respondents.

In addition, the existing literature does not reconcile why these purportedly 'impartial' processes of inquiry include many instances of conflict between employers and workers, including respondents. Underpinning these conflicts is a tension between the 'inquisitorial' function of workplace investigations and the presence of 'adversarial' features. An inquisitorial process is one where 'it is the adjudicator who takes the initiative in seeking evidence, formulating legal argument and who controls the course of the case' whereas an adversarial process is a forum where the parties 'control how the case will be argued and the evidence which will be adduced' with the judge taking a 'neutral role'.[194] Inquisitorial processes are centrally concerned with finding the 'truth' while adversarial processes are concerned with the adjudication of evidence.[195] As noted by James Mattson and Mark Paul, '[i]nvestigations are not meant to be adversarial but inquisitorial . . . [h]owever, employers and respondent lawyers would equally be forgiven for feeling that the process has become adversarial'.[196]

Existing texts often describe workplace investigations as 'inquiries' that are conducted by an 'impartial' investigator who may seek evidence from the employer and workers. However, the sources reveal many features of workplace investigations that are more commonly associated with adversarial processes. For example, employers may work with the investigator to determine the scope of the investigation.[197] In addition, it is apparent that the investigation file prepared by the investigator (and the investigation report) is ordinarily not open to both parties but only to the employer,[198] and employers treat investigation reports as their property.[199] Employers may not give respondents witness statements or investigators' reports and may claim legal professional privilege over the contents.[200] Commentators also observe that, where an employer engages a lawyer as an investigator, that lawyer has a responsibility to act in the interests of the employer as its client while also being required to impartially conduct the inquiry.[201] These features indicate that workplace investigations can include a conflation of inquisitorial and adversarial attributes in Australia. This raises a range of

192 Fox and others (n 3) 356–60.
193 Jenkins, Winefield, and Sarris (n 4).
194 Tom Thawley, 'Adversarial and Inquisitorial Procedures in the Administrative Appeals Tribunal' (1997) 4 Australian Journal of Administrative Law 61, 62–63.
195 ibid 63.
196 Mattson and Paul (n 104) 3.
197 Rose (n 169); Turnbull (n 52) 21; Cornes (n 168) 93.
198 See, eg, Amy Oppenheimer, 'Workplace Harassment Investigations Worldwide' (2019) 10 Association of Workplace Investigators Journal 1, 5.
199 Thornton, Sivaraman, and James (n 131).
200 Wyborn, Matthews, and Beasley (n 114).
201 See, eg, Turnbull (n 52) 37; Workplace Express (n 138). See also Robertson (n 165) 237–38.

implications that are overlooked in the literature, including that employers participate in workplace investigations as interested parties, while also commissioning and commanding the investigator, who is expected to act impartially.[202]

The HRM texts also do not critically consider how employers may use workplace investigations to prepare for future legal claims.[203] The inclination to prepare for future legal claims may explain why some employers adopt such elaborate workplace investigation processes featuring many organizational actors. Within the Australian legal system, these civil proceedings will mostly take place within a (formal or informal) adversarial system. For example, a workplace investigation enables an employer to gather evidence of misconduct that it can rely upon to take disciplinary action against a worker.[204] It may have been conducted following a 'preliminary inquiry' which also involved the employer collecting evidence.[205] If that worker is an employee who is eligible to make a claim of unfair dismissal under pt 3-2 of the *FW Act*, the employer can rely upon the investigation report (and the evidence collected) to defend the disciplinary action at the subsequent hearing of the matter before the FWC. The literature indicates that, by the time an employer is required to respond to a legal claim about disciplinary action taken in response to a worker's alleged misconduct, it may have had multiple opportunities to rehearse the evidence and assess its prospects of defending the interests of the employer before a court or tribunal. These internal steps can be seen as ways employers 'construct the meaning of compliance in a way that meets legal demands yet preserves managerial interests'.[206] The HRM texts overlook how preliminary inquiries and workplace investigations can amplify disparities in information, preparation, and power, which might fundamentally disadvantage respondent workers in later legal proceedings.

VI Conclusion

In this chapter, I have consolidated and critically examined a broad body of HRM texts to identify common employer practices and central conflicts and controversies between parties during workplace investigations. The analysis problematizes the concept of a workplace investigation from a legal perspective.

Employers commence workplace investigations for many different reasons and have diverse practices. Key controversies relate to how employers exercise managerial power and the existence of 'poor' workplace investigation practices. Central contests relate to the meaning of 'procedural fairness' during workplace investigations and the

202 Roos and Tredwell (n 121).

203 The connection between employer practices and concern about future legal proceedings is noted by James Mattson, 'Workplace Scandals: Some Lessons for Employers' (*Bartier Perry Lawyers*, 29 March 2018) 5 <https://www.bartier.com.au/insights/articles/workplace-scandals-some-lessons-for-employers> accessed 31 July 2025.

204 Williamson (n 112) 2.

205 Storm Carnie, 'How to Cull Misconduct Allegations to Those That Really Matter—a Preliminary Assessment Approach' (*Worklogic*, 21 July 2021) <https://www.worklogic.com.au/workplace-investigations/how-to-cull-misconduct-allegations-to-those-that-really-matter-a-preliminary-assessment-approach/> accessed 31 July 2025; Turnbull (n 52) 23.

206 Edelman (n 160) 1532.

need for employers to manage purportedly 'independent' internal inquiries in which they are fundamentally interested. Personnel, such as HRM practitioners, sometimes embody this conflict by being required to perform multiple roles, although lawyers often warn that they should not do so.[207] Many of these contests and controversies are amplified by the absence of direct and clear legal regulation about workplace investigations.

Respondents' own voices and perspectives on workplace investigations are lacking in the HRM texts. Of significance are sources that reveal that even properly conducted workplace investigations can cause psychiatric harm and injury to respondents.[208] Some HRM texts written by practitioners who represent respondents express concern that poor employer practices can worsen the risk of harm or injury to respondents. The texts also illuminate that commentators are concerned about the prevalence of poor workplace investigations and recognize that these processes are inherently complex and difficult for employers. Yet there is little detail about the views or experiences of respondents in HRM texts.

This analysis of HRM texts indicates that it is necessary to develop a theory of justice in workplace investigations that focuses on respondents as subjects of the law and inquire into respondents' perspectives and experiences of workplace investigations. It is also necessary to better understand the specific legal constraints that apply to employer conduct towards respondents under judge-made and statute law in Australia. In chapter 3, I construct an idea of justice in workplace investigations. This theoretical framework is applied in chapter 7 to evaluate the legal regulation of workplace investigations and propose an agenda for reform.

207 Turnbull (n 52) 34–35.
208 See, eg, Djurkovic and others (n 34).

3

A Framework of Justice for Respondents in Workplace Investigations

I Introduction

In chapter 2, I explored how management power is prevalent in workplace investigations and the dimensions of risk of harm and injury to workers, including respondents. This chapter is informed by the preceding analysis and develops a framework of justice in workplace investigations with the respondent as the subject of the law. I argue that achieving justice in workplace investigations involves implementing work laws that promote a multidimensional framework of individual and collective work rights for respondents that is pragmatic and advances citizenship at work. The theoretical and normative examination proceeds in six key steps.

II The Normative Concept of Justice at Work in Legal Scholarship

As a first step in developing a theory of justice through work regulation applicable to respondents in workplace investigations, I examine the concept of justice at work within legal scholarship. In this section, I argue that a central concept of justice at work has traditionally been, and continues to be, the protection of workers having regard to the subordination of labour to capital.

There is an array of perspectives regarding the idea of 'justice' in the context of work, and these ideas span several fields of research. For example, a large body of literature considers ethical and political questions about justice at work. This literature views work through the lens of philosophy to suggest different forms of justice for workers. These texts examine ideas such as contributive justice, which pertains to the right to work,[1] and productive justice, which relates to workers' choices of jobs and overall contributions to society.[2] Another example is the extensive body of literature, in the field of HRM, which is concerned with workers' perceptions of fairness regarding workplace processes and outcomes. This literature has developed a concept of organizational justice,[3] which is defined as comprising distributive, procedural,

[1] See, eg, Jon Elster, 'Is There (or Should There Be) a Right to Work?' in Amy Gutmann (ed), *Democracy and the Welfare State* (Princeton University Press 1988).

[2] See, eg, Michael Cholbi, 'The Duty to Work' (2018) 21 Ethical Theory and Moral Practice 1119.

[3] The first enunciation of the concept is set out in Jerald Greenberg, 'A Taxonomy of Organizational Justice Theories' (1987) 12 Academy of Management Review 9. See further Russell S Cropanzano and Maureen L Ambrose, 'Organizational Justice: Where We Have Been and Where We Are Going' in Russell S Cropanzano and Maureen L Ambrose (eds), *The Oxford Handbook of Justice in the Workplace* (OUP 2015).

Workplace Investigations. Adriana Orifici, Oxford University Press. © Adriana Orifici 2026.
DOI: 10.1093/9780198970019.003.0003

interpersonal, and informational justice.[4] These fields of scholarship rarely engage in discussions about justice through work regulation.[5]

Legal scholars have developed their own distinct idea of what is meant by 'justice' at work. The idea of justice at work is central to the traditional normative foundation of work regulation.[6] According to this rationale, justice is achieved through legal regulation that addresses the unequal bargain between workers and capital. This idea is encapsulated in the often-cited vision of Otto Kahn-Freund that '[t]he main object of labour law has always been, and we venture to say always will be, to be a countervailing force to counteract the inequality of bargaining power which is inherent and must be inherent in the employment relationship.'[7] This idea of justice has been developed and debated in the scholarship about work regulation over time.[8]

As Brian Langille has suggested, it is crucial to recognize that justice is not automatically secured by workers when they commence work.[9] This is because workers face inequality in bargaining power in the contracting process and this 'will generate poor results, both in terms of concern and respect'.[10] Similarly, Hugh Collins identifies justice at work as essentially comprising 'robust guarantees against possible abuses of power at work' and 'respect for the humanity of all workers'.[11] Richard Mitchell has also reflected that justice for workers involves ensuring that they receive 'a fair share for their labours'.[12] The scholars present a normative idea of justice for workers through work regulation that is concerned with imbalance of power and underpinned by concepts of fairness and respectful treatment. This idea of justice through work regulation continues to underpin the legal scholarship across diverse subject matter.[13]

[4] Jason A Colquitt and others, 'Justice at the Millennium: A Meta-Analytic Review of 25 Years of Organizational Justice Research' (2001) 86 Journal of Applied Psychology 425, 425.

[5] The lack of interaction between the fields of legal and organizational justice is discussed in further detail in Barry Goldman, 'Organizational Justice and Legal Justice: How Are They Related?' in Russell S Cropanzano and Maureen L Ambrose (eds), *The Oxford Handbook of Justice in the Workplace* (OUP 2015).

[6] Brian Langille, 'Labour Law's Back Pages' in Guy Davidov and Brian Langille (eds), *Boundaries and Frontiers of Labour Law: Goals and Means in the Regulation of Work* (Hart 2006) 22–23; Brian Langille, 'Labour Law's Theory of Justice' in Guy Davidov and Brian Langille (eds), *The Idea of Labour Law* (OUP 2011) 111; Brian Langille, 'What Is International Labor Law For? Labor Rights in the Era of Globalization' (2009) 3 Law & Ethics of Human Rights 48.

[7] Otto Kahn-Freund, *Labour and the Law* (Stevens for the Hamlyn Trust 1972) 6.

[8] See, eg, Guy Davidov, *A Purposive Approach to Labour Law* (OUP 2016) 53–54; Guy Davidov, 'Re-Matching Labour Laws with Their Purpose' in Guy Davidov and Brian Langille (eds), *The Idea of Labour Law* (OUP 2011) 181; Christopher Arup and others (eds), *Labour Law and Labour Market Regulation: Essays on the Construction, Constitution and Regulation of Labour Markets and Work Relationships* (The Federation Press 2006); Guy Davidov and Brian Langille (eds), *Boundaries and Frontiers of Labour Law: Goals and Means in the Regulation of Work* (Bloomsbury 2006); Richard Mitchell, 'Where Are We Going in Labour Law? Some Thoughts on a Field of Scholarship and Policy in Process of Change' (2011) 24 Australian Journal of Labour Law 45, 45; Alan Bogg, *The Democratic Aspects of Trade Union Recognition* (Bloomsbury 2009) 3–32.

[9] Langille, 'What Is International Labor Law For?' (n 6) 53.

[10] ibid.

[11] Hugh Collins, 'Justice at Work' (2020) 1 Judiciary Forum Review 59, 61. For an account that integrates how private law theory might augment a public law or regulatory approach to answer questions about justice at work, see further Hugh Collins, 'Relational and Associational Justice in Work' (2023) 24 Theoretical Inquiries in Law 26.

[12] Mitchell (n 8) 48.

[13] See, eg, Alan Bogg, 'Employment Status in the Social Democratic Constitution: Law and Politics' in Alan Bogg, Jacob Rowbottom, and Alison Young (eds), *The Constitution of Social Democracy: Essays in Honour of Keith Ewing* (Hart Publishing 2020); Douglas Brodie, 'The Irrepressible Common Law: The

The International Labour Organization (ILO) also integrates the just treatment of workers into its normative instruments and its concept of decent work.[14] Article 23, regarding work, in the United Nations Universal Declaration of Human Rights,[15] is underpinned by concepts of just treatment. It provides that:

> (1) Everyone has the right to work, to free choice of employment, to just and favorable conditions of work and to protection against unemployment. (2) Everyone, without any discrimination, has the right to equal pay for equal work. (3) Everyone who works has the right to just and favorable remuneration ensuring for himself and his family an existence worthy of human dignity, and supplemented, if necessary, by other means of social protection. (4) Everyone has the right to form and to join trade unions for the protection of his interests.[16]

The ILO's recognition of the imbalance of bargaining power experienced by workers is encapsulated in the *Declaration Concerning the Aims and Purposes of the International Labour Organization*, which states that 'labour is not a commodity'.[17]

Just treatment of workers also forms part of the concept of decent work as set out in the Decent Work Agenda of the ILO and the *2030 Agenda for Sustainable Development*.[18] The idea of justice for workers promoted by the ILO through the concept of decent work is broad. It has four elements: full and productive employment, fundamental principles and rights at work, social protection, and the promotion of social dialogue.[19] The notion of decent work includes the protection of workers' fundamental rights in the workplace including through legal regulation.[20] I turn to consider the function of work law in promoting this idea of justice at work below.

Economic Torts and the Right to Strike' in Alan Bogg, Jacob Rowbottom, and Alison Young (eds), *The Constitution of Social Democracy: Essays in Honour of Keith Ewing* (Hart 2020); Navraj Singh Ghaleigh, 'Just Transitions for Workers: When Climate Change Met Labour Justice' in Alan Bogg, Jacob Rowbottom, and Alison Young (eds), *The Constitution of Social Democracy: Essays in Honour of Keith Ewing* (Hart 2020). On the difference between the traditional goal and public policy goals of governments in work regulation see, eg, Harry Arthurs, 'Can Davidov's Legal Slingshot Slay the Goliath of Political Economy? On Guy Davidov's *A Purposive Approach to Labour Law*' (2017) 16 Jerusalem Review of Legal Studies 1, 7.

[14] Labour standards can comprise conventions, recommendations, declarations, and protocols of the ILO.

[15] 'Universal Declaration of Human Rights (Adopted 10 December 1948)' UNGA Res 217 (III), UN GAOR, UN Doc A/810 <https://www.un.org/en/development/desa/population/migration/generalassembly/docs/globalcompact/A_RES_217(III).pdf> accessed 28 July 2025.

[16] ibid.

[17] 'Declaration Concerning the Aims and Purposes of the International Labour Organization' annex l(a) to the *Constitution of the International Labour Organisation and Standing Orders of the International Labour Conference, 1994* (adopted at Philadelphia 10 May 1994).

[18] 'Transforming Our World: The 2030 Agenda for Sustainable Development (Adopted 25 September 2015, Entered into Force 1 January 2016)' GA Res 70/1, UN GAOR, 70th sess, 4th plen mtg, Agenda Items 15 and 116, UN Doc A/RES/70/1 <https://sdgs.un.org/2030agenda> accessed 28 July 2025. See Harry Arthurs, 'Labour Law After Labour' in Guy Davidov and Brian A Langille (eds), *The Idea of Labour Law* (OUP 2011) 27.

[19] 'Transforming Our World: The 2030 Agenda for Sustainable Development (Adopted 25 September 2015, Entered into Force 1 January 2016)' (n 18).

[20] ILO, 'Decent Work Indicators: Guidelines for the Producers and Users of Statistical and Legal Framework Indicators' (2nd edn, ILO Manual, 2013).

III The Role of Work Law in Promoting Justice at Work

As a second step in developing a theory of justice through work regulation applicable to respondents in workplace investigations, I analyse the role of work regulation in achieving justice at work. This regulation takes the form of statutory intervention, judicial decision-making, and collective bargaining and industrial action in common law countries. In this section, I argue that work regulation continues to be crucial to advancing social goals and/or universal values for employees,[21] but recognize that work regulation faces a central tension. This tension relates to the requirement for work law to support employers to extract labour from workers and efficiently run their organizations, but also to adhere to its normative tradition by resisting the unacceptable exploitation or treatment of workers in the labour market, or denial of freedom of association.

Scholars have long debated the role of work law in achieving justice for workers, and whether work law should be aimed towards achieving social justice. For example, some scholars in the 1980s argued that market forces should be left to determine the distribution of wealth and rights to workers without legal intervention.[22] This theoretical perspective received support from policymakers in jurisdictions including Australia at various times,[23] but was broadly seen to reinforce the power disparity between labour and capital.

In the 1990s, theorists proposed that the regulation of work should be aimed at regulating the labour market to achieve economic goals.[24] This proposal received attention, but critics argued that it shifted the focus away from social goals and reduced focus on issues such as power and equity within work relations.[25] The debates reflect a continuous tension within work regulation. On the one hand, it must navigate between supporting employers to extract labour from workers and efficiently run their organizations. On the other hand, it must ensure that workers are not subjected to unacceptable exploitation or treatment, or denial of freedom of association. For work law to function and promote justice, it must, arguably, negotiate this tension.[26]

[21] This reflects a purposive view of work law. See further Davidov, *A Purposive Approach to Labour Law* (n 8); Simon Deakin, 'Labor Law: The Pragmatist's Guide—Comments on *A Purposive Approach to Labor Law*' (2017) 16 Jerusalem Review of Legal Studies 28; Guy Mundlak, 'The Power of Purpose: Comments on *A Purposive Approach to Labour Law*' (2017) 16 Jerusalem Review of Legal Studies 40; Ruth Dukes, 'Identifying the Purposes of Labor Law: Discussion of Guy Davidov's *A Purposive Approach to Labour Law*' (2017) 16 Jerusalem Review of Legal Studies 52. For a critique of this approach see, eg, Zoe Adams, *Labour and the Wage: A Critical Perspective* (OUP 2020) 1–4.

[22] Two key proponents of this theory were Frederich Hayek and Richard Epstein. See, eg, Friedrich August Hayek, *1980s Unemployment and the Unions: Essays on the Impotent Price Structure of Britain and Monopoly in the Labour Market* (Institute of Economic Affairs 1980); Richard A Epstein, 'A Common Law for Labor Relations: A Critique of the New Deal Labor Legislation' (1983) 92 The Yale Law Journal 1357.

[23] Andrew Stewart, Anthony Forsyth, and Mark Irving, *Creighton and Stewart's Labour Law* (7th ed, The Federation Press 2025) 7–8.

[24] See, eg, Arup and others (n 8); Andrew Frazer, 'Reconceiving Labour Law: The Labour Market Regulation Project' (2008) 8 Macquarie Law Journal 21, 31–32.

[25] Hugh Collins, 'Labour Law as a Vocation' (1989) 105 Law Quarterly Review 468, 472–73; Frazer (n 24) 38.

[26] Hugh Collins, *Employment Law* (2nd edn, OUP 2010) 5; Gordon Anderson, 'Employment Rights in an Era of Individualised Employment' (2007) 38 Victoria University of Wellington Law Review 417, 420.

More recently, scholars have questioned whether work law can advance justice for all workers.[27] These debates refer to the profound changes caused by factors such as the fissuring of the workplace,[28] rise of the on-demand economy,[29] decline of trade unions,[30] and globalization.[31] For example, some theorists have suggested that work regulation should be untethered from the contract of employment and linked instead to all people who work and all enterprises where work is performed to achieve justice.[32] Mark Freedland has suggested the desirability of a unified system of work law for 'employees' as well as 'workers' who are not engaged under contracts of employment.[33] These important debates recognize the challenges that contemporary work arrangements pose for promoting justice through work law. However, they do not eclipse the rationale that work regulation plays a crucial role in promoting justice for workers who are engaged under contracts of employment.[34] As shown in chapter 2, these workers include respondents who are vulnerable to harm and injury in workplace investigations.

These debates are augmented by scholarly analysis of the three main dimensions of work law and how they can promote justice for employees.[35] First, scholars assert that legal regulation that facilitates collective bargaining and industrial action advances justice for employees,[36] including because they promote procedural justice.[37] Second, scholars maintain that statutory intervention that rewrites the agreement struck in the contracting process can promote justice for employees, including by establishing minimum standards or individual rights.[38] Third, scholars contend that in common law countries such as Australia, judicial decisions also promote justice for employees.[39] For example, Anderson et al have recognized that courts can intervene to

[27] Adrian Goldin, 'Social Justice for an Ongoing Theoretical Reconfiguration of Labour Law' in Brian Langille and Anne Trebilcock (eds), *Social Justice and the World of Work: Possible Global Futures* (Hart 2023) 356–57; Judy Fudge, 'Blurring Legal Boundaries: Regulating for Decent Work' in Judy Fudge, Shae McCrystal, and Kamala Sankaran (eds), *Challenging the Legal Boundaries of Work Regulation* (Bloomsbury 2012) 1.

[28] See further David Weil, *The Fissured Workplace: Why Work Became So Bad for So Many and What Can Be Done to Improve It* (Harvard University Press 2014).

[29] See further Jeremias Prassl, *Humans As a Service: The Promise and Perils of Work in the Gig Economy* (OUP 2018); Sarah Kaine and Emmanuel Josserand, 'The Organisation and Experience of Work in the Gig Economy' (2019) 61 Journal of Industrial Relations 479.

[30] See further Anthony Forsyth, *The Future of Unions and Worker Representation: The Digital Picket Line* (Hart 2022); Jelle Visser, 'Trade Unions in the Balance' (2019) ILO/ACTRAV Working Paper <https://www.ilo.org/wcmsp5/groups/public/---ed_dialogue/---actrav/documents/publication/wcms_722482.pdf> accessed 28 July 2025.

[31] See, eg, Eddy Lee, 'Globalization and Labour Standards: A Review of Issues' (1997) 136 International Labour Review 173; Fudge, 'Blurring Legal Boundaries' (n 27) 2.

[32] Goldin (n 27) 356.

[33] Mark Freedland, *The Personal Employment Contract* (OUP 2005) 519–23.

[34] Simon Deakin, 'The Comparative Evolution of the Employment Relationship' in Guy Davidov and Brian Langille (eds), *Boundaries and Frontiers of Labour Law: Goals and Means in the Regulation of Work* (Hart 2006) 104–06.

[35] These mechanisms may operate concurrently. See further Langille, 'What Is International Labor Law For?' (n 6) 54; Anderson (n 26) 419.

[36] Langille, 'What Is International Labor Law For?' (n 6) 54.

[37] See, eg, ibid; Hugh Collins, *Justice in Dismissal: The Law of Termination of Employment* (OUP 1992) 2.

[38] Langille, 'What Is International Labor Law For?' (n 6) 54–55; Anderson (n 26) 419, 420.

[39] See, eg, Alan Bogg, 'Can We Trust the Courts in Labour Law? Stranded Between Frivolity and Despair' (2022) 38 International Journal of Comparative Labour Law and Industrial Relations 103.

prevent employers transferring undue risk to employees because of the inequality of bargaining power between the parties.[40] The literature also reinforces that these three dimensions of legal regulation may need to work complementarily to promote justice for employees. Together the framework 'stands and speaks fairness, or "decency" to the superior bargaining power of capital'.[41]

Scholars are also continually evaluating whether these three aspects of work regulation are capable of securing justice for employees. The critiques are grounded in analysis that is concerned with the contemporary conditions in which work is performed. For example, scholars have recognized that the capacity for collective bargaining to achieve justice for employees continues to depend on the practice being widespread and facilitated by laws that allow a broad scope of workers to organize and bargain.[42] These debates reinforce that the role that each dimension of work regulation plays in advancing justice needs to be critically and contextually considered in developing a theory of justice in workplace investigations.

IV Debates About the Goals and Values That Advance Justice at Work

As a third step in developing a theory of justice in workplace investigations, I critically consider debates between scholars regarding the social goals and/or universal values that work law should promote to further justice for workers. I suggest that different values will have potency depending on the issue or problem at hand and that workplace democracy and citizenship are apposite values when considering the subject of respondents in workplace investigations. This is because respondents are less often seen as requiring the protection of work law to mitigate their vulnerability to employer power, and citizenship at work presents a lens through which all workers are equally entitled to legal protection.

While debates abound amongst scholars about the social goals and/or universal values that work law needs to promote to achieve justice, there are three key schools of thought in the literature.[43] First, there are scholars who connect the idea of justice for workers with the capacity of work law to achieve values drawn from liberal theories of justice.[44] Within that school of thought are experts who nominate diverse values, which they argue underpin work law,[45] such as dignity,[46]

[40] Gordon Anderson, Douglas Brodie, and Joellen Riley, 'Development and Character of the Contract of Employment: A Comparative Study' in Gordon J Anderson, Douglas Brodie, and Joellen Riley (eds), *The Common Law Employment Relationship: A Comparative Study* (Edward Elgar 2017) 17.

[41] Langille, 'Labour Law's Theory of Justice' (n 6) 106–07 (citation omitted).

[42] Forsyth, *The Future of Unions* (n 30) 219–33.

[43] These approaches are not necessarily mutually exclusive, and there are studies that adopt a framework of social values that encompass all three bases for achieving justice.

[44] Hugh Collins, 'Theories of Rights as Justifications for Labour Law' in Guy Davidov and Brian Langille (eds), *The Idea of Labour Law* (OUP 2011). On the concept of a liberal theory of justice see, in particular, John Rawls, *John Rawls, A Theory of Justice* (Otfried Höffe ed, Joost den Haan tr, Brill 2013).

[45] Liberal values, which are identified by scholars as essential to securing justice for workers, are not necessarily compatible or interchangeable, although there is potential overlap.

[46] See, eg, Pablo Gilabert, 'Dignity at Work' in Hugh Collins, Gillian Lester, and Virginia Mantouvalou (eds), *Philosophical Foundations of Labour Law* (OUP 2018); Manfred Weiss, 'Re-Inventing Labour Law?' in Guy Davidov and Brian A Langille (eds), *The Idea of Labour Law* (OUP 2011) 121.

freedom,[47] capability,[48] and human rights.[49] Yet critics of this approach argue that these theorizations of justice at work rely on broad and opaque concepts that are difficult to adapt into practical protections,[50] and lead to unpredictability when interpreted by judges, lawyers, and academics.[51]

Second, there are scholars who argue that justice is best advanced through work regulation that protects democratic values.[52] This approach sees justice as dependent on the promotion of democracy in the workplace,[53] including through collective bargaining,[54] strike action,[55] union representation and recognition,[56] worker voice, and participation in managerial decision-making.[57] Some scholars challenge this template of justice on the basis that democratic goals have lost relevance in the context of work due to factors such as a global decline in trade union membership,[58] and the increasingly diverse interests that divide groups of workers.[59] These critiques are countered by arguments that although the mechanisms for advancing collectivism need to be adjusted to respond to contemporary work arrangements, the goal of democracy at

[47] See, eg, Brian Langille, 'Human Development: A Way out of Labour Law's Fly Bottle' in Hugh Collins, Gillian Lester, and Virginia Mantouvalou (eds), *Philosophical Foundations of Labour Law* (OUP 2018). On freedom in liberal theory see, eg, Amartya Sen, *Development As Freedom* (OUP 2001).

[48] Langille, 'Labour Law's Theory of Justice' (n 6) 112.

[49] See, eg, Philippa Collins, 'The Role of Human Rights in Labour Law' in Philippa Collins (ed), *Putting Human Rights to Work: Labour Law, The ECHR, and The Employment Relation* (OUP 2022); Virginia Mantouvalou, 'Human Rights and Unfair Dismissal: Private Acts in Public Spaces' (2008) 71 The Modern Law Review 912.

[50] On dignity as a broad justification for legally regulating work with potentially limited practical content see, eg, Christoper McCrudden, 'Labour Law as Human Rights Law: A Critique of the Use of "Dignity" by Freedland and Kountouris' in Alan Bogg, Cathryn Costello, and ACL Davies (eds), *The Autonomy of Labour Law* (Bloomsbury 2015).

[51] See, eg, on the potential of dignity to give rise to unpredictability in interpretation, see further Alysia Blackham, 'Interrogating the "Dignity" Argument for Mandatory Retirement: An Undignified Development?' (2019) 48 Industrial Law Journal 377.

[52] See, eg, Bob Hepple, 'Four Approaches to the Modernisation of Individual Employment Rights' in Roger Blanpain and Manfred Weiss (eds), *Changing Industrial Relations and Modernisation of Labour Law: Liber Amicorum in Honour of Professor Marco Biagi* (Kluwer Law International 2003) 182; Keith Ewing, 'Democratic Socialism and Labour Law' (1995) 24 Industrial Law Journal 103, 111.

[53] See, eg, Martin O'Neil and Stuart White, 'Trade Unions and Political Equality' in Hugh Collins, Gillian Lester, and Virginia Mantouvalou (eds), *Philosophical Foundations of Labour Law* (OUP 2018) 257.

[54] See, eg, Guy Davidov, 'Collective Bargaining Laws: Purpose and Scope' (2004) 20 International Journal of Comparative Labour Law and Industrial Relations 81, 82; Collins, *Employment Law* (n 26) 120–21.

[55] See, eg, Alan Bogg and Cynthia Estlund, 'The Right to Strike and Contestatory Citizenship' in Hugh Collins, Gillian Lester, and Virginia Mantouvalou (eds), *Philosophical Foundations of Labour Law* (OUP 2018) 250.

[56] See Bogg, *Trade Union Recognition* (n 8).

[57] See, eg, O'Neil and White (n 53) 261–62; Bogg, *Trade Union Recognition* (n 8) 148–49; Davidov, *A Purposive Approach to Labour Law* (n 8) 56.

[58] A comprehensive review of this body of literature is outside the scope of this study. For an overview of these debates see, eg, Gillian Lester, 'Beyond Collective Bargaining: Modern Unions as Agents of Solidarity' in Guy Davidov and Brian A Langille (eds), *The Idea of Labour Law* (OUP 2011) 334–37.

[59] See, eg, Lester (n 58). A range of scholarship asserts that collective self-regulation is adaptable to these new conditions. On 'community unions' and capacity for the union movement to evolve see, eg, Janice Fine, 'A Marriage Made in Heaven? Mismatches and Misunderstandings between Worker Centres and Unions' (2007) 45 British Journal of Industrial Relations 335. On the potential to reform work law to give workers institutionalized roles in self-regulation in pursuit of 'workplace democracy' see, eg, Cynthia Estlund, 'Rebuilding the Law of the Workplace in an Era of Self-Regulation' (2005) 105 Columbia Law Review 319, 402–04.

work remains central to advancing justice.[60] For example, Ruth Dukes and Wolfgang Streeck have developed a broad and dynamic idea of workplace democracy and citizenship at work that they argue is relevant to contemporary work contexts,[61] and can exist under capitalism.[62]

Third, there are scholars who argue that justice is best achieved through regulation aimed at redistributing power and economic resources from employers to workers.[63] There is consensus in this scholarship that work regulation has distributive goals.[64] However, scholars who support this approach debate which workers should receive the benefits of redistributive efforts and why.[65] For example, some scholars support the concept of 'desert-based' redistribution, which involves workers getting what they deserve given their contribution, effort or other moral quality,[66] while others advocate for distributional equality, which involves consideration of how redistribution can eliminate workers' previous disadvantages.[67] Critics of this approach have raised concerns that work law can itself contribute to distributional unfairness between workers,[68] including by promoting rights that prioritize a privileged group of workers to the disadvantage of others such as unemployed persons, workers in insecure employment, and migrant workers.[69]

Scholars vigorously debate which social goals and/or universal values best advance justice for workers.[70] Within the three main schools of thought, there are some scholars who argue that one specific goal or value needs to be prioritized,[71] while other scholars contend that work law should be underpinned by multiple goals or values.[72]

The scholarship of Harry Arthurs is of assistance at this juncture. Arthurs challenges the idea that aspirational social goals and/or universal values (such as dignity or redistribution) can be easily translated into pragmatic legal rights for workers.[73] He notes that:

[60] Ruth Dukes and Wolfgang Streeck, *Democracy at Work: Contract, Status and Post-Industrial Justice* (Polity Press 2023) 108–39.

[61] ibid 48–71, 108–39.

[62] ibid 139. See also Ruth Dukes and Wolfgang Streeck, 'Labour Law after Neoliberalism?' (2023) 50 Journal of Law and Society 165, 182.

[63] See, eg, Guy Mundlak, 'The Third Function of Labour Law: Distributing Labour Market Opportunities among Workers' in Guy Davidov and Brian A Langille (eds), *The Idea of Labour Law* (OUP 2011); ACL Davies, 'Identifying "Exploitative Compromises": The Role of Labour Law in Resolving Disputes Between Workers' (2012) 65 Current Legal Problems 269.

[64] Mundlak, 'The Third Function of Labour Law' (n 63) 316.

[65] ibid 317–22; Davies (n 63) 270.

[66] Guy Davidov, 'Distributive Justice and Labour Law' in Hugh Collins, Gillian Lester, and Virginia Mantouvalou (eds), *Philosophical Foundations of Labour Law* (OUP 2018) 143–47.

[67] ibid 151–53.

[68] Davies (n 63) 270–73; Mundlak, 'The Third Function of Labour Law' (n 63) 317.

[69] Davies (n 63) 273–78.

[70] The purposive approach to work law proposes the aims of work law but does not reconcile these debates about which social goals and/or universal values best achieve these aims: Davidov, *A Purposive Approach to Labour Law* (n 8) 68.

[71] Langille, 'Human Development' (n 47) 21.

[72] Davidov, *A Purposive Approach to Labour Law* (n 8) 68.

[73] Harry Arthurs, 'Foreword: Mining the Philosophers' Stone: Sixteen Tons and What Do You Get? Another Day Older and Deeper in Doubt' in Hugh Collins, Gillian Lester, and Virginia Mantouvalou (eds), *Philosophical Foundations of Labour Law* (OUP 2018) v.

> [s]ome of us believe, like alchemists, that we can convert higher order ideals . . . into legally enforceable workers' rights. Perhaps so, but surely not by simply tweaking legal doctrine or patching leaky legislation, nor even by the clever channelling of traditional constitutional theory. If we want to propose ideas about rights that might be able to transform relations of work, they must be big ideas . . . and we must advocate them aggressively . . . [s]ubordination, injustice, and indignity are endemic in our society; they are not confined to the employment context.[74]

Arthurs suggests that a way forward is for scholars to synthesize aspirational views of justice with the traditional narrative of justice in work law. This narrative points towards practical ways that workers can resist the unequal power that underpins work contracts 'through a show of political and/or industrial force'.[75]

According to Arthurs, it is unnecessary to hold out one set of values or goals as offering a definitive template for justice at work.[76] Instead, it is suitable to change the lens of justice depending on the question or issue at hand.[77] In this context, I am seeking to identify the values or goals that support a theory of justice in workplace investigations through legal regulation that focuses on respondents as the subjects of the law. The values of workplace democracy and citizenship at work are apposite here as respondents are rarely seen as requiring the protection of work law to mitigate their vulnerability to management power. The value of citizenship at work presents a lens through which all workers are equally entitled to legal protection, including with respect to dismissal and WHS.[78] The concept also promotes the need for work regulation to ensure all workers are given an opportunity to provide input into the processes that employers use to make decisions that affect them and to seek representation.[79]

V Workplace Democracy and Citizenship at Work as Foundations of Justice

As a fourth step, recognizing the potency of these values in this context, I examine justice at work through the lens of workplace democracy and citizenship at work in detail. I start by unpacking the original idea of labour rights within the framework of citizenship theory by Thomas Humphrey Marshall,[80] and his concept of 'industrial citizenship'. I then examine how scholars have built on the concept of industrial citizenship to develop contemporary ideas about workplace democracy and citizenship at work. In this section, I argue that scholars have developed compelling ideas about workplace democracy and citizenship at work that originate in the concept of

[74] ibid vii.
[75] ibid vi.
[76] ibid viii.
[77] ibid.
[78] Ronald C McCallum, 'Citizenship at Work: An Australian Perspective' (2011) Sydney Law School Research Paper No 11/17 <https://papers.ssrn.com/abstract=1769271> accessed 28 July 2025; Collins, *Employment Law* (n 26) 24–25.
[79] McCallum, 'Citizenship at Work' (n 78).
[80] TH Marshall, *Class, Citizenship and Social Development* (Anchor, 1965) republished in TH Marshall and Tom Bottomore, *Citizenship and Social Class* (Pluto Press 1987).

industrial justice. These ideas promote justice for workers and can be adapted to contemporary work contexts.

A The original idea of industrial citizenship as a source of justice

Theories of citizenship and labour did not overlap until the 1950s, when the work of Marshall incorporated labour rights into the framework of citizenship.[81] In his pathbreaking treatise *Citizenship and Social Class*, Marshall described citizenship as advancing equality as it envisaged that all citizens had full membership within a community.[82] He argued that the largest community to which a citizen belonged was the nation-state and so the theory of citizenship was centrally preoccupied with determining the rights and obligations owed by the nation-state to citizens, and vice versa.

For Marshall, this framework of citizenship comprised civil, political, and social pillars.[83] However, Marshall also saw the potential for citizenship to operate distinctly in the context of work. He argued that collective bargaining and the rise of trade unions in the post-war era caused workers to use their civil rights collectively.[84] Following this idea, Marshall conceptualized the workplace as a secondary community in which workers participated as industrial citizens. Marshall argued that this produced a parallel system of citizenship that could be understood as 'industrial citizenship'.[85] In this parallel system, workers were citizens who used collective civil rights to bargain and engaged in collective action in a way that resembled the collective political rights exercised by citizens in public life.[86] Marshall's revelatory framework produced a concept of justice that was grounded in the rights that workers had as citizens in a collective, having regard to the workplace as a sphere of public interest.[87]

While Marshall's explanation of industrial citizenship is quite brief, other scholars have developed the idea.[88] First, scholars identified that industrial citizenship

[81] ibid 3.

[82] The civil element of citizenship includes the 'intensely individual' rights needed to secure a person's freedom and autonomy. The political element comprises people's collective rights to exercise political power to determine the composition of government. The social element includes rights to economic welfare and security that counter the effects of market capitalism through regulation by the nation-state: ibid 6.

[83] Marshall identifies these civil rights to include, for example, personal liberty, freedom of speech, freedom of thought and belief, and the right to justice: ibid 8.

[84] ibid 41.

[85] Marshall did not explain whether, by describing the system as 'secondary' he intended to denote it is subordinate to the other systems described, or rather that it was secondary because it arose in the specific realm of work. On Marshall affording of industrial rights 'secondary' status, see further Judy Fudge, 'After Industrial Citizenship: Market Citizenship or Citizenship at Work?' (2006) 60 Relations Industrielles 631, 635–36.

[86] Marshall also asserted that this parallel system produces a distinct range of rights from those that citizens might always hold (arising from their civil rights), as they were collectively held and exercised, rather than individually held: Marshall and Bottomore (n 80) 26.

[87] Guy Mundlak, 'Industrial Citizenship, Social Citizenship, Corporate Citizenship: I Just Want My Wages' (2007) 8 Theoretical Inquiries in Law 719, 719. See also Joanna Howe, *Rethinking Job Security: A Comparative Analysis of Unfair Dismissal Law in the UK, Australia and the USA* (Routledge 2017) 19–20.

[88] Key theorizations include Harry W Arthurs, 'The New Economy and the New Legality: Industrial Citizenship and the Future of Labour Arbitration Commentary' (1999) 7 Canadian Labour & Employment

involved community, collectivism, equality of access, inclusion, and active participation.[89] Second, industrial citizenship was aspirational[90] and concerned with norm creation and realization.[91] Third, the idea was about freedom from arbitrary power and domination, as an extension of political rights.[92] Fourth, industrial citizenship was about the subordination of rights and duties under contract to rights conferred by citizenship status.[93] Fifth, it invested industrial citizens with both industrial rights and duties,[94] including the duty of active participation.[95] Sixth, as Walter Korpi identified, industrial citizenship aided redistribution because 'laws regulating rights and duties of citizenship [could] constitute formal institutions of basic importance for distributive processes.'[96] Seventh, the framework eschewed the exclusionary framework of the employment relationship because it did not rely on the contract of employment to give workers rights.[97] Scholars also recognized that industrial citizenship rights could be reinforced in statutes but these rights originated from the status of workers as citizens and the duties that communities (such as workplaces or the nation-state) owed to citizens.[98]

B From industrial citizenship to workplace democracy and citizenship at work

Scholars until the 1990s optimistically discussed how industrial citizenship could promote justice at work, but many discussions of the concept after that time focused on its limitations. These discussions developed in the context of the global rise of neoliberal

Law Journal 45, 45–64; Fudge, 'After Industrial Citizenship' (n 85); Keith Ewing, 'Australian and British Labour Law: Differences of Form or Substance?' (1998) 11 Australian Journal of Labour Law 44.

[89] Marshall and Bottomore (n 80) 41; Michel Coutu and Gregor Murray, 'Towards Citizenship at Work? An Introduction' (2005) 60 Relations Industrielles 617; Mundlak, 'Industrial Citizenship, Social Citizenship, Corporate Citizenship' (n 87) 724. On the distinction between active and passive citizenship see further Einat Albin and Virginia Mantouvalou, 'Active Industrial Citizenship of Domestic Workers: Lessons Learned from Unionizing Attempts in Israel and the United Kingdom' (2016) 17 Theoretical Inquiries in Law 321, 327–28.

[90] Arthurs, 'The New Economy and the New Legality' (n 88) 46–47; Fudge, 'After Industrial Citizenship' (n 85) 630–31; Marcel Paret, 'Citizenship and Work in Global Capitalism: From Domination to Aspiration' (2018) 12 Sociology Compass e12602.

[91] Marshall and Bottomore (n 80) 92; Mundlak, 'Industrial Citizenship, Social Citizenship, Corporate Citizenship' (n 87) 724.

[92] Marshall and Bottomore (n 80) 41; Arthurs, 'The New Economy and the New Legality' (n 88) 46.

[93] Marshall and Bottomore (n 80) 41.

[94] ibid 42.

[95] Albin and Mantouvalou (n 89) 325.

[96] Walter Korpi, 'The Iceberg of Power below the Surface: A Preface to Power Resources Theory' in Julia S O'Connor and Gregg M Olsen (eds), *Power Resource Theory and the Welfare State: A Critical Approach* (University of Toronto Press 1998) x. On the connection between the related theory of 'industrial justice' and 'dignity' see Philip Selznick, *Law, Society, and Industrial Justice* (Russell Sage Foundation 1969) 225; Arthurs, 'Foreword: Mining the Philosophers' Stone: Sixteen Tons and What Do You Get? Another Day Older and Deeper in Doubt' (n 73).

[97] On the potential for broader application of industrial citizenship to workers other than employees see, eg, Albin and Mantouvalou (n 89).

[98] See, eg, Wolfgang Streeck, 'Industrial Citizenship under Regime Competition: The Case of the European Works Councils' (1997) 4 Journal of European Public Policy 643.

regulation, and the scholarship reflected this development in its two main critiques of industrial citizenship, which are that the concept was either vague and/or outdated.[99] Connected to these critiques were more specific concerns that industrial citizenship was difficult to distinguish from the concept of industrial justice. Yet deeper examination of the two concepts indicates that they are based on different ideas of justice for workers.

The work of Phillip Selznick provides a helpful starting point for understanding industrial justice and its connection to industrial citizenship.[100] Selznick argued that the concept of industrial justice comprised three central components: procedural justice, substantive justice, and cooperation by parties in performing their contractual obligations.[101] Selznick explained that industrial justice sought formal and substantive justice by balancing considerations about procedural justice against individual circumstances and broader inequality.[102] Selznick suggested that legality at work also had a moral dimension that was reflected in the restitutive potential of parties' obligations under categories of private law including contract.[103] He described this as a 'morality of cooperation'.[104]

In contrast, Selznick viewed the concept of citizenship as a mechanism for achieving industrial justice. He regarded citizenship as the most effective means of articulating the 'public rights accruing to the individual who occupies that status' as a citizen with plural polities, including the polity of the workplace.[105] Selznick argued that this approach could potentially enable a 'return to the traditional concept of public law and yet [could provide capacity to] transcend it. The relation between government and the individual has long been taken as the touchstone of public law'.[106] In short, according to Selznick's model of industrial justice, citizenship was the conduit through which workers realized procedural justice, substantive justice, and the morality of cooperation. However, his approach presumed that industrial citizenship had the same goals as industrial justice.

Alternatively, Joanna Howe has argued that industrial citizenship can be seen as a potential successor to industrial justice.[107] Howe examined the concepts of industrial citizenship and industrial justice in the course of analysing the development of statutory unfair dismissal protections in Australia and elsewhere.[108] As Howe has noted, 'community, fair play and freedom from arbitrary power or domination are central to the normative ideal of citizenship.'[109] These characteristics illuminate a more

[99] See, eg, Fudge, 'After Industrial Citizenship' (n 85) 631; Mundlak, 'Industrial Citizenship, Social Citizenship, Corporate Citizenship' (n 87) 728.
[100] Selznick (n 96).
[101] ibid 11–26.
[102] ibid 13–14.
[103] ibid 13, 20. On this theory, see further the work of Emile Durkheim in George Simpson (tr), *Emile Durkheim on the Division of Labour in Society* (New York 1933), as cited in ibid 19. On the relational interest underpinning contract, see further discussion at ibid 65–70.
[104] Selznick (n 96) 13.
[105] ibid 249. On the concept of a business as a governmental institution, see further ibid 269–74.
[106] Selznick (n 96) 249–50 (citation omitted). On the two key requirements of citizenship (legitimate authority and objective rules) see further ibid 274.
[107] Selznick (n 96) 274.
[108] Howe (n 87) 18–21.
[109] ibid 19.

extensive idea of justice for workers than those embodied in the components of industrial justice. Howe's explanation of the idea of industrial citizenship as including a broader vision of justice for workers is also supported by other scholarship.[110] These examinations reinforce that it is possible to see industrial citizenship and industrial justice as having complementary goals, but to also understand that industrial citizenship includes a broader concept of rights for workers.

The literature also includes debates about whether Marshall viewed the industrial citizenship rights of workers as exclusively collective, or both collective and individual in nature.[111] While the literature on this subject is diverse, a clear thread amongst scholars is to either view the individual rights of workers as industrial citizens as limited to rights that ultimately promote their collective rights, or as constituting a broader framework of civil and social rights at work. Examinations of industrial citizenship by Guy Mundlak and Hugh Collins illustrate these two approaches.

On the one hand, Mundlak suggests that all industrial citizenship rights are linked to membership within a community. Interpreting Marshall, Mundlak argues that the individual rights of industrial citizens can be seen as 'process-oriented rights' that do not secure end-norms (labour standards) but rather are mechanisms for a more just outcome.[112] This includes, for example, the right of a worker to join a trade-union or participate in collective bargaining. Mundlak's approach delineates rights of industrial citizens from human rights, but also notes that the distinction is not clear because all rights associated with citizenship are also regarded as human rights.[113]

On the other hand, Collins presents an inclusive catalogue of individual and collective rights that, he argues, provide a 'modern vision of citizenship' rights at work for the European Union.[114] These include rights derived from the civil rights (eg, privacy and whistleblowing) and social rights traditions (eg, freedom of association, work health and safety, fair treatment, and fair pay).[115] Collins also draws on international conventions to identify industrial rights comprising: rights to access vocational training; freedom to choose an occupation; right to freedom from workplace discrimination; right to information and consultation; right to fair and just working conditions; and protection from unjustified dismissal.[116] Collins' approach recognizes that the citizenship rights of workers are derived from membership of the community, as well as from other sources, such as binding international standards and the translation of civil and social rights into protections at work. It develops a broad-based template of justice for workers that is grounded in the legal regulation of work in the nation-state and is transformative in its ambition and scope. It shows how the concept of

[110] See, eg, Ruth Dukes and Wolfgang Streeck, 'From Industrial Citizenship to Private Ordering? Contract, Status, and the Question of Consent' (MPIfG Discussion Paper 20/13, Max Planck Institute for the Study of Societies, 18 November 2020) 32 <http://hdl.handle.net/21.11116/0000-0007-6AAA-3> accessed 29 July 2025.

[111] For an overview of these debates see Paul Bagguley, 'Industrial Citizenship: A Re-conceptualisation and Case Study of the UK' (2013) 33 International Journal of Sociology and Social Policy 265, 268–71.

[112] Mundlak, 'Industrial Citizenship, Social Citizenship, Corporate Citizenship' (n 87) 722–24.

[113] ibid 726–33.

[114] Collins, *Employment Law* (n 26) 25.

[115] ibid.

[116] Collins acknowledges that these Charter rights are not 'directly legally enforceable' but nevertheless 'have profound implications for employment law': ibid.

industrial citizenship can potentially be adapted and updated to develop an idea of justice through citizenship at work with collective and individual dimensions.[117]

Rather than seeing these debates about the concept of industrial citizenship as eroding its legitimacy, Judy Fudge has argued that the indeterminacy of the concept is 'part of the concept's appeal'.[118] Similarly, for Michel Coutu and Gregory Murray, the concept of industrial citizenship 'is itself in movement',[119] as the rights of citizenship must be negotiated and then, through participation, civil rights can be negotiated and realized.[120] They suggest that industrial citizenship provides 'one avenue of analysis for the complex re-regulation of working lives . . . [as] both a work in progress and a transformative narrative for social actors seeking to bring about change at work.'[121] They view the dynamism of the concept as enabling it to evolve.

In addition to critiques of industrial citizenship that argue it presents a vague idea of rights at work, there is scholarship that debates its relevance to contemporary work arrangements and contexts.[122] Some scholars have posited that industrial citizenship is predicated on a model of work that prioritized the male breadwinner from the industrial era,[123] and overlooked the possibility that contractual freedom could benefit workers as well as employers.[124] Scholars have emphasized that Marshall conceived of industrial citizenship by having regard to British industrial practices in the 1950s and that these practices are far removed from contemporary work conditions in developed and developing countries.[125] They have suggested that the concept is rigid and incapable of adaptation to a post-industrial, digital era.

In contrast to these critiques is work by scholars who have shifted their focus towards related ideas of workplace democracy and other forms of citizenship at work.[126] They have argued that industrial justice (or post-industrial justice) remains a relevant goal of work regulation and that the ideas that underpin industrial citizenship remain pertinent but require reframing and updating.[127] Three central examples arise in the work of Edelman, Mundlak, and Dukes and Streeck.

Edelman was inspired by Selznick in her exploration of how organizations created institutionalized models of the law.[128] Edelman empirically found that legal

[117] See also Bagguley (n 111) 271–73.

[118] Fudge, 'After Industrial Citizenship' (n 85) 631.

[119] Coutu and Murray (n 89) 621.

[120] ibid.

[121] ibid 628.

[122] See, eg, Dukes and Streeck, *Democracy at Work* (n 60) 13–21; Mundlak, 'Industrial Citizenship, Social Citizenship, Corporate Citizenship' (n 87) 724; Judy Fudge, 'The New Discourse of Labor Rights: From Social to Fundamental Rights' (2007) 29 Comparative Labor Law & Policy Journal 29, 48–49.

[123] See, eg, Fudge, 'After Industrial Citizenship' (n 85) 632; Di Zetlin and Gillian Whitehouse, 'Gendering Industrial Citizenship' (2003) 41 British Journal of Industrial Relations 773.

[124] Dukes and Streeck, *Democracy at Work* (n 60) 10.

[125] See, eg, Arthurs, 'The New Economy and the New Legality' (n 88) 46; Coutu and Murray (n 89) 619; Fudge, 'After Industrial Citizenship' (n 85) 641–47.

[126] See, eg, Federico Tomasello, 'From Industrial to Digital Citizenship: Rethinking Social Rights in Cyberspace' (2023) 52 Theory and Society 463; Guy Standing, *Work after Globalization: Building Occupational Citizenship* (Edward Elgar 2009); Dukes and Streeck, *Democracy at Work* (n 60) 107–39; Fudge, 'After Industrial Citizenship' (n 85).

[127] See, eg, Dukes and Streeck, *Democracy at Work* (n 60) 110; Standing (n 126) 10, 13–17.

[128] Dukes and Streeck, *Democracy at Work* (n 60) 108–09; Lauren B Edelman, 'Organizations, Institutions, and Law: The Sociological Significance of Philip Selznick's Law, Society, and Industrial Justice' in Paul van Seters (ed), *The Anthem Companion to Philip Selznick* (Cambridge University Press 2021) 77.

managerialism produced signifiers of legal compliance that did not substantively advance fairness or equality for workers.[129] Edelman noted that these findings demonstrated Selznick's concept of industrial justice via 'legality' was 'an ideal to strive for but one that was extremely difficult to achieve'.[130] Edelman's work emphasized the aspirational dimension of workplace democracy and revealed that it must contend with the 'interplay of organisational governance and the public legal ideal', particularly in settings with low unionism and collective bargaining.[131]

Mundlak has suggested two contemporary models of citizenship that could be used to update Marshall's original concept to fit 'post-union institutions'.[132] The first model he suggested was workplace democracy, which assumes workers have status, constituency, or standing in a corporation.[133] The second model was corporate citizenship, which purports to impose obligations on corporations akin to those traditionally vested in 'human citizens', such as the obligation to pay taxes, and envisages that the corporations are citizens of the state.[134]

Recognizing that 'relations of solidarity' may persist among workers despite the privatization of work relations,[135] Dukes and Streeck have argued that industrial citizenship could be pursued by contemporary workers 'through either the internalisation or the rejection of the status ascribed to them by their employers'.[136] They have argued that social norms and prevailing beliefs among workers at a particular workplace have continued to produce shared understandings of a 'just order'.[137] They have posited that workers who form 'occupational communities' develop social norms in common.[138] In their treatise on workplace democracy and citizenship, Dukes and Streeck developed these notions to posit a concept of post-industrial justice for workers and a new 'labour constitution'.[139] A similar approach is taken by Guy Standing, who advocates for egalitarianism and community-building produced by new forms of 'civic friendship and social solidarity' within occupations, coupled with a universal basic income.[140]

The scholarship includes compelling arguments that industrial citizenship can be developed to produce a contemporary vision of workplace democracy and citizenship at work. Selznick and Edelman illuminate the struggle between the development of social norms through worker participation in managerial decision-making, and the pressures of markets and the managerialization of law. Mundlak and Dukes and Streeck provide templates that reframe industrial citizenship for contemporary workers. However, the scholarship that updates and develops the concept of industrial citizenship mainly focuses on case studies from the United States, United Kingdom,

[129] Edelman (n 128) 73. See further Lauren B Edelman, 'Legal Environments and Organizational Governance: The Expansion of Due Process in the American Workplace' (1990) 95 American Journal of Sociology 1401.
[130] Edelman (n 128) 79.
[131] ibid 83. See further Dukes and Streeck, 'Labour Law after Neoliberalism?' (n 62) 108.
[132] Mundlak, 'Industrial Citizenship, Social Citizenship, Corporate Citizenship' (n 87) 737.
[133] ibid 721.
[134] ibid.
[135] Dukes and Streeck, *Democracy at Work* (n 60) 110, 111.
[136] Dukes and Streeck, 'From Industrial Citizenship to Private Ordering?' (n 110) 30.
[137] ibid 32.
[138] Dukes and Streeck, *Democracy at Work* (n 60) 111–25.
[139] ibid 1–22.
[140] Standing (n 126) 10.

European Union, or from Canada. In the following section, I consider how the idea of industrial citizenship has been understood and developed in the context of Australian law.[141]

VI Forging an Idea of Justice Using the Concepts of Workplace Democracy and Citizenship at Work

As a fifth step towards developing a theory of justice in workplace investigations, I examine a small body of literature that is spearheaded by the work of Ron McCallum to understand how scholars have conceptualized industrial citizenship in the context of Australian work law.[142] I consider how Australian law developed to feature a tradition of egalitarianism and a presumption of social and political rights at work that have produced a distinct concept of citizenship at work. In this section, I argue that the *Charter* is underscored by this distinct concept of citizenship at work and presents a cogent vision of justice that is fitting for respondents in workplace investigations.[143]

A The idea of justice for Australian workers grounded in the concept of citizenship at work

Taking a historical perspective, McCallum has examined how scholars have used the concept of industrial citizenship as a construct to explain approaches to legal regulation of work in a nation-state.[144] Applying this approach to Australia, McCallum analysed the legal rights of workers through the lens of industrial citizenship.[145] He argued that the compulsory system of conciliation and arbitration, which was a defining feature of the legal regulation of work in Australia under Commonwealth law for most of the twentieth century,[146] promoted industrial citizenship by securing 'industrial

[141] ibid 147.

[142] Ronald C McCallum, 'The New Millennium and the Higgins Heritage: Industrial Relations in the 21st Century' (1996) 38 Journal of Industrial Relations 294; Ronald C McCallum, 'Crafting a New Collective Labour Law for Australia' (1997) 39 Journal of Industrial Relations 405; Ronald C McCallum, 'Collective Labour Law, Citizenship and the Future' (1998) 22 Melbourne University Law Review 42; Ronald C McCallum, 'The Australian Constitution and the Shaping of Our Federal and State Labour Laws' (2005) 10 Deakin Law Review 460; Ronald C McCallum, 'Justice at Work: Industrial Citizenship and the Corporatization of Australian Labour Law' (2006) 48 Journal of Industrial Relations 131; Ronald C McCallum, 'Australian Labour Law after the Work Choices Avalanche: Developing an Employment Law for Our Children' (2007) 49 Journal of Industrial Relations 436; Ronald C McCallum, 'Australian Labour Law and the Rudd Vision: Some Observations' (2008) 18 Economic and Labour Relations Review 23; McCallum, 'Citizenship at Work' (n 78); Ronald C McCallum and Hannah Michelle Martin, 'A Forgotten Cohort: Citizenship through Work and Persons with Disabilities' (2016) 41 Queen's Law Journal 317.

[143] Mordy Bromberg and Mark Irving (eds), *Australian Charter of Employment Rights* (Hardie Grant Books 2007).

[144] McCallum refers to scholarship that focuses on Australia, the United States, and Canada that uses industrial citizenship in this way, see, McCallum, 'Citizenship at Work' (n 78) 10.

[145] ibid. For other applications, see, eg, Ewing (n 88); Zetlin and Whitehouse (n 123) 781–84; Carol Fox, 'Union Democracy and Collective Bargaining: Public Policy in Transition' (1999) 41 Journal of Industrial Relations 393.

[146] *Commonwealth of Australia Constitution Act 1900 (Cth) s 51(xxxv)*. See also *Conciliation and Arbitration Act 1904 (Cth)*. This was repealed and replaced by *Industrial Relations Act 1988 (Cth)*.

peace',[147] as well as 'ensuring that workers received fair outcomes . . . adequate remuneration and fair terms and conditions of employment'.[148]

McCallum has recognized that Australian labour courts and industrial relations commissions also played central roles 'in fashioning Australian industrial citizenship' until the mid-1990s.[149] Their roles were to set safety nets of wages and conditions and develop principles informed by binding international labour conventions and evolving community standards.[150] McCallum noted that workers' rights were also augmented by 'remedial statutes' that were enacted by Commonwealth and state governments over time. These statutes covered subjects such as work health and safety and equality at work that were 'appropriate and beneficial having regard to the major changes in social attitudes of Australian industrial citizens'.[151]

McCallum has also explained that this integrated system led workers to expect outcomes in labour disputes that promoted values such as fairness, reasonableness, equality, and legitimate constraints upon managerial power.[152] It produced a tradition of egalitarianism, and the presumption of social and political rights at work, that defined the concept of industrial citizenship in a specific way in Australia.

McCallum has also considered how legal regulation shifted away from promoting citizenship rights at work in the mid-1990s.[153] He attributed this change to government policies that sought to respond to factors such as the economic impacts of globalization on the Australian economy,[154] and preference towards corporatizing the legal regulation of work.[155] McCallum viewed the enactment of the *Workplace Relations Amendment (WorkChoices) Act 2005* (Cth) (*WorkChoices*) by the Commonwealth government in 2005 as the culmination of this trend.[156] *WorkChoices* effectively displaced s 51(xxxv) of the Constitution by relying on s 51(xx), known as the corporations power, to establish a national statutory labour regime.[157] Despite a

[147] McCallum, 'Citizenship at Work' (n 78) 10. Industrial peace views justice for workers as achievable through the implementation of evenly conferred benefits, such as parental leave and casual entitlements, via test cases determined by federal and state industrial tribunals, without recourse to strikes.

[148] ibid 11. On the 'social obligation' owed by the state to citizens at work, see further Ewing (n 88) 47.

[149] McCallum identifies that the roles of courts and commissions became more limited from the mid-1990s onwards when the Commonwealth and state governments shifted the focus of labour regulation away from conciliation and arbitration and towards standard setting at workplace level through collective and individual bargaining: See further McCallum, 'Justice at Work' (n 142) 139–40. For an overview of the changes made by the federal government in the 1990s see further Stewart, Forsyth, and Irving (n 23) 52–65.

[150] McCallum also addresses paternalistic and exclusionary issues of justice for workers, noting particularly that for women, indigenous Australians and persons from non-English speaking backgrounds, full industrial citizenship was withheld and depended on the evolving community standards: McCallum, 'Citizenship at Work' (n 78) 13–14.

[151] McCallum, 'Justice at Work' (n 142) 142.

[152] McCallum, 'Citizenship at Work' (n 78) 10.

[153] ibid 6.

[154] McCallum, 'The Australian Constitution' (n 142) 466; McCallum, 'Justice at Work' (n 142) 143.

[155] McCallum, 'Justice at Work' (n 142) 133.

[156] These laws commenced operating on 27 March 2006. See also McCallum, 'The Australian Constitution' (n 142); McCallum, 'Australian Labour Law after the Work Choices Avalanche' (n 142).

[157] For a detailed overview of *WorkChoices*, see further Stewart, Forsyth, and Irving (n 23) 65–68. On the government's policy objective to establish a national system of regulating labour see, eg, George Williams, 'The Constitution and a National Industrial Relations Regime' (2005) 10 Deakin Law Review 498; Anna Chapman, 'Unfair Dismissal Law and Work Choices: From Safety Net Standard to Legal Privilege' (2006) 16 The Economic and Labour Relations Review 237, 239–40.

legal challenge by state governments, a majority of the HCA upheld the validity of *WorkChoices* and the use of the corporations power to make Commonwealth laws that regulate work.[158]

McCallum has described the system of conciliation and arbitration as an 'industrial citizen's constitutional charter . . . [that guarantees outcomes through] independent machinery possessing broad powers of conciliation and arbitration for the benefit of employees, employers, trade unions and employer associations.'[159] He contrasted this with the use of the corporations power to enact work regulation under *WorkChoices*, which he argued prioritized corporate economic productivity and made the rights and needs of workers an ancillary consideration.[160] In this way, McCallum regarded the corporatization of legal regulation as disturbing the values that protected citizens at work, such as through the elevation of managerial prerogative over fair outcomes for workers.[161]

Considering these changes, McCallum's theorization also identified how industrial citizenship had been used by scholars as a normative template for promoting the rights of citizens at work.[162] From the mid-1990s onwards, McCallum discussed the gap between the legal regulation of work in Australia and upholding the values that defined industrial citizenship. He developed an aspirational agenda for reforming collective and individual industrial citizenship rights. This agenda proposed that trade unions be recognized and regarded as 'the exclusive spokespersons for all of the workers in the industries over which the unions had coverage.'[163] With respect to the content of individual rights, McCallum observed that:

> [i]t is trite to state that workers require fair terms and conditions of employment that give them adequate wages to sustain themselves and their families. However, I wish to focus upon less publicised needs. All employees have the right to be secure in body and mind while at work. Workers require freedom from physical, genetic and mental injuries. This not only includes hazards like chemicals, but sexual and other forms of harassment and bullying that occur in the modern enterprise. Employees also have the right to seek redress against arbitrary power, whether on an individual or a systemic basis. This covers unfair dismissals and demotions, as well as other forms of discriminatory and arbitrary conduct.[164]

McCallum's formulation of aspirational citizenship did not call for the reinstatement of the regime of conciliation and arbitration but for a new formulation of citizenship at work that drew on the values that were embodied in that former regime.

[158] *New South Wales v Commonwealth* (2006) 229 CLR 1 [422] (Gleeson CJ, Gummow, Hayne, Heydon, and Crennan JJ).
[159] McCallum, 'Justice at Work' (n 142) 147.
[160] McCallum, 'The Australian Constitution' (n 142) 469.
[161] See further ibid 436.
[162] McCallum, 'Citizenship at Work' (n 78) 17–18.
[163] McCallum, 'The New Millennium' (n 142) 297.
[164] McCallum, 'Crafting a New Collective Labour Law for Australia' (n 142) 408 (citation omitted).

In this way, McCallum argued for the realization of rights through membership within a community at work and worker voice through representation,[165] although his adherence to trade unions could be updated to encompass other forms of collectivism as proposed by Mundlak and Dukes and Streeck. McCallum's vision recognized that promoting citizenship at work requires standard setting through worker participation at workplace level and the protection of rights that limits abuse of managerial power by employers. This comprised McCallum's idea of justice for Australian workers that was framed by the aspirational concept of citizenship.

A small body of scholarship has built on McCallum's examination of industrial citizenship having regard to Australian workers and organizations. Mostly, this scholarship emerged while the *WorkChoices* regime remained in operation.[166] Joe Isaac, Iain Ross, and Paul Munro each set out key analyses that have added to the normative concept of justice for Australian workers through the lens of citizenship.[167] These experts also emphasized collective and individual dimensions of the framework.

Isaac has proposed that citizenship rights should entail access to trade unions, collective bargaining, and collective action.[168] Isaac has also proposed that workers have rights to minimum terms of employment, representation in individual grievances, and protection of health and safety.[169] Ross has envisaged a framework of citizenship rights that included minimum entitlements to notice and paid and unpaid leave, minimum wages and entitlements such as to penalty rates and overtime, collective bargaining rights and associated rights to consultation, information and freedom of association, and protections against unlawful termination, unsafe working conditions and discriminatory treatment at work.[170] Ross has also argued that the framework of industrial citizenship enlivened obligations for workers, which he suggested could be drawn from the duties that applied to employees under the contract of employment.[171] Munro has also advocated for a framework that protected economic and social rights, an 'adequate standard of living' and 'fair dealing' at work.[172] These complementary perspectives used the lens of citizenship to propose an ideal framework of individual and collective rights that were aligned with the broad principles of citizenship at work, although these discussions generally require more detailed development.

[165] ibid 410.

[166] McCallum, 'Australian Labour Law after the Work Choices Avalanche' (n 142) 445.

[167] Iain Ross, 'Commentary: Industrial Citizenship' in Joe Isaac and Russell Lansbury (eds), *Labour Market Deregulation: Rewriting the Rules* (The Federation Press 2005); Joe Isaac, 'Reforming Australian Industrial Relations?: The 21st Foenander Lecture, 28 August 2006' (2007) 49 Journal of Industrial Relations 410; Paul Munro, 'Changes to the Australian Industrial Relations System: Reforms or Shattered Icons? An Insider's Assessment of the Probable Impact on Employers, Employees and Unions' (2006) 29 University of New South Wales Law Journal 128.

[168] Isaac contends that the establishment of these standards by an independent umpire is part of Australia's industrial history, see Isaac (n 167) 414.

[169] ibid.

[170] Ross suggests that other citizenship rights at work that might be more contentious include redundancy pay for employees in small businesses, unfair dismissal protections, industrial democracy, and privacy: Ross (n 167) 42. cf Standing (n 126) 40–41.

[171] Ross (n 167) 42.

[172] Munro (n 167) 161–62.

B The Charter as a framework of rights for contemporary Australian workers grounded in citizenship at work

The *Charter* is arguably the most considered and broad-ranging elaboration of a framework of rights for citizens at work in Australia. Published by the Australian Institute of Employment Rights (AIER),[173] the *Charter* was written in 2007 in response to the *WorkChoices* regime.[174] It followed after a similar charter of employment rights was developed in the United Kingdom.[175] The *Charter* was intended to sit alongside international charters of labour rights.[176] Mordy Bromberg, one of the authors of the *Charter*, has described it as a 'back to basics' template of workers' rights for contemporary Australian workplaces.[177] The *Charter* can also be seen as promoting an agenda of aspirational citizenship at work.

Bromberg has acknowledged that the *Charter* can be used to critique current work regulation and sets out an ideal framework of collective and individual rights.[178] The *Charter* is not legally binding but articulates an idea of justice for workers that the authors assert is supported by Australia's international obligations, the institutional 'guarantee of industrial fairness and reasonableness' that characterized Australia's industrial tradition under the system of conciliation and arbitration,[179] and the common law of the contract of employment.[180] It is a practical as well as aspirational template.

The *Charter* is underpinned by the concept of citizenship at work. The authors of the *Charter* took on McCallum's challenge to forge a new template of Australian industrial citizenship and have articulated ten core rights.[181] They have proposed that employees, and workers who are dependent contractors, be entitled to those ten core rights at work.[182] In turn, the core rights can be seen as comprising a contemporary idea of justice for workers in Australia. Each of the core rights is underpinned by a protective rationale for labour regulation.

The core rights effectively translate citizens' political and social rights into the realm of the workplace and have individualistic and collective dimensions. They address good faith performance of work, work with dignity, freedom from discrimination and

[173] Bromberg and Irving (n 143).

[174] ibid 6–7.

[175] Keith D Ewing, John Hendy, and Carolyn Jones, 'Rolling out the Manifesto for Labour Law' (Institute of Employment Rights 2018) <https://www.ier.org.uk/wp-content/uploads/RollingOutTheManifestoForLabourLaw.pdf> accessed 28 July 2025. See also Jane Carolan and others, 'Charter of Workers' Rights' (Draft for Consultation, Institute of Employment Rights 2019) <https://strathprints.strath.ac.uk/67615/1/Carolan_etal_IER_2019_A_Charter_of_Workers_Rights_for_Scotland.pdf> accessed 28 July 2025.

[176] See, eg, Mordy Bromberg, 'Introduction' in Mordy Bromberg and Mark Irving (eds), *Australian Charter of Employment Rights* (Hardie Grant Books 2007) 2–3.

[177] ibid 1.

[178] ibid.

[179] ibid.

[180] ibid 2–6. The question of how rights that stem from these sources are to be enforced is not addressed in the *Charter*, although the AIER, which published the *Charter*, subsequently established a campaign for a voluntary system of accreditation to be established for employers who adopt the *Charter*. See further AIER, 'The Australian Charter of Employment Rights' <https://www.aierights.com.au/charter/> accessed 29 July 2025.

[181] Bromberg (n 176) 5.

[182] Mordy Bromberg and Mark Irving, 'The Scope of the Charter' in Mordy Bromberg and Mark Irving (eds), *Australian Charter of Employment Rights* (Hardie Grant Books 2007) 125–26.

harassment, a safe and healthy workplace, workplace democracy, trade union participation and representation, protection from unfair dismissal, fair minimum standards, fairness and balance in bargaining, and effective dispute resolution.[183] The core rights were revisited in 2015 and examined with reference to several regulatory developments, including the changes instituted by the commencement of the *FW Act*.[184] The 2015 publication reinforced the ongoing salience of the core rights set out in the *Charter*. In 2022, the AIER also published *A New Work Relations Architecture*,[185] with the *Charter* providing a principles-based approach that guided that volume's vision for reforming the approach to legally regulating work.[186]

The ten core rights are specific to the Australian context, and this is centrally achieved through the authors' recognition of the distinct concept of fairness, which has emerged from the tradition of regulating work in Australia.[187] This value resonates in each core right under the *Charter*. Fairness has cultural significance in the tradition of work regulation in Australia.[188] The guarantee of 'a fair go all round' featured as a rationale for the system of conciliation and arbitration,[189] and the concept of a 'fair and reasonable wage' on a national basis.[190] Fairness is also reflected in the inclusion in the principle of a 'fair go all round' for parties in a dispute about unfair dismissal under the current *FW Act*.[191] As noted by Joanna Howe, the concept of a 'fair go' is 'deeply embedded' in Australian work regulation, and the concept has evolved and developed over time.[192]

The literature also includes broader assertions about the cultural resonance of a 'fair go' as a right of citizens at work in Australia.[193] A central example is set out in a dissenting judgment, in the *WorkChoices Case*, by Kirby J.[194] The judgment referred to the related concept of 'industrial fairness' as entailing the resolution of disputes through collective bargaining that took into account factors including 'the ideal of "a fair go", due process, [and] transparent negotiations',[195] and the development of Australian work standards consistent with 'an egalitarian principle not always present in the pure operation of the market or the laws and practices of other countries.'[196] His Honour described the concept of fairness as 'an important part of the nation's institutional history and the egalitarian and idealistic values that such history has reinforced

183 Bromberg and Irving (n 143) 145.
184 *Fair Work Act 2009 (Cth)*. Clare Ozich (ed), *Employment Rights Now: Reflections on the Australian Charter of Employment Rights* (Hardie Grant Books 2015).
185 James Fleming (ed), *A New Work Relations Architecture: The AIER Model for the Future of Work* (Hardie Grant Books 2022).
186 Joellen Riley Munton, 'Preface' in James Fleming (ed), *A New Work Relations Architecture: The AIER Model for the Future of Work* (Hardie Grant Books 2022) 13–14.
187 Bromberg (n 176) 4–5.
188 See further McCallum, 'Justice at Work' (n 142) 139.
189 *Re Loty and Holloway v Australian Workers' Union* [1971] AR (NSW) 95.
190 *McKay, Ex parte* (1907) 2 CAR 1. See also Stephen Bell and Michael Keating, *Fair Share: Competing Claims and Australia's Economic Future* (Melbourne University Publishing 2018) 158.
191 *FW Act s 381(2).*
192 Howe (n 87) 101–02.
193 See, eg, ibid 101; Joellen Riley, 'Good Faith Performance' in Mordy Bromberg and Mark Irving (eds), *Australian Charter of Employment Rights* (Hardie Grant Books 2007).
194 *WorkChoices Case* (n 158) [423]–[616] (Kirby J).
195 ibid [519] (Kirby J).
196 ibid [524] (Kirby J).

in the field of industrial disputes and employment standards.'[197] The Australian cultural tradition of the 'fair go all round' can be seen as a specific expression of egalitarianism, which is a hallmark of the concept of citizenship at work arising in the original theorization by Marshall. The tradition articulates a central dimension of the idea of justice for workers as citizens and a rationale for the legal regulation of work.[198]

Upon its publication in 2007, there was considerable engagement with the *Charter*, although more recently there has been far less discussion about this template in Australian circles.[199] Generally, the views expressed about the content and efficacy of the *Charter* over time have been positive.[200] However, some scholars have critiqued the approach taken. For example, Guy Standing asserted that the *Charter* should have included a broader idea of a 'worker', to include, for example, outworkers and unpaid care workers.[201] Elsewhere, Standing has observed that the definition of a worker proposed in the *Charter* was convoluted and arbitrary as 'extension still [left] a dichotomy'.[202]

Standing has suggested that this problem could be overcome by linking rights to work, rather than workers.[203] He has also argued that the *Charter* exhibited a 'paternalistic bias'.[204] This bias was reflected in the descriptions of employers as duty holders in the *Charter* that could deny workers agency and undermine self-determined routes to dignity at work. Standing has suggested that a preferable approach would be to recognize occupational rights and develop a system of occupational regulation rather than focusing any longer on the workplace.[205] Overall, this critique arises from a difference in views about how to conceptualize work and workers and whether to situate rights in occupational or workplace citizenship. These are valid debates that reveal the potential challenges of making these rights enforceable through regulatory mechanisms. Yet, Standing's approach does not deny the legitimacy of the core rights set out in the *Charter* or the validity of its overarching agenda.[206] In fact, Standing described the values set out in the *Charter* as progressive.[207] It is these values that are central to the idea of justice through work regulation applicable to workplace investigations, which is set out below.

After the *Charter* was published, *WorkChoices* was repealed and replaced by the *FW Act*,[208] and this produced further reflections on the rights of citizens at work in

[197] ibid [530] (Kirby J). For further discussion, see Michael Kirby, 'Securing a "Fair Go"–ILO, Australia and the World' (International Industrial Relations Association, 15th World Congress, Sydney, 2009) <https://www.michaelkirby.com.au/images/stories/speeches/2000s/2009%2B/2391.Speech_-_Iira_-_Darling_Harbour%2C_26_August_2009.pdf> accessed 29 July 2025.

[198] McCallum, 'Crafting a New Collective Labour Law for Australia' (n 142) 422.

[199] Note, however, James Fleming, 'Introduction' in James Fleming (ed), *A New Work Relations Architecture: The AIER Model for the Future of Work* (Hardie Grant Books 2022) 19.

[200] See, eg, Gordon Anderson, 'Grasping the Moment: Some Cross-Tasman Thoughts on Australian Labour Law Reform' (2008) 18 Economic and Labour Relations Review 113, 115–16; Braham Dabscheck, 'Book Review: *Australian Charter of Employment Rights*' (2020) 18 The Economic and Labour Relations Review 155; Ben French, 'Australian Charter of Employment Rights' (2008) 16 International Journal of Employment Studies 131.

[201] Guy Standing, 'The Australian Charter of Employment Rights: The Missing Dimensions' (2008) 50 Journal of Industrial Relations 355.

[202] Standing (n 126) 269.

[203] Standing (n 201) 358.

[204] ibid.

[205] ibid 360–61.

[206] Standing (n 126) 283.

[207] Standing (n 201) 356.

[208] *Workplace Relations Amendment (Transition to Forward with Fairness) Act 2008 (Cth).*

Australia. The *FW Act*, which commenced in 2009, sought to reinstate key protections for eligible workers that had been removed or undermined by *WorkChoices*, but also continued to rely on the corporations power under the Constitution.[209] The overarching object of the *FW Act* is to 'provide a balanced framework for cooperative and productive workplace relations that promotes national economic prosperity and social inclusion for all Australians[.]'[210] Perhaps because the *FW Act* sought to strike a balance, groups representing employers and workers respectively argued that it did not adequately address their concerns or interests.[211]

Between 2009 and 2022, the framework of regulating work under Commonwealth legislation remained quite stable, despite a review by the Productivity Commission,[212] and some unsuccessful attempts by governments to change key aspects of the framework.[213] The Labor Government, which was elected in 2022, then embarked on a series of substantial reforms to work law including to the *FW Act* such as through the enactment of the *Fair Work Legislation Amendment Act 2022 (Secure Jobs, Better Pay) Act* (Cth) (*SJBP Act*),[214] *Fair Work Legislation Amendment (Closing Loopholes Act 2023* (Cth),[215] and *Fair Work Legislation Amendment (Closing Loopholes No 2) Act 2024* (Cth) (collectively, *Closing Loopholes Acts*).[216] The Minister for Employment and Workplace Relations, the Hon. Tony Burke MP, stated in October 2022 that the amendments set out in the *SJBP Act* aimed 'to promote job security, help close the gender pay gap, modernise the workplace bargaining system and get wages moving'.[217] The *Closing Loopholes Acts* enacted and extended a range of individual rights for workers including with respect to gender equality,[218] and provisions aimed at revitalizing collective bargaining.[219]

While these amendments to the *FW Act* aim to improve and extend individual statutory rights, strengthen and extend collective bargaining, and promote workplace democracy,[220] they do not displace the relevance of the *Charter* rights. Russell Lansbury argued in 2009 that, beyond the architecture of the *FW Act*, 'a more ambitious vision

[209] *Constitution s 51(xx).*
[210] *FW Act s 3.*
[211] Productivity Commission, 'Workplace Relations Framework (Inquiry Report No. 76)' (2015) 5–8.
[212] ibid.
[213] See, eg, Andrew Stewart and others, 'The (Omni)Bus That Broke Down: Changes to Casual Employment and the Remnants of the Coalition's Industrial Relations Agenda' (2021) 34 Australian Journal of Labour Law 132.
[214] Assented on 6 December 2022. The Commonwealth Parliament also passed other key legislation that amends the *FW Act* such as the *Fair Work Legislation Amendment (Protecting Worker Entitlements) Act (2023)* (Cth) and *Fair Work Legislation Amendment (Closing Loopholes) Act (2023)* (Cth).
[215] Assented on 14 December 2023.
[216] Assented on 26 February 2024.
[217] Tony Burke, 'Delivering Secure Jobs, Better Pay and a Fairer System' (*Ministers' Media Centre*, 27 October 2022) <https://ministers.dewr.gov.au/burke/delivering-secure-jobs-better-pay-and-fairer-system> accessed 29 July 2025.
[218] See further, eg, Michael Rawling, 'Regulating beyond the Employment Relationship to Protect Road Transport and "Gig" Workers: The Regulated Worker Provisions' (2024) 37 Australian Journal of Labour Law 178.
[219] See further Rosalind Read, 'A Loophole Big Enough to Walk a Stolen Horse Through: Delegates' Rights and the Precarity of Workplace Activism under the Fair Work Act' (2024) 37 Australian Journal of Labour Law 157; Anthony Forsyth, 'Closing the Labour Hire Loophole: Legislative Enshrinement of the "Same Job, Same Pay" Principle for Australian Labour Hire Workers' (2024) 37 Australian Journal of Labour Law 135.
[220] On the democratizing potential of new rights for union delegates see further Read (n 219).

is needed that asserts the rights of Australians to both decent work and a democratic workplace that will provide a beacon for the rest of the world.'[221] This salient observation remains relevant. Arguably the formulation set out in *A New Work Relations Architecture*, which is underpinned by the *Charter*, constitutes an ambitious agenda of reform of this kind.[222] This agenda reinforces, rather than displaces, the necessity of the *Charter*.

VII A Framework of Justice for Respondents in Workplace Investigations

Building on the idea that a distinct idea of justice at work has emerged in the Australian context, as a sixth step, I critically analyse the rights under the *Charter*. I propose a template of justice as applicable to the legal regulation of workplace investigations that builds on those rights that include nine key elements.

The idea of justice articulated in the core rights under the *Charter* forms an apposite template with which to critically examine the legal regulation of employer conduct towards respondents in workplace investigations, and normatively evaluate the regulatory response to these internal processes. This idea of justice embodies a distinctly Australian conceptualization of citizenship at work that is informed by the tradition of legally regulating work in Australia and binding obligations under international law.[223]

I propose that there are three ways to augment the *Charter* to further promote justice for respondents in workplace investigations.[224] First, the *Charter* overlooks the importance of rights of access by workers and their representatives to information about employer practices that impact on them.[225] As shown in chapter 2, workplace investigations can be shrouded in secrecy and employers can withhold information from affected workers including regarding the process of an investigation. For formal and informal expressions of solidarity amongst workers to flourish, workers need access to information and data about matters that affect them, and the ability to communicate with each other.[226] The importance of information to securing the rights of citizens at work is overlooked in the *Charter*.[227] This requires expansion of the concept of workplace democracy developed in *Charter Right 5*, which promotes the rights of workers to express their views and participate in decision-making matters that significantly affect them.

Second, the concept of dispute resolution in *Charter Right 10* is primarily focused on parties having access to an independent tribunal. That is, it is concerned with

[221] Russell D Lansbury, 'Workplace Democracy and the Global Financial Crisis' (2009) 51 Journal of Industrial Relations 599, 613.

[222] Fleming (n 185).

[223] On the interaction between industrial regulation in Australia and international labour standards see further Michael Kirby, 'Human Rights and Industrial Relations' (2002) 44 Journal of Industrial Relations 562, 575–76.

[224] The core right of 'fairness and balance in industrial bargaining' is not included in the framework of justice in workplace investigations as it is not relevant to this issue.

[225] See, eg, Cynthia Estlund, 'Just the Facts: The Case for Workplace Transparency' (2011) 63 Stanford Law Review 351.

[226] Forsyth, *The Future of Unions* (n 30) 215–16.

[227] On the benefits of mandatory disclosure of information requirements in the workplace see further Estlund (n 225).

resolution of disputes through recourse to external institutions. However, as Dukes and Streeck identify, workplace democracy is promoted by conflict facilitation as well as adjudication.[228] This indicates that mechanisms for internal resolution of conflict are also important to promoting justice for workers. Workers and their representatives must also be involved in designing these mechanisms if they are to promote democracy at work and not reinforce managerialization of the law in organizations. This requires rethinking of *Charter Right 10* to include rights for workers to shape and have access to both internal and external dispute resolution options, having regard to individual and collective dimensions of disputes and the role of worker representatives.

Third, *Charter Right 4* recognizes a right to a safe and healthy workplace.[229] This right encompasses mental and physical health and safety of workers. The right is predicated on minimizing illness and injury to workers, but it does not reinforce that an employer should have a proactive duty to eliminate risks to health and safety. Similarly, the right considers how workers' health and safety representatives can use consultation to address workers' concerns about risks. This aspect of the *Charter* needs to be extended to have regard to the necessity for work law to confer individual and collective mechanisms that enable workers to enforce their right to a safe and healthy workplace.

The relevant core rights in the *Charter*, adapted to workplace investigations and augmented by the additional elements I have proposed above, present a framework of justice for respondents in workplace investigations. Justice for respondents in workplace investigations under this framework has nine elements:

- good faith performance of the contract of employment by the parties;[230]
- dignified treatment of respondents;[231]
- freedom from discrimination and harassment;[232]
- elimination of risk to respondents' physical and psychiatric health and safety so far as reasonably practicable;[233]
- promotion of workplace democracy, augmented by consultation with nominated representatives and giving respondents access to information;[234]
- rights to representation for respondents;[235]
- a procedurally and substantively fair process where it could result in dismissal of the respondent;[236]

[228] Dukes and Streeck, *Democracy at Work* (n 60) 131.

[229] Peter Rozen, 'A Safe and Healthy Workplace' in Mordy Bromberg and Mark Irving (eds), *Australian Charter of Employment Rights* (Hardie Grant Books 2007).

[230] Riley (n 193).

[231] Greg Bamber and Bob Russell, 'Work with Dignity' in Mordy Bromberg and Mark Irving (eds), *Australian Charter of Employment Rights* (Hardie Grant Books 2007).

[232] Carol Andrades, 'Freedom from Discrimination and Harassment' in Mordy Bromberg and Mark Irving (eds), *Australian Charter of Employment Rights* (Hardie Grant Books 2007).

[233] Rozen (n 229).

[234] Anthony Forsyth, 'Workplace Democracy' in Mordy Bromberg and Mark Irving (eds), *Australian Charter of Employment Rights* (Hardie Grant Books 2007).

[235] Mark Irving, 'Union Membership and Representation' in Mordy Bromberg and Mark Irving (eds), *Australian Charter of Employment Rights* (Hardie Grant Books 2007).

[236] Marilyn Pittard, 'Protection from Unfair Dismissal' in Mordy Bromberg and Mark Irving (eds), *Australian Charter of Employment Rights* (Hardie Grant Books 2007).

- fair and relevant minimum standards mandated by law;[237] and
- effective dispute resolution,[238] augmented by mandatory procedures and internal dispute resolution mechanisms.

These elements are broad-ranging and form a fitting framework of justice for respondents that can be used to evaluate the legal regulation of employer conduct during workplace investigations positively and normatively. They are underpinned by a rights-based approach, which recognizes that employers and respondents will legitimately have divergent interests, and the law contributes to mediating these conflicting interests.[239]

VIII Conclusion

In this chapter, I have developed a framework of justice for respondents through work regulation applicable to workplace investigations. While philosophical texts about workplace democracy, participation, and citizenship at work have often focused on case studies from jurisdictions like the United Kingdom and European Union, I have examined how these ideas have evolved in the Australian context. I have identified that a central aim of the field of work law remains the protection of workers, and that democracy and citizenship at work are key values that can be enabled through law to achieve justice.

I have considered compelling arguments in the scholarship that the concept of citizenship at work is dynamic and has individual and collective aspects. It includes pragmatic and aspirational dimensions. I have argued that citizenship at work is apposite to considering respondents in workplace investigations because they are rarely conceptualized as requiring protection against employer power during these processes. In addition, the concept allows rights at work to be viewed as matters that need to be negotiated and re-regulated and so is suited to considering questions of law reform.

By translating and adapting the template of rights in the *Charter*, which is underpinned by the concept of citizenship at work, I have established a framework of justice as applicable to the legal regulation of workplace investigations for respondents with nine elements. The template envisages implementing work laws that promote a multi-dimensional framework of individual and collective work rights for respondents that advances citizenship at work.

This framework offers a pragmatic resource that is underpinned by aspirational ideals about workplace citizenship. In chapter 7, I use the framework to positively and normatively evaluate the legal regulation of employer conduct towards respondents in workplace investigations and suggest a practical agenda of law reform.

[237] Paul Munro, David Peetz, and Barbara Pocock, 'Fair Minimum Standards' in Mordy Bromberg and Mark Irving (eds), *Australian Charter of Employment Rights* (Hardie Grant Books 2007).
[238] Sean Reidy, 'Effective Dispute Resolution' in Mordy Bromberg and Mark Irving (eds), *Australian Charter of Employment Rights* (Hardie Grant Books 2007).
[239] Collins, *Justice in Dismissal* (n 37) 82.

4
The Regulation of Employer Conduct Towards Respondents During Workplace Investigations Through Judge-Made Law

I Introduction

Chapters 2 and 3 explored ways that employers exercise managerial power towards respondents during workplace investigations and provided a theoretical template for justice towards respondents during these processes. There is no direct statutory regulation of employer conduct under work law, and so, in this chapter, I examine decisions of superior and appellate courts in Australia, in the areas of contract and tort law, that develop principles that apply to employer conduct towards respondents during workplace investigations.

I explain the method that I have used to collect and analyse the decisions in part II. In part III, I firstly analyse key cases that relate to claims by respondents under contract and/or tort law for negligent employer conduct during workplace investigations. I identify judicial principles that constrain negligent employer conduct towards respondents and key gaps in the law. Secondly, I examine key court decisions involving claims by respondents about unreasonable employer conduct during workplace investigations. Each of these decisions relates to a claim made by a respondent that their employer's conduct during a workplace investigation breached a term of the contract of employment. I pinpoint judicial principles that constrain unreasonable employer conduct towards respondents. I argue that key principles are unsettled and underdeveloped, and some courts have been reluctant to develop the law in ways that would further constrain employer conduct during workplace investigations.

II Method

I used a doctrinal legal research method to identify and analyse the cases in this chapter. This method involved inductive reasoning, and 'synthesizing facts, values and law' from relevant decisions.[1] I first searched for all decisions in the areas of contract and/or tort law that were decided between 1 January 2000 and 1 June 2025 in which a Commonwealth, state, or territory superior or appellate court considered a claim by a respondent in a workplace investigation about negligent or unreasonable employer conduct. I produced a database of decisions and systematically analysed the

[1] P Ishwara Bhat, *Idea and Methods of Legal Research* (1st edn, OUP 2020) 151.

Workplace Investigations. Adriana Orifici, Oxford University Press. © Adriana Orifici 2026.
DOI: 10.1093/9780198970019.003.0004

facts and legal reasoning to identify any instances where a court explained and/or substantively developed principles that constrain the employer's conduct towards those respondents during workplace investigations under contract and/or tort law.[2]

III The Development of Judicial Principles About Negligent Employer Conduct in Workplace Investigations

Superior and appellate courts have developed key judicial principles that relate to employer conduct during workplace investigations as part of determining claims pursued by respondents that the employer breached the duty of reasonable care owed to them. Specifically, in these claims, respondents have alleged that the employer's conduct during a workplace investigation breached the duty of reasonable care that was owed to them and caused or exacerbated a psychiatric injury.[3] Respondents have pursued these claims under contract and/or tort law. Three central principles established by case law are that under contract and tort:

- an employer owes a duty of reasonable care towards a respondent;[4]
- the duty of reasonable care requires an employer to take all reasonable steps to provide a respondent with a safe system of work;[5] and
- the duty of reasonable care requires an employer to provide adequate support for a respondent in the workplace while a workplace investigation is ongoing, so as to avoid reasonably foreseeable psychiatric injury to the respondent.[6]

A close examination of the judgments reveals key gaps in the judicial development of an employer's duty of reasonable care as applicable during a workplace investigation in contract and tort. Courts have left open the question of whether the duty of reasonable care generally extends to require an employer to provide a respondent with a safe system of:

- workplace investigation or decision-making so as to avoid reasonably foreseeable psychiatric injury;[7] or
- decision-making when directing a respondent not to perform work during a workplace investigation so as to avoid reasonably foreseeable psychiatric injury.[8]

I examine the development of the law and the gaps in the obligations of employers in detail below.

[2] Each decision that I identified and analysed using this process referred to a workplace investigation by an employer about alleged misconduct by an employee.

[3] On the recoverability of damages for psychiatric injury in these circumstances, see *Elisha v Vision Australia Ltd* (2024) 421 ALR 184, 186 (Gageler CJ, Gordon, Edelman, Gleeson, and Beech-Jones JJ).

[4] *Koehler v Cerebos (Australia) Ltd* (2005) 222 CLR 44, 57 (McHugh, Gummow, Hayne, and Heydon JJ).

[5] ibid 53 (McHugh, Gummow, Hayne, and Heydon JJ).

[6] *Hayes v Queensland* (2017) 1 Qd R 337 360–61 (Dalton J, Mullins J agreeing at 336–37).

[7] *New South Wales v Paige* (2002) 60 NSWLR 371, 405 (Spigelman CJ, Mason P agreeing at 416, Giles JA agreeing at 419).

[8] *Potter v Gympie Regional Council* [2022] QCA 255 [36] (Flanagan JA, Mullins P agreeing at [1], Williams J agreeing at [83]).

A The duty of reasonable care and the context of workplace investigations

An implied duty to take reasonable care is owed by an employer towards an employee under the employment contract.[9] The duty broadly requires employers to take reasonable care to protect employees from reasonably foreseeable physical or psychiatric injury during employment.[10] The duty is non-delegable and also exists separately in tort.[11] The contractual and tortious duties are broadly concurrent and coextensive,[12] and each derives from the relationship of employer and employee. There are differences between a claim for breach of the contractual duty to take reasonable care and a claim of negligence in tort, and a court's assessment of damages can also differ.[13] However, as noted by Sappideen et al, claimants rarely find an advantage in pursuing a claim in one area rather than the other.[14]

As identified in chapter 2, if an employer conducts a workplace investigation process negligently, there is a risk that this will cause psychiatric injury to a respondent. As will be explored further in chapter 5, employees may seek redress under workers' compensation legislation for psychiatric injuries incurred at work, although there are exclusions from compensation, and the statutes generally limit the quantum and type of compensation available.[15] Alternatively, an employee may be entitled to pursue a claim in tort in these circumstances,[16] or a claim that the employer breached the implied duty of reasonable care under the employment contract,[17] subject to any statutory limitations.

The content of the duty of care in contract and tort is shaped by the 'fundamental aspects of the relationship between the parties',[18] including the terms of the contract of employment.[19] The HCA has noted that the 'standard of care for an employee's

[9] For a discussion of the duty of reasonable care see, eg, Carolyn Sappideen, Paul O'Grady, and Joellen Riley, *Macken's Law of Employment* (9th edn, Thomson Reuters 2022) 260–68. Employees owe employers an implied contractual duty to exercise reasonable care and skill in the performance of their duties, see ibid 215–21.

[10] See, eg, *Tame v New South Wales* (2002) 211 CLR 317, 365 (McHugh J); *Nationwide News Pty Ltd v Naidu* (2007) 71 NSWLR 471, 475 (Spigelman CJ), 519 (Beazley JA). On the scope of the duty as encompassing physical and psychiatric injury, see, eg, *Koehler* (n 4) 52 (McHugh, Gummow, Hayne, and Heydon JJ); *Hegarty v Queensland Ambulance Service* [2007] QCA 366 [41] (Keane JA).

[11] It arises in the tort of negligence, see, eg, *Matthews v Kuwait Bechtel Corp* (1959) 2 QB 57, 65–67; *Astley v Austrust Ltd* (1999) 197 CLR 1, 20–23 (Gleeson CJ, McHugh, Gummow, and Hayne JJ). On the non-delegable nature of the duty, see *Kondis v State Transport Authority* (1984) 55 ALR 225, 229 (Mason J).

[12] *Goldman Sachs JBWere Services Pty Ltd v Nikolich* [2007] FCAFC 120 [72] (Black CJ).

[13] Kit Barker and others, *The Law of Torts in Australia* (5th edn, OUP 2012) 9–10.

[14] See further Sappideen, O'Grady, and Riley (n 9) 227.

[15] See chapter 5 IV(C). An employer may also be prosecuted under work health and safety laws for the primary duty owed to persons including employees, see chapter 5 IV(B).

[16] Workers' compensation laws may restrict an employee's capacity to make this type of claim and/or restrict the type and quantum of damages that a court may award, see, eg, *Workplace Injury Rehabilitation and Compensation Act 2013 (Vic) ss 335, 340, 342, 371.* In the Northern Territory, common law claims are not permitted: *Return to Work Act 1986 (NT) s 52.* If an employee obtains damages from a claim in tort and has also received compensation pursuant to a workers' compensation scheme, that employee may have to repay some or all of the statutory benefit depending on the state or territory in which the employee resides, see, eg, *WIRC Act (Vic) s 343.*

[17] See, eg, *Nikolich* (n 12) [31] (Black CJ).

[18] *Koehler* (n 4) 53 (McHugh, Gummow, Hayne, and Heydon JJ).

[19] ibid 55 (McHugh, Gummow, Hayne, and Heydon JJ).

safety is not a low one'.[20] The duty to take reasonable care includes obligations on employers to provide competent staff, adequate materials, effective supervision, and a safe system of work.[21]

Disputes about the duty to take reasonable care during workplace investigations often focus on the concept of a safe system of work. Judicial reasoning has established that the features of a safe system of work are factually specific and vary depending on the type of work an employee performs.[22] The duty is continuous and owed by employers to employees as individuals.[23] A system of work encompasses matters such as the tasks to be performed, the conditions in which work is performed, and the permanent 'practice, method or system' adopted for the work.[24]

However, there is uncertainty about whether a system of work also includes incidents of the employment contract, such as disciplinary processes. Courts have been required to grapple with this question in the context of claims by respondents that negligent conduct by their employer during a workplace investigation caused or worsened a psychiatric injury. Respondents have pursued these claims in tort and/or contract. The key decisions of superior and appellate courts that develop the law on this question are examined below.

I first examine the reasoning in *New South Wales v Paige*, which was the first decision of an appellate court to comprehensively consider this question.[25] Next, I analyse six key decisions in which courts have considered, applied, or distinguished *Paige*. These decisions are *Hayes v Queensland*,[26] *Govier v Uniting Church in Australia Property Trust (Q)*,[27] *Potter v Gympie Regional Council*,[28] *Lloyd v Healthscope Operations Pty Ltd*,[29] *Ackers v Cairns Regional Council*,[30] and *Elisha (HCA)*.[31]

B The duty of reasonable care during workplace investigations—principles developed in Paige

Paige was the first decision of an appellate court to comprehensively consider whether an employer owed a respondent a duty of reasonable care to avoid reasonably foreseeable psychiatric injury during a workplace investigation.

[20] *O'Connor v Commissioner for Government Transport* (1954) 100 CLR 225, 230.

[21] On each of these aspects, see further Sappideen, O'Grady, and Riley (n 9) 282–85.

[22] *Koehler* (n 4) 53; *Robertson v State of Queensland* [2021] QCA 92 [112] (Henry J, Fraser JA agreeing at [1], McMurdo JA agreeing at [2]). For example, a safe system of work for police officers was found to include a system that enabled them to work in pairs and remain together wherever possible so that they could psychologically support each other during traumatic events: *New South Wales v Fahy* (2007) 232 CLR 486, 561 (Crennan J).

[23] Mark Irving, *The Contract of Employment* (2nd edn, LexisNexis Butterworths 2019) 671–72.

[24] ibid 687.

[25] *Paige* (n 7).

[26] *Hayes* (n 6).

[27] *Govier v Uniting Church in Australia Property Trust (Q)* [2017] QCA 12.

[28] *Potter v Gympie Regional Council* [2022] QSC 9. This decision was considered and affirmed on appeal in *Potter (Appeal)* (n 8) [82] (Flanagan JA, Mullins P agreeing at [1], Williams J agreeing at [83]).

[29] *Lloyd v Healthscope Operations Pty Ltd* [2020] VCC 2032. This decision was considered and affirmed in *Lloyd v Healthscope Operations Pty Ltd* [2021] VSCA 327 [62]–[72].

[30] *Ackers v Cairns Regional Council* (2021) 311 IR 378.

[31] *Elisha (HCA)* (n 3).

The claim was pursued by Mr Paige, who was a school principal employed by the State of New South Wales. In 1992, students made a complaint to Mr Paige that another teacher at the school had engaged in sexual misconduct (the Complaint). Mr Paige notified the New South Wales Department of Education (the Department) about some aspects of the Complaint and decided to transfer the teacher to another school. In February 1997, the Department asked principals to advise it of any complaints of sexual misconduct that had not been adequately investigated. Mr Paige told the Department about the Complaint. In May 1997, the Department commenced an investigation into the Complaint. During that investigation, the Department told Mr Paige that his conduct was not under investigation but that he was required to participate in an interview as a witness.

In August 1997, the Department commenced a separate investigation into allegations that Mr Paige had breached the *Teaching Service Act 1980* (NSW) (*TS Act*) because he had not responded to the Complaint in a manner that complied with the Department's procedures. The Department ultimately determined that Mr Paige had breached the *TS Act*.[32] In March 1998, Mr Paige's employment with the Department ceased. Mr Paige pursued a claim in tort that he had suffered a psychiatric injury and lost income because the State, as his employer, had negligently conducted the workplace investigation into his alleged misconduct.[33]

At first instance, the District Court of New South Wales confirmed that the State was 'under a duty of care to take reasonable steps to prevent psychiatric injury to its employees'.[34] Graham DCJ determined that the duty of care:

> to provide a safe system of work encompasse[d] the provision of a safe system of investigation and decision making . . . that is subject to the necessity involved in discharging contractual, common law or statutory obligations in relation to the conducting of inquiries. Any teacher who is subject to a disciplinary inquiry is likely to suffer stress and, possibly psychiatric injury, as a result of the conduct of such an inquiry.
>
> The breach of the duty of care in those circumstances will only come about where the system of investigation or decision making is not a proper or reasonable system or is carried out otherwise than in accordance with the rights of the employer to regulate its activities in accordance with contract, common law or statute.[35]

Graham DCJ considered 'the requirements of the law and statutes governing [Mr Paige's] form of employment' and held that the State had breached its tortious duty of reasonable care to Mr Paige.[36]

[32] *Paige* (n 7) 374 (Spigelman CJ). See *Teaching Service Act 1980 (NSW) s 83(e)*.

[33] During the workplace investigation, Mr Paige submitted (and then withdrew) a notice of retirement. After the charges were found proven, the Department sought to accept the notice of retirement. The validity of Mr Paige's withdrawal of the notice of retirement was the subject of a separate claim of breach of contract in the proceedings. This contractual claim was not relevant to the Court's reasoning regarding the Department's duty of reasonable care. On the decision of the Court with respect to this contractual claim, see further *Paige* (n 7) 407–12 (Spigelman CJ), 419–21 (Giles JA).

[34] *Paige v New South Wales* DC 3492/99, cited in *Paige* (n 7) 376–77 (Spigelman CJ).

[35] ibid, cited in *Paige* (n 7) 376–77 (Spigelman CJ).

[36] ibid, cited in *Paige* (n 7) 377 (Spigelman CJ).

Graham DCJ determined that the State had breached the duty of reasonable care for five reasons. These reasons were that the State had: misled and falsely assured Mr Paige that he would be given 'full protection against legal action' when re-notifying the Department about the Complaint in 1997; falsely assured Mr Paige that his conduct was not under investigation when he was interviewed as a witness in May 1997; failed to conduct a full investigation into the allegations against Mr Paige in accordance with the *TS Act*; adopted a 'paper or explanation type inquiry' that was inconsistent with the principles of procedural fairness; and erroneously acted upon Mr Paige's purportedly withdrawn resignation notice to terminate his employment. His Honour determined that this conduct negligently caused Mr Paige to suffer a reasonably foreseeable psychiatric injury and awarded him damages.[37] The State appealed the decision, including on the basis that the Graham DCJ had erred because no relevant duty of reasonable care existed in tort.[38]

The appeal was determined by a Full Court of the Supreme Court of New South Wales, and Spigelman CJ provided the leading judgment, with which Mason P and Giles JA agreed.[39] Spigelman CJ noted that Graham DCJ had characterized the duty of reasonable care as, firstly, requiring the employer 'to take reasonable steps to prevent psychiatric injury to its employees' and, secondly, to 'provide a safe system of work [including] ... a safe system of investigation and decision making[.]'[40] On appeal, the State had accepted that it had a duty to avoid the risk of reasonably foreseeable psychiatric injury, but that no duty existed under the law that required it to provide a safe system of investigation and decision-making.[41]

Spigelman CJ noted that previous cases that had considered the concept of a safe system of work were only concerned with the 'conduct of tasks' that an employee was contracted to perform.[42] For example, the HCA had previously considered the materials, machinery, and physical actions that an employee was required to use to drill, lift, and pack a heavy pipe.[43] His Honour noted that no authority had extended the concept of a safe system of work 'to matters concerning the ... incidents of the contract of employment' such as disciplinary procedures.[44]

His Honour characterized the employer's 'system of workplace investigation and decision-making' as an 'incident' of the contract of employment that was not encompassed within the system of work that applied to Mr Paige.[45] On this basis, Spigelman CJ determined that the Court needed to decide whether to recognize a 'novel category of duty ... [that would involve] an extension of employers' duties'.[46]

37 ibid, cited in *Paige*, 379–80 (Spigelman CJ). Graham DCJ also determined that the employer breached express terms of Mr Paige's contract of employment.
38 *Paige* (n 7) 386 (Spigelman CJ Mason P agreeing at 416, Giles JA agreeing at 419).
39 ibid 378, 416, 419.
40 *Paige First Instance* (n 34) cited in *Paige* (n 7) 387.
41 *Paige* (n 7) 387.
42 ibid 387 (Spigelman CJ).
43 *Bankstown Foundry Pty Ltd v Braistina* (1986) 160 CLR 301, 310 (Mason, Wilson, Dawson JJ).
44 *Paige* (n 7) 387 (Spigelman CJ).
45 ibid 377–78 (Spigelman CJ). As discussed further in chapter 5 IV(B), an employer also has obligations under work health and safety legislation to, so far as is reasonably practicable, provide and maintain a work environment that is safe and without risk to health. These obligations exist alongside the contractual and tortious duties of care.
46 ibid 387 (Spigelman CJ). The Court observed that it was specifically considering a duty of care with respect to the exercise of statutory powers of investigation: ibid 390.

To determine whether the Court should extend the employer's duty to take reasonable care in the circumstances, Spigelman CJ applied the approach enunciated by the HCA in *Sullivan v Moody* (*Sullivan*).[47] In *Sullivan*, the Court held that courts needed to adopt a multifactorial approach to determine if a 'novel category of duty' in tort should be recognized. The Court in *Sullivan* stated that:

> [d]ifferent classes of case give rise to different problems in determining the existence and nature or scope, of a duty of care... Sometimes they may concern the need to preserve the coherence of other legal principles, or of a statutory scheme which governs certain conduct or relationships. The relevant problem will then become the focus of attention in a judicial evaluation of the factors which tend for or against a conclusion, to be arrived at as a matter of principle.[48]

Spigelman CJ applied this approach from *Sullivan* to evaluate the factors in *Paige*. His Honour stated that the Court was required to 'consider the requirements of a coherent system of law in Australia' when determining whether to recognize the 'novel category of duty'.[49] His Honour determined that the proceedings raised three factors concerning legal coherence and compatibility that suggested the Court should not recognize the 'novel duty of care'.

First, his Honour noted that the proceedings raised considerations concerning how the 'novel category of duty' would interact with applicable statutory powers and duties.[50] Spigelman CJ recognized that there would be 'at least a level of tension, and perhaps of conflict' between the State's obligations under the *TS Act* and under tort law if the Court recognized the 'novel category of duty'.[51] His Honour identified that the tension or conflict would arise where the State, on the one hand, was required under the *TS Act* to conduct an efficient and effective workplace investigation and, on the other hand, was required to ensure a safe system of workplace investigation and decision-making. Spigelman CJ reasoned that an:

> inhibiting effect on the process of investigation and decision making... would arise if the law were to impose a duty of care to avoid the risk of mental trauma to the person whose conduct was being investigated.
>
> As a general rule, in my opinion, it is undesirable to inhibit an investigation into the exercise of a statutory power which protects public interests by imposing the chilling effect of a risk of civil liability.[52]

His Honour determined that the charging, inquiry, and determination steps prescribed by the *TS Act* were underpinned by objectives of temporal and cost efficiency

[47] *Sullivan v Moody* (2001) 207 CLR 562, 579–80, 580–81. See *Paige* (n 7) 390 (Spigelman CJ).
[48] *Sullivan* (n 47) 579–80.
[49] *Paige* (n 7) 391 (Spigelman CJ).
[50] ibid 387 (Spigelman CJ).
[51] ibid 392 (Spigelman CJ).
[52] ibid 393–94 (Spigelman CJ).

(in the public interest) that were inconsistent or incompatible with extending an employer's duty of reasonable care to encompass the 'novel category of duty'.[53]

Second, Spigelman CJ identified that the proceedings raised considerations regarding how the 'novel category of duty' would intersect with administrative law, including the law regarding judicial review of administrative action.[54] His Honour explained that this issue arose because the State was required to follow a statutory workplace investigation process under the *TS Act*, and its actions and decisions were subject to judicial review under administrative law. Spigelman CJ identified the overlap between 'the specific negligence alleged . . . [and] the heartland of judicial review of administrative conduct'.[55] So, his Honour reasoned that if the Court recognized the 'novel category of duty', it could 'well overwhelm the traditional remedies of administrative law' which are not compensatory.[56]

Third, his Honour discerned that the proceedings raised considerations about how the 'novel category of duty' would interact with the law that applied to termination of employment,[57] which Spigelman CJ described as 'the law of contract, as modified by statute'.[58] His Honour observed that judge-made law about termination of employment struck a 'balance of conflicting interests found to be appropriate as a matter of contract or by intervention of statute',[59] and statutory unfair dismissal protections under Commonwealth, state, and territory laws comprised a 'well developed alternative mechanism for adjusting the interests' of employers and employees.[60] Spigelman CJ expressed concern about developing the law of tort in a manner that could disturb these legal frameworks or create 'a parallel remedy of unlimited scope' in which claims could be made 'in the general jurisdiction'.[61] His Honour observed that *Addis v Gramophone Co Ltd* had 'long been cited as authority against recovery of damages for the manner of dismissal', and that while *Baltic Shipping Company v Dillon* provided an exception in relation to physical injury, it did not extend to 'psychiatric damage'.[62]

Spigelman CJ also noted that three factors pointed in favour of recognizing the 'novel category of duty'. First, the 'novel category of duty' would apply to the relationship between an employer and employee, which was a relationship where courts had incrementally developed a wide range of non-delegable duties.[63] Second, respondents were vulnerable to negligent conduct by the State during workplace investigations under the *TS Act* and were 'not able to protect [themselves from harm caused

[53] ibid 393–95 (Spigelman CJ).
[54] ibid 389 (Spigelman CJ).
[55] ibid 400 (Spigelman CJ).
[56] ibid 404 (Spigelman CJ).
[57] ibid 389 (Spigelman CJ).
[58] ibid.
[59] ibid 398 (Spigelman CJ). The applicable framework in this case was the *Industrial Relations Act 1996 (NSW) s 83*.
[60] *Paige* (n 7) 400 (Spigelman CJ).
[61] ibid 398 (Spigelman CJ). Gageler J referred to this approach with approval and noted that '[c]ommon law obligations in contract, like common law obligations in tort, ought not to be developed by courts other than in a manner that is sensitive to their interaction with legislation' in *Commonwealth Bank of Australia v Barker* (2014) 253 CLR 169, 387.
[62] *Paige* (n 7) 395 (Spigelman CJ). See *Addis v Gramophone Co Ltd* [1909] AC 488; *Baltic Shipping Co v Dillon* (1993) 176 CLR 344.
[63] *Paige* (n 7) 404–05 (Spigelman CJ).

by negligent employer conduct], other than by way of protest and proceedings for judicial review[.]'[64] The third factor was that the employer was in control of the disciplinary process.[65]

His Honour considered these factors, but ultimately determined that they did not outweigh the concern that a decision to recognize the 'novel category of duty' would cause legal incoherence and conflict with statutory duties.[66] His Honour overturned the reasoning of Graham DCJ and declined to recognize the 'novel category of duty'.[67] In practical terms, the decision meant that the duty of reasonable care owed by the employer did not include a duty to ensure a safe system of workplace investigation and decision-making.

C The duty of reasonable care during workplace investigations—the development of principles after Paige

Superior and appellate courts have considered, applied, or distinguished the reasoning in *Paige* in subsequent cases about negligent employer conduct towards respondents during workplace investigations.[68] Four key decisions of appellate courts that have considered *Paige* and substantively developed the law are *Hayes*,[69] *Govier*,[70] *Potter*,[71] and *Elisha (Court of Appeal)*.[72] The HCA briefly considered *Paige* in *Elisha (HCA)*,[73] but ultimately determined the appeal based on a claim concerning breach of contract, which is discussed further below.

In *Hayes*, a Court of Appeal of the Supreme Court of Queensland considered a key aspect of the boundary between an employer's system of work and system of work place investigation and decision-making.[74] *Hayes* involved four employees of a government department who were all respondents in the same workplace investigation.

[64] ibid 405 (Spigelman CJ).

[65] Ibid.

[66] ibid 387–88 (Spigelman CJ, Mason P agreeing at 416, Giles JA agreeing at 419) citing *Hill v Van Erp* (1997) 188 CLR 159 (Gummow J).

[67] ibid 395, 405 (Spigelman CJ).

[68] Subordinate courts have considered *Paige* in cases where employees have made claims in contract and/or tort, see, eg, *Heptonstall v Gaskin* [2004] NSWSC 80 [63], [66]–[67]; *Irving v Kleinman* [2005] NSWCA 116 [31]–[33]; *New South Wales v Rogerson* [2007] NSWLR 346 [2], [39] (Handley AJA, McColl JA agreeing at [1], Hoeben J agreeing at [44]); *Blows v Townsville City Council* [2018] QSC 234 [6]–[8]; *Knight v Queensland* [2019] QSC 86 [6]; *Elisha v Vision Australia Ltd* [2022] VSC 754 [511]; *Robertson v Queensland* [2020] QDC 185 [322]–[333] undisturbed on appeal in *Robertson v Queensland* [2021] QCA 92. A Full Court of the Supreme Court of New South Wales affirmed the principles in *Paige* in *Shaw v New South Wales* (2012) 219 IR 87 [1], [2], [123]–[127], [136]. The FCA has referred to the reasoning in *Paige* with approval but has not applied the ratio or considered it in detail, see *Fitzpatrick v Keelty* [2008] FCA 35, [54]; *Dafallah v Fair Work Commission* (2014) 225 FCR 559, 593.

[69] *Hayes* (n 6).

[70] *Govier* (n 27).

[71] *Potter* (n 28).

[72] *Vision Australia Ltd v Elisha* (2023) 328 IR 299.

[73] *Elisha (HCA)* (n 3).

[74] *Hayes* (n 6). The duty to take reasonable care towards employees during workplace investigations has also been considered in latter decisions of subordinate courts, see, eg, *Robinson v State of Queensland* [2017] QSC 165 [193], where it was held that an employer's duty of care included a duty to investigate complaints of harassment.

The employer had directed the employees to continue to perform their duties in the workplace during the workplace investigation, which the employees alleged was a hostile environment. The findings of the investigation were that the allegations against the respondents were unproven. The employees each claimed that the employer had breached its duty of care in tort by failing to give them adequate support during the investigation, and this had caused them to suffer psychiatric injuries. At first instance, the trial judge considered *Paige*, determined that no duty of care arose, and dismissed the employees' claims.[75] The employees appealed this decision.

On appeal, McMurdo P, Mullins J, and Dalton J delivered separate judgments. Their Honours each affirmed the reasoning in *Paige*[76] but distinguished the application of the principles in the case. Their Honours each reasoned that the employees' claims focused on alleged breaches by the employer of the duty of reasonable care that arose from failing to provide them with adequate support in the workplace during the investigation.[77]

Their Honours each held that the employer owed a duty of care to provide adequate support so as to avoid psychiatric injury to the employees who 'were vulnerable in a hostile workplace while their conduct was being investigated'.[78] Their Honours each reasoned that the duty of care to provide adequate support was owed from the time the complaints of misconduct were made, and throughout the investigation, in circumstances where the employer was on notice that the employees were vulnerable to psychiatric injury because it was a hostile workplace.[79] In the majority, Mullins and Dalton JJ determined that the employer had breached its duty of care to three of the employees.[80]

In *Govier*, a Full Court of the Supreme Court of Queensland considered whether the principles in *Paige* applied where an employer was not bound by a statutory process of workplace investigation. That is, the Court in *Govier* was required to decide if the 'novel category of duty' should be recognized in a case that did not raise concerns about incompatibility between tort and administrative law, or about tension or conflict between tortious duties and statutory rights and powers.

The claim was pursued by Ms Govier, who was a disability care worker. In December 2009, Ms Govier was physically assaulted by a colleague. Ms Govier immediately told her supervisor about the attack and admitted herself to hospital. On the same day, the employer commenced a workplace investigation into the assault and formed a view that Ms Govier (as well as the colleague who had attacked her) had potentially engaged in misconduct. The employer visited Ms Govier in hospital and gave her a letter that set out allegations of misconduct against her. The letter included a direction for Ms Govier to attend an interview with an investigator the next day. The

75 *Hayes* (n 6) [7] (McMurdo P), [169] (Dalton J, Mullins P agreeing at [100]).
76 ibid [6]–[7] (McMurdo P), [100] (Mullins J), [113]–[125] (Dalton J).
77 ibid [121] (Dalton J).
78 ibid [7] (McMurdo P), [100] (Mullins J), [121] (Dalton J).
79 The employees' claim was, however, ultimately unsuccessful. One employee failed to show that there was a breach of the duty in her circumstances. The three other employees failed to establish that their psychiatric injuries had been caused by a breach of the duty, see ibid [34], [43], [47], [80], [82] (McMurdo P), [102] (Mullins J), [177], [267] (Dalton J).
80 ibid [100]–[103] (Mullins J), [133]–[301] (Dalton J). In dissent, McMurdo P held that the employer owed a duty of care to each of the four employees in the circumstances: ibid [15]–[95].

letter also advised Ms Govier that she would continue to be paid but should not attend work during the investigation. Ms Govier subsequently gave her employer a medical certificate that stated she was unfit for work and did not attend the interview.

The employer sent a second letter to Ms Govier while she remained absent because of her illness. That letter suggested that Ms Govier had refused to attend the proposed interview and stated that the employer had made preliminary findings that Ms Govier had engaged in 'violent and inappropriate' behaviour towards her colleague. Ms Govier never returned to work, and her employment ultimately ceased due to her ongoing unfitness for work. Ms Govier made a claim in tort that her employer had breached the duty of reasonable care because the timing and content of its letters during the workplace investigation had aggravated a psychiatric injury.[81]

At trial, Ms Govier accepted that the decision in *Paige* was correctly decided but argued it was distinguishable because it, firstly, involved a statutory investigation process and, secondly, involved concerns about incoherence between administrative law and tort law.[82] Ms Govier argued that these factors were not relevant in her case, including because the employer was not obliged to follow an investigation process prescribed by statute.

The trial judge held that the employer had been 'insensitive' and careless in sending the two letters to Ms Govier.[83] However, the trial judge did not distinguish *Paige*, and held that the employer did not owe Ms Govier a duty to take reasonable care when sending the letters because this conduct arose in its 'system of workplace investigation and decision-making'.[84] Ms Govier appealed the judgment, including on the basis that the trial judge had erred in declining to distinguish *Paige*.

On appeal, Fraser JA (with whom Gotterson JA and North J agreed) affirmed the approach of the trial judge.[85] Fraser JA did not apply the multifactorial approach enunciated in *Sullivan*, which was endorsed in *Paige*, to Ms Govier's circumstances to determine whether the Court should recognize the 'novel category of duty'. Instead, his Honour adopted the reasoning set out in *Paige* and determined that the outcome in *Paige* was not the result of a concern about the cumulative effect of each of the factors that pointed towards legal inconsistency or incoherence in the case.[86] Rather, Fraser JA accepted that the factor of incoherence between tort law and the law of employment was determinative in *Paige*, and that there were no grounds to distinguish the principles in the proceedings.[87]

Govier seems to treat the factor of incompatibility between tort and administrative law as an ancillary consideration. However, Spigelman CJ emphasized in *Paige* that the decision not to recognize the 'novel category of duty' derived from weighing the specific factors concerning legal incoherence and incompatibility that applied in the

[81] *Govier* (n 27) [2]–[9], [64] (Fraser JA).
[82] *Govier v Unitingcare Community* [2016] QDC 56 [180]–[181].
[83] ibid [4], [178]. See further *Govier* (n 27) [73] (Fraser JA, Gotterson JA, and North J agreeing at [87]–[88]).
[84] *Govier Trial* (n 82) [178].
[85] *Govier* (n 27) [77] (Fraser JA, Gotterson JA, and North J agreeing at [87]–[88]).
[86] ibid [77] (Fraser JA, Gotterson JA, and North J agreeing at [87]–[88]). See *Paige* (n 7) 405 (Spigelman CJ).
[87] *Govier* (n 27) [77] (Fraser JA, Gotterson JA, and North J agreeing at [87]–[88]).

proceedings.[88] It is unclear, from the reasoning in *Govier*, why Fraser JA concluded that the ratio in *Paige* should operate to exclude the 'novel duty of care' in any dispute where there may be concern about incoherence between tort law and the law regarding termination of employment.

A key difference arises in the facts of *Govier*, as compared to those in *Paige*, which may explain why Ms Govier pursued her claim under tort law. In *Govier*, the employer did not rely on the findings of the investigation to dismiss the employee. Rather, Ms Govier remained absent from work due to illness for two years. Her employment ceased because she remained medically unfit for work. This meant that, unlike Mr Paige, she could not seek a review of her employer's conduct during the investigation through the law of termination of employment. Ms Govier was also not entitled to seek a review of her employer's conduct under administrative law, as her employer was not bound by a statutory framework of investigation or decision-making. Ms Govier specifically claimed a remedy in tort for an injury that was caused by the employer's negligent conduct in the workplace investigation process.

Govier and *Hayes* raise the question of what the ratio of *Paige* really is and when it will apply. This crucial question remains unsettled. It is unclear whether *Paige* applies to factual circumstances where a respondent is not dismissed, where an employer's investigation and decision-making process is not prescribed by statute, and/or where a claim is based in contract rather than tort. These questions were central to an application in 2017 by Ms Govier for special leave to appeal the decision of the Court of Appeal to the HCA (Special Leave Application). The High Court initially granted,[89] but ultimately revoked, the Special Leave Application.[90]

A close examination of the transcript of the hearing of the Special Leave Application reinforces that the case raised questions of law that need attention. The Honours' comments indicate that Ms Govier raised questions of merit in the Special Leave Application, but these questions could not be determined having regard to the tendered evidence. Ms Govier pleaded in the Special Leave Application that her employer had breached its duty of reasonable care in both tort and contract.[91] Yet Ms Govier's contract of employment document was never tendered into evidence.[92] At the hearing of the Special Leave Application, their Honours observed that the absence of the contract document was inimical to determining the 'questions of compatibility and coherence' raised by the dispute as the contract formed part of the 'broader legal context' beyond the tortious context.[93]

Nettle J specifically indicated that the questions raised by the Special Leave Application not only related to the scope of an employer's duty of care in tort but also whether the proposed duty comprised an implied obligation under the common law contract of employment.[94] Edelman J observed that the dispute seemed to raise

[88] See, eg, *Paige* (n 7) 396 (Spigelman CJ).
[89] *Govier v Uniting Church in Australia Property Trust (Q)* [2017] HCATrans 183.
[90] *Govier v Uniting Church in Australia Property Trust (Q)* [2018] HCATrans 65.
[91] The Court in *Govier* had referred to the new category of duty without explaining whether it arose as an implied contractual term or a duty in tort, and the trial judge seemed to presume that the new category of duty arose in tort.
[92] *Govier HCATrans* (n 90).
[93] ibid (Gageler J).
[94] *Govier HCATrans* (n 90).

questions about tort and about whether 'an implied [contractual] obligation [existed] to exercise power . . . in a reasonable way so as to avoid psychological injury [to Ms Govier]'.[95] Their Honours also questioned how, if a duty of care arose in contract or tort, it was shaped by the terms of the contract.[96] It was the evidentiary deficiencies that led the Court to revoke the Special Leave Application.[97]

The legal principles in *Paige* were also considered and developed by the Supreme Court of Queensland in *Potter.* The claim was made by Mr Potter, who alleged that he had suffered a psychiatric injury, including because his employer had acted negligently when it directed him to not perform work during a workplace investigation into allegations that he had engaged in serious misconduct.[98] A central question in the proceedings was whether the employer's duty of reasonable care extended to the decision to direct Mr Potter to not perform work during the investigation.[99] Mr Potter argued that the employer's decision to direct him not to perform work was an alteration of work duties, and so the employer's duty to provide a safe system of work applied to that decision.[100] On the other hand, the employer relied on *Paige* and *Govier* to argue that its duty of reasonable care did not extend to ensuring a safe system of workplace investigation or decision-making,[101] nor did it extend to its decision to direct Mr Potter to not perform work during the investigation or while he was suspended from work.[102]

Brown J rejected Mr Potter's characterization of the employer's decision to direct him to not perform work during the investigation. Brown J determined that:

> [t]he effect of the decision to suspend an employee or direct the employee not to perform work while an investigation is carried out requires an employee not to perform work at all during that period at the workplace. It alters the employee's state from working to not working whilst still being employed not the employee's work duties. The decision to suspend is therefore outside of the employer's duty to provide a safe system of work.[103]

Her Honour reasoned that it was appropriate to distinguish the facts in the case from those in *Hayes*, where the employees continued to perform duties during the workplace investigation.[104]

Brown J noted that no Australian court had previously found that an employer owed a duty of reasonable care with respect to any decision to suspend an employee. Brown J observed that the employer had relied on its implied contractual right to issue lawful

[95] ibid (Edelman J).
[96] ibid.
[97] ibid.
[98] *Potter* (n 28) [114]. The employer paid Mr Potter during his absence from work. The decision describes the employer's action as a 'suspension' of the employee.
[99] ibid [258]. The Court also determined that the principles in *Paige* and *Govier* were to be distinguished from the facts in the case that related to a process of conducting 'work performance management' rather than an investigation of allegations of misconduct: ibid [258].
[100] *Potter* (n 28) [368].
[101] ibid [271].
[102] ibid [272].
[103] ibid [379].
[104] ibid.

and reasonable directions when it directed Mr Potter not to perform work during the investigation.[105] Brown J relied on the principles in *Paige* and *Govier* to conclude that the employer did not owe a duty of reasonable care with respect to its decision to direct Mr Potter to not perform work during the investigation.[106] Ultimately, Brown J dismissed Mr Potter's claim.[107] Mr Potter appealed the decision, including on the basis that Brown J had erred by applying the decisions of *Paige* and *Govier*, rather than *Hayes*, to determine that the employer did not owe a duty of reasonable care with respect to its decision to suspend Mr Potter.[108] A Court of Appeal of the Supreme Court of Queensland upheld her Honour's reasoning on this matter.[109] The reasoning of Brown J in *Potter*, as affirmed on appeal, indicates that an employer will not owe a duty of reasonable care with respect to a decision to direct an employee whose conduct is under investigation to not perform work.

The legal principles in *Paige* were also considered in detail by a Court of Appeal of the Supreme Court of Victoria in *Elisha (Court of Appeal)*.[110] Vision Australia Limited (Vision Australia) engaged Mr Elisha as an adaptive technology consultant under a written contract of employment in September 2006. In May 2015, Vision Australia was informed that a hotel staff member had complained that Mr Elisha had been 'aggressive and intimidating' towards her in March 2015, while he was staying at the hotel overnight on a work trip (the 'hotel incident').

When Mr Elisha's manager, Ms Hauser, was told about the hotel incident, she told staff at Vision Australia who were involved in investigating the incident that Mr Elisha had allegedly engaged in a pattern of aggressive behaviour prior to the hotel incident (the 'other allegations').

On 19 May 2015, Vision Australia provided Mr Elisha with a letter that included allegations he had breached certain policies and 'values' of Vision Australia because of his conduct during the hotel incident. The letter set out a direction from Vision Australia to Mr Elisha to not attend work while the allegations were investigated, to not communicate with any staff member about the matter unless they were a support person, and to attend a meeting to respond to the allegations that would be 'conducted in accordance with the due process clause of the Vision Australia Unified Enterprise Agreement 2013 ("Vision EA")'. The letter attached appendices, relevant terms of the Vision EA, and the 'Vision Australia Disciplinary Procedure', effective April 2015. The letter did not mention the other allegations.

Mr Elisha attended the disciplinary meeting on 26 May 2015, with Mr Nunns of the Australian Services Union (ASU) as his support person. At that meeting, he denied the allegations arising from the hotel incident. Again, Vision Australia did not disclose to Mr Elisha that it was considering the other allegations, nor did it give him an opportunity to respond to them. Vision Australia provided Mr Elisha with a letter on 29 May 2015, which advised him that his employment was terminated with immediate effect. The letter stated Vision Australia 'consider[ed] that on the balance of probability'

105 ibid [391].
106 ibid [400]–[401].
107 ibid [711].
108 *Potter (Appeal)* (n 8) [30] (Flanagan JA, Mullins P agreeing at [1], Williams J agreeing at [83]).
109 ibid [82] (Flanagan JA, Mullins P agreeing at [1], Williams J agreeing at [83]).
110 *Elisha (Court of Appeal)* (n 72).

Mr Elisha had behaved in the manner described by the hotel staff member during the hotel incident, and this comprised 'serious misconduct'.[111]

Mr Elisha was diagnosed with a serious and ongoing psychiatric injury and was found to have no capacity for work in the foreseeable future. Mr Elisha made a claim in the Supreme Court of Victoria for damages principally arising from the termination of his employment.[112] Specifically, Mr Elisha made a claim for breach of contract on the basis that Vision Australia had breached express terms of his contract of employment. Mr Elisha made an alternate claim in tort that the conduct of Vision Australia had breached the implied duty of reasonable care that it owed towards him.[113]

O'Meara J determined at first instance that Vision Australia had breached express terms of Mr Elisha's contract of employment and made orders for damages.[114] His Honour also set out observations about Mr Elisha's alternative claim in tort, but noted it was unnecessary to 'fully determine' the issues raised by that claim. O'Meara J turned to examine the reasoning in *Paige*, decisions applied in *Paige*, including *Addis*, and decisions that have considered or applied *Paige*, including *Govier* and *Potter*.

His Honour reasoned that the duty of care as contended by Mr Elisha 'concerning the termination of [Mr Elisha's] contract of employment, as distinct from performance under that contract', was 'not presently recognised by the common law'.[115] O'Meara J observed that the 'central reasoning' in *Paige* and *Govier* had not been displaced[116] but also expressed doubt that *Paige* 'wholly' foreclosed 'any possible claim in negligence'.[117] O'Meara J made four key observations about *Paige*. First, the two statutes applicable in *Paige* were not relevant in Mr Elisha's case. Second, the *FW Act* was relevant to Mr Elisha's case and (unlike the statutes applicable to Mr Paige) it did not permit an award of compensation for psychiatric injury. Third, it was not easy to see how a much later common law claim directed to psychiatric injury could distort a claim under the unfair dismissal protection in pt 3-1 of the *FW Act*. Fourth, 'real issues may well arise' regarding the point where any preclusion from the duty of reasonable care 'starts and finishes' including in the context of procedures for discipline and dismissal.[118] His Honour also observed Spigelman J had identified incoherence between the proposed duty in *Paige* and the principles in *Addis* and *Baltic Shipping*.[119]

O'Meara J observed that absent contractual terms that would permit Mr Elisha's claim, 'the common law seem[ed] to stand against a negligence claim such as the present that is directed to the termination of [Mr Elisha's] contract of employment',[120] but that if the duty as claimed by Mr Elisha did arise under the law, Vision Australia

[111] *Elisha (First Instance)* (n 68) [39].
[112] Mr Elisha also made a claim under the unfair dismissal protection under pt 3-2 of the *FW Act*, which was settled prior to adjudication: ibid [237]–[238].
[113] ibid [48]–[53].
[114] See further chapter 4 IV.
[115] *Elisha (First Instance)* (n 68) [467], [529].
[116] ibid [518].
[117] ibid [525].
[118] ibid [483]–[489].
[119] ibid [513].
[120] ibid [516]. His Honour noted that in *Aldersea v Public Transport Corporation* (2001) 3 VR 499, the principles in *Addis* had been held to apply to 'damages for personal injury resulting from wrongful termination of a contract of employment': ibid [514].

had breached the duty by its conduct during the disciplinary process leading to the termination.[121]

Vision Australia appealed the decision at first instance to the Court of Appeal of the Supreme Court of Victoria. Vision Australia contended that the trial judge had erred in finding that Vision Australia had breached express terms of the contract of employment, including by breaching terms of the Vision EA and 2015 Disciplinary Procedure, which his Honour had found to be incorporated into the terms of the contract. Vision Australia also raised that O'Meara J had erred in not concluding that damages would be limited to a maximum of one month's pay under the contract, were not available in law for any psychiatric harm suffered by Mr Elisha, and were not available because the psychiatric harm to Mr Elisha was too remote. Mr Elisha alternatively contended that the trial judge had erred by holding that Vision Australia 'did not owe a duty of care to [him] to take reasonable care to avoid injury . . . in its implementation of the processes leading to and resulting in' his dismissal.[122]

In a unanimous joint judgment, McLeish, Kennedy, and Macaulay JJA overturned the decision of O'Meara J regarding Mr Elisha's claim of breach of express terms of his contract.[123] Their Honours also considered Mr Elisha's alternative claim in tort. Their Honours affirmed the reasoning of Spigelman J in *Paige*, confirmed its broad application as reflected in *Govier*, and declined to accept that either *Paige*, or cases that have applied *Paige*, were 'plainly wrong'.[124] Their Honours affirmed O'Meara J had 'made no error in holding that Vision did not owe the alleged duty of care'.[125]

Mr Elisha obtained special leave to appeal the decision of the Court of Appeal to the HCA and alleged that Vision Australia was liable to pay damages for his psychiatric injury because it had breached express contractual terms,[126] and the duty of reasonable care arising in tort. The joint judgment of Gageler CJ, Gordon, Edelman, Gleeson, and Beech-Jones JJ,[127] and the judgment of Jagot J, determined the appeal based on the issue of whether Vision Australia had breached express terms of the contract. On this issue, their Honours upheld the judgment and orders of the trial judge, and Jagot J agreed.[128] The contractual claim pursued by Mr Elisha before the HCA is considered further below.

In this context, the majority judges held that it was not necessary to further consider the issue pursued by Mr Elisha based in tort,[129] which 'raise[d] very different issues'.[130] Their Honours observed that Mr Elisha alleged that the duty of care owed by employers included to 'provide "a safe system of investigation and decision-making with respect to discipline and termination of employment"' and, as this would be a duty imposed by law, it could 'be shaped by, and must be coherent with, relevant

[121] *Elisha (First Instance)* (n 68) [532].
[122] *Elisha (Court of Appeal)* (n 72) 312.
[123] See further chapter 4 IV.
[124] *Elisha (Court of Appeal)* (n 72) 352–54.
[125] ibid 304.
[126] See further chapter 4 IV.
[127] Hereinafter, for brevity, the decision of their Honours is referred to as the 'joint judgment'.
[128] *Elisha (HCA)* (n 3) 207 (joint judgment), 226 (Jagot J), 207 (Steward J, dissenting).
[129] ibid 186 (joint judgment).
[130] ibid 206 (joint judgment).

legislation'.[131] Their Honours observed that the parties had not made comprehensive submissions on the issue of coherence between the duty of care that Mr Elisha alleged was owed by Vision Australia and statute. Their Honours noted that comprehensive submissions had not been made about the scope and availability of compensation for psychiatric injury under specific parts of the *FW Act* and state WHS regimes.[132] The majority judges determined it was unnecessary to determine the scope of an employer's duty to provide a safe system of work or further address the issue.

A central argument raised by Vision Australia was that the law precluded Mr Elisha from recovering damages for breach of a contractual duty that concerned the manner of dismissal. The majority judges held that, subject to the terms and context of the particular contract, an employee could recover damages for psychiatric injury caused by an employer's breach of a term of a contract, including if that term is about the manner of dismissal.[133] This displaced the long-held understanding that *Addis*, as applied by Australian courts, precluded an employee from recovering damages for psychiatric injury caused by the manner of termination of a contract of employment. A claim for psychiatric damages caused by an employer's breach of the duty of reasonable care during a workplace investigation might now be alternately pursued under contract or tort, without the possibility that the contractual claim is precluded on this basis.

In a dissenting judgment, Steward J determined that Mr Elisha's appeal should be dismissed.[134] His Honour considered Mr Elisha's claim in negligence in further detail and affirmed the reasoning of the Court of Appeal in *Paige* and *Elisha (Court of Appeal)* on this issue.[135] Steward J stated that '[t]he reason why there is no duty of care of the kind claimed by [Mr Elisha] is the need for coherence of the law'.[136] His Honour noted, with approval, the reasoning of Spigelman CJ in *Paige* and affirmed that 'matters concerning the creation and termination of a contract of employment should be left to the law of contract and statute, and no additional duty of care should be imposed over this extensive legal regime'.[137] His Honour's observations in dissent provide a further interpretation of the ratio in *Paige*. These observations add to ambiguity regarding the content of that ratio.

The decisions examined above, culminating in *Elisha (HCA)*, illustrate that the legal principles regarding the scope of an employer's duty of reasonable care during a workplace investigation process are ambiguous and unsettled. The delineation between the system of work and the system of workplace investigation is uncertain. Courts have consistently grappled with the scope and content of an employer's duty of reasonable care, and with the reasoning and precise ratio in *Paige*. The doubt expressed by O'Meara J about where 'any such preclusion [from the duty] starts and ends' affects employers, respondents, advisors, union representatives, and policymakers.

[131] ibid 206 (joint judgment) (citations omitted).
[132] ibid 206–07 (joint judgment).
[133] ibid 186 (joint judgment). See further Adriana Orifici,'Reframing Addis: A Clarification of the Law of Damages for Psychiatric Injury in Dismissal in Elisha v Vision Australia Ltd' (2025) 38(3) Australian Journal of Labour Law 1.
[134] ibid 204 (Steward J).
[135] ibid 210 (Steward J).
[136] ibid.
[137] ibid.

Divergent approaches to interpreting *Paige* and *Govier* have discernible effects on the legal reasoning of subordinate courts.[138] The differing approaches are exemplified in the reasoning in *Lloyd*[139] and *Ackers*.[140]

On the one hand, in *Lloyd*,[141] the County Court of Victoria observed that 'the application of *Govier* [was] not absolute',[142] but:

> [a]t any [step in an investigation] there might arise a real or appreciable risk of psychological harm to an employee, depending on what he or she is aware is taking place or becomes subsequently aware has occurred. To impose a duty of care as formulated to so many moving parts that constitute an investigation is not readily reconcilable with a duty of care to provide a safe system of work.[143]

This reasoning suggests that courts may decline to recognize the 'novel category of duty' in any circumstance where it would be undesirable to inhibit an employer's investigation process, despite the indicia of proximity, vulnerability, and control.[144]

On the other hand, *Ackers* closely followed the approach taken in *Hayes* and distinguished and confined the principles in *Paige*. In *Ackers*, an employee claimed that his employer had breached the duty of reasonable care in tort because of its conduct during an investigation into allegations that he had engaged in misconduct and because of its negligent implementation of a Performance Improvement Action Plan (PIAP).[145] Mr Ackers alleged that this conduct caused, and then exacerbated, a psychiatric injury.

In *Ackers*, the Supreme Court of Queensland held that *Paige* and *Govier* precluded Mr Ackers' first claim.[146] However, Henry J rejected an argument put by the employer that *Paige* and *Govier* also precluded Mr Ackers' claim regarding the PIAP.[147] The employer made this argument on the basis that the investigation into performance could similarly lead to Mr Ackers' dismissal and so gave rise to possible incompatibilities between the law of tort and the law of dismissal.[148] In rejecting this argument, Henry J observed:

138 See, eg, *Lloyd* (n 29); *Knight* (n 68); *Blows* (n 68); *Potter* (n 28).
139 *Lloyd* (n 29).
140 *Ackers* (n 30).
141 *Lloyd* (n 29). This reasoning was affirmed in *Lloyd Appeal* (n 29) [62]–[72].
142 *Lloyd* (n 29) [288].
143 ibid [288].
144 Similar reasoning was applied by the FCA in *Sklavos v Australasian College of Dermatologists* [2016] FCA 179, [407] where Jagot J cited the principles from *Paige* with approval and adopted a similar approach to *Paige* to hold that a training college does not owe a duty to provide reasonable care to a trainee to avoid foreseeable psychological harm when investigating allegations of misconduct. Jagot J emphasized that recognizing the proposed duty could have a 'chilling effect' on the college's investigations, which had a 'protective' purpose in the public interest: *Sklavos v Australasian College of Dermatologists* [406]–[408].
145 *Ackers* (n 30).
146 ibid 409–10. The Court also determined that, even if the Court could recognize the new category of duty, the employer would not have breached that duty because there was no foreseeable risk of psychiatric injury to the employee at the time: ibid 417.
147 *Ackers* (n 30) 417.
148 ibid 430.

> [t]here is no logical incompatibility between the existence of the right to require competent job performance and liability in negligence for a breach of the duty of care to avoid foreseeable risk of psychiatric injury, if the breach involves a process of purported correction of job performance which is carried out in bad faith or contrary to the employer's own processes and procedures. Such conduct bespeaks an other than genuine purported exercise of the contractual right[.][149]

The approach in *Ackers* differs from the broad interpretation of the ratio in *Paige* that is set out in *Lloyd*. In *Ackers*, the Court described the facts as 'quite different than both *Paige* and *Govier*'.[150] Henry J declined to construe *Paige* as applying to employer conduct during a process that was designed to investigate and address employee underperformance, even though the process could lead to dismissal. *Ackers* and *Lloyd* show that the outcome of a claim currently pivots on the Court's approach to interpreting *Paige*.

A central aspect of the reasoning in *Paige* was also cited with approval in *Commonwealth Bank of Australia v Barker* (*Barker*), in which the HCA unanimously determined that there was no implied term of mutual trust and confidence in employment contracts.[151] In the joint judgment, their Honours explained that it was necessary for courts to develop obligations in contract or tort in a manner that was sensitive to legislation.[152] Their Honours recognized that this was especially important where those obligations 'intrude[d] a common law policy choice of broad and uncertain scope into [Commonwealth and state statutory unfair dismissal law, which was] an area of frequent, detailed and often contentious legislative activity'.[153] The Court cited the reasoning of Spigelman CJ in *Paige* as an example of where this issue had arisen.[154]

Barker reinforces that *Paige* exemplifies a broader reluctance by courts to develop obligations that are at the 'intersection with the [statutory] law of unfair dismissal'.[155] The reasoning of Steward J in dissent in *Elisha (HCA)*, noted above, also reflects this approach. Courts have, in decisions like *Paige* and *Barker*, stated that the statutory law of unfair dismissal should be regarded as a comprehensive scheme that was developed by the Australian Parliament to exclude the judicial development of any additional common law remedies.[156] The judicial reluctance to develop common law obligations arising from the termination of employment, which will interact with statutory unfair dismissal law, indicates that courts will continue to regard the development of obligations, such as the 'novel category of duty', as matters to be addressed by the legislature.

[149] ibid.
[150] ibid.
[151] *Barker* (n 61) 370–71.
[152] ibid 387.
[153] ibid.
[154] ibid.
[155] ibid.
[156] On concern regarding the enlivenment of additional remedies, see *Barker* (n 61) 387.

D Discussion

Courts have developed principles that apply to negligent employer conduct during workplace investigations, but the law is inadequate because key principles remain unclear and unresolved. The HCA is yet to determine if a cause of action in negligence is available to claimants where employers breach the duty of reasonable care while conducting a workplace investigation. The collection of legal principles under *Paige, Hayes, Govier, Potter,* and *Elisha (Court of Appeal)* on this issue is complex, and the boundaries between an employer's system of work and its system of workplace investigation are hard to discern. Crucially, the ratio in *Paige* remains unclear but has been central to judicial determinations of subsequent disputes. This is reinforced by the observations about *Paige* in the dissenting judgment of Steward J in *Elisha (HCA).*

The location of key principles in decisions of state-based appellate courts also adds to the uncertainty and complexity of the law. It is possible for the principles to differ between jurisdictions based on the claims that have arisen for determination before the courts. For example, the decision in *Ackers* was determined in Queensland. An appellate court in another jurisdiction, such as Victoria, is not required to apply the principle from that case but may be persuaded to do so.

There are also gaps in the development of an employer's duty of reasonable care as applicable during a workplace investigation. *Paige* and *Govier* determined that the duty of reasonable care owed by the employer towards the respondent in contract and tort did not generally include a duty to ensure a safe system of workplace investigation and decision-making. *Potter* built on these decisions and determined that an employer did not have a duty when directing a respondent not to perform work during a workplace investigation. *Hayes* and *Ackers* demonstrated how the ratio in *Paige* may be distinguished and confined but also contributed to uncertainty about how that ratio will be interpreted and applied by courts in future.

Paige and *Govier* provide some insights into why gaps in the development of the law have persisted since 2002. Courts have demonstrated reluctance to develop a new remedy in tort that is about a subject matter that interacts with the statutory law on unfair dismissal. In these decisions, courts have viewed the statutory framework as a comprehensive scheme that covers the field. The dissenting judgment of Steward J in *Elisha (HCA)* also reflects this approach. Courts appear to regard it as a matter for the legislature to decide whether the law of contract or tort should be developed to extend the duty of reasonable care to require an employer to ensure a safe system of workplace investigation and decision-making because it raises complex questions about the interactions between fields of law and new remedies.

A close examination of the trial decision in *Elisha* illuminates that Mr Elisha's claim was, fundamentally, about the damage caused to him by his employer's negligence, but the HCA ultimately determined the claim based on Vision Australia's breach of the express terms of his contract of employment. It seems the most salient aspect of the claim was not definitively determined by the HCA. In these circumstances, *Elisha (HCA)* seems to lead to a troubling asymmetry in possible outcomes for claimants. Respondents can pursue a claim in contract for psychiatric injury if the employer breaches express contractual terms that relate to the workplace investigation process, including in a manner that is negligent. However, it is yet to be determined by the HCA whether a claim in contract or tort for breach of the duty of reasonable care is available, or would succeed, if a respondent was psychiatrically injured by the same employer conduct but was not covered by a contract that included relevant express terms.

Paige is also underpinned by public policy considerations that are now over two decades old. Spigelman CJ regarded it as a matter of public policy that the State should be allowed to conduct an efficient workplace investigation under the *TS Act* despite the risk of foreseeable psychiatric injury to Mr Paige. However, since 2002, workplace investigations have become more prevalent, and the Australian Parliament has galvanized its policy objective to ensure 'safe and healthy work for all' through the legal regulation of WHS.[157] There is now significant tension between the policy considerations underlying judge-made law and statute on this subject. It is arguable that the finely balanced public policy rationale that underpins the decision of Spigelman CJ in *Paige* is no longer convincing without qualification and requires judicial scrutiny in future decisions and/or legislative intervention.

IV The Development of Judicial Principles About Unreasonable Employer Conduct in Workplace Investigations

Superior and appellate courts have also determined claims by respondents that their employer exercised a contractual power or discretion under the contract of employment in a manner that was unreasonable, or in a manner that breached an express or implied contractual term.

A close examination of key judicial decisions reveals central principles that an employer:

- must act reasonably (to the standard set out in *Associated Provincial Picture Houses Ltd v Wednesbury Corp*,[158] and honestly (consistent with the principle in *Service Station Association Ltd v Berg Bennett & Associates Pty Ltd*),[159] when exercising rights and powers under the express terms of an employment contract at least so far as its workplace investigation process goes, as distinct from the result;
- may be required to initiate a workplace investigation for a bona fide purpose and in a manner that enables the respondent to fairly respond to allegations as part of the implied contractual duty of cooperation;[160]

[157] Safe Work Australia, 'Australian Work Health and Safety Strategy 2023–2033' (2023) Strategy Paper <https://www.safeworkaustralia.gov.au/awhs-strategy_23-33> accessed 24 August 2025.

[158] *Bartlett v Australia & New Zealand Banking Group Ltd* (2016) 92 NSWLR 639, 639, 651–52 (Macfarlan JA, Meagher HA agreeing at 662, Simpson JA dissenting on this matter at 664–69). See *Associated Provincial Picture Houses Ltd v Wednesbury Corp* (1948) 1 KB 223, 233–34 (Lord Greene MR). Application of the *Wednesbury* standard invalidates a decision that is 'so unreasonable that no reasonable [decision-maker] could ever have come to it': *Braganza v BP Shipping Ltd* [2015] WLR 1661, 1671 [24] (Baroness Hale DPSC) quoting Wednesbury, 233–34 (Lord Greene MR).

[159] *Service Station Association Ltd v Berg Bennett & Associates Pty Ltd* (1993) 45 FCR 84, 94. See *Avenia v Railway & Transport Health Fund Ltd* (2017) 272 IR 151, 203.

[160] The interrelationship between the implied duty of cooperation, and the concepts regarding good faith and reasonableness in the exercise of contractual powers, is yet to be clearly enunciated in case law regarding

- must comply with an internal policy about a workplace investigation where the policy is directive and places sufficient emphasis on mutual compliance.[161]

However, these principles are underpinned by judicial reasoning that is unsettled and underdeveloped. There are central gaps and uncertainties in the development of judge-made law.

I examine case law that develops key judicial principles in three parts. First, I analyse two decisions that discuss the extent of an employer's obligation to exercise powers under the employment contract reasonably during a workplace investigation: *Bartlett v Australia & New Zealand Banking Group* (*Bartlett*),[162] and *Avenia v Railway & Transport Health Fund Ltd* (*Avenia*).[163] Second, I examine *Cummins South Pacific Pty Ltd v Keenan* (*Cummins*) and identify judicial observations about how an employer's implied duty of cooperation applies during workplace investigations.[164] Third, I consider decisions that enunciate principles about the obligation of an employer to abide by an internal policy about workplace investigations: *Romero v Farstad Shipping (Indian Pacific) Pty Ltd* (*Romero*),[165] *Tucker v Victoria* (*Tucker (No 1)*),[166] and *Elisha (HCA)*.[167]

A The scope of an employer's duty to exercise contractual powers reasonably during a workplace investigation

As noted in chapter 1, an employer may rely on express or implied powers and rights to conduct a workplace investigation. Contracts of employment may include express terms that relate to workplace investigation processes. For example, express terms might prescribe how an employer must conduct a workplace investigation or how it will make disciplinary decisions based on the findings of an investigation. An employer may also prepare internal policies about workplace investigations, which may or may not be contractually binding.[168] Alternatively, the employment contract might not include any relevant terms about workplace investigations. In these circumstances, an employer that wishes to conduct a workplace investigation will rely on rights and powers arising from implied contractual terms.[169]

the contract of employment. This analysis discusses these obligations separately but recognizes that they are related. There is similar uncertainty regarding the relationship between these concepts in commercial contracts, see, eg, Geoffrey Kuehne, 'Implied Obligations of Good Faith and Reasonableness in the Performance of Contracts: Old Wine in New Bottles?' (2006) 33 University of Western Australia Law Review 63, 76.

161 *Romero v Farstad Shipping (Indian Pacific) Pty Ltd* (2014) 231 FCR 403, 420.
162 *Bartlett* (n 158).
163 *Avenia* (n 159).
164 *Cummins South Pacific Pty Ltd v Keenan* (2020) 281 FCR 421.
165 *Romero* (n 161).
166 *Tucker v Victoria* [2018] VSC 389 [6]–[7].
167 *Elisha (HCA)* (n 3).
168 Courts have considered circumstances where these policies will be legally binding. See further chapter 4 IV(C) below.
169 On terms implied in law in the contract of employment, see further Sappideen, O'Grady, and Riley (n 9) 192–266.

Courts have held that employers must exercise express contractual powers reasonably during workplace investigations, but it is unclear whether employers must also exercise implied contractual powers reasonably in this context. In cases about commercial contracts, the obligation to act reasonably has been variously described as an obligation to not act irrationally, dishonestly, or for a collateral purpose.[170] Australian employment contracts do not include an implied obligation for employers to act reasonably when exercising contractual rights or powers, but courts have developed various principles that establish that employers must exercise specific rights and powers reasonably under employment contracts.[171] Courts have ordinarily considered the terms of the contract and the objective intention of the parties to determine the content of a duty to act reasonably.[172] The development of principles relevant to employer conduct towards respondents during workplace investigations is situated in the decisions of *Bartlett* and *Avenia*.[173]

In *Bartlett*, a Full Court of the Supreme Court of New South Wales considered whether an employer was required to act reasonably when exercising express contractual powers during a workplace investigation. Mr Bartlett's employer, the Australia and New Zealand Banking Group Ltd (ANZ), had summarily dismissed him for serious misconduct. ANZ had relied on an express term in Mr Bartlett's employment contract to do so. Mr Bartlett made a claim in contract that, firstly, challenged how ANZ had construed the express term,[174] and secondly, argued that the contractual term was subject to an implied obligation on ANZ to act reasonably and/or in good faith.[175]

At trial, ANZ accepted that it was required to act in good faith; however, Mr Bartlett did not contend that it had failed to do so. Instead, Mr Bartlett claimed that the employer's decision to summarily dismiss him was made unreasonably. ANZ argued that it did not have an implied obligation to exercise the express contractual power reasonably and, in any case, denied it had failed to do so. The trial judge rejected Mr Bartlett's claim,[176] and Mr Bartlett subsequently appealed that decision.

On appeal, Macfarlan JA (with whom Meagher and Simpson JJA agreed on this matter) decided that ANZ was required to establish the objective existence of misconduct by Mr Bartlett to dismiss him for misconduct under the contract of employment.[177] Specifically, Macfarlan JA determined that ANZ had to ensure that the decisions it made following the workplace investigation were based on the objective existence of misconduct rather than an opinion that misconduct had occurred.[178]

[170] Irving (n 23) 707–11. Other cases have equated the concept of 'reasonableness' with good faith, see discussion in Kuehne (n 160) 64.

[171] Irving (n 23) 404–05. These cases often relate to contractual terms that provide employers with discretion to pay an employee a bonus, see discussion in Matthew Moir, 'Discretion, Good Faith and Employer Control over Executive Remuneration' (2011) 24 Australian Journal of Labour Law 121.

[172] Joellen Riley, 'Siblings But Not Twins: Making Sense of "Mutual Trust" and "Good Faith" in Employment Contracts' (2012) 36 Melbourne University Law Review 521, 543.

[173] *Bartlett* (n 158); *Avenia* (n 159).

[174] *Bartlett* (n 158) 648 (Macfarlan JA).

[175] ibid 649 (Macfarlan JA).

[176] This decision overturned *Bartlett v Australia and New Zealand Banking Group Ltd* (2014) 246 IR 190.

[177] *Bartlett* (n 158) 648–49 (Macfarlan JA, Meagher JA agreeing at 662, Simpson JA agreeing at 665). On the other hand, the Court determined that the employer was not required to act reasonably when exercising its power to dismiss without reason and with reasonable notice: ibid 648–49, 662, 665.

[178] *Bartlett* (n 158) 648 (Macfarlan JA).

Their Honours held that ANZ had failed to establish that it was entitled to summarily dismiss Mr Bartlett in the circumstances.[179]

Macfarlan JA also considered Mr Bartlett's second argument, that the contractual term was subject to an implied obligation on ANZ to act reasonably and/or in good faith.[180] His Honour held that, in forming an opinion under the express term, ANZ was 'obliged to act reasonably, at least in the *Wednesbury* sense and at least so far as its [investigation] process, as distinct from the result, was concerned'.[181] The *Wednesbury* standard of reasonableness effectively renders a decision made under an express contractual term invalid where it is so irrational that it would not have been made by any reasonable decision-maker.[182]

Macfarlan JA elaborated that the conclusion was warranted, having regard to the reasoning in *Service Station Association*,[183] and the reasoning in other authoritative or persuasive decisions regarding the obligation of a party to exercise express contractual power reasonably, including in the context of employment.[184] In *Service Station Association*, the FCA held:

> [w]here one party has an express power the exercise of which will significantly affect the interests of the other party (e.g. by cancellation of their supply contract) if the holder of the power is satisfied that a certain state of affairs exists, the words of the contract are fairly readily construed (and the more so when the parties have given such a power to a third party) as requiring a reasonable as well as honest state of satisfaction . . . But this is a result arrived at by a process of construction of the express terms in the setting of the contract as a whole. It is best not seen at all as the implication of a further term.[185]

His Honour also observed that the reasoning of the Supreme Court of the United Kingdom in *Braganza* relevantly highlighted that the requirement to act reasonably focused on 'the rationality of the decision-making process rather than [concentration] on the outcome'.[186]

His Honour determined that ANZ was required to act reasonably when it formed an opinion under the express contractual term, but it had not done so.[187] His Honour held that ANZ had limited the scope of its workplace investigation into allegations of Mr Bartlett's misconduct in a manner that was 'unwarranted' and had not afforded Mr Bartlett procedural fairness.[188] For these reasons, Macfarlan JA determined that

[179] ibid 658 (Macfarlan JA, Meagher JA agreeing at 662, Simpson JA agreeing at 665).
[180] ibid 649–52 (Macfarlan J). Meagher JA determined that it was 'unnecessary' to consider this further argument: ibid 652. Simpson JA declined to determine this question: ibid 669.
[181] *Bartlett* (n 158) 652 (Macfarlan JA).
[182] *Wednesbury* (n 158) 33–34 (Lord Greene MR).
[183] *Bartlett* (n 158) 652 (Macfarlan JA).
[184] His Honour referred to *Braganza* (n 158); *Burger King Corporation v Hungry Jack's Pty Ltd* (2001) 69 NSWLR 558; *Barker* (n 61). See *Bartlett* (n 158) 651–52 (Macfarlan JA, Meagher JA agreeing at 662).
[185] *Service Station Association* (n 159) 303–04 (Gummow J). See *Bartlett* (n 158) 651–52 (Macfarlan JA).
[186] *Bartlett* (n 158) 652 (Macfarlan JA).
[187] ibid 652–53 (Macfarlan JA).
[188] ibid 653 (Macfarlan JA).

ANZ had not satisfied the *Wednesbury* standard of reasonableness.[189] However, Macfarlan JA also emphasized that this conclusion was not determinative in the case.[190] This was because their Honours had accepted Mr Bartlett's primary argument that ANZ was required to establish the objective existence of misconduct in order to summarily dismiss him under the express term, and had determined that ANZ had not done so.

The reasoning of Macfarlan JA in *Bartlett* comprises a step towards recognizing that the *Wednesbury* standard of reasonableness applies to actions taken by an employer so far as its workplace investigation process goes.[191] It indicates that an employer may be required to act reasonably when it exercises rights and powers pursuant to express contractual terms during a workplace investigation process. The *Wednesbury* standard does not incorporate other concepts of reasonableness (such as fair or honest conduct). However, the principles are nascent and underdeveloped.

In *Avenia*, the FCA considered and affirmed the reasoning of Macfarlan JA in *Bartlett*. The case involved Dr Avenia, who had been the respondent in a workplace investigation conducted by his employer, the Railway & Transport Health Fund Ltd (RTHF). RTHF had relied on express and implied contractual terms to conduct the workplace investigation.[192] RTHF had conducted the investigation and made findings of misconduct. RTHF decided to dismiss Dr Avenia, who then commenced proceedings in which he claimed RTHF had breached express and implied contractual terms. One claim pursued by Dr Avenia was that RTHF was obliged 'to exercise contractual powers in good faith [and this] extended to an obligation to act reasonably when exercising powers which may adversely affect Dr Avenia's employment'.[193]

Dr Avenia argued that, according to *Bartlett*, this obligation included a requirement for RTHF to exercise contractual powers 'in accordance with the principles of procedural fairness'.[194]

The Court determined that the decision in *Bartlett* did not establish the 'very broad propositions' articulated by Dr Avenia.[195] Lee J held that the reasoning in *Bartlett*:

> is best seen . . . as an application of the principle explained by Gummow J in *Service Station Association Ltd v Berg Bennett & Associates Pty Ltd* . . . that 'where one party has an express power which will significantly affect the interests of the other party . . . the words of the contract are fairly readily construed . . . as requiring a reasonable as well as honest state of satisfaction', but this construction 'is best not seen at all as the implication of a further term'.[196]

[189] ibid 652–53. Macfarlan JA rejected an argument by Mr Bartlett that the employer was obliged to act reasonably if exercising a specific contractual power that allowed the employer to dismiss Mr Bartlett 'for any reason' with four months' notice: ibid 660.

[190] *Bartlett* (n 158) 649 (Macfarlan JA).

[191] See further Richard Naughton, 'Termination of Employment and Workplace Investigations' (2016) 22 Employment Law Bulletin 186, 186; Natalie Williams, '*Bartlett v Australia & New Zealand Banking Group Ltd* [2016] NSWCA 30 (7 March 2016)' (2016) 37 Adelaide Law Review 571, 579.

[192] *Avenia* (n 159) 201.

[193] ibid 201.

[194] ibid 203.

[195] ibid 205.

[196] ibid 203 quoting Service Station Association, 94 (Gummow J) (citations omitted).

The approach taken by Lee J affirmed the reasoning of Macfarlan JA in *Bartlett* but also confined the application of the principles to circumstances where an employer exercises an express contractual power.

It remains unclear whether an employer is also required to act in good faith or reasonably when it exercises implied contractual powers during a workplace investigation process, or whether the requirement to act reasonably requires an employer to ensure procedural fairness.[197] In *Avenia*, Lee J stated that it was not necessary to decide these 'large questions which are primarily directed to the standard of reasonableness to be observed in the exercise of a discretionary contractual power' having regard to the matters in dispute and the content of express contractual terms that bound the parties.[198]

As noted by Lee J, the broader question of whether an employer must generally act in good faith and/or reasonably when it exercises a discretionary power under a contract of employment is uncertain, having regard to the decision in *Barker*.[199] In *Barker*, the HCA left open the question of 'whether contractual powers and discretions may be limited by good faith and rationality requirements analogous to those applicable in the sphere of public law'.[200] Lee J observed that Dr Avenia's claim raised these 'large questions', but it was unnecessary to determine these questions in the context of the dispute.[201]

An implied contractual obligation to exercise discretionary contractual powers in good faith and/or in a reasonable way would constrain employer conduct towards respondents in various ways. For example, employers could possibly be required to ensure procedural fairness[202] or reasonable notice before holding an interview with an investigator. However, the law remains uncertain and underdeveloped. *Bartlett* and *Avenia* only develop principles about how employers must exercise express contractual powers during workplace investigations.

B The application of the implied duty of cooperation during a workplace investigation

The duty of cooperation is owed by both parties under the contract of employment. The meaning of the duty was set out in *Mackay v Dick* as requiring each party 'to do all that is

[197] On the potential for development of an implied duty to conduct disciplinary processes fairly, see Philippa Collins and Gabrielle Golding, 'An Implied Term of Procedural Fairness During Disciplinary Processes: Into Contracts of Employment and Beyond?' (2024) 53 Industrial Law Journal 125; Douglas Brodie, 'Disavowing an Implied Term of Fairness' (2024) 53 Industrial Law Journal 157.

[198] *Avenia* (n 159) 205.

[199] ibid 203 (emphasis omitted). See *Barker* (n 61) 371.

[200] *Avenia* (n 159) 201 quoting Barker (n 60) 195–96 (citations omitted). See also the discussion in *Barker* (n 61) 212–13. For consideration of the implications of a possible implied term of good faith in employment contracts, see Riley (n 172) 356–45; Gabrielle Golding, 'Rethinking the Rationale for Implying Terms by Law into Australian Employment Contracts' (2020) 39 University of Tasmania Law Review 1.

[201] *Avenia* (n 159) 204.

[202] On the role of the court and current issues arising from implying terms by law into employment contracts, see further Golding (n 200) 13–21.

necessary on [their] part to enable the other party to have the benefit of the contract'.[203] The source of the duty of cooperation remains uncertain, even though it is central to the contract of employment. There are divergent views regarding whether the duty arises as a matter of construction or, alternatively, as a term implied in fact or law.[204]

Cummins is a decision of a Court of Appeal of the FCA.[205] It includes a dissenting judgment in which Anastassiou J has discussed how the implied duty of cooperation applies to employer conduct towards respondents during workplace investigations.[206] The central claim in *Cummins* was pursued under the general protections in pt 3-1 of the *FW Act*.[207] The claim was made by Mr Keenan, who was a senior executive who had been employed by Cummins South Pacific Pty Ltd (Cummins) for more than two decades. Mr Keenan became involved in an interpersonal dispute with an employee whom he managed, Ms Baldota. Mr Keenan and Ms Baldota made complaints about each other to senior management. Ultimately, Cummins rejected Mr Keenan's complaints about Ms Baldota, but accepted Ms Baldota's complaints about Mr Keenan, and dismissed Mr Keenan. The central dispute in the case related to whether Mr Keenan could pursue his claim under s 340 of the *FW Act* on the basis that he had experienced adverse action because he had made various complaints to Cummins.[208]

One complaint made by Mr Keenan related to a formal process initiated by his manager, which involved placing Mr Keenan on a Performance Improvement Plan (PIP). Mr Keenan was contractually required to comply with policies and procedures of his employer, including a policy that set out the PIP process. Mr Keenan asserted the PIP prepared by his manager included metrics that were subjective and/or ambiguous.[209] He asserted that Cummins needed to clarify or modify the metrics to enable him to respond to them and properly participate in the process. Mr Keenan's capacity to pursue his claim was first determined by the Federal Circuit Court.[210] The trial judge upheld all of Mr Keenan's claims and made an order for compensation. Cummins appealed that decision.[211]

In the majority, Bromberg and Mortimer JJ set aside substantial parts of the primary judgment.[212] Mr Keenan did not pursue claims of breach of contract in the proceedings, and the majority judgments of Bromberg and Mortimer JJ did not comment on the implied duty of cooperation. However, Anastassiou J provided a dissenting judgment that includes reasoning that is relevant in the context of workplace investigations.

As part of that judgment, Anastassiou J set out observations regarding Mr Keenan's entitlement to complain about the PIP process. These observations related to the

[203] *Mackay v Dick* (1881) 8R. HL 37, 37 (Blackburn LJ).
[204] Irving (n 23) 718–21.
[205] *Cummins* (n 164).
[206] ibid 471–500 (Anastassiou J).
[207] *Fair Work Act 2009 (Cth).*
[208] For a discussion of the case, see Joellen Riley Munton, 'Executive Employment Grievances Brought Under the *Fair Work Act*: A New Challenge to Orthodox Contract Law?' (2021) 37 Journal of Contract Law 105, 112–13.
[209] *Cummins* (n 164) 490 (Anastassiou J).
[210] *Keenan v Cummins South Pacific Pty Ltd* (2018) 283 IR 31.
[211] ibid 185.
[212] *Cummins* (n 164) 426–40 (Bromberg J, Mortimer J agreeing at 470–71).

content of the implied duty of cooperation in the context of a workplace investigation. His Honour reasoned that the PIP process was 'not consensual' but a process that 'Mr Keenan was subject to under his employment contract'.[213] In the dissenting judgment, his Honour stated:

> Mr Keenan was entitled, and thus 'able to' in the relevant sense, to voice his complaint . . . Mr Keenan was entitled to expect that such a right would not be exercised capriciously or in a manner which would deprive him of the benefit of his contractual bargain with the employer.
>
> The implied obligation of cooperation in the sense identified in *Mackay v Dick* (1881) 6 App Cas 251 and followed in many cases thereafter, see in particular *Secured Income Real Estate (Australia) Ltd v St Martins Investments Pty Ltd* [1979] HCA 51; 144 CLR 596 and *Commonwealth Bank of Australia v Barker* [2014] HCA 32; 253 CLR 169 at [30], required that Cummins should not exercise its right to instigate its PIP policy in a way that would deprive the employee of the right to fairly respond to the matters raised by the employer.[214]

These observations have not been considered or elaborated on in subsequent judgments. They are nevertheless significant because they are underpinned by a nascent idea that an employer must initiate an investigation for a proper purpose and in a manner that enables the respondent to respond to matters raised. His Honour reasoned that this obligation arose under the implied duty of cooperation.

These observations in *Cummins* relate to a performance-related disciplinary process. Yet they are arguably also applicable to a disciplinary process about alleged misconduct. Anastassiou J posited that an employer may breach the implied duty of cooperation by initiating an investigation process for an improper purpose and/or by conducting that process in a manner that does not enable the employee to fairly respond to the concerns raised by the employer. This is because these actions would deprive the employee of the benefit of the contract. These observations were included in a dissenting judgment and require further judicial consideration.

C The extent of the requirement to abide by internal policies and procedures during workplace investigations

Courts have also examined the extent of an employer's contractual obligation to abide by internal policies that set out a workplace investigation process. In general, a term in an internal policy will only have contractual force if it is incorporated into the employment contract by signature of the employee,[215] by the employer giving the employee reasonable notice,[216] through a course of dealings,[217] or by reference.[218] An employer

213 ibid 490 (Anastassiou J).
214 ibid 491 (Anastassiou J).
215 *Nikolich* (n 12) [23] (Black CJ).
216 ibid [23].
217 Irving (n 23) 392–93.
218 ibid 393–94.

will breach the contract of employment if it breaches a term of an internal policy that has been incorporated into the contract expressly or by implication.[219] In some instances, the contractual incorporation of an internal policy is explicit and clear. In other cases, the contractual force of an internal policy is highly contested.[220]

In *Romero*, a Full Court of the FCA developed principles regarding an employer's obligation to abide by internal policies that are relevant to respondents in workplace investigations. The claim was pursued by Ms Romero, who alleged her employer, Farstad Shipping (Indian Pacific) Pty Ltd (Farstad), had breached her employment contract by failing to follow an investigation process that was set out in its Workplace Harassment and Discrimination Policy (WHD Policy).

Farstad argued that the WHD Policy was not incorporated as a term of the contract, including because the terms of the policy principally consisted of directions to employees.[221] Ms Romero argued that the WHD Policy had contractual force, including because her employment contract stated that all Farstad policies were 'to be observed at all times', she was provided training on the policies when she commenced employment, and she was required to sign an acknowledgement that she had read the policies.[222] The trial judge applied principles regarding the contractual incorporation of employer policies and determined that the WHD Policy was not contractually binding.[223] Ms Romero appealed the decision including on the basis that the trial judge was incorrect in holding that the WHD Policy did not constitute part of her employment contract.[224]

On appeal, the Court observed that an employer policy would generally be contractually binding if it used clear language and placed sufficient emphasis on the need for mutual compliance.[225] The Court held that the WHD Policy included directions to employees on how to make complaints about alleged workplace harassment or discrimination and set out 'a responsive assurance' that the employer would treat the complaints in a certain way.[226] The Court reasoned that this established a need for mutual compliance, and this, in turn, indicated that the terms of the WHD Policy were contractual.[227] The Court also observed that other matters, when considered cumulatively, reinforced that the WHD Policy was incorporated into the employment contract.[228] These matters were that the WHD Policy was the subject of an education

[219] *Nikolich* (n 12) [120]–[127] (Marshall J); *Romero* (n 161) 431–32. See also Irving (n 23) 393–97.

[220] See, eg, *Riverwood International Australia Pty Ltd v McCormick* (2000) 177 ALR 193; *Nikolich* (n 12).

[221] *Romero* (n 161) 418–19 (Marshall J).

[222] ibid 408–13.

[223] *Romero v Farstad Shipping (Indian Pacific) Pty Ltd* [2014] FCA 439 [30]–[31] cited in Romero 407. On the established principles, see *Nikolich* (n 12) [49]–[63].

[224] *Romero* (n 161) 421.

[225] ibid 420 [55]–[56]. In the case, the Court recognized that the elements of the policy were more than merely 'directive . . . on proper analysis they are more in the nature of a bargain with an exchange of undertakings and assurances or promises'. For a contrary view on mutuality, see *Westpac Banking Corporation v Wittenberg* [2016] FCR 505, 527 (Buchanan J).

[226] *Romero* (n 161) 420.

[227] ibid 420. The Court did observe that there may be difficulties inherent in this type of claim, namely the need to prove additional elements such as reliance. A term in a policy or procedure will not have contractual force if it is intended to operate as a guideline only, see, eg, *Yousif v Commonwealth Bank of Australia* (2010) 193 IR 212 [95]–[96].

[228] *Romero* (n 161) 421.

program, the benefit provided under the WHD Policy was consistent with benefits conferred by statute, and that the employer regularly reinforced its policies through mandatory training.

According to the reasoning in *Romero*, if an employer's policy states how employees must make complaints about misconduct and sets out how the employer will investigate any complaints, it is likely to establish mutual obligations that are contractually binding.[229] The reasoning in *Romero* revealed a nascent principle that employers are contractually bound to comply with an internal policy that describes how it will respond to a complaint through a workplace investigation process.

While it did not refer to *Romero*, the interlocutory decision of *Tucker (No 1)* articulated a similar idea. Mr Tucker claimed that his employer, the State Revenue Office (SRO), had breached an implied term of his employment contract by failing to adhere to the process set out in its 'Managing Misconduct Policy May 2017' when conducting a workplace investigation into allegations that he had engaged in misconduct.[230] The SRO argued that Mr Tucker's claim had no prospect of succeeding because his employment contract stated that the SRO's policies and procedures were 'not incorporated as terms of [the] contract but [the employee] must nonetheless abide by them because they are lawful and reasonable directions'.[231] The Supreme Court of Victoria observed that:

> [a] failure by the plaintiff [employee] to comply with SRO policies and procedures arguably constitutes a breach of the contract. This conclusion is not altered by reason of the policies and procedures not being incorporated into the contract. If there is an express contractual obligation upon the plaintiff [employee] to comply with SRO policies and procedures, he has a real prospect of establishing an implied term that his employer is also subject to a contractual obligation to comply with all SRO policies and procedures.[232]

Like *Romero*, this reasoning focused on the existence of mutual obligations under the internal policy, with respect to the process the employer will follow to conduct a workplace investigation. Considered together, *Romero* and *Tucker (No 1)* presented an emerging idea that respondents should be entitled to expect that internal policies, which set out directions regarding when and how an employer will conduct a workplace investigation, will be contractually binding on their employer.

These ideas were developed further in *Elisha*. Specifically, the issue of whether relevant terms of the Vision EA and Disciplinary Procedure 2015 were contractually

[229] ibid 420. This argument was raised by the applicant in proceedings culminating in *Riverwood* (n 220). However, the Court determined that it was not necessary to address this argument, see ibid 199 (Lindgren J). See *Farrell v Choosewell Health Link Pty Ltd* [2021] FCCA 910 [162] where the Court declined to recognize that a policy about commission payments was contractually binding. In *Southern Migrant and Refugee Centre Inc v Shum (No 3)* [2022] FCA 481 [165] (Snaden J).

[230] *Tucker (No. 1)* (n 166) [6].

[231] ibid [8].

[232] ibid [10]. Despite this observation, the plaintiff did not pursue the argument in the proceedings, see *Tucker v Victoria* [2019] VSC 420. Nor was the argument considered as part of the appeal of the decision of the associate judge, see *Tucker v Victoria* [2021] VSCA 120.

binding was central in the proceedings. This issue was considered at first instance, by a Court of Appeal of the Supreme Court of Victoria, and by the HCA. At first instance, O'Meara J determined that the relevant terms of the Vision EA and Vision Australia Disciplinary Procedure were incorporated into Mr Elisha's contract, and Vision Australia's conduct during the disciplinary process had breached contractually binding terms.[233] O'Meara J accepted that if a proper disciplinary process had been followed, Vision Australia would not have summarily dismissed Mr Elisha, and he would not have developed the serious psychiatric injury. His Honour held that it was reasonably within the contemplation of the parties at the time when the contract was made that 'distress and potential psychiatric illness was a risk that was a "serious possibility" ... in the event that the protective processes directly contemplated by the terms of the contract were not followed'.[234] His Honour held that the plaintiff's employment was therefore wrongly terminated, and so the damages claimed by Mr Elisha were not too remote.[235]

In its unanimous judgment, the Court of Appeal of the Supreme Court of Victoria affirmed the reasoning of the trial judge that the Disciplinary Procedure 2015 was contractually binding, but held that the terms of the Vision EA were not contractual. Their Honours determined that Vision Australia had breached a contractually binding term of the Disciplinary Procedure 2015 by failing to inform Mr Elisha about the other allegations, or an opportunity to respond to them.[236] However, their Honours determined that damages were not available to Mr Elisha for psychiatric injury caused by the breach because these damages were 'precluded' by the long-held understanding of the law in Australia following *Addis* and *Baltic Shipping*, and were too remote.[237] On this basis, their Honours overturned the judgment made at first instance and set aside the orders for damages.[238]

Mr Elisha received special leave to appeal the decision of the Court of Appeal to the HCA. With respect to Mr Elisha's claim in contract, Mr Elisha argued that the Court of Appeal had erred in concluding that he was not entitled to recover damages for his psychiatric injury. The majority judgment confirmed that the terms of the 2015 Disciplinary Procedure were incorporated to Mr Elisha's employment contract.[239] Their Honours affirmed the reasoning of the FCA in *Romero* and accepted that it was the common intention of the parties that Vision Australia's policies and procedures would be contractually binding. This was reinforced by 'the existence of clear language with sufficient emphasis upon the need for compliance'.[240] As noted, their Honours determined that, subject to the specific terms and context of a particular contract, liability for damages for psychiatric injury was not beyond the scope of a contractual duty concerned with the manner of dismissal under the common law in Australia, and Mr Elisha's psychiatric injury was not too remote, particularly in the

[233] *Elisha (First Instance)* (n 68) [428].
[234] ibid [566]–[568].
[235] ibid.
[236] *Elisha (Court of Appeal)* (n 72) 325.
[237] ibid 346.
[238] ibid 304.
[239] *Elisha (HCA)* (n 3) 186 (joint judgment).
[240] ibid 194–95 (joint judgment).

serious circumstances of the breach by Vision Australia.[241] *Elisha (HCA)* set out an important clarification that damages are available for psychiatric injury (as a physical injury for which damages may be claimed) to a respondent caused by employer conduct during a workplace investigation process that breaches a contractually binding term, including if that process leads to dismissal.

D Discussion

A close reading of decisions that determine contractual disputes shows that courts have developed key principles that apply to employer conduct towards respondents during workplace investigations. However, the analysis also reveals that judge-made law is inadequate because the judicial reasoning is often unclear, and courts give deference to the express terms of the contract.

Bartlett and *Avenia* establish that employers must exercise express contractual powers reasonably (at least to the *Wednesbury* standard of reasonableness) so far as a workplace investigation process is concerned. The decisions suggest that the principle set out in *Service Station Association* also applies in this context and requires an employer to exercise express contractual rights and powers honestly. However, courts have not yet determined whether employers must also exercise implied contractual rights and powers reasonably and/or in good faith so far as their workplace investigation processes go.

The comments by Anastassiou J in *Cummins* indicate that the implied contractual duty of cooperation may require employers to initiate workplace investigations for a bona fide purpose and ensure that a respondent has the opportunity to fairly respond to allegations. His Honour's comments articulate how the duty of cooperation may translate into practical constraints on employer conduct during a workplace investigation. However, these comments are not binding principles. *Cummins* did not involve a claim of breach of contract, and his Honour's observations about the duty of cooperation were peripheral to the dispute. The principles require further judicial consideration and development.

Romero developed a helpful principle that employers must abide by policies during workplace investigations where those policies set out directions regarding when and how a workplace investigation process will be conducted and are predicated on mutual compliance. These principles have potentially broad application, as the practical aim of internal policies about a workplace investigation is often to describe when and how an employer will investigate a complaint. This is exemplified by the outcome in *Elisha (HCA)*, which clarified that damages were available for psychiatric injury caused by breach of an express contractual duty concerned with the manner of dismissal.

In *Elisha (HCA)*, the HCA gave primacy to the express terms of the contract and so ensured that claims remain individualized and contingent on an individual respondent's specific contractual terms and context. Employers will likely respond to *Elisha (HCA)* by ensuring that contracts of employment do not include express

[241] ibid. See further Orifici (n 133).

terms about disciplinary procedures, and do not incorporate terms of enterprise agreements, policies, or procedures so far as possible. The decision also seems to discourage an employer from preparing any policies or procedures about workplace investigations or disciplinary processes, except insofar as it is statutorily required to do so.[242] The important clarification of the common law of the contract in *Elisha (HCA)*, with respect to the availability of damages for psychiatric injury for breach of contract concerned with the manner of dismissal, should make it possible for more respondents to pursue claims for damages for psychiatric injuries caused by negligent or arbitrary employer conduct during workplace investigations. However, the availability of any claim remains individualized and dependent on an employee identifying a breach of a relevant express or implied contractual term and on demonstrating that the damages arising from their psychiatric injury was not too remote in the circumstances.

V Conclusion

In this chapter, I have examined how courts have developed principles in contract and tort that apply to employer conduct towards respondents during workplace investigations. I have conducted close readings of a body of key decisions and synthesized the reasoning to identify central principles that apply to constrain negligent or unreasonable employer conduct in specific circumstances.

I have also scrutinized the decisions and discerned instances where courts have declined to develop the law. The first key instance is that courts have declined to recognize that the duty of reasonable care owed by the employer to the respondent in contract and tort extends to requiring a safe system of workplace investigation or decision-making, or decision-making when directing a respondent not to perform work during a workplace investigation.

The second key instance is that judge-made law has not clearly established that an employer must exercise an implied right or power under the employment contract reasonably (at least to the *Wednesbury* standard of reasonableness) so far as its workplace investigation process goes, as distinct from the result. I have identified how the legal principles that have been developed by courts are nascent or uncertain, how key principles are underdeveloped, and factors that potentially impede the development of judge-made law in future. One central reason that the law is underdeveloped is that courts seem to view it as a matter for the Australian Parliament to determine principles that interact with statutory law about termination of employment. This is apparent in decisions from *Paige* and *Govier*, to *Avenia* and *Barker*, and *Elisha (Court of Appeal)* and the dissenting judgment of Steward J in *Elisha (HCA)*. Significantly, the joint majority judgment in *Elisha (HCA)* clarified an important aspect of the law of contract but did not extend or develop principles in the context of a tortious dispute about psychiatric injury arising from a workplace investigation process. Overall, principles developed through judge-made law are inadequate in terms of ensuring that employers exercise their powers safely and reasonably towards respondents during workplace investigations.

[242] See chapter 5 IV(B).

5
The Regulation of Employer Conduct Towards Respondents During Workplace Investigations Through Statute

I Introduction

In chapter 4, I mapped how key principles developed under judge-made law constrain employer conduct towards respondents during workplace investigations and identified key uncertainties and gaps in the law. In this chapter, I build on this analysis to critically analyse how provisions, which span across seven key areas of Australian statute, apply to employer conduct towards respondents during workplace investigations and impose constraints on employer conduct towards respondents.

In part II, I explain the method used to conduct the analysis. Part III maps the provisions under four areas of the *FW Act* that apply to employer conduct towards respondents during workplace investigations, and part IV examines provisions that apply to employer conduct during workplace investigations in six other key areas of legislation. These areas are anti-discrimination laws, WHS laws, workers' compensation laws, laws that apply to employees in the public service, whistleblowing laws, and evidence laws. Part V synthesizes the statutory analysis and critically considers gaps, issues, and inconsistencies in the law. I argue that relying on existing statutory regulation to constrain how employers exercise managerial power towards respondents during workplace investigations is unsatisfactory because applicable provisions are fragmented, and their application is frequently uncertain and dependent on judicial interpretation.

II Method

I have used a doctrinal research method in this chapter to locate decisions where Commonwealth, state, or territory superior or appellate courts or the FWC applied, discussed, or interpreted a statutory provision that applies to employer conduct towards a respondent during a workplace investigation. I have examined all relevant decisions made between 1 January 2000 and 30 June 2025 and produced a database of all decisions and analysed these decisions to understand the legal reasoning.[1]

[1] Most decisions identified using this method refer to a workplace investigation by an employer into the conduct of a respondent who was engaged as an employee. A smaller number of decisions about principals and independent contractors were determined under *Fair Work Act 2009 (Cth) pt 3-1*. See, eg, *Construction, Forestry, Maritime, Mining and Energy Union v BM Alliance Coal Operations Pty Ltd (No 3)* [2022] FCA

Workplace Investigations. Adriana Orifici, Oxford University Press. © Adriana Orifici 2026.
DOI: 10.1093/9780198970019.003.0005

III Regulation of Employer Conduct During Workplace Investigations Through the *FW Act*

The principal statute that regulates work by Australian employees is the *FW Act*.[2] The *FW Act* does not include provisions that directly and completely regulate employer conduct during workplace investigations. However, four key areas of the *FW Act* include provisions that apply to employer conduct towards respondents during workplace investigations.[3] These areas are the general protections against adverse action,[4] the protection against unfair dismissal,[5] protections against bullying at work,[6] and the framework for making and enforcing enterprise agreements.[7] As I argue below, these provisions regulate aspects of employer conduct towards respondents in a fragmented and incomplete manner.

A General protections

The general protections against adverse action under the *FW Act* originated in anti-victimization protections for trade unionists, which have existed in Commonwealth labour legislation since 1904.[8] In the 1990s, these protections were extended to non-unionists and independent contractors.[9] Provisions prohibiting dismissal on discriminatory grounds have also existed in Commonwealth labour legislation since the 1990s. The *FW Act* rationalized and, in some cases, expanded these protections in pt 3-1 of the *FW Act*, which commenced operation in 2009.[10]

One of the main protections set out under pt 3-1 is that certain persons (including employers) are prohibited from taking 'adverse action' against certain other persons (including employees) for a proscribed reason.[11] Three prohibited reasons for

1345; *Construction Forestry, Maritime, Mining and Energy Union v BM Alliance Coal Operations Pty Ltd* [2023] FCA 30.

[2] *FW Act s 11.* For completeness, it is noted the principal statute that regulates principals and independent contractors does not include any provisions that regulate workplace investigations, see *Independent Contractors Act 2006 (Cth).*

[3] For an overview of the statutory regulation of work in Australia, see Carolyn Sappideen, Paul O'Grady, and Joellen Riley, *Macken's Law of Employment* (9th edn, Thomson Reuters 2022) 1–12.

[4] *FW Act pt 3-1.*

[5] ibid pt 3-2.

[6] ibid pt 6-4B.

[7] ibid pt 2-4.

[8] Kathleen Love, 'Union Victimisation, the Reverse Onus and the Causal Link: The Development of Principles Prior to the Fair Work Act' (2014) Melbourne Law School Working Paper 52 10–14 <https://labourlawresearch.net/union-victimisation-the-reverse-onus-and-the-causal-link-the-development-of-principles-prior-to-the-fair-work-act/> accessed 10 August 2025.

[9] ibid 15.

[10] Anna Chapman, 'Protections in Relation to Dismissal: From the *Workplace Relations Act* to the *Fair Work Act*' (2009) 32 University of New South Wales Law Journal 746, 751.

[11] 'Adverse action' by an employer includes dismissal of an employee, injuring an employee in his or her employment, altering the position of an employee to their prejudice, and discriminating between the employee and other employees of the employer: *FW Act s 342 item 1.*

'adverse action' are included in pt 3-1. These reasons are because of a 'workplace right',[12] where a person is or is not a union member or has or has not engaged in industrial activities,[13] and because of one or more protected grounds of discrimination.[14] Several exceptions apply that deem conduct to be lawful where it would otherwise constitute 'adverse action'.[15]

There are several key aspects of the protection against adverse action under pt 3-1. First, there must be a 'causal link' between the adverse action and one of the prohibited reasons.[16] This means that the adverse action must have been taken because of one or more of the prohibited reasons. Second, the prohibited reason need only be one reason why the employer took the adverse action.[17] Third, there is a shifting onus of proof.[18] Fourth, the prohibited reason needs to be a substantial and operative reason for the adverse action, but does not need to be the sole or dominant reason.[19] All protections set out in pt 3-1 are civil remedy provisions.[20]

Courts have applied and interpreted pt 3-1 in claims pursued by respondents against employers that involve workplace investigations. Courts have determined that an employer can engage in adverse action against a respondent under s 342 by commencing or conducting a workplace investigation. However, that adverse action will only be unlawful if the employer took the action for a prohibited reason. For example, in *Jones v Queensland Tertiary Admissions Centre Ltd (No 2)* (*Jones*),[21] Collier J accepted that commencing a workplace investigation could constitute 'adverse action' even if the investigation was initiated in good faith.[22] Her Honour observed that:

[12] ibid s 340. The term 'workplace right' is broadly defined. A 'workplace right' includes being 'entitled to the benefit of, or [having] a role or responsibility under, a workplace law, workplace instrument or order made by an industrial body': ibid s 341(1)(a). It also includes being 'able to initiate, or participate in, a process or proceedings under a workplace law or workplace instrument' and being 'able to make a complaint or inquiry . . . to a person or body having the capacity under a workplace law to seek compliance with that law or a workplace instrument [or, where] the person is an employee—in relation to his or her employment': ibid s 341(1)(b)–(c).

[13] *FW Act s 346.*

[14] These grounds are 'race, colour, sex, sexual orientation, breastfeeding, gender identity, intersex status, age, physical or mental disability, marital status, family or carer's responsibilities, subjection to family and domestic violence, pregnancy, religion, political opinion, national extraction or social origin': ibid s 351.

[15] ibid ss 342(3), (4), 351(2)(a)–(c).

[16] Anna Chapman, Kathleen Love, and Beth Gaze, 'The Reverse Onus of Proof Then and Now: The Barclay Case and the History of the Fair Work Act's Union Victimisation and Freedom of Association' (2014) 37 University of New South Wales Law Journal 471.

[17] *FW Act s 360.*

[18] ibid s 361. The shifting onus of proof means that where an applicant establishes there was adverse action and one of the prohibited reasons applies, the onus shifts to the employer to prove that the adverse action was not taken for a prohibited reason. See further Chapman, Love, and Gaze (n 16); Beth Gaze and Belinda Smith, *Equality and Discrimination Law in Australia: An Introduction* (Cambridge University Press 2017) 236–41.

[19] *Board of Bendigo Regional Institute of Technical and Further Education v Barclay* (2012) 248 CLR 500, 534, 542 (Gummow and Hayne JJ).

[20] *FW Act s 539(2) items 11, 12.* Where a provision is a civil remedy provision under the *FW Act*, an affected person can apply to an applicable court for orders in relation to a contravention or proposed contravention of provision, including an order for a financial penalty or any other order that the court considers appropriate subject to the Act: ibid pt 4-1.

[21] *Jones v Queensland Tertiary Admissions Centre Ltd (No 2)* (2010) 186 FCR 22.

[22] ibid 46.

> [w]hile an investigation into allegations of bullying may be appropriate and indeed warranted in the circumstances of an individual case, this does not mean that the employee will not be 'injured' or their position altered to their prejudice by the investigation. I do not agree that, as a general proposition, amenability to a disciplinary investigation is a 'normal' incident of employment, even if the investigation is commenced in good faith and on a proper *prima facie* evidentiary basis.[23]

The central question in *Jones* was whether the employer had commenced the workplace investigation for a reason that was prohibited under pt 3-1.[24] Collier J ultimately accepted the employer's evidence that the adverse action (as pleaded) was not for a prohibited reason and so was not unlawful.[25]

Subsequent decisions have similarly recognized that commencing a workplace investigation can comprise adverse action under s 342.[26] Uniting these decisions is a view that the commencement of a workplace investigation will comprise adverse action if it substantively diminishes or prejudicially alters the position of the respondent in their employment.[27] For example, in *Avard v Australian Capital Territory*, Kennett J reasoned that the commencement of a workplace investigation by the employer constituted adverse action because:

> [b]eing under investigation is stressful and a drain on a person's time, financial resources or both. It is often damaging to a person's reputation. Repeated investigations can be an effective tool of harassment. The existence of a proper basis to commence the investigation is relevant to an assessment of whether or not the action was taken [for a proscribed reason]; it is not relevant at the anterior stage of considering whether the action was 'adverse'. That question is objective.[28]

His Honour took a broad view of the effect of the commencement of a workplace investigation on the respondent in her employment, and observed that the employer's step of commencing the workplace investigation was adverse action even though it had not yet made any adverse findings against the respondent or taken any disciplinary action.[29]

Cases also establish that certain procedural steps taken by an employer during a workplace investigation can comprise separate instances of adverse action against a respondent.[30] For a procedural step to comprise adverse action, it must meet the definition

23 ibid 47 (emphasis omitted).

24 See also *Automotive, Food, Metals, Engineering, Printing and Kindred Industries Union v Visy Packaging Pty Ltd (No 3)* (2013) 216 FCR 70, 91.

25 *Jones* (n 21) 47. A persistent source of evidentiary complexity in proceedings that involve workplace investigations is the identification and attribution of reasons for decisions where there are multiple decision-makers in the employer, or where two or more decision-makers acted together. See, eg, *Pilbrow v University of Melbourne* [2024] FCA 1140, [136]; *Han v St Basil's Homes* (2023) 325 IR 190 [77]–[82].

26 See, eg, *Visy* (n 24) [101]–[103]; *The Environmental Group Ltd v Bowd* [2019] FCA 951 [163]; *Green v Preston Motors Pty Ltd (No 2)* [2022] FedCFamC2G 840 [143]–[146]. cf *Iyengar v Commonwealth* [2025] FedCFamC2G 608 [143].

27 *Visy* (n 24) 91.

28 *Avard v Australian Capital Territory* [2024] FCA 690 [136].

29 ibid.

30 See, eg, *Bowd* (n 26) [143]–[146].

of adverse action under s 342.[31] For example, an employer's direction to a respondent to not attend work during a workplace investigation, with pay, can comprise an instance of adverse action.[32] This means that pt 3-1 prohibits employers from commencing a workplace investigation, and from taking procedural steps during an investigation that detriment the respondent, where the act is causally linked to a prohibited reason.[33]

Court decisions also articulate that, subject to a key exception, the question of whether an employer conducted a procedurally or substantively fair workplace investigation is ordinarily not relevant to determining if an employer acted unlawfully under pt 3-1. This is because courts have interpreted 'adverse action' under s 342(1) to require more than evidence of 'mere unfairness or injustice' towards an employee, absent 'some practical detriment or harm'.[34] For example, *Ermel v Duluxgroup (Australia) Pty Ltd (No 2)* (*Ermel*) was a claim of unlawful adverse action on the basis that the respondent had exercised a 'workplace right'.[35] In *Ermel*, Bromberg J relevantly observed that a claim under pt 3-1 was 'not a broad inquiry as to whether the [employee] has been subjected to a procedurally or substantively unfair outcome' but a specific interrogation of whether the respondent had been subjected to 'adverse action' for a prohibited reason.[36]

An exception to this approach arises if an employer's conduct or decision-making during a workplace investigation was so unreasonable that it indicated the employer had acted for a prohibited reason, having regard to the shifting onus under s 361. For example, in *Serpanos*, the Court was required to consider whether Mr Serpanos' employer had taken adverse action against him, including by dismissing him for misconduct following a workplace investigation.[37] Snaden J observed that the existence of evidence that showed an employer and/or its workplace investigator had acted unreasonably could lead a court to determine that the employer has not discharged the onus of proof.[38] This is because it could lead a court to dismiss the evidence provided by the employer that any adverse action was not taken for a prohibited reason.[39] His Honour noted:

> the court's task presently is not to assess whether [the investigator's] reasons were well-founded or justified or even fair; the court's task presently is to assess whether

[31] *Bartolo v Doutta Galla Aged Services Ltd (No 2)* [2015] FCCA 345, 345. For an outcome where the court determined that the circumstances evidenced that the employer commencing a workplace investigation was not adverse action see, eg, *Green* (n 26) [145].

[32] *Bowd* (n 26) [166]. cf *Avard* (n 28), [113], [137]–[138].

[33] The term 'detriment' is taken to mean 'any disadvantage': *Mount v Dover Castle Metals Pty Ltd* (2024) 339 IR 1 [148].

[34] *Lamont v University of Queensland (No 2)* [2020] FCA 720 [66]. See, eg, *Jones* (n 21) [121]–[122]; *Tsilibakis v Transfield Services (Australia) Pty Ltd* [2015] FCA 740 [16]; *Celand v Skycity Adelaide Pty Ltd* (2017) FCR 306 [101]; *Taylor v Department of Health (Cth)* [2020] FCA 1364 [23]; *Serpanos v Commonwealth* [2022] FCA 1226 [276].

[35] *Ermel v DuluxGroup (Australia) Pty Ltd (No 2)* [2015] FCA 17.

[36] ibid [48]. This reasoning was accepted in *Serpanos* (n 34) [125]; *Heal v Sydney Flames Basketball Pty Ltd* [2024] FCA 401 [218]. See also *Khiani v Australian Bureau of Statistics* [2011] FCAFC 109 [33]; *Mishra v Monash Health* [2022] FedCFamC2G 240 [62] citing *Musgrove v Murrayland Fruit Juices Pty Ltd* (1980) 47 FLR 156.

[37] *Serpanos* (n 34).

[38] ibid [275]. cf *Construction, Forestry, Mining and Energy Union v BHP Coal Pty Ltd* [2012] FCA 1201.

[39] ibid [275]. cf *Barclay* (n 19) 517, 542, 544.

> they were, in fact, the reasons that actuated her to make and communicate the findings that she made. If there were simply no basis upon which [the investigator] could credibly have formed the views that she said that she formed, then I would be more inclined to accept that she was not actuated by the reasons that she identified. But it could not be said that her conclusions were wholly beyond what might reasonably have formed in her mind (or that of anybody in her situation).[40]

Snaden J assessed the evidence and determined that it was reasonably open to the employer to rely on the findings of the investigation to dismiss Mr Serpanos. Snaden J concluded the employer had discharged the rebuttable presumption under s 361 that required it to demonstrate that it had not acted for a prohibited reason.[41]

Court decisions confirm that pt 3-1 provides a central protection for respondents against unlawful employer conduct, but that protection is confined and limited. Part 3-1 specifically requires an employer to ensure it does not act for a prohibited reason during a workplace investigation. Judicial interpretations indicate that wholly unreasonable conduct by an employer might lead a court to decide that the employer has not discharged the shifting onus of proof.[42] However, pt 3-1 does not limit an employer's power to commence a workplace investigation, nor does it generally require an employer to conduct a workplace investigation in a procedurally or substantively fair way.[43]

B Unfair dismissal

The *FW Act* (and its predecessor) has provided eligible employees with a statutory right to seek redress with respect to unfair dismissal since the 1990s.[44] Part 3-2 of the *FW Act* currently sets out the protection against unfair dismissal. Employees who have been dismissed can apply to the FWC for an order granting a remedy on the basis that their dismissal was unfair,[45] if they meet the prescribed criteria.[46] The test applied by the FWC to determine if a dismissal was unfair is set out in s 385 of the *FW Act*. Among other things, s 385 provides that a dismissal will be unfair if it was 'harsh, unjust or unreasonable'.[47]

Section 387 prescribes the factors that the FWC must consider when determining whether a dismissal was 'harsh, unjust or unreasonable'. Specifically, the FWC must consider whether there was a 'valid reason for the dismissal related to the person's capacity or conduct'.[48] The FWC must also consider procedural factors. These factors are

[40] *Serpanos* (n 34) [276].
[41] ibid [5]. For a similar approach in the context of an unfounded and incomplete workplace investigation, see *Han* (n 25) [234]–[240].
[42] *Serpanos* (n 34) [276].
[43] ibid [276].
[44] See, eg, Chapman (n 10); Anna Chapman, 'Unfair Dismissal Law and Work Choices: From Safety Net Standard to Legal Privilege' (2020) 16 The Economic and Labour Relations Review 237.
[45] *FW Act s 390.* On the definition of 'dismissal', see ibid ss 385(a), 386.
[46] A person must have completed the 'minimum employment period', earn less than the 'high income threshold' and be covered by a modern award or enterprise agreement: *FW Act ss 382–84.*
[47] ibid s 385(b).
[48] ibid s 387(a).

whether the employer notified the employee of the reason for the dismissal,[49] gave the employee an 'opportunity to respond to any reason [that] related to [their] capacity or conduct',[50] and did not unreasonably refuse 'to allow [the employee] to have a support person present to assist at any discussions relating to dismissal'.[51] The FWC must also have regard to whether 'the size of the employer's enterprise' or 'the degree to which the absence of dedicated human resource management specialists or expertise in the enterprise would be likely to impact on the procedures followed in effecting the dismissal'.[52] Finally, the FWC must take into account 'any other matters' that it considers relevant.[53]

The FWC's decision involves balancing all relevant criteria. The object of pt 3-2 includes a requirement for the FWC to ensure a 'fair go all round' to the parties when determining an application.[54] Part 3-2 sets out exclusions from the prohibition against unfair dismissal for small businesses that have followed the Small Business Code,[55] and in cases where a dismissal constitutes a 'genuine redundancy'.[56] If the FWC determines that an employee has been unfairly dismissed under pt 3-2, it may order the employer to reinstate the employee,[57] or if reinstatement is inappropriate, the FWC may order compensation in accordance with s 392.[58] The FWC is required to reduce the remedy it would otherwise order if it is satisfied that the employee's misconduct contributed to the employer's decision to dismiss them.[59] Crucially, in the context of the risk of psychiatric injury of respondents arising from workplace investigations, an order for compensation must not include any component that is compensation for 'shock, distress or humiliation, or other analogous hurt, caused ... by the manner of the person's dismissal'.[60]

The FWC is required to determine whether an employer followed a fair procedure based on the facts of a dispute and having regard to the factors set out in s 387 and in the context of the object in s 381. An employer's workplace investigation can comprise a substantive factor in a dispute under pt 3-2 for a range of reasons. The *Unfair Dismissals Benchbook*, written by the FWC, draws on decisions made under pt 3-2.[61] It provides guidance on the relevance of workplace investigations to the determination of an unfair dismissal application and explains that '[w]here the dismissal is based upon the alleged misconduct of the employee, the employer will satisfy the evidentiary onus which is cast upon it if it demonstrates that insofar as was within its power, before dismissing the employee' it took steps including conducting 'as full and

[49] ibid s 387(b).
[50] ibid s 387(c).
[51] ibid s 387(d).
[52] ibid ss 387(f), 387(g).
[53] ibid s 387(h).
[54] ibid s 381(2). See *Re Loty v Australian Workers' Union* [1971] AR (NSW) 95.
[55] *FW Act ss 385, 388(1).* See also *FW Act, Declaration under subsection 388(1), Small Business Fair Dismissal Code 2009 (Cth).*
[56] *FW Act s 389.*
[57] ibid ss 390, 391.
[58] ibid ss 390, 392. *FW Act* ss 390, 392.
[59] ibid s 392(3).
[60] ibid s 392(4).
[61] FWC, 'Unfair Dismissals Benchbook' (2025) <https://www.fwc.gov.au/benchbook/unfair-dismissals-benchbook> accessed 15 July 2025.

extensive investigation into all of the relevant matters surrounding the alleged misconduct as was reasonable in the circumstances'.[62] This explanation highlights how an employer's workplace investigation into alleged misconduct by a respondent can comprise a substantive factor in the dispute.

The decisions of the FWC under pt 3-2 provide further guidance about the relevance of workplace investigations to how its Members determine claims. These decisions are factually dependent and, as these are arbitrations, there is no formal doctrine of precedent.[63] Caution is therefore warranted in generalizing from their content. Nonetheless, some themes are apparent. First, the FWC has decided that a substantively unfair workplace investigation can lead to the lack of a 'valid reason' under s 387(a) and a determination that the dismissal of a respondent was 'harsh, unjust or unreasonable'.[64] The FWC has determined that substantive unfairness in workplace investigations includes making findings based on insufficient evidence,[65] that could not have been reasonably drawn from the available evidence,[66] or without a thorough inquiry.[67]

Second, the FWC has determined that an investigation procedure that is inconsistent with one or more of the factors set out in ss 387(b)–(d) can result in a finding that the dismissal was 'harsh, unjust or unreasonable',[68] although the approach between decisions varies widely.[69] For example, the FWC has found that a dismissal was 'harsh' because the employer had conducted an incomplete investigation and failed to investigate each of the explanations for the misconduct provided by the respondent.[70] It has also determined that a dismissal was because a workplace investigator did not keep an 'open mind' and so the respondent was not given a genuine opportunity to respond to allegations.[71]

Third, the FWC has considered conduct by employers during workplace investigations as relevant when taking into account 'any other matters' in s 387(h). For instance, the FWC has determined that a dismissal was 'harsh, unjust or unreasonable' because the evidence indicated the employer had modified the scope and detail of the allegations of misconduct to ensure that the investigator made findings that the allegations were proven.[72] The FWC has also found that extensive delay in a workplace investigation,[73] and overly broad allegations that left unclear the specific concerns of the employer,[74] are relevant matters under s 387(h).

[62] ibid 113.
[63] See *Kirkbright v K&S Freighters Pty Ltd* [2016] FWC 1555; *Cowan v Sargeant Transport Services Pty Ltd* [2014] FWC 5330.
[64] *IW McLauchlan v Australia Meat Holdings Pty Ltd* [1998] AIRC 379. The AIRC was the principal Australian industrial tribunal between 1997 and 2009 and a predecessor to the FWC.
[65] *Dewson v Boom Logistics Limited* [2012] FWA 9027 [72]; *Sydney Trains v Hilder* [2020] FWC 1373 [111].
[66] *Meat Holdings* (n 64).
[67] *Dragicevich v Me Trading Group Pty Ltd* [2024] FWC 1017 [38].
[68] See, eg, *Maltby v Trustee for Kingston Family Trust* [2024] FWC 2987 [29]–[31].
[69] See, eg, *Michalitsis v Dig Dig Demolition Pty Ltd* [2024] FWC 1034 [138]–[142].
[70] *Ryan v Department of Human Services* [2013] FWC 4060 [128]–[137].
[71] *Weule v Central Queensland Services Pty Ltd* [2025] FWC 1219 [158].
[72] *Lupson v Australian Pacific Airports (Melbourne) Pty Ltd* [2020] FWC 6721 [88].
[73] *Owczarek v The University of Melbourne* [2024] FWC 1368 [316].
[74] *Brandies v Secrets Shhh Pty Ltd* [2024] FWC 2069 [364].

While HRM texts pay much attention to decisions of the FWC under pt 3-2,[75] the provisions only apply to employer conduct during workplace investigations in an indirect manner. Part 3-2 does not explicitly refer to workplace investigations, nor does it prohibit conduct by employers that leads to a 'harsh, unjust or unreasonable' dismissal. The decisions highlight that the FWC will consider facts about an employer's workplace investigation when evaluating the factors under s 387. However, each dispute is factually dependent, and decision-makers have sometimes expressed inconsistent ideas about how employer conduct during a workplace investigation is relevant to the factors set out under s 387.[76]

C Protections against bullying

The FWC has been able to make orders to stop bullying under pt 6-4B since 2014.[77] An application for an order to stop bullying can be made by a 'worker', including an employee.[78] Specifically, a worker in a 'constitutionally-covered business'[79] who 'reasonably believes that he or she has been bullied at work' can apply to the FWC for an order to stop the bullying.[80] A worker has been 'bullied' if an individual or group of individuals 'repeatedly behaves unreasonably towards the worker, or a group of workers of which the worker is a member' and 'that behaviour creates a risk to health and safety'.[81] The test for 'unreasonable behaviour' is objective, being what 'a reasonable person, having regard to the circumstances, may consider to be unreasonable'.[82] Part 6-4B states that 'reasonable management action carried out in a reasonable manner' does not constitute bullying.[83]

For the FWC to make an order to stop bullying, it must be satisfied that there is a risk that while the worker is at work, they will continue to be bullied by the relevant

[75] See further chapter 2.

[76] cf *Kirkbright* (n 63); *Cowan* (n 63).

[77] *Fair Work Amendment Act 2013 (Cth) s 3 sch 3, commencing 1 January 2014.* Between 11 September 2021 and 5 March 2023, pt 6-4B also provided the FWC with jurisdiction to make stop sexual harassment orders on similar terms to stop bullying orders: *FW Act ss 789FD, 789FC, 789FF(b)(ii).* These provisions were repealed by the *Fair Work Legislation Amendment (Secure Jobs, Better Pay) Act 2022 (Cth) pt 8 sch 1.* Pt 3-5A commenced on 6 March 2023: ibid s 2. Under pt 3-5A, a person including a 'worker' may apply to the FWC for a stop sexual harassment order: *FW Act ss 527F, 527J.* Decisions that relate to applications for orders to stop sexual harassment have not, to date, considered matters relevant to the conduct of employers towards workers who are respondents in workplace investigations.

[78] A 'worker' is defined by reference to the *Work Health and Safety Act 2011 (Cth) s 7.* See *FW Act s 789FC(2).*

[79] *FW Act s 789FD(1)(a).*

[80] ibid s 789FC(1). The FWC has noted that a reasonable belief is one that is genuinely held and 'objectively speaking, there must be something to support it or some other rational basis for the holding of the belief and it is not irrational or absurd': *Mac v Bank of Queensland Ltd* [2015] FWC 774 [79].

[81] *FW Act s 789FD(1).*

[82] *Re SB* [2014] IR 127 136.

[83] *FW Act s 789FD(2).* To determine the 'reasonableness' of the action, the FWC will make 'an objective assessment of the action in the context of the circumstances and knowledge of those involved at the time': *Re SB* (n 82). The specific 'attributes and circumstances' of the situation including the emotional state and psychological health of the worker involved may also be relevant. The FWC has emphasized that the test relates to whether the management action was reasonable, not whether it could have been 'more reasonable' or 'more acceptable: *Re SB* (n 82) 137.

person or group.[84] If the FWC is satisfied that bullying has taken place, the FWC can also make 'any order it considers appropriate' to prevent the worker from being bullied by a person or group of persons.[85] Orders are generally tailored to the specific circumstances of the worker and employer.[86]

There are two central ways that the provisions of pt 6-4B apply to employer conduct during workplace investigations. First, when making an order, the FWC must take into account factors including 'any final or interim outcomes arising out of an investigation into the matter that is being, or has been, undertaken by another person or body', and any grievance or dispute resolution procedures available to the worker and any final or interim outcomes arising out of those procedures.[87] These provisions seem to invite examination by the FWC of the procedural and substantive aspects of any workplace investigation conducted by the employer when it determines an application. Some decisions of the FWC under pt 6-4B include detailed consideration of an employer's workplace investigation procedure and practices.[88] Decisions also include orders by the FWC for employers to implement or improve procedures for investigating allegations of bullying.[89]

Second, the FWC has interpreted 'bullying' to include unreasonable employer conduct during a workplace investigation in determinations made under pt 6-4B. The FWC has reasoned that an employer's conduct during a workplace investigation will constitute 'reasonable management action' if it is 'carried out in a reasonable manner',[90] but that unreasonable employer conduct during a workplace investigation can amount to bullying.[91] For example, the FWC has determined that bullying includes an employer conducting 'an investigation in a grossly unfair manner',[92] and unreasonably refusing to provide a respondent with redacted findings.[93] The FWC has made orders that intervene in an employer's workplace investigation in each of these circumstances.[94] This includes orders that have prevented an employer from taking any further procedural steps to finalize an investigation or to

[84] *FW Act s 789FF(1).* For a critique, see Amber Sharp, 'Workplace Bullying: Are Stop Bullying Orders Really the Answer?' (2014) 1 *Law Society Journal* 82.

[85] *FW Act s 789FF(1).* The FWC cannot make orders requiring payment of a pecuniary amount.

[86] See, eg, *Applicant v Respondent* (PR548852) (21 March 2014).

[87] *FW Act s 789FF(2)(a)–(c).*

[88] See, eg, *Application by Sharon Bowker* [2015] FWC 7312 [32]–[45], [116]; *Re Inderjeet Kaur* [2024] FWC 3096.

[89] See, eg, *Re appln by Sharma* [2024] FWC 2634 [49].

[90] See *Re SB* (n 82) 140. See, eg, *EE v Australian Association of Social Workers* [2022] FWC 3019 [24]; *Vine v Central Bayside Community Health Services* [2020] FWC 5910 [55] where the FWC declined to recognize that a workplace investigation constituted bullying.

[91] The FWC has determined that procedural flaws on their own do not amount to bullying, see, eg, *Application by Nady Antoun* [2021] FWC 4585 [11]; *Harrison v Trustee for UBT Marketing Trust* [2024] FWC 1422 [85].

[92] *Re SB* (n 82) 128. See also *Fletcher v Eastern Australian Airlines Pty Ltd t/as Qantas Link* [2022] FWCFB 56 [155].

[93] *Application by Peter Farac* [2021] FWC 5107 [585].

[94] The FWC has clarified it will only intervene in an employer's workplace investigation process (through the terms of an order) where it is reasonable to do so. One factor the FWC will consider is if any evidence that the worker's application for an order is an attempt to interfere with the workplace investigation process or delay disciplinary action. See, eg, *Application by Tanka Jang Karki* [2019] FWC 3147 [235]; *Application by Stephen Cain* [2020] FWC 1914 [234]–[239].

take disciplinary action against a respondent based on the findings of the workplace investigation.[95]

Part 6-4B therefore allows the FWC to make orders that constrain ongoing employer conduct towards respondents during a workplace investigation where it constitutes 'bullying', and to make other orders in relation to an employer's workplace investigation process. Part 6-4B therefore provides respondents with a key protection in the context of workplace investigations, and this protection is, importantly, oriented towards preventing further harm. Yet this protection relies, in part, on the way the FWC has interpreted pt 6-4B in its determinations. The FWC is not bound by these determinations when making subsequent decisions, and the reasoning has not been judicially considered or affirmed. The application of pt 6-4B to workplace investigations is confined and uncertain.

D Enterprise agreements

The FWC may approve enterprise agreements which have been agreed between employers and employees in accordance with the *FW Act*.[96] Enterprise agreements set terms and conditions of employment, which apply to the employer and employees covered by the agreement, for a period of up to four years.[97] The *FW Act* prescribes how bargaining begins, proceeds, and ends.[98] It also sets out when the FWC must approve an enterprise agreement.[99]

The *FW Act* also sets out rules regarding the content of enterprise agreements. A term included in an enterprise agreement must be a 'mandatory term' or about a 'permitted matter'.[100] Mandatory terms must be included in all enterprise agreements. Among other things, it is mandatory for an enterprise agreement to include a term providing for a procedure for settling disputes about matters arising under the agreement.[101] Permitted matters are set out in s 172(1) and, to the extent that a term is not about a permitted matter, it has no effect and is not enforceable.[102] If a party to an

[95] *Application by Lynette Bayly* [2017] FWC 1886 [49]. cf *Application by Katherine Burbeck (PR596356)*; *Application by Jennifer Watts (PR601077)* [3].

[96] *FW Act pt 2-4.* The *FW Act* also regulates the system of modern awards, which apply to employers and relevant employees based on industry and occupation: ibid pt 2-3. Modern awards do not currently include terms that regulate employer conduct towards respondents in workplace investigations. It seems that a term about when, or how, an employer will conduct a workplace investigation would not be about a matter that is permitted to be included in a modern award: ibid s 139.

[97] *FW Act s 186(5)(b).* On the development of the statutory rules regarding agreement-making, see further, Carolyn Sutherland, 'Making the "BOOT" Fit: Reforms to Agreement-Making from Work Choices to Fair Work' in Anthony Forsyth and Andrew Stewart (eds), *Fair Work: The New Workplace Laws and the Work Choices Legacy* (The Federation Press 2009).

[98] *FW Act pt 2-4 div 3.*

[99] ibid pt 2-4 div 4.

[100] ibid pt 2-4 div 5, ss 186, 172(1)(a). A 'permitted matter' includes any matter that pertains to the employment relationship between the employer and employees who will be covered by the enterprise agreement. Whether a term pertains to the employment relationship is contextually specific. It depends on the form of the clause, its content and effect, as well as its precise construction and the circumstances surrounding the particular employment relationship.

[101] ibid s 186(6).

[102] ibid s 253(1)(a).

enterprise agreement contravenes its terms, another party to that enterprise agreement (and other prescribed persons) may apply to the FCA, the Federal Circuit and Family Court of Australia, or an 'eligible State or Territory court' for remedies.[103] The court can order remedies such as a monetary penalty, an award of compensation, or injunctive relief.[104]

Enterprise agreements may include terms about when and/or how an employer will conduct a workplace investigation into allegations of misconduct. Terms that regulate employer conduct during workplace investigations can, for example, prescribe the type of alleged misconduct which an employer must investigate,[105] whether the employer can make an initial/preliminary assessment of any alleged misconduct before commencing a formal workplace investigation,[106] whether procedural fairness applies during the workplace investigation,[107] when an employer may direct an employee to not attend work during a workplace investigation (with or without pay),[108] procedural steps an employer must follow during a workplace investigation,[109] possible disciplinary outcomes that can follow a finding of misconduct,[110] and how the FWC must deal with disputes about these terms.[111] An employer's compliance with the terms of an enterprise agreement may be reviewed by the FWC in accordance with the dispute settlement procedures prescribed in the agreement.[112]

Decisions of the FWC illustrate how the conduct of an employer towards a respondent can be constrained by the terms of an enterprise agreement. First, employers must carefully comply with any terms in an applicable enterprise agreement that prescribe when or how they will conduct a workplace investigation. For example, the FWC has made findings that employers have acted inconsistently with terms in enterprise agreements during workplace investigations,[113] and orders that direct an employer to follow a workplace investigation procedure as set out in an enterprise agreement.[114]

Second, an employer must act reasonably and fairly when exercising rights or powers under the terms of an applicable enterprise agreement.[115] The FWC has

[103] ibid ss 50, 539(2) item 4.

[104] ibid ss 545–47. Parties to enterprise agreements can also seek to enforce the terms of the agreement through invoking the dispute resolution process under the agreement. These applications are made to the FWC.

[105] See, eg, *Nurses and Midwives (Victorian Public Sector) (Single Interest Employers) Enterprise Agreement 2020–2024* [2022] FWCA 521 cl 15.2(b); *Visy Recycling—NSW and ACT Operations Enterprise Agreement 2021* [2023] FWCA 190 cl 36.

[106] See, eg, *Victorian Public Service Enterprise Agreement 2020* [2020] FWCA 5215 cl 25.7(a)(i); *The Australian National University Enterprise Agreement 2017–2021* [2020] FWCA 3514 cl 71.24.

[107] See, eg, *VPSEA* (n 106).

[108] See, eg, ibid cl 25.7(b); *ANUEA* (n 106); *VisyEA* (n 105).

[109] See, eg, *VPSEA* (n 106); *ANUEA* (n 106); *NMEA* (n 105); *VisyEA* (n 105).

[110] See, eg, *VPSEA* (n 106); *ANUEA* (n 106); *NMEA* (n 105).

[111] See, eg, *VPSEA* (n 106); *NMEA* (n 105).

[112] See, eg, *Construction, Forestry, Maritime, Mining and Energy Union (105N) v BHP Coal Pty Ltd* [2022] FWC 1699 [195]; *Automotive, Food, Metals, Engineering, Printing and Kindred Industries Union v CSL Limited t/as CSL Behring* [2020] FWC 6068 [3], [32].

[113] See, eg, *Richardson v Ambulance Victoria* [2024] FWC 1313 [112]–[113].

[114] See, eg, *Communications, Electrical, Electronic, Energy, Information, Postal, Plumbing and Allied Services Union of Australia (128V) v Ausgrid Management Pty Ltd* [2022] FWC 963 [113]–[115].

[115] *Construction, Forestry, Mining and Energy Union (105N) v BHP Coal Pty Ltd* [2014] FWC 1526 [76]; *Towns v Community Services Directorate ACT Government* [2018] FWC 4271 [29]–[31]; *Gonzalezv ACT Community Services Directorate* [2021] FWC 1049 [30]–[33].

specifically determined that employers must act reasonably and fairly when exercising rights and powers under enterprise agreement terms about workplace investigations. In these decisions, the FWC has generally applied the broad principle in *Australian Federated Union of Locomotive Enginemen and State Rail Authority of New South Wales* (*XPT Case*) that the FWC must:

> examine all the facts and not to interfere with the right of an employer to manage [its] own business unless [it] is seeking from the employees something which is unjust or unreasonable. The test of injustice or unreasonableness would embrace matters of safety and health because a requirement by an employer for an employee to perform work which was unsafe or might damage the health of the employee would be both unjust and unreasonable.[116]

This approach is exemplified in the decision of *Communications, Electrical, Electronic, Energy, Information, Postal, Plumbing and Allied Services Union of Australia v Ausgrid Management Pty Ltd* (*Ausgrid*).[117]

In *Ausgrid*, the employer had relied on terms in an enterprise agreement to conduct a preliminary investigation, and then a workplace investigation, into alleged misconduct by eleven employees who were electricians.[118] The employer's decision to investigate was triggered by a complaint from a third party who was protected by whistleblowing laws.[119] The FWC was required to determine if any of the employees under investigation had engaged in conduct that justified the employer taking disciplinary action against them.[120] The FWC considered evidence from the parties about whether the process, findings, and disciplinary outcomes of the workplace investigation were justified,[121] and undertook 'a detailed review of the actions and decisions taken by [the employer]',[122] including by considering 'the reasonableness or otherwise of the [employer's] decisions . . . having regard for the circumstances and material[.]'[123] The FWC identified 'major issues of concern' with the employer's actions and decisions,[124] and held that the steps taken to investigate and discipline the eleven employees were 'unreasonable and unjustifiable'.[125] The FWC observed that:

> [u]nfortunately, the circumstances in this case have revealed an approach where Ausgrid management was motivated to provide a perception that it took stringent action in response to a whistleblower complaint, irrespective of the validity of the

116 *Australian Federated Union of Locomotive Enginemen and State Rail Authority of New South Wales* [1984] CAR 432, 191 (the Commission). See, eg, *Boxsell v ACT Government* [2018] FWC 141, [25]–[26] (Kovacic DP).

117 *Ausgrid* (n 114).

118 ibid [6]–[7] (Commissioner Cambridge). The process was conducted under the *Ausgrid Enterprise Agreement 2018* [2018] FWCA 2960.

119 See further chapter 5 IV(E).

120 *Ausgrid* (n 114).

121 ibid.

122 *Ausgrid* (n 114) [57].

123 ibid [59].

124 ibid [61].

125 ibid [117].

> complaint, and in a way which protected Ausgrid management from any scrutiny, and instead, sought to have some Ausgrid employees disciplined as scapegoats to appease any complaint or criticism.[126]

The FWC held that it was not just or reasonable for the employer to discipline the employees in these circumstances. In other decisions that follow a similar approach, the FWC has held that workplace investigations that unnecessarily or disproportionately affected the health and/or reputations of respondents were unreasonable and unjustified.[127]

These decisions reinforce that the extent of an employer's managerial prerogative in a workplace investigation will be limited by terms in an applicable enterprise agreement that expressly forego or constrain that right.[128] However, this protection is only afforded to respondents who are covered by applicable terms in enterprise agreements[129] and requires that respondents individually, or through their union,[130] pursue legal action to challenge employer conduct. The legal regulation of workplace investigations through the terms of enterprise agreements is contingent and relatively confined.

IV Regulation of Employer Conduct During Workplace Investigations Through Other Key Statutes

Other areas of statute law also apply to employer conduct towards respondents during workplace investigations. I examine provisions under six central areas of statute law below. I argue that these provisions include important constraints on employer conduct towards, and protections for, respondents. However, the statutory framework is fragmented, unduly complex, and primarily relies on individual respondents pursuing legal claims for enforcement.

A Anti-discrimination laws

Anti-discrimination laws apply to dimensions of employer conduct towards respondents during workplace investigations, although they do so indirectly. All Australian jurisdictions have adopted legislation that prohibits discrimination based on

[126] ibid [116].

[127] See, eg, *Construction, Forestry, Mining and Energy Union (105N) v MSS Strategic Medical Pty Ltd* [2015] FWC 6937 [84]-[85]; *Australian Rail, Tram and Bus Industry Union (139V) v NSW Trains* [2016] FWC 1553 [77].

[128] *Richardson v Ambulance Victoria* (n 113) [109]–[110].

[129] In March 2025, about one third of all employees in the Australian labour market were covered by an enterprise agreement made and approved under the *FW Act*: Department of Employment and Workplace Relations, 'Trends in Federal Enterprise Bargaining—March Quarter 2025' (2025) 5 <https://www.dewr.gov.au/enterprise-agreements-data/resources/trends-federal-enterprise-bargaining-march-quarter-2025> accessed 1 August 2025.

[130] See, eg, *Australian Workers' Union v SSX Services Pty Ltd* [2025] FWC 906.

attributes such as sex, race, or disability, although the legislation is not uniform.[131] Protections under anti-discrimination laws apply in employment and other contexts. Anti-discrimination laws prohibit unlawful direct and indirect discrimination, including by employers. Under anti-discrimination statutes, unlawful discrimination also includes sexual harassment,[132] sex-based harassment and a hostile working environment,[133] and sometimes disability harassment.[134] Employers can be vicariously liable for unlawful conduct by their employees or agents,[135] although an employer generally has a defence to a claim of vicarious liability if it is able to establish that it took 'all reasonable steps' to prevent the unlawful conduct from occurring.[136] Anti-discrimination statutes also include provisions that prohibit persons, including employers, from inciting, causing, instructing, inducing, aiding, or permitting another to commit an act of unlawful conduct.[137]

Some anti-discrimination laws are augmented by positive duties,[138] and duties to reasonably accommodate persons, such as employees, in certain circumstances. For example, the *Sex Discrimination Act 1984* (*SDA*) includes a positive duty on employers, and others, to take 'reasonable and proportionate measures to eliminate, as far as possible' conduct such as sex discrimination, sexual harassment, harassment on the ground of sex, a hostile work environment and acts of victimization,[139] and the *Disability Discrimination Act 1992* (Cth) (*DDA*) requires an employer to ensure it does not directly,[140] or indirectly,[141] discriminate against a worker, such as an employee,[142] by failing to make reasonable adjustments or accommodations.[143] Anti-discrimination laws include mechanisms by which complaints of unlawful conduct

[131] *Age Discrimination Act 2004 (Cth); Disability Discrimination Act 1992 (Cth); Australian Human Rights Commission Act 1986 (Cth); Sex Discrimination Act 1984 (Cth); Racial Discrimination Act 1975 (Cth); Discrimination Act 1991 (ACT); Anti-Discrimination Act 1977 (NSW); Anti-Discrimination Act 1992 (NT); Anti-Discrimination Act 1991 (Qld); Equal Opportunity Act 1984 (SA); Anti-Discrimination Act 1998 (Tas); Equal Opportunity Act 2010 (Vic); Equal Opportunity Act 1984 (WA).* Grounds of discrimination vary in each jurisdiction. The complex framework of discrimination protections in Australia has been the subject of scholarly discussion, see, eg, Neil Rees, Simon Rice, and Dominique Allen, *Australian Anti-Discrimination and Equal Opportunity Law* (3rd edn, The Federation Press 2018) 301–02.

[132] SDA ss 28A, 28AA; DA (ACT) ss 58–64; ADA (NSW) s 22; ADA (NT) ss 22A–22J; ADA (Qld) ss 118–20; EOA (SA) s 87; ADA (Tas) s 17; EOA (Vic) ss 92–102; EOA (WA) ss 24–26.

[133] *SDA ss 28AA, 28M.*

[134] *DDA s 35.*

[135] See, eg, *SDA s 106; RDA s 18A, 18E; DDA s 123; EOA (Vic) s 102.*

[136] *SDA s 106; RDA s 18A.* See also 'reasonable precautions': *ADA s 57; DDA s 123.* In the case of the *DDA*, the employer must show it also exercised 'due diligence': ibid ss 123(2), (4).

[137] *SDA s 105; RDA s 17; DDA ss 43, 122.*

[138] See, eg, *EOA (Vic) s 15.*

[139] *SDA ss 47B, 47C.* The positive duty operates concurrently with state and territory laws about WHS and anti-discrimination, which may provide affected employees with mechanisms by which to complain about unlawful conduct by employers, and others, or seek compensation.

[140] *DDA s 5(1).*

[141] ibid s 6(2).

[142] ibid s 15.

[143] An exception to this requirement applies if making the adjustment or accommodation would cause the employer 'unjustifiable hardship': ibid ss 5(2), 6(b), 15(4)(b). State and territory anti-discrimination laws also include the requirement that employers make reasonable adjustments for employees with a disability, see, eg, *EOA (Vic) s 20.* For a critique of judicial interpretations of the duty to make reasonable adjustments under the *DDA*, see Alice Taylor, 'Disability Discrimination, the Duty to Make Adjustments and the Problem of Persistent Misreading' (2019) 45 Monash University Law Review 461.

can be filed, conciliated, and determined.[144] In most instances, complainants bear the onus of establishing that unlawful discrimination or sexual harassment occurred.[145] If a claim is successful, the complainant may seek orders, including compensation for economic and non-economic loss.[146]

Anti-discrimination laws can indirectly apply to the conduct of employers towards respondents during workplace investigations, although there are no provisions in the statutes that explicitly refer to workplace investigations. It is unlawful for an employer to directly or indirectly discriminate against a respondent to whom a protected ground applies during a workplace investigation.[147] An employer must also comply with any applicable obligations to reasonably accommodate a respondent under anti-discrimination statutes. However, few court decisions relate to claims by respondents under anti-discrimination laws regarding the conduct of their employer during a workplace investigation. There is limited guidance regarding how the provisions apply in this context.

A decision that provides helpful guidance is *Dare v Hurley* (*Dare*), in which Ms Dare had claimed that her employer had unlawfully discriminated against her on the grounds of pregnancy when it dismissed her following a workplace investigation.[148] The employer had denied that it had unlawfully discriminated against Ms Dare. It submitted that it had dismissed her after conducting a workplace investigation that found she had engaged in misconduct.

In *Dare*, the Court considered evidence from the workplace investigation as part of determining the claim. Driver FM accepted that the employer had not followed an internal guide that set out its investigation process during its investigation,[149] had not afforded Ms Dare procedural fairness during the workplace investigation,[150] and had made findings that Ms Dare had engaged in misconduct when the evidence indicated she had not done so.[151] His Honour held that the employer had directly discriminated against Ms Dare in breach of the *SDA*,[152] and observed that the:

> reason for [the] dismissal was Ms Dare's pregnancy and the consequential request for maternity leave. The password protection of the two stationery order forms and the SMS message to Mrs Hurley on 23 May 2003 were merely convenient pretexts . . . In dismissing Ms Dare, Mr Hurley treated Ms Dare less favourably than the hypothetical comparator because of her need for maternity leave, a characteristic that appertains to women who are pregnant.[153]

[144] See, eg, *EOA (Vic) pt 8*.
[145] See further Dominque Allen, 'Reducing the Burden of Proving Discrimination in Australia' (2009) 31 Sydney Law Review 579.
[146] See, eg, *EOA (Vic) pt 8*.
[147] For a decision that considers an investigation of misconduct in the context of an employee with an impairment see, eg, *Victoria v Grant* (2014) 246 IR 441.
[148] *Dare v Hurley* [2005] FMCA 844. See *SDA ss 5(1), 7(1), 14(2)*.
[149] *Dare* (n 148).
[150] *Dare* (n 148) [109]. For a decision involving an employee where a claim of this type was rejected see, eg, *Li v Edith Cowan University (No 3)* [2013] WASCA 277. For a claim pursued under s 351 of the *FW Act* see, eg, *Victoria v Grant* (n 147).
[151] *Dare* (n 148).
[152] The claim was brought under the *Human Rights and Equal Opportunity Act 1986 (Cth) s 46PO*. Ms Dare also made a claim of breach of contract.
[153] *Dare* (n 148).

Dare illustrates that courts may be willing to scrutinize evidence about a workplace investigation to determine if an employer has engaged in unlawful discrimination under anti-discrimination statutes. It highlights that courts may be willing to examine the evidence about an employer's workplace investigation process to determine whether that process is bona fide, and that the employer did not commence or continue that process for a reason that was proscribed under anti-discrimination statutes. The decision highlights that protections under anti-discrimination laws apply to respondents in workplace investigations, but judicial consideration of these statutes in the context of workplace investigations is very limited.

B WHS laws

WHS laws include important duties that apply to employer conduct towards respondents during workplace investigations. Commencing in January 2012, all states and territories except Victoria proceeded to adopt the Model Work Health and Safety Bill 2011 (Cth). These statutes are collectively described as the harmonized *WHS Acts*.[154] The *WHS Acts* impose a primary duty of care on a person conducting a business or undertaking (PCBU) to 'ensure, so far as is reasonably practicable, the health and safety of workers engaged . . . workers engaged, or caused to be engaged by the person by the person; and workers whose activities in carrying out work are influenced or directed by the person'.[155] This duty is owed to workers while they are at work in the business or undertaking. The *WHS Acts* provide examples of the steps that PCBUs must take to discharge the primary duty such as providing and maintaining 'a work environment without risks to health and safety' and 'information, training, instruction or supervision that is necessary to protect all persons from risks to their health and safety'.[156] The *WHS Acts* also impose other duties that supplement the primary duty of care.[157]

As noted, PCBUs must comply with the primary duty, and additional duties under ss 20–26 of the *WHS Acts*, so far as is 'reasonably practicable'. Section 18 of the *WHS Acts* defines 'reasonably practicable' as 'that which is, or was at a particular time, reasonably able to be done in relation to ensuring health and safety, taking into account and weighing up all relevant matters'. Section 18 also lists matters that are relevant to determining if a step was 'reasonably practicable'. There are various mechanisms under the *WHS Acts*, which are intended to enable enterprises to address risks to health and safety. The *WHS Acts* facilitate the appointment of health and safety

[154] *Work Health and Safety Act 2011 (NSW); Work Health and Safety Act 2011 (ACT); Work Health and Safety Act 2011 (Qld); Work Health and Safety (National Uniform Legislation) Act 2011 (NT); Work Health and Safety Act 2012 (Tas); Work Health and Safety Act 2012 (SA)*. These are, collectively, the *Work Health and Safety Acts*. In Victoria, substantively similar obligations to the *WHS Acts* are set out in the *Occupational Health and Safety Act 2004 (Vic)*. For an examination of the *WHS Acts*, see Andrew Stewart, Anthony Forsyth, and Mark Irving, *Creighton and Stewart's Labour Law* (7th ed, The Federation Press 2025) 659–740; Sappideen, O'Grady, and Riley (n 3) 283–312.

[155] *WHS Acts s 19(1)*. Workers are defined as any persons who carry out work 'in any capacity' for a PCBU: ibid s 7(1).

[156] *WHS Acts ss 19(3)(a), 19(3)(f)*.

[157] ibid ss 20–26.

representatives and committees to address risks.[158] Health and safety representatives also have the power to issue Provisional Improvement Notices (PINs) if they reasonably believe a person (including a PCBU) is contravening the *WHS Act* or has, and is likely to continue to, contravene the *WHS Act*.[159] A PCBU may also be prosecuted for breach of the *WHS Act*.[160]

The *WHS Acts* are supported by model *Work Health and Safety Regulations 2011* (Cth) (*WHS Regulations*) that elaborate how PCBUs must discharge the primary duty under the *WHS Acts*. To complement the harmonized *WHS Acts*, states and territories have adopted harmonized *WHS Regulations*.[161] The *WHS Regulations* relevantly prescribe that, to manage hazards to health and safety, a PCBU must: identify hazards;[162] eliminate the risk so far as is reasonably practicable, and if it is not reasonably practicable to eliminate the risk, minimize the risk so far as is reasonably practicable;[163] implement 'risk control measures' in accordance with the hierarchy of measures prescribed in regulation; maintain and review those control measures that are implemented;[164] and provide information, training, and instruction to support the control measures implemented.[165]

In 2022, the *WHS Regulations* were amended to address psychosocial risks.[166] The *WHS Regulations* expressly state that PCBUs must manage 'psychosocial hazards',[167] as well as hazards that may cause a person physical harm.[168] At the time of writing, these amendments have legal effect in all states and territories except Victoria.[169] The *WHS Regulations* provide that, where a PCBU needs to implement control measures to manage a psychosocial hazard, it must determine what measures to implement by having regard to all relevant matters.[170] Non-compliance with these obligations can constitute an offence under the *WHS Act*.

[158] ibid ss 60–69, 75–82.

[159] ibid s 90(1).

[160] ibid s 230. On enforcement and compliance under the *WHS Acts*, see further Elizabeth Bluff and Richard Johnstone, 'Supporting and Enforcing Compliance with Australia's Harmonised WHS Laws' (2017) 30 Australian Journal of Labour Law 30.

[161] *Work Health and Safety Regulations 2011 (Cth)*. Again, Victoria differs in its approach to work health and safety legislation, cf *Occupational Health and Safety Regulations 2017 (Vic)*.

[162] *WHS Regulations reg 34*.

[163] ibid reg 35.

[164] ibid regs 37–38.

[165] ibid reg 39.

[166] ibid regs 55A–55D.

[167] ibid reg 55C. The *WHS Regulations* define a psychosocial hazard as a hazard that may cause a worker or other person psychological harm, which arises from or relates to the design or management of work, the working environment, the plant at a workplace, or workplace interactions or behaviours: ibid reg 55A. The *WHS Regulations* also define a 'psychosocial risk' as a risk to health and safety arising from a psychosocial hazard: ibid reg 55B.

[168] The amendments were enacted by the *Work Health and Safety Amendment (Managing Psychosocial Risk and Other Measures) Regulations 2022*. See *WHS Regulations pts 3.1-3.2*.

[169] Work Health and Safety Amendment Regulation 2022 (NSW); Work Health and Safety (Psychosocial Risks) Amendment Regulation 2022 (Qld); Work Health and Safety (General) Regulations 2022 (WA); Work Health and Safety Regulations 2022 (Tas); Work Health and Safety (National Uniform Legislation) Amendment Regulations 2022 (NT); Work Health and Safety (Managing Psychosocial Hazards at Work Code of Practice) Approval 2023 (ACT). In Victoria, see Ben Carroll MP, 'New Rules to Protect Workers' Mental Health' (21 February 2025) <https://www.premier.vic.gov.au/new-rules-protect-workers-mental-health> accessed 4 August 2025.

[170] *WHS Regulations reg 55D*. Relevant matters are inclusively defined in ibid reg 55D(2).

The *WHS Acts* add a central dimension to the regulation of employer conduct towards respondents during workplace investigations. The primary duty of care under the *WHS Acts* is expressed to be 'without limitation' and applies to employer conduct during workplace investigations.[171] The obligation on PCBUs to manage psychosocial hazards applies during workplace investigations. A national model *Managing Psychosocial Hazards at Work Code of Practice* (*Psychosocial Hazards Code of Practice*) provides practical guidance to PCBUs about how to comply with the *WHS Acts* and *WHS Regulations*.[172] States and territories have implemented codes of practice on psychosocial hazards that are aligned with the *Psychosocial Hazards Code of Practice*.[173]

The *Psychosocial Hazards Code of Practice* notes that a PCBU's investigation of a potential psychosocial hazard is different from a workplace investigation.[174] However, if a PCBU decides not to undertake a workplace investigation or conducts a workplace investigation poorly, it can enliven psychosocial hazards. For example, the *Psychosocial Hazards Code of Practice* states that psychosocial hazards can arise from 'poor organisational justice', which includes hazards from 'failing to appropriately address (actual or alleged) underperformance, inappropriate or harmful behaviour, or misconduct', and from having 'no or inadequate processes for making decisions affecting workers (e.g. policies and processes do not set out the key considerations for disciplinary decisions)'.[175] This reveals that the *Psychosocial Hazards Code of Practice* indirectly interacts with workplace investigations and contemplates how workplace investigations can include psychosocial hazards including for respondents.

The clarification that an employer's primary duty under *WHS Acts* includes a duty to manage hazards arising from management processes for addressing misconduct provides a clear and important limitation on employer conduct during workplace investigations that protects respondents. However, these statutory obligations are discordant with the position under judge-made law regarding the limits of an employer's duty of reasonable care during workplace investigations.[176] In addition, the *WHS Acts* do not enable individual respondents to pursue complaints about the risk of psychosocial harm that arises from their involvement in a workplace investigation. Statutory workers' compensation schemes complement the *WHS Acts* and provide employees with compensation for injuries incurred at work, but they are subject to key limitations.

[171] *WHS Acts s 19(1)*.

[172] Work Health and Safety (Managing Psychosocial Hazards at Work) Code of Practice 2024 (Cth); *WHS Acts s 274*. A code of practice is admissible as evidence in court proceedings under the *WHS Acts* and a court may rely on the code as evidence of what is known about a hazard, risk, or control method and may rely on the code to determine what is reasonably practicable in the circumstances to which the code relates: ibid s 275(2)–(3).

[173] See, eg, Work Health and Safety (Managing Psychosocial Hazards at Work Code of Practice) Approval 2023 (ACT).

[174] *Psychosocial Hazards Code of Practice* 43.

[175] ibid 58.

[176] See further chapter 4 III.

C Workers' compensation laws

Workers' compensation laws are relevant to employers and respondents in circumstances where a respondent sustains a mental injury during a workplace investigation. Statutory workers' compensation schemes operate in each Australian state and territory,[177] and separate Commonwealth schemes apply to workers such as employees of the Commonwealth government.[178] The schemes differ between jurisdictions. Each scheme provides no-fault compensation to employees, and other eligible workers,[179] who have suffered an injury arising out of or in the course of their employment.[180] The type of compensation a worker can receive with respect to an injury or disease under these schemes depends on the circumstances and includes income replacement,[181] medical, hospital and like costs,[182] permanent impairment payments,[183] and payments to support rehabilitation and return to work.[184]

Workers' compensation laws operate alongside other areas of law that may also provide workers with the ability to pursue claims for compensation for injuries and illnesses incurred at work.[185] Workers' compensation laws in some states and territories permit common law claims for damages in tort or contract with respect to a work-related injury or disease,[186] although the statutory scheme may limit the availability and quantum of the claim.[187] Separate avenues of compensation under anti-discrimination laws might also be available to a worker who incurs an injury at work

[177] See Workplace Injury Management and Workers Compensation Act 1998 (NSW); Workplace Injury Rehabilitation and Compensation Act 2013 (Vic); Return to Work Act 2014 (SA); Workers' Compensation and Rehabilitation Act 2003 (Qld); Workers' Compensation and Injury Management Act 1981 (WA); Workers Rehabilitation and Compensation Act 1988 (Tas); Return to Work Act 1986 (NT); Workers Compensation Act 1951 (ACT). For an historical overview of the development of the state and territory schemes and each statute, see Safe Work Australia, 'Comparison of Workers' Compensation Arrangements in Australia and New Zealand' (2021) 28th edn <https://www.safeworkaustralia.gov.au/doc/comparison-workers-compensation-arrangements-australia-and-new-zealand-2021> accessed 20 August 2025.

[178] The Commonwealth schemes are regulated by the *Safety, Rehabilitation and Compensation Act 1988 (Cth); Safety, Rehabilitation and Compensation (Defence-Related Claims) Act 1988 (Cth); Seafarers Rehabilitation and Compensation Act 1992 (Cth); Military Rehabilitation and Compensation Act 2004 (Cth); Veterans' Entitlements Act 1986 (Cth).*

[179] Eg, a worker is an individual who performs work for an employer or agrees with an employer to perform work at the employer's direction, instruction or request, whether under a contract of employment (whether express, implied, oral, or in writing) or otherwise, or who is deemed to be a worker under the *WIRC Act* (Vic) schedule: *WIRC Act (Vic) s 3.*

[180] Each scheme sets out a specific definition of an injury and how it must be related to employment to be compensable. See, eg, ibid s 39(1).

[181] See, eg, ibid ss 160–79.

[182] See, eg, ibid ss 223–33.

[183] See, eg, ibid ss 210–21.

[184] See, eg, ibid s 230.

[185] On the distinction and interrelationship between compensation in a workers' compensation claim and under the *FW Act s 545*, see *Reynolds v Harrier Group Pty Ltd* [2023] FedCFamC2G 930 [24].

[186] On the scope of common law claims permitted under each state and territory, see further Safe Work Australia (n 177) 253–57.

[187] Eg, in Victoria, an employee must be granted a 'serious injury' certificate to pursue a claim for damages under the common law, and maximum damages for economic and non-economic loss apply: *WIRC Act (Vic) ss 327, 333, 340.*

due to discrimination, although the statutory schemes prevent employees from receiving the same type of compensation for the same injury twice.[188]

Workers' compensation laws apply to some injuries to respondents incurred during workplace investigations. However, workers' compensation laws in each jurisdiction relevantly exclude from compensation a psychological injury incurred by an employee that is wholly or partly caused by the employer's reasonable management action conducted in a reasonable manner in respect of an employee's employment.[189] The statutory exclusion was intended to 'insulate' management action 'from [the] need for concern about the psychological effect of the [decision-making] on the employee',[190] provided the employer acted reasonably. The test of reasonableness is objective but is to be assessed by reference to all the subjective facts.[191]

Each state and territory scheme sets out this exclusion in different terms. The *Workplace Injury Rehabilitation and Compensation Act 2013 (Vic)* (*WIRC Act (Vic)*) specifically defines management action to include an employer conducting a workplace investigation into allegations of misconduct.[192] The other state and territory schemes define management action as including action with respect to discipline,[193] which has been interpreted to include conducting a workplace investigation.[194]

This indicates that, where an employer conducts a workplace investigation in an unreasonable way and this causes psychological injury to an employee under investigation, that employee is potentially entitled to workers' compensation. However, decisions where an employer has been found to have conducted a workplace investigation in an unreasonable manner are factually specific and often finely balanced.[195] These decisions usually include evidence of the cumulative impact of multiple and significant procedural or substantive errors on the psychological health of the respondent.[196] A decision-maker might recognize that an employer took particular steps that were not reasonable, but that overall the workplace investigation was a reasonable action taken in a reasonable manner.[197]

Workers' compensation laws, therefore, provide an avenue of redress for respondents who incur a psychological injury because of an employer's unreasonable management action during a workplace investigation. However, respondents who incur a

188 See, eg, ibid s 48. For a discussion of these parallel jurisdictions, see Carol Andrades, 'When Worlds Collide—Intersections Between Anti-Discrimination Law and Workers' Compensation Law—the Decision in "Friend v Comcare"' (2021) 26 Employment Law Bulletin 82.

189 *WIMWC Act (NSW) s 111A; WIRC Act (Vic) s 40; RTW Act (SA) s 7(4); WCR Act (Qld) s 32(5); WCIM Act (WA) s 5(4); WRC Act (Tas) s 25(1A); RTW Act (NT) s 3A(2); WC Act (ACT) s 4(2).* On causation, see further *Comcare v Martin* (2016) 339 ALR 1 9–10.

190 *Comcare v Martin* (n 189) 9.

191 *Jeffery v Lintipal Pty Ltd* [2008] NSWCA 138 [4] (Hodgson JA); [44] (Basten JA); [81] (Rein J).

192 *WIRC Act (Vic) s 40(7).*

193 *WIMWC Act (NSW) s 111A; WIRC Act (Vic) s 40; RTW Act (SA) s 7(4); WCR Act (Qld) s 32(5); WCIM Act (WA) s 5(4); WRC Act (Tas) s 25(1A); RTW Act (NT) s 3A(2); WC Act (ACT) s 4(2).*

194 See, eg, *Bryant and National Australia Bank Limited (Compensation)* [2021] AATA 2769 [293]–[299].

195 See, eg, *Read v Workers' Compensation Regulator* [2017] QIRC 072.

196 See, eg, *Queensland (Queensland Health) and Q-COMP and Tracy Connors* [2012] (WC/2010/173) [68].

197 *Department of Education and Training v Sinclair* [2005] NSWCA 265 [97] (Spigelman CJ); [99] Hodgson JA; [100] (Bryson JA).

psychological injury due to an employer's conduct during a workplace investigation face evidentiary barriers and uncertainty if they seek to claim workers' compensation. The regulatory scheme is also not designed to prevent unreasonable employer conduct but to retrospectively compensate employees who are injured after the conduct has occurred.

D Public service employment laws

Employers within the Australian public sector are subject to specific statutory obligations, which apply when they conduct workplace investigations.[198] Different statutes regulate entities within the public sector. The Australian public sector is broad and diverse and consists of numerous Commonwealth, state and territory public services, police services, state and territory public education systems, thousands of statutory authorities, and government business enterprises.[199] In this section, I refer to the statutory regulation of the Australian public service (APS) as a frame of reference to examine how statute law applies during workplace investigations to employers that are governments, as the APS is a key segment of the Australian public sector.[200]

At the Commonwealth level, the *Public Service Act 1999* (Cth) (*PS Act*) governs the employment of persons in the APS.[201] The *PS Act* sets out the APS values and principles,[202] and the *APS Code of Conduct (Code of Conduct)*.[203] The *PS Act* devolves the rights, duties, and powers of an employer to 'Agency Heads',[204] and the *PS Act* and *Public Service Regulations 2023 (Cth) (PS Regulations 2023)* set out the obligations of employees of the APS within the *Code of Conduct*.[205] The *PS Act* prescribes that an Agency Head may discipline an employee for breaching the *Code of Conduct*, and must establish written procedures for determining if an APS employee has breached the *Code of Conduct*, and, if so, the sanction that is to be imposed.[206] The procedures must comply with the *Australian Public Service Commissioner's Directions (APSC Directions)*,[207] and 'have due regard to procedural fairness'.[208]

The *APSC Directions* include the 'basic procedural requirements' for investigations of suspected breaches of the *Code of Conduct*. Any specific procedures established

[198] Phillipa Weeks, 'The Reshaping of Australian Public Service Employment Law' in Marilyn Pittard and Phillipa Weeks (eds), *Public Sector Employment in the Twenty-First Century* (ANU Press 2007) 11.

[199] On the features and governance of the Australian public service, see further John R Nethercote, 'The Australian Public Service: Statutory, Doctrinal and Institutional Arrangements for Its Governance' in Marilyn Pittard and Phillipa Weeks (eds), *Public Sector Employment in the Twenty-First Century* (ANU Press 2007).

[200] Weeks (n 198) 11.

[201] *Public Service Act 1999 (Cth).*

[202] ibid ss 10, 10A.

[203] ibid s 13 (*Code of Conduct*).

[204] ibid s 20. An Agency Head is defined as the Secretary of a Department, the Head of an Executive Agency, and the Head of a Statutory Agency, as defined: ibid ss 7, 65. The employer powers of Agency Heads are as prescribed: ibid ss 20–33; Public Service Regulations 2023 (Cth) regs 3.1–3.12.

[205] *PS Act ss 13–14.* For the definition of an employee of the Commonwealth public service (known as an 'APS employee'), see ibid ss 7, 22, 72. The *Code of Conduct* also applies to statutory office holders: *PS Regulations regs 8, 56.*

[206] *PS Act ss 15(1), 15(3)–15(8), 29.*

[207] Australian Public Service Commissioner's Directions 2022 (Cth) pt 5; *PS Act 15(4)(a).*

[208] *PS Act s 15(4)(b).*

by an Agency Head must comply with these basic requirements.[209] In summary, the framework establishes basic procedural requirements for a workplace investigation that reflect the requirements of procedural fairness, as discussed further below, but also requires as little formality as possible.

Taken together with the *PS Act* and *PS Regulations* and any relevant terms in applicable enterprise agreements, the *APSC Directions* establish statutory parameters that apply to the workplace investigation procedure of an APS employer.[210] A respondent may seek redress for a breach through a review of actions, including by the Agency or the Merit Protection Commissioner,[211] or an application for judicial review.[212] A breach by an Agency Head of procedures may also lead to a decision by a court that the procedure was not properly established.[213]

APS employers have a statutory obligation to comply with the central requirements of procedural fairness established under judge-made administrative law. As explained in chapter 2, procedural fairness has two key aspects. These aspects are the 'hearing rule' and 'bias rule'. The *APSC Directions* include directions that the content of the procedures, which must be established by Agency Heads, reflect the 'hearing rule',[214] and 'bias rule',[215] and the *PS Act* more broadly requires that the procedures must, in general, 'have due regard to procedural fairness'.[216] This statutory framework prescribes a legislated standard of procedural fairness that applies to workplace investigations conducted by APS employers towards respondents.

Courts have interpreted key statutory provisions in this context. In *Lohse v Arthur* (*Lohse*),[217] the FCA considered the content of the principles of procedural fairness as applicable to a workplace investigation in the Commonwealth public sector. Mr Lohse sought judicial review with respect to his employer's proposed sanction of dismissal based on the findings of an investigation that he had breached the *Code of Conduct*.[218] Mr Lohse claimed that his employer had breached the requirements of procedural fairness during the workplace investigation and sought a writ of prohibition that prevented it from imposing the sanction.[219] He alleged that one way his employer had

[209] *APSC Directions ss 57, 59(a), 60, 61, 62, 63.*

[210] The *PS Act* and *PS Regulations* also impose some additional conditions on decision-making by Agency Heads relevant to workplace investigations, see, eg, *PS Act s 28; PS Regulations reg 14.*

[211] *PS Act s 33; PS Regulations regs 36–39, 41–42, 43–45.* Note a review of action is not available where the sanction imposed was dismissal: *PS Act s 33(1).*

[212] Note, however, that uncommon for employees to seek judicial review of decisions made under the *PS Act (Cth).* See discussion in Marilyn Pittard and Phillipa Weeks (eds), *Public Sector Employment in the Twenty-First Century* (ANU Press 2007) 31–32.

[213] *Tucker v Victoria* [2019] VSC 420, [118] (Ierodiaconou AsJ).

[214] *APSC Directions ss 59(b), 60(b).*

[215] ibid s 61.

[216] *PS Act s 15(4)(b).* Courts have been required to consider, for example, the requirements owed by public sector employers regarding disclosure of documents during workplace investigations, having regard to the obligation to afford procedural fairness, see, eg, *Tucker (No 2)* (n 213). On the requirements of procedural fairness during a statutorily prescribed workplace investigation into alleged misconduct by a doctor, see also *Vega Vega v Hoyle* [2015] QSC 111 [170]–[189].

[217] *Lohse v Arthur (No 3)* (2009) 205 IR 1118.

[218] The employer was an agency that comprised a division of a Commonwealth government department. The employee was entitled to seek the review pursuant to *PS Act s 33.*

[219] Mr Lohse claimed he was denied procedural fairness and natural justice. Courts have noted that natural justice and procedural fairness are related, but not identical, concepts. The HCA has determined that

denied him procedural fairness was by engaging an investigator (an external consultant) who had acted with actual or apprehended bias.[220]

In *Lohse*, Graham J considered the requirements of procedural fairness as applicable during the workplace investigation and specifically scrutinized the issue of bias by an investigator. Graham J observed that procedural fairness was a 'flexible obligation to adopt fair procedures which are appropriate and [needed to be] adapted to the circumstances' including during workplace investigations.[221] His Honour noted that procedural fairness was broadly concerned with giving 'a person such as Mr Lohse a fair go' during the investigation process and described a workplace investigator as 'a decision-maker obliged to be fair'.[222] Graham J also held that the principles of procedural fairness applied to the investigation process conducted by an investigator where the finding would be used by the employer to make an administrative decision.

Graham J then applied these concepts when considering whether the investigator had demonstrated actual or apprehended bias towards Mr Lohse. His Honour held that the investigator had shown actual bias because he 'did not approach the task which was entrusted to him with an open mind and he was not open to persuasion'.[223] Graham J found that presumptive comments by the investigator to witnesses captured in interview recordings, and other contemporaneous records, indicated actual bias.[224]

Graham J also considered whether the investigator had demonstrated apprehended bias. His Honour examined the apprehended bias rule in the context of a workplace investigation, where decisions were made in private.[225] His Honour observed that apprehended bias would be proven where:

> a hypothetical fair-minded lay person properly informed as to the nature of the process which [the investigator] was engaged in and the possible sanctions which might be imposed upon [the employee], might reasonably apprehend that [the investigator] might not have brought an impartial mind to the making of his decision on alleged breaches [by the employee].[226]

Graham J determined that, even if the investigator's comments during interviews were not sufficient to establish actual bias, those same comments were sufficient to support a finding of apprehended bias. His Honour determined that the investigator's bias resulted in the denial of procedural fairness to Mr Lohse.[227] Graham J quashed

in the context of administrative decision-making it is suitable speak of a duty to act fairly or accord procedural fairness, see *Kioa v West* (1985) 159 CLR 550, 550, [583] (Mason J).

[220] *Lohse* (n 217) 2017, 219, 220.
[221] ibid 227. A similar approach was adopted in *Henzell v Centrelink* [2006] FCA 1844 [34].
[222] *Lohse* (n 217) 228.
[223] ibid 229.
[224] His Honour observed that it may also be possible to find, on the facts, that the investigator exhibited actual bias through having a 'closed mind' at the commencement of the investigation. The investigator had intimated, through his comments, that he agreed with or supported comments made by witnesses. For example, the investigator stated and repeated 'I'm not doubting that' in response to comments by a witness: ibid 229.
[225] ibid 225.
[226] ibid 229.
[227] ibid.

the investigator's determinations that found the allegations of misconduct by Mr Lohse were proven,[228] and the employer's proposed decision to impose a sanction of termination based on the investigator's findings.[229]

Lohse illuminates the meaningful difference that the statutory requirement of procedural fairness can have for a respondent who is faced with a sanction of dismissal. The possibility of internal and judicial reviews enables an employee to apply to set aside the decision to dismiss and preserve their employment.

The statutory obligations that apply to employers that conduct workplace investigations in the public and private sectors differ significantly. Statutory obligations that require applicable employers in the public sector to establish written procedures and ensure procedural fairness (as defined by statute) impose important constraints on employer conduct towards respondents. However, the application of these statutory provisions is confined and, as noted, there are no similar provisions that apply to employers in the private sector.

E Whistleblowing and public interest disclosure laws

Two central regimes that regulate whistleblowing are set out under the *Corporations Act 2001* (Cth) (*CA*) and *Public Interest Disclosure Act 2013* (Cth) (*PIDA*),[230] and these regimes apply to employers that conduct workplace investigations in specific circumstances. Statutory protections for whistleblowers were first introduced by the Commonwealth government in Australia in 2004. Commonwealth protections applicable to persons who report misconduct about companies and other prescribed commercial organizations are set out in pt 9.4AAA of the *CA*. These protections are complemented by a regime that is applicable to persons who report misconduct about the Commonwealth government or related entities under the *PIDA*. Separate regimes also apply to persons who report misconduct about governments and associated entities of each Australian state and territory.[231]

The *CA* and *PIDA* set out circumstances where an entity that is covered by the regime may or must investigate a report about disclosable conduct.[232] Both statutes contemplate that, when an entity investigates a disclosure, this may involve an investigation into the conduct of an employee mentioned in the report. This means that these two regimes apply to the conduct of employers towards respondents during workplace investigations to which the regimes apply.[233]

First, the *CA* prescribes that an entity needs to have a whistleblower policy that includes information about how it will investigate a disclosure and how it will ensure fair

228 ibid 236.
229 ibid.
230 *Corporations Act 2001 (Cth); Public Interest Disclosure Act 2013 (Cth).*
231 *Public Interest Disclosures Act 2002 (Tas); Public Interest Disclosure Act 2003 (WA); Public Interest Disclosure Act 2010 (Qld); Public Interest Disclosures Act 2012 (Vic); Public Interest Disclosure Act 2012 (ACT); Public Interest Disclosure Act 2018 (SA); Public Interest Disclosures Act 2022 (NSW); Independent Commissioner Against Corruption Act 2017 (NT).*
232 *CA s 1317AI; PIDA Div 2.*
233 *CA s 1317AI; PIDA Div 2.*

treatment of any employees of the entity who are mentioned in the disclosure, which includes any respondents.[234] Failure to comply with this requirement is an offence of strict liability.[235] The Australian Securities and Investments Commission (ASIC),[236] has published *Regulatory Guide 270 Whistleblower Policies* (*Regulatory Guide*), which sets out best practice principles for entities covered by the *CA*.[237] The *Regulatory Guide* provides examples of procedural steps that entities may choose to include in policies to promote compliance with the obligation to ensure fair treatment of employees during investigations. Recommended steps include entities handling disclosures confidentially whenever possible, ensuring the investigation is 'objective, fair and independent' and advising an employee who is the subject of a disclosure about the subject matter of the disclosure 'as and when required by principles of natural justice and procedural fairness and prior to any actions being taken'.[238]

Second, the *PIDA* sets out requirements regarding how entities covered by the regime may or must investigate disclosures, and prescribes that investigations that involve allegations of misconduct against employees comply with statutory requirements that generally apply to these investigations.[239] Among other things, these statutory requirements include an obligation that the employer afford procedural fairness to an employee under investigation.[240]

The regimes apply to employer conduct and prescribe that an employer must fairly investigate alleged misconduct by an employee when it forms part of a broader investigation of disclosable conduct.[241] The *CA* establishes a statutory obligation to provide 'fair treatment'. These statutory provisions constrain employer conduct towards respondents during workplace investigations in specific circumstances. They contribute to the fragmentation and complexity of statutory regulation of employer conduct during workplace investigations.

F Evidence law

Courts have interpreted two key dimensions of the law of evidence in the context of disputes pursued by respondents about workplace investigations. The first dimension relates to the capacity of employers to claim legal professional privilege over communications and documents that were produced during a workplace investigation. The

[234] *CA s 1317AI.*

[235] ibid s 1317AI.

[236] ASIC is the agency that oversees the administration and enforcement of the *CA:* see ibid s 5B.

[237] ASIC, 'Regulatory Guide 270 Whistleblower Policies' (2019) 270 <https://download.asic.gov.au/media/5702691/rg270-published-13-november-2019-20200727.pdf> accessed 20 August 2025.

[238] ibid 38.

[239] *PIDA s 53(5).* Investigations that relate to alleged breaches of the *Code of Conduct*, within the meaning of the *Parl S Act* or *PS Act (Cth)*, respectively, must comply with the procedures established under s 15(3) of those statutes.

[240] *PS Act s 15(4)(b); Parliamentary Service Act 1999 (Cth) 15(4)(b).*

[241] The *CA* states that reports that are solely about workplace complaints or grievances are not protected: *CA s 1317AADA(1)(b).* See also Revised Explanatory Memorandum, *Treasury Laws Amendment (Enhancing Whistleblower Protections) Bill* 2018 22 [2.38]. Under the *PIDA*, a disclosure is not protected including if it relates only to a policy, or proposed policy, of the Commonwealth Government with which a person disagrees: *PIDA s 31.*

second dimension relates to the ability of employees who are respondents in workplace investigations to refuse to answer questions by claiming the privilege against self-incrimination.

Legal professional privilege and the privilege against self-incrimination are enshrined in the *Evidence Act 1995* (Cth) (*Evidence Act*), which applies in Commonwealth courts.[242] The same rules are set out in uniform legislation, which is based on the *Evidence Act*, in each Australian territory,[243] as well as in New South Wales, Victoria, and Tasmania.[244] These rules apply to trials held in courts in these jurisdictions. The States of South Australia, Western Australia, and Queensland are yet to enact uniform legislation.[245]

Under the *Evidence Act*, persons may claim legal professional privilege or the privilege against self-incrimination as bases on which to refuse to disclose information to a court in legal proceedings. First, a person may claim legal professional privilege over confidential communications or documents that have been prepared for the dominant purpose of obtaining legal advice or, alternatively, for the dominant purpose of a lawyer providing legal services relating to litigation.[246] Legal professional privilege can be lost,[247] or waived,[248] in certain circumstances. Second, the *Evidence Act* provides a privilege against self-incrimination that a person may invoke to refuse to answer questions in civil court proceedings.[249] To claim the privilege, a person must show there are reasonable grounds to find that the evidence they give could prove the person committed an offence or is liable for a civil penalty.[250] If the privilege applies, the person claiming the privilege is not required to answer questions or produce documents, where they would otherwise be statutorily obliged to do so.[251]

Disputes about legal professional privilege that refer to workplace investigations generally involve applications by employees, such as respondents, for orders (from a court or the FWC) that require their employer to disclose communications or documents.[252] Two key decisions that have examined claims of legal professional privilege

[242] *Evidence Act 1995 (Cth) ss 118–19.*
[243] *Evidence Act 2011 (ACT) ss 118–19;* ibid.
[244] *Evidence Act 1995 (NSW) ss 118–19; Evidence Act 2008 (Vic) ss 118–19; Evidence Act 2001 (Tas) ss 118–19.* On the historical development of statutory evidence law, see Stephen Odgers, *Uniform Evidence Law* (15th edn, Thomson Reuters 2020) 1–4.
[245] *Evidence Act 1929 (SA); Evidence Act 1977 (Qld); Evidence Act 1906 (WA).* In these jurisdictions, the Legal professional privilege and the privilege against self-incrimination are established under judge-made law.
[246] *Evidence Act (Cth) ss 118–19.* See also *Esso Australia Resources Ltd v Federal Commissioner of Taxation* (1999) 201 CLR 49 64 (Gleeson CJ, Gaudron and Gummow JJ); *Daniels Corporation International Pty Ltd v Australian Competition & Consumer Commission* (2002) 213 CLR 543 552 (Gleeson CJ, Gaudron, Gummow, and Hayne JJ). The 'dominant purpose' of a communication predominates over other purposes and must be determined objectively: *AWB Ltd v Cole* (2006) 152 FCR 382 411–12.
[247] *Evidence Act (Cth) ss 121–26.*
[248] ibid s 122. The HCA has determined that 'what brings about the waiver is the inconsistency, which the courts, where necessary informed by considerations of fairness, perceive, between the conduct of the client and maintenance of the confidentiality; not some overriding principle of fairness operating at large': *Mann v Carnell* (1999) 201 CLR 1 13 (Gleeson CJ, Gaudron, Gummow, and Callinan JJ).
[249] *Evidence Act (Cth) ss 128.*
[250] ibid ss 128(2). See also *Sorby v Commonwealth* (1983) 152 CLR 281, 294 (Gibbs CJ); *Reid v Howard* (1995) CLR 1, 14 (Toohey J, Gaudron J, McHugh J, and Gummow J).
[251] See, eg, *Evidence Act (Cth) s 128(4)(b).*
[252] See, eg, *Stephen v Seahill Enterprises Pty Ltd* [2021] FWCFB 2623.

by employers in workplace investigations are *Bartolo v Doutta Galla Aged Services Ltd* (*Bartolo*),[253] and *Komlotex Pty Ltd v AMP Ltd* (*Komlotex*).[254]

In *Bartolo*, Mr Bartolo applied to the Federal Circuit Court for an order directing his employer to provide him with a copy of a workplace investigation report that had been prepared by a lawyer.[255] Mr Bartolo's employer, Doutta Galla Aged Services Ltd (Doutta Galla), had instructed its lawyer to investigate allegations that Mr Bartolo had engaged in misconduct. The lawyer conducted the investigation, prepared a report with findings, and gave the report to the Board of Directors of Doutta Galla. The Board had relied on the report and advice provided by the lawyer, to recommend to Doutta Galla to dismiss Mr Bartolo. Doutta Galla had relied on the Board's recommendation to dismiss Mr Bartolo and claimed legal professional privilege over the report. Mr Bartolo argued the report was not protected by legal professional privilege and that, even if it was protected, the employer had waived privilege by referring to the report in its pleadings and witness evidence in the main proceedings under the *FW Act*.

The Court in *Bartolo* reasoned that a workplace investigation was not work for which being a lawyer was required.[256] So, engaging a lawyer to perform this work did not necessarily mean that an employer could presume that any communications or documents produced by the lawyer comprised legal advice to which legal professional privilege applied.[257] Whelan J held that, for an employer to claim legal professional privilege over a particular communication or document produced during a workplace investigation, it needed to specifically establish that it was produced for the dominant purpose of legal advice or for use in current or anticipated litigation.[258]

Whelan J accepted the evidence of the chairperson of the Board that the dominant purpose of the report was to obtain legal advice about 'the Board's exposure to legal liability'.[259] Her Honour did not have access to the report in the proceedings, but surmised that it may have also included 'a range of matters some of which . . . in the normal course may not [attract legal professional privilege]'.[260] Whelan J determined that the possible existence of other matters in the investigation report did not prevent the employer from claiming legal professional privilege over it, provided that the evidence demonstrated its dominant purpose was legal advice.[261]

Her Honour then turned to the question of whether the employer had waived privilege over the report. Whelan J observed that Doutta Galla had referred to the recommendations of the Board in pleadings, and this opened up for scrutiny the basis for those recommendations, which were potentially the findings set out in the investigation report.[262] Her Honour concluded that this conduct was inconsistent

[253] *Bartolo v Doutta Galla Aged Services Ltd* [2014] FCCA 1517.
[254] *Komlotex Pty Ltd v AMP Ltd* [2022] NSWSC 1525.
[255] The application arose in proceedings initiated by Mr Bartolo against his employer under the *FW Act*, see *Bartolo (No 2)* (n 31).
[256] ibid [77].
[257] ibid.
[258] ibid.
[259] ibid [51].
[260] ibid [95].
[261] ibid [85].
[262] ibid [95].

with maintaining legal professional privilege over the report and so Doutta Galla had waived privilege.[263] Whelan J reasoned that it would be unfair to Mr Bartolo to allow Doutta Galla to withhold the factual basis on which the Board had based its recommendations and yet rely on them in the substantive proceedings. His Honour ordered that the employer give Mr Bartolo the report.[264]

Bartolo recognized that the report set out factual findings that the Board had relied on to make disciplinary recommendations. The reasoning does not provide much detail regarding how Whelan J determined that the dominant purpose of the workplace investigation report was legal advice, rather than a source of information to make a disciplinary decision, beyond it being clear that Whelan J was prepared to accept the uncontested evidence of the chairperson. It is, however, possible to construe the decision of Whelan J that Doutta Galla had waived privilege over the document as an approach that sought to reconcile the tension between the competing purposes of the document.

A similar tension is apparent in the decision of the Supreme Court of New South Wales in *Komlotex*. In that case, the Court was required to consider two central challenges to a claim of legal professional privilege made by AMP Limited (AMP) over documents produced by lawyers during a workplace investigation into allegations of misconduct by several employees of AMP.[265] AMP's external lawyers had instructed another legal firm, Workdynamic Australia, to conduct the workplace investigation.[266] AMP claimed legal professional privilege over all communications and documents produced by Workdynamic Australia on the basis that its lawyers had engaged the firm to provide it with advice about matters of employment law in connection with the workplace investigation.

The plaintiffs in the dispute in *Komlotex* were shareholders. They challenged AMP's claim of legal professional privilege and argued, among other things, that there was 'a real difference between an engagement to provide legal advice and an ordinary workplace investigation'.[267] The plaintiffs asserted that if AMP's lawyers had engaged Workdynamic Australia for the dominant purpose of conducting a workplace investigation that AMP would rely on when deciding whether to take disciplinary action against the employees, then the report was not privileged because it formed part of an 'ordinary workplace investigation'.[268]

[263] ibid.

[264] ibid.

[265] AMP Limited had discovered approximately 29,000 documents in the proceedings and made claims of legal professional privilege over part or all of approximately 9,000 documents.

[266] The allegations related to potential breaches of the AMP code of conduct by employees involved in obtaining ongoing fees for providing financial advice that was not actually provided: *Komlotex* (n 254) [16], [76]. AMP had been investigated by ASIC about these matters for nearly two years before the legal practice commenced this workplace investigation. The Board of AMP had been previously advised that these matters were because of an 'administrative error' but due to a previous investigation, the Board had become aware that this advice was wrong and instead these matters were potentially due to employee misconduct: ibid [30] (Rees J).

[267] *Komlotex* (n 254). This argument cited the decision of *Stephen FWCFB*, which upheld the decision in *Stephen v Seahill Enterprises Pty Ltd* [2021] FWC 972 972. A Full Bench of the FWC had considered whether the employer could rely on legal professional privilege to resist production of documents pursuant to *FW Act s 590*.

[268] *Komlotex* (n 254) [79].

The Court in *Komlotex* took a similar approach to Whelan J in *Bartolo* and accepted the evidence of AMP's Group General Counsel that the dominant purpose of the workplace investigation was for AMP's external lawyers to provide AMP with legal advice and to assist AMP to prepare for possible future legal proceedings by the employees under investigation.[269] The Court determined that the employer could therefore claim legal professional privilege over all communications and documents between AMP and its lawyers as part of the workplace investigation.

The Court observed that an employer could conduct a workplace investigation in a manner that ensured the 'product of the investigation was privileged, as long as the dominant purpose of the investigation was the provision of legal advice'.[270] Rees J did not directly address the argument raised by the plaintiffs that the product of an 'ordinary workplace investigation', comprising factual findings used by the employer to make disciplinary decisions, could be distinguished from any legal advice that followed from those findings. Instead, the Court accepted AMP's assertion that the workplace investigation was conducted for the purpose of legal advice and to prepare for legal action despite the factual import of the inquiry.

Courts have also examined whether the privilege against self-incrimination can be relied on by respondents in workplace investigations, including in the decisions *Murray Irrigation Ltd v Balsdon* (*Murray Irrigation*),[271] and *Grant v BHP Coal Pty Ltd* (*Grant Full Bench*).[272] *Murray Irrigation* comprised a claim of unfair dismissal by Mr Balsdon, who had been charged with criminal offences and was under police investigation. Mr Balsdon's employer had commenced a workplace investigation into allegations that were about the same subject matter as the police investigation. Mr Balsdon had refused to answer questions from the investigator so as not to affect his rights in potential future criminal proceedings. The employer insisted that Mr Balsdon respond to the investigator's questions and, when he continued to refuse to do so, summarily dismissed him for failing to give the information as directed. Mr Balsdon argued his dismissal was 'harsh, unjust or unreasonable' because he was entitled to invoke the privilege against self-incrimination. Mr Balsdon's claim succeeded at trial.[273] The employer appealed the decision.

On appeal, a Full Court of the Supreme Court of New South Wales observed that the 'high value of the privilege against self-incrimination should be brought to bear' when considering the lawfulness of the employer's decision to dismiss Mr Balsdon.[274] The Court noted that:

> [t]here are powerful elements in the circumstances supporting the pursuit by the [employer] of its own interests, but powerful as they are, they have to be weighed

[269] ibid [88].
[270] ibid [81].
[271] *Murray Irrigation Ltd v Balsdon* (2006) NSWLR 73.
[272] *Grant v BHP Coal Pty Ltd* (2017) 247 FCR 295 [108].
[273] At trial, the court determined that the employer had breached a term of the enterprise agreement that applied to the parties, which required the employer to ensure termination of the employee was not harsh, unjust, or unreasonable: *Murray Irrigation* (n 271). An application for special leave to the HCA to appeal this decision was refused: *Balsdon v Murray Irrigation Ltd* [2007] HCATrans 406.
[274] *Murray Irrigation* (n 271).

> with the [employee's] own interest in resisting criminal prosecutions, avoiding furnishing any basis for any further prosecutions and defending his personal liberty against the criminal law.[275]

The Court determined that, despite the employer's 'understandable business need to know what had happened', it was harsh, unjust, and unreasonable for it to insist that Mr Balsdon answer questions that could affect his rights in criminal proceedings and dismiss him for refusing to do so.[276] The Court upheld the decision of the trial judge.[277]

These principles were elaborated by a Full Bench of the FCA in *Grant Full Bench*.[278] The dispute involved Mr Grant, who had pursued a claim before the FWC and, later, the FCA that disputed his employer's decision to dismiss him for refusing its direction to attend a workplace investigation interview. Mr Grant argued before the FCA that he had refused his employer's direction because he would have been asked questions about alleged misconduct which, if proven, could constitute a statutory offence.[279] Mr Grant argued that he was entitled to rely on the privilege against self-incrimination to refuse the direction to attend the interview. In the proceedings, the employer argued that the privilege against self-incrimination did not apply to 'questions asked in the sphere of employment'.[280]

The Court determined that the privilege against self-incrimination was 'at least capable of applying to questions asked of the [employee] in the workplace interview'.[281] The Court noted that it was necessary to apply the 'test traditionally applied' to decide if the privilege applied to the employee's circumstances.[282] The Court determined that it could not apply this test to Mr Grant's specific circumstances because he had not raised the issue of privilege in the initial proceedings, and this led to 'a vacuum of [relevant] facts'.[283] The Court also held that Mr Grant had not enlivened the privilege against self-incrimination because he had not made the claim at the time of the interview and '[i]t is for the person claiming privilege to assert it and to identify its precise basis'.[284]

275 *Murray Irrigation* (n 271) [40] (Bryson JA).
276 ibid [40] (Bryson JA).
277 ibid [41] (Bryson JA).
278 *Grant Full Bench* (n 272).
279 The relevant provisions were ss 34, 39(2)(d) of the *Coal Mining Safety and Health Act 1999* (Qld): ibid [107] (Collier J). Mr Grant did not raise this argument in his initial claim before the FWC: *Grant v BHP Coal Pty Ltd* [2014] FWC 1712. Mr Grant raised the argument as part of his appeal from that decision. A Full Bench of the FWC declined to 'consider new arguments of this kind on appeal' but observed that the privilege against self-incrimination would not apply to a workplace investigation interview that inquired about an employee's misconduct: *Grant v BHP Coal Pty Ltd* [2014] FWCFB 3027, [146]. Mr Grant sought orders from the FCA that quashed both decisions of the FWC including on the basis that the Full Bench of the FWC had been in error in rejecting his argument that he was entitled to claim the privilege against self-incrimination. Collier J initially dismissed Mr Grant's application: *Grant v BHP Coal Pty Ltd (No 2)* [2015] FCA 1374. Mr Grant appealed that judgment to a Full Bench of the FCA.
280 *Grant Full Bench* (n 272) [108].
281 ibid [108]. On this matter, the Court cited *Police Service Board v Morris* (1985) 156 CLR 397 397, 403, 408, and 411 (Gibbs CJ).
282 *Grant Full Bench* (n 272) [109].
283 ibid [110].
284 ibid [111].

While Mr Grant's claim was not successful, considered together with the approach in *Murray Irrigation*, the reasoning in *Grant Full Bench* indicates that the privilege against self-incrimination is at least capable of being enlivened during a workplace investigation to limit the capacity of an employer to direct a respondent to answer questions. This idea has not been developed in any subsequent court decisions, although these cases have been cited by the FWC as supporting an employee's right to refuse to answer questions during a workplace investigation.[285]

The decisions prioritize an employee's ability to rely on the privilege against self-incrimination over the employer's interests in making findings during a workplace investigation. The novel extension of the privilege against self-incrimination to the sphere of work in these decisions suggests that courts consider that the privilege is not just a rule of evidence that applies in judicial and non-judicial proceedings but a fundamental right with no exception except as explicitly set out in statute.[286]

Judicial interpretations have illuminated how statutory evidence law applies to disputes about employer conduct towards respondents during workplace investigations. The decisions regarding legal professional privilege illustrate that employers have a broad scope to claim the privilege over communications and documents produced in workplace investigations. This has the effect of reducing the information available to respondents who participate in workplace investigations by employers that claim the privilege.

The decisions that recognize that the privilege against self-incrimination may be invoked by a respondent in a workplace investigation show that respondents can rely on this privilege to resist a direction by an employer to answer certain questions in an interview. However, there are few court decisions on this subject, which makes the law less certain. It also seems an employer might still draw an adverse inference if a respondent relies on the privilege to refuse to answer a question in these circumstances.

V The Implications of Uncertainty in the Statutory Regulation of Workplace Investigations

The analysis above reveals that:

- four key areas of the *FW Act* apply to aspects of employer conduct towards respondents during workplace investigations, but the provisions are fragmented and apply in particular circumstances;
- the *WHS Acts* and *WHS Regulations* in all states and territories except Victoria explicitly require employers to manage psychosocial hazards as part of the primary duty, and the *Psychosocial Hazards Code of Practice* provides helpful guidance that this includes ensuring fair and reasonable treatment of respondents during workplace investigations;[287]

[285] *Sydney Trains v Bobrenitsky* [2023] FCAFC 96 [137]. See also *Newton v Toll Transport Pty Ltd* (2021) 307 IR 140 [156].

[286] *Sorby* (n 250); *Reid* (n 250).

[287] Safe Work Australia, 'Managing Psychosocial Hazards at Work' (2022) Model Code of Practice <https://www.safeworkaustralia.gov.au/doc/model-code-practice-managing-psychosocial-hazards-work> accessed 9 August 2025.

- rather than imposing explicit constraints on employer power, provisions of the *FW Act* allow eligible respondents to seek redress if their employer breaches pt 3-1 or pt 3-2 of the *FW Act*, engages in 'bullying' under pt 6-4B, or breaches (or behaves unreasonably or unfairly when acting pursuant to) a term in an enterprise agreement that applies during the workplace investigation;
- six other areas of statute law include key provisions that apply to aspects of employer conduct towards respondents, but the rules are fragmented and unduly complex for employers and respondents;
- the application of key statutory provisions to employer conduct during workplace investigations towards respondents depends on statutory interpretation, and this means that the law as it applies to this subject is indirect and could change. For example, this affects how pt 6-4B of the *FW Act* and the *Evidence Act* apply in this context.

The analysis also illuminates gaps, issues, and inconsistencies in the statutory regulation of employer conduct towards respondents during workplace investigations. Notably:

- there is no direct or comprehensive regulation of workplace investigations under work law;
- key statutory provisions only apply to employer conduct towards respondents in specific circumstances and jurisdictions, and this results in legal complexity and inconsistency. This is exemplified in key differences between *WHS Regulations* in each state and territory and the application of the *CA* and *PIDA* to only some workplace investigations;
- there is no consistent articulation or standard of fair treatment of respondents under statute law, but at least three statutes require employers to ensure some form of fairness/fair treatment towards respondents in prescribed circumstances;[288]
- there is no consistent obligation under statute for employers to establish an internal policy that explains how they will conduct a workplace investigation, but some employers must establish internal policies in accordance with statutes such as the *PS Act*, *CA*, or *PIDA*; and
- the disparate packages of legislation that apply to aspects of employer conduct towards respondents during workplace investigations have produced a statutory framework that is unsatisfactory as being fragmented, unduly complex and unsystematic.

As shown in chapter 2, workplace investigations are an important and prevalent HRM tool, and there is a risk of harm and injury to respondents during these processes. Parliament has not articulated a policy position regarding the regulation of employer conduct towards respondents in workplace investigations. This means the application of statutory rules to this context has been unsystematic and sporadic and, arguably, inadequate. Different statutory rules apply to employer conduct depending

[288] These statutes are the: *FW Act pt 3-1, 6-4B; PS Act; CA; PIDA.*

on the circumstances, and some only do so indirectly or incidentally. The rules are fragmented and lack cohesion. Clear and consistent minimum standards of employer conduct are required through targeted development of the law.

In chapter 7, I positively and normatively evaluate the framework of legal regulation that I have examined in detail in this chapter and in chapter 4. Applying the nine elements of the framework of justice that I have enunciated in chapter 3 to that framework of legal regulation, I propose an agenda for law reform.

6
An Empirical Profile of Respondents' Views and Experiences of Workplace Investigations from Tribunal Decisions

I Introduction

As shown in chapters 1 and 2, respondents face the risk of harm and injury during workplace investigations but legal scholarship and HRM texts rarely provide insights into their views or experiences.[1] In this chapter, I use qualitative content analysis to examine a sample of 183 decisions of the FWC made under the unfair dismissal protection under pt 3-2 of the *FW Act*. I make findings about how respondents in the sample of decisions viewed and experienced workplace investigations and consolidate these findings to discern four central themes. These themes relate to informational asymmetry between employers and respondents, denial/minimization by employers of respondents' voices and opportunities for advocacy, denial by employers of respondents' needs or requests for accommodation, and harm to respondents' mental health. These findings and themes inform proposals for law reform provided in chapter 7.

II The Context and Utility of Tribunal Decisions as Sources of Information About Respondents

In chapter 5, I discussed the substantive rules regarding the meaning of an unfair dismissal under pt 3-2 of the *FW Act*. To contextualize the empirical analysis in this chapter, I add to this explanation below. Specifically, I set out an overview of the dispute resolution procedure through which the FWC handles unfair dismissal applications under pt 3-2 of the *FW Act*. I also explain the rationale for using a sample of decisions of the FWC under pt 3-2 to draw out information about how respondents viewed and experienced workplace investigations.

[1] An exception is Moira Jenkins, Helen Winefield, and Aspa Sarris, 'Consequences of Being Accused of Workplace Bullying: An Exploratory Study' (2011) 4 International Journal of Workplace Health Management 33. See further chapter 2 III.

Workplace Investigations. Adriana Orifici, Oxford University Press. © Adriana Orifici 2026.
DOI: 10.1093/9780198970019.003.0006

A The procedure used by the FWC to handle applications under pt 3-2 of the *FW Act*

Under pt 3-2 of the *FW Act*, employees who meet prescribed criteria and regard their dismissal as unfair[2] can apply to the FWC for an order granting a remedy.[3] The FWC must deal with an application by holding a conference if it involves facts that are in dispute between the parties.[4] This conference is known as a conciliation. At a conciliation, the parties are assisted to voluntarily negotiate a settlement of the dispute in private.[5] Most applications are resolved during or after conciliation, through a settlement or discontinuance.[6] If an application is not settled or discontinued, a Member of the FWC may hold a hearing and make a binding determination.[7] The Member must conduct a conference or hold a hearing in relation to any application that involves 'facts the existence of which is in dispute'.[8]

Parties can provide wide-ranging written and verbal information to the FWC, and each other, when they make an application, respond to an application, prepare for a hearing, or participate in a hearing.[9] Prior to a hearing, the Member ordinarily makes directions to the parties to provide (to the FWC and each other) outlines of submissions, witness statements for each person who the party intends to call to give evidence at the hearing, and documentary material.[10] At the hearing, the FWC may seek verbal submissions from the parties.[11] Witness statements stand as the evidence of witnesses, subject to verbal statements made during examination and cross-examination.[12] The process is intended to proceed with as little formality at possible,[13] and the FWC is not bound by the rules of evidence and

[2] The employee must earn less than the 'high income threshold' (as defined in s 333) or be covered by a modern award or enterprise agreement and must have completed the 'minimum employment period' (as defined in ss 383 and 384): *FW Act s 382.*

[3] ibid s 394(1). The FWC may order the remedy of reinstatement or compensation: ibid ss 391, 392.

[4] *FW Act ss 397, 398.*

[5] FWC, 'What Is Conciliation?' <https://www.fwc.gov.au/job-loss-or-dismissal/unfair-dismissal/conciliation-unfair-dismissal/what-conciliation> accessed 2 August 2025.

[6] Eg, the FWC reported that in the 2018/2019 financial year, of the 13,928 unfair dismissal applications lodged, 78% of applications conciliated by staff conciliators (8,161) were resolved by the agreement of the parties, and 5% of applications (728) were resolved by the FWC through an order granting a remedy: FWC, 'Annual Report 2018–19' (FWC 2019) 27. Note, more recent annual reports of the FWC do not include this data.

[7] *FW Act s 399.* This is known as an 'arbitration'.

[8] *FW Act s 536LX.*

[9] The FWC may inform itself in such a manner as it considers appropriate when dealing with an application: *FW Act ss 590(1).* The FWC may inform itself including by: requiring a person to attend before the FWC; requiring written or oral submissions; requiring a person to provide copies of documents, records, or any other information; taking evidence under oath or affirmation; conducting inquiries or undertaking or commissioning research; or holding a conference or a hearing: ibid s 590(2). Commonly, parties submit sworn witness statements to the FWC as part of their submissions. See, eg, *Boris v Metcash Trading Limited t/as Metcash* [2019] FWC 3993.

[10] FWC, 'Practice Note: Unfair Dismissal Proceedings' (FWC 2014) para [54] <https://www.fwc.gov.au/hearings-decisions/practice-notes/practice-note-unfair-dismissal-proceedings> accessed 2 August 2025.

[11] *FW Act ss 590(2)(b).*

[12] FWC, 'Practice Note' (n 10) para [59].

[13] *FW Act ss 577(1)(b).*

procedure.[14] Parties must seek permission from the FWC to be represented by a lawyer or paid agent at the hearing.[15]

The FWC usually publishes a written decision when it determines an application by an employee made under pt 3-2.[16] The decision is written by the decision-maker who is a Member of the FWC. Decisions include descriptions of relevant verbal and written submissions made by the parties, the material that the parties have provided in support of their submissions and the written and verbal evidence of witnesses. The extent to which a decision describes relevant material varies. In most decisions, the material is set out in sub-sections entitled 'Background', 'Applicant's Materials', or 'Case for the Applicant', although the decisions might quote or describe submissions and oral evidence in further detail in sub-sections that consider the application of the law to the factual dispute.[17]

B Decisions under pt 3-2 of the *FW Act* as a source of information about respondents' views and experiences

Few scholarly studies use empirical legal research methods to understand the views and experiences of respondents during workplace investigations. Workers are, in general, a hard-to-access group for the purposes of empirical research,[18] and workers who are respondents in workplace investigations are particularly hard to access. As identified in chapter 2, employers conduct workplace investigations confidentially and legal disputes about workplace investigations that involve respondents are likely to settle prior to hearing.[19] Parties routinely agree to keep the terms of settlement private,[20] and respondents might agree to terms of settlement that prohibit them from disclosing that a complaint was made or any detail about the complaint.[21] This means that it is challenging to identify workers who have been respondents in workplace investigations to invite them to participate in an interview or survey.

Decisions made under pt 3-2 of the *FW Act* are a rich source of information about the views and experiences of workers who were respondents in workplace investigations.[22] Applications were made by 14,772 workers under pt 3-2 in the 2023–24

[14] The FWC cannot ignore these rules to the extent that doing so would cause unfairness between the parties: ibid s 591.
[15] *FW Act ss 596.*
[16] FWC, 'Practice Note' (n 10) para [61].
[17] See, eg, *Abarra v Toyota Motor Corporation Australia Ltd* [2018] FWC 3761.
[18] See further Dominique Allen and Alysia Blackham, 'Under Wraps: Secrecy, Confidentiality and the Enforcement of Equality Law in Australia and the United Kingdom' (2019) 43 Melbourne University Law Review 384.
[19] ibid 389–96.
[20] ibid. In context of the United Kingdom, see Lizzie Barmes, 'Silencing at Work: Sexual Harassment, Workplace Misconduct and NDAs' (2023) 52 Industrial Law Journal 68.
[21] For a discussion of these terms and their impact on workers, see AHRC, 'Respect@Work: Sexual Harassment National Inquiry Report' (Final Report 2020) 556–64.
[22] An empirical study found that unfair dismissal applications that proceed to arbitration are commonly about 'policy and procedure' and employees seeking to 'clear their name' against allegations of misconduct, see further, Andrew See, Michael Barry, and David Peetz, 'The Australian Unfair Dismissal Regime: Exploring How Applications for Unfair Dismissal Remedy Resolve' (2022) 35 Australian Journal of Labour Law 27, 41–42.

financial year.[23] Over 200 applications were determined via arbitration in the 2017–18 financial year,[24] and the FWC ordinarily publishes a written decision in relation to an arbitration. As noted, written decisions describe and quote from sources such as witness statements, supporting materials, and transcripts of verbal evidence provided by parties. The open-textural test for determining if a dismissal was 'harsh, unjust or unreasonable' under s 387 of the *FW Act* invites parties to provide detailed material.

Each decision that I examined in this study included information about a respondent's views or experiences during a workplace investigation. This was because the FWC regarded the process and/or findings of the employer's workplace investigation as a substantive factor in the dispute. While the views and experiences of respondents during workplace investigations are also set out in decisions made in other relevant jurisdictions,[25] the information available in decisions made under pt 3-2 of the *FW Act* was the most voluminous and detailed.

By examining published decisions of the FWC, I overcame the barriers to accessing respondents as a hard-to-reach group. I accessed digitized versions of the decisions and searched for keywords using the electronic database administered by the FWC.[26] This method of collecting the data was unobtrusive and cost-effective. It did not require respondents in workplace investigations to be identified, recruited, or interviewed/surveyed. It did not raise barriers to participation arising from the prevalence of settlement and non-disclosure agreements because the decisions were on the public record.

Some limitations need to be kept in mind in terms of generalizing from the findings of the study. First, the decisions include respondents who were pursuing claims against their employers in which they challenged their dismissal. The study only provides an insight into the views and experiences of respondents who were dismissed and were so aggrieved as to pursue claims under pt 3-2 of the *FW Act*. Second, the study examined information that was provided by respondents to the FWC during litigious disputes where evidence could be highly contested. Respondents provide witness statements and verbal evidence under oath or affirmation.[27] While the veracity and legal validity of their submissions and materials were of concern to the decision-maker, they are not the focus of the study. Their accounts are subjective and comprise their perceptions and experiences including about workplace investigations.

Third, the study examined information provided to the FWC by respondents that was summarized in the decisions, alongside direct quotations from respondents' written materials and verbal evidence. The translation of respondents' evidence by the decision-maker can be seen as limiting access to workers' own voices and perspectives. Yet the written and verbal submissions by representatives are based on workers'

[23] FWC, 'Fair Work Commission Annual Report 2022–23' (FWC 2023) 21.

[24] See FWC, 'Annual Report 2018–19' (n 6) 29, which notes 13,928 unfair dismissal applications were filed and 229 arbitrated decisions were made. Reports for more recent years set out the number of unfair dismissal applications but not the number of arbitrated decisions.

[25] Eg, employee perspectives are also included in decisions under the 'General Protections' jurisdiction in pt 3-1 of the *FW Act*, and the common law of the contract of employment.

[26] FWC, 'Hearings and Decisions' <https://www.fwc.gov.au/hearings-and-decisions> accessed 26 July 2023.

[27] FWC, 'Practice Note' (n 10).

instructions and, in many decisions, they are quoted in detail.[28] The decisions describe at length, and directly quote from, the written and verbal witness statements provided by the workers in their own words.[29]

Fourth, the decisions analysed in this study each relate to workers who were dismissed by their employers and then made claims under pt 3-2 of the *FW Act* that reached final determination.[30] The study only made findings about the views and experiences of respondents who were in these specific circumstances. Yet many decisions included detailed information about their views and experiences and so it is helpful to consider them given the paucity of insights in legal scholarship. The decisions provided a 'chorus' of voices that the study reflected across central themes.[31]

III Study Setting, Data, and Method

I explain the study setting, approach to selecting decisions of the FWC, and method for coding and analysing the data below.

A Using qualitative content analysis to analyse the decisions in the sample

While doctrinal analysis aims to systematize legal texts, content analysis is concerned with discerning themes in texts.[32] Bernard Berelson described content analysis in 1952 as 'a research technique for the objective, systematic, and quantitative description of the manifest content of communication'.[33] More recent definitions expand the method to include both qualitative and quantitative content analysis.[34] For example, James Drisko and Tina Maschi described qualitative content analysis as 'a set of techniques for the systematic analysis of texts of many kinds, addressing not only manifest content but also the themes and core ideas found in texts as primary content'.[35] Qualitative content analysis allows conceptual themes and categories to emerge from data and for consideration of textual features that are latent, hidden, or contextual.[36]

[28] See and others found that materials provided by employees who are represented in their applications can also be clearer and more coherent: See, Barry, and Peetz (n 22) 40.

[29] The form in which the employee's reported experience of a workplace investigation is set out in each decision (ie, in a verbal or written statement, supporting document, or written or verbal submission) was recorded and is noted in the study.

[30] See and others found that unfair dismissal claims that proceed to arbitration are more likely to involve: matters of principle for either party; an employee applicant who has been emotionally impacted by the dismissal; an employee applicant who seeks reinstatement; and/or an employee applicant who has unrealistic expectations due to a lack of understanding of the law or process for resolving the dispute via conciliation: See, Barry, and Peetz (n 22) 42–46.

[31] Mark A Hall and Ronald F Wright, 'Systematic Content Analysis of Judicial Opinions' (2008) 96 California Law Review 63, 76.

[32] Klaus Krippendorff, *Content Analysis: An Introduction to Its Methodology* (4th edn, SAGE 2019) 1.

[33] Bernard Berelson, *Content Analysis in Communication Research* (Hafner 1971) 18.

[34] On this dichotomy see further, Lindsay Prior, 'Content Analysis' in Patricia Leavy (ed), *The Oxford Handbook of Qualitative Research* (2nd edn, OUP 2020) 543–44.

[35] James W Drisko and Tina Maschi, *Content Analysis* (OUP 2015) 82.

[36] Michael Pickering, 'Qualitative Content Analysis' in Michael S Lewis-Beck, Alan Bryman, and Tim F Liao (eds), *The SAGE Encyclopedia of Social Science Research Methods* (SAGE 2004) 890; Hall and Wright (n 31) 118.

Scholars have regarded content analysis, including qualitative content analysis,[37] as a suitable method to use in legal research settings,[38] and have used the approach to analyse a broad range of legal documents.[39] In a leading treatise on the use of content analysis in law, Mark Hall and Ronald Wright have noted that the method 'allow[ed] the researcher to deal with larger numbers of cases, which provide[d] a truer measure of broad patterns in the case law'.[40] In turn, this enabled the researcher to 'assemble a chorus, listening to the sound that the cases [made] together'.[41]

This method was suited to the current study as it involved analysing many decisions of a similar precedential weight and format of presentation. Each case comprised a decision of the FWC under pt 3-2 of the *FW Act*, which was determined between 2018 and 2020 (inclusive) where the employer's workplace investigation process and/or findings comprised a substantive factor in the dispute. I used the method to investigate what could be known about the views and recounted experiences of respondents during workplace investigations from the sample of decisions. I produced findings and identified patterns and themes from the body of decisions.[42]

B Case identification and eligibility

I extracted data for this study from written decisions of the FWC under pt 3-2 of the *FW Act* that were determined in the calendar years of 2018–20 (inclusive). I determined the time frame on the basis that it produced a sufficiently large body of decisions to enable in-depth understanding of the experiences of workers who were respondents in workplace investigations. The coding of decisions became consistent (and no new codes were generated) after the coding of cases for two calendar years (2019–20) was completed. I also coded a further year of decisions (2018) to check whether any additional coding was generated. This step resulted in several minor additions to coding but no substantial changes.[43]

I identified decisions using the publicly accessible online database of the FWC.[44] All decisions of the FWC for the three-year period of the study were available on the database. I used the database to search for all decisions made under pt 3-2 of the *FW*

[37] Lisa Webley, 'Qualitative Approaches to Empirical Legal Research' in Peter Crane and Herbert M Kritzer (eds), *The Oxford Handbook of Empirical Legal Research* (OUP 2010) 940–41; Hall and Wright (n 31) 64.

[38] See, eg, Kylie Burns and Terry Hutchinson, 'The Impact of "Empirical Facts" on Legal Scholarship and Legal Research Training' (2009) 43 The Law Teacher 153; Chris Dent and Andrew T Kenyon, 'Defamation Law's Chilling Effect: A Comparative Content Analysis Of Australian And US Newspapers' (2004) 9 Media & Arts Law Review 89.

[39] Hall and Wright (n 31) 67.

[40] ibid 65.

[41] ibid 76.

[42] ibid 66.

[43] Although the COVID-19 pandemic was mentioned in twenty-two decisions in the study sample, there is no mention in any of these decisions that the pandemic impacted on how the employer conducted its workplace investigation.

[44] FWC, 'Find Decisions and Orders' <https://www.fwc.gov.au/hearings-decisions/find-decisions-and-orders> accessed 31 July 2025.

Act that included the phrase 'workplace investigation' or 'investigation',[45] and identified 309 relevant decisions in the study period.

Of the 309 decisions, three related to interlocutory applications in connection with an unfair dismissal application. I did not exclude them as they set out descriptions of relevant worker submissions and the focus of the study was on workers' experiences of workplace investigations, rather than the legal outcome of the claim. There were also twenty-seven decisions that were the subject of an appellate review during the study period.[46] I generally only included the original decision because the appeals determined whether there was an error in the original decision.[47] Parties' submissions related to grounds of appeal and referred to the materials and evidence that were provided in the original hearing and so added little further data about the experiences of respondents.

Once I had excluded twenty-seven appeal decisions, I divided the remaining 282 decisions into two mutually exclusive groups according to whether they were of 'low relevance' or 'high relevance' to the study. I categorized ninety-nine decisions as 'low relevance' to the study. These decisions included only brief or peripheral references to a 'workplace investigation' or referred to 'workplace investigations' involving persons other than the worker who had made the application to the FWC.[48] This approach resulted in a study sample of 183 decisions that were categorized as of 'high relevance'. In each of these 183 decisions, the employer's workplace investigation process and/or findings comprised a substantive factor in the dispute and/or the decision included text that provided details about a respondent's views or experience during the workplace investigation.[49]

C Data coding

The purpose of coding in qualitative content analysis is to assign a 'truncated, symbolic meaning' to individual sections of the data so it can be categorized, classified, and (later) reorganized into emergent categories for analysis.[50] Coding is 'a method of discovery' to the meaning of data.[51] Data can consist of textual sources (eg interview transcripts or survey responses) or visual sources (eg photographs or artefacts).[52] The study sample of relevant decisions of the FWC comprised a form of data that was text that could be coded.

[45] The search term 'workplace investig*' was used to search. This method means that no sampling issues arose. Decisions that included stemmed words, eg, 'investigating', 'workplace investigations', and 'workplace investigator' were also included. A broader search of decisions using the broader term 'investigation' (and stemmed words) was also conducted, with decisions that used this term to describe a 'workplace investigation' added to the study sample.

[46] See *FW Act ss 400, 604*.

[47] The error may relate to an error of law or significant error of fact: ibid ss 400(2), 604(1).

[48] See, eg, *Ghee v Staffing Options for Community Services Pty Ltd* [2020] FWC 6067 [33].

[49] A list of all decisions in the dataset is set out in Appendix 3.

[50] Johnny Saldaña, 'Qualitative Data Analysis Strategies' in Patricia Leavy (ed), *The Oxford Handbook of Qualitative Research* (2nd edn, OUP 2020) 882–83.

[51] ibid 882.

[52] ibid 883.

There is no standard method for coding data that is accepted for qualitative content analysis, and sociological scholarship endorses a range of approaches.[53] It is possible to code data deductively or inductively. Deductive coding involves commencing with a set of predetermined codes.[54] It is mostly used to test and refine theories and where the researcher is certain that various codes or themes will appear in the data.[55] On the other hand, inductive coding (which is also known as grounded theory) involves developing codes directly from the data.[56] Experts have observed that most qualitative researchers code inductively.[57]

This study was focused on the content of written and verbal material that was quoted or summarized in relevant decisions of the FWC. The text described the views or experiences of a respondent in a workplace investigation who ultimately made a claim of unfair dismissal under pt 3-2 of the *FW Act*. The aim of the analysis was to give voice to the experiences of respondents as their perspectives were generally marginalized. I did not commence with presumptions regarding the codes or themes that would appear in the data apart from understanding from HRM texts that respondents risked injury or harm during workplace investigations. An inductive coding method was selected to enable the codes and themes to emerge from the data.

Although there is no standard method of inductive coding for qualitative content analysis, one widely accepted inductive coding method is initial coding.[58] Initial coding is a method that is endorsed for studies that seek to explore subjects' actions/ processes and perceptions as found in data.[59] I used this approach in the study as it was suited to the aim, which was to develop new understanding about respondents' views and experiences of workplace investigations.

Initial coding has no guidelines with respect to how codes are created. I therefore selected a code creation methodology to conduct the initial coding. I identified 'process coding' as a suitable and helpful code creation method.[60] Process coding 'uses gerunds ("-ing" words) exclusively to represent action suggested by the data'.[61] The action coded in process coding can consist of observable human actions (eg requesting information, reading), or more general conceptual action (eg evaluating, negotiating, assuming).[62] I used process coding because the study focused on the respondents' experiences in the specific context of a workplace investigation. It became apparent that this usually involved the employer taking three key steps, and it was possible to systematically build and link concepts within and between these steps.[63] These steps

[53] For example, Saldaña has identified thirty-five different approaches: Johnny Saldaña, *The Coding Manual for Qualitative Researchers* (4th edn, Thousand Oaks 2021) 97. See also six approaches in Saldaña (n 50) 876–911.
[54] Saldaña (n 53) 40.
[55] ibid.
[56] ibid 41.
[57] ibid.
[58] This method is also known as open coding: ibid 72.
[59] ibid 91.
[60] Saldaña (n 50) 883–91.
[61] ibid 883.
[62] ibid.
[63] Juliet Corbin and Anselm Strauss, *Basics of Qualitative Research: Techniques and Procedures for Developing Grounded Theory* (3rd edn, SAGE Publications 2008) 270.

are: commencing the investigation, conducting the investigation (including information gathering and interviewing), and making findings and any decisions to discipline a respondent.

I coded text (sentence or paragraph) in each decision in the study sample ('data') that described, or directly quoted from, the worker's written or verbal submissions or witness statements where it referred to a respondent's participation in, or view about, a workplace investigation.[64] The data was coded cyclically by reading through the text and assigning codes to sentences and paragraphs. I repeated this process several times. I first conducted coding manually and then used Nvivo data analysis software.[65] I assigned multiple codes to some passages of text. Once all the relevant text was coded, I collated a coding framework. I conducted the coding iteratively with the initial broad categories incrementally refined into sub-categories. The codebook for the initial coding cycle is set out in Appendix 1.

D Data analysis and interpretation to produce themes

Data analysis in qualitative research frequently involves the researcher making interpretations. Interpretation involves researchers assigning meaning to the data after careful consideration to uncover new concepts or relationships in data.[66] The interpretation of data in the study comprised a further step towards bringing to life the lived experiences of workplace investigations of a hard-to-access group (in this study, the respondents). It enabled dimensions of their recounted experiences to be better understood.[67]

The first cycle of coding of the data in the study revealed that the recounted experiences of respondents were diverse, but many of the experiences that they described were connected to broader concepts.[68] To identify these broader concepts, a second cycle of coding the data was conducted with a focus on interpretation. This coding was more analytical and sought to identify concepts and then categories.[69] Concepts were derived from the data to group similar events and actions/interactions. Categories are more abstract terms that build a major theme from the underpinning concepts.[70] By coding for concepts and categories, I identified how patterns/themes emerged in the data. A list of all second cycle concepts and categories applied to the data in the study is set out in Appendix 2.

64 ibid 119. A pilot test of coding choices was conducted using a randomly chosen decision to assess the possibilities of the code.

65 All cases were coded using the electronic PDF version available on the FWC Online Database. On the advantages of using a combination of manual coding and electronic coding software, see Carmel Maher and others, 'Ensuring Rigor in Qualitative Data Analysis: A Design Research Approach to Coding Combining NVivo With Traditional Material Methods' (2018) 17 International Journal of Qualitative Methods 1.

66 Corbin and Strauss (n 63) 11.

67 ibid 12.

68 Eg, many of the codes were concerned with experiences that related to notice, proof, information, and advocacy.

69 Saldaña (n 50) 885–87.

70 Corbin and Strauss (n 63) 113–21.

IV Findings

The findings about respondents' recounted views and experiences during workplace investigations from decisions in the study sample are organized in three parts and correlate to the three central stages of a workplace investigation. These stages are commencing the investigation, conducting the investigation (including information gathering and interviewing), and making findings and decisions to discipline a respondent.

A Commencing the investigation

Decisions in the study sample provide understanding about how respondents viewed and experienced being notified (or not) by their employer about the commencement of a workplace investigation, directed by their employer to ensure confidentiality, and directed by their employer to not attend the workplace during the investigation.[71]

(a) Notice regarding commencement of investigation

Most respondents in the sample of decisions discussed being told by their employer that it had commenced a workplace investigation. However, some respondents recounted that they had been unaware or unsure of whether their employer had commenced a workplace investigation into their conduct.[72] There were respondents who recounted that their employers had directed them to attend meetings where they were asked to respond to allegations of misconduct without notice, or with limited notice.[73]

Absence of notice that an investigation had commenced

There were some respondents in the study who described participating in informal discussions or inquiries about incidents in the workplace without knowing that the information they provided was for the purpose of a workplace investigation,[74] or would be later used for that purpose.[75] Some respondents recounted that their employers described these discussions as 'information gathering' sessions,[76] 'informal discussion[s]',[77] 'walk/talk' sessions,[78] 'fact finding exercise[s]',[79] or 'mediation[s]',[80]

[71] This is often described in decisions as a 'suspension' of the employee from work during the investigation.

[72] This sub-group comprised thirty-seven decisions.

[73] This sub-group comprised seventy-five decisions.

[74] See, eg, *Barber-Fleming v Billi Australia Pty Ltd* [2020] FWC 6029 [58] (Cambridge C) (written evidence, summarized); *Linfox Armaguard Pty Ltd v Symes* [2018] FWC 7142 [45] (Ashbury DP) (verbal submission, summarized).

[75] See, eg, *Moylan v Gosnells Golf Club Inc* [2020] FWC 3130 [35]–[38] (Beaumont DP) (written witness statement, summarized); *Steel v Hitachi Power Tools Australia Pty Ltd* [2019] FWC 1195, [118] (Sams DP) (verbal evidence, summarized).

[76] See *Fisher v Cabra-Vale Ex-Active Servicemen's Club Ltd* [2020] FWC 5703 [72] (Riordan C) (written witness statement, summarized); *Symes* (n 74) [44] (verbal evidence, summarized).

[77] *Steel* (n 75) [118] (verbal evidence, summarized).

[78] *Natoli v Envision Employment Services* [2018] FWC 4034 [115] (Cribb C) (verbal evidence, summarized).

[79] *Waite v Serco Australia Pty Ltd* [2018] FWC 3113 [87] (Ashbury DP) (verbal evidence, summarized).

[80] *Johns v Zone RV Pty Ltd* [2020] FWC 5049 [195] (Simpson C) (verbal evidence, summarized).

rather than investigation interviews. For example, one decision set out the following summary, by a Member of the FWC, of a worker's recounted experience of an 'informal' meeting:

> [the employee] said that he was not advised of any allegations in advance of the 15 July 2020 meeting, was not advised of his rights and did not know it was a meeting about possible disciplinary action to be taken against him. During that meeting the [employee] said he was asked a series of questions which he answered truthfully. He said that he was never given a copy of the recording or transcript of the interview. He said at no time was he advised that he was being investigated for possible fraud or bribery offences.[81]

There were respondents who stated that they did not get the opportunity to consider if they needed a support person prior to the discussion/meeting.[82]

There were also respondents who recounted that they were asked by their employers to attend a formal meeting but did not understand that they were participating in a meeting or discussion that was the start of a workplace investigation.[83] Some respondents said they refused to answer further questions,[84] or asked for meetings to be postponed.[85] Some respondents said that their employers refused their requests to leave meetings,[86] or that the investigator/manager insisted they answer questions.[87] For example, one worker said that he had told his manager 'he would rather put his statement in writing than answer the question verbally' and, in response, his manager had 'started to shout at him that he should answer the question'.[88]

Absence of notice to attend an interview

There were also respondents in the sample of decisions who stated that their employers gave them the allegations of misconduct and directed them to attend investigation interviews immediately or at short notice,[89] or only provided them with details of the allegations at the interview.[90] Respondents recounted being given very little

[81] *Katrib v Commonwealth Insurance Limited t/as CommInsure* [2020] FWC 6872 [145] (Bisset C) (verbal evidence, summarized).

[82] See, eg, *Eagland v BMW Melbourne Pty Ltd* [2018] FWC 649 [54], [98] (Harper-Greenwell C) (written witness statement, summarized); *Allen v Kandeena Pty Ltd* [2020] FWC 761 [51] (Hunt C) (written/verbal statements, summarized).

[83] See, eg, *Akpey v Perth Re Pty Ltd* [2018] FWC 5699 [11] (Beaumont DP) (verbal evidence, summarized); *Fisher* (n 76).

[84] See, eg, *Akpey* (n 83) [11] (verbal witness evidence, summarized); *Pickering v Linfox Australia Pty Ltd* [2020] FWC 6595 [21] (McKenna C) (verbal evidence, summarized).

[85] *McCouaig v Colliers International (SA) Pty Ltd* [2019] FWC 1517 [83] (written evidence, summarized/quoted).

[86] *Akpey* (n 83) [11] (verbal evidence, summarized); *McCouaig* (n 85) [84] (written evidence, summarized/quoted); *Pickering* (n 84) [21] (written submissions and evidence, summarized).

[87] *Pickering* (n 84) [21] (written submissions and evidence, summarized).

[88] *Akpey* (n 83) [11] (verbal evidence, summarized).

[89] See, eg, *Puszka v Ryan Wilks Pty Ltd* [2019] FWC 1132 [21] (Cambridge C) (written submissions, summarized); *Waite* (n 79) [54] (written statement and evidence, summarized); *Ward v TRG Administration Pty Ltd* [2018] FWC 1475 [64] (Asbury DP) (verbal evidence, summarized).

[90] *Waite* (n 79) [54] (verbal evidence, summarized); *Kandeena* (n 82) [52] (verbal evidence, summarized).

information about the allegations in these circumstances.[91] Some respondents used the word 'ambush' to describe these experiences.[92] For example, one respondent said that her employer had only told her she was required to attend a meeting about concerns regarding 'a business account' and her employer did not provide her with any information about allegations of misconduct before the meeting. At the meeting, the respondent said she was required to answer questions for about 40 minutes, where it was put to her that she had breached the employer's policies, and she was asked to respond to documents. The respondent submitted 'she was very upset and emotional at the time, and this caused her to be confused and uncertain about what was being put to her'.[93] Another respondent stated she had declined to attend an interview with her manager about the investigation because she had not been given any details of the allegations.[94]

(b) Directions regarding confidentiality

Respondents in the sample of decisions sometimes referred to directions from their employers to maintain confidentiality over the investigation and/or have no contact with other workers, access to emails or documents, or the workplace generally.[95] Some respondents said that they did not comply with employers' directions regarding confidentiality because they had wanted to collect relevant evidence to respond to allegations, and this led to warnings or disciplinary action.[96] There were respondents who recounted how managers had not kept details of the investigation into their alleged misconduct confidential.[97] For example, one respondent stated that her manager had shared a letter setting out allegations, and her response, with three other managers who she believed were involved in the investigation, and this left her 'upset'.[98]

(c) Directions not to perform work

Respondents in the sample who were directed by their employers not to perform work during the workplace investigation sometimes said that their employers did

[91] See, eg, *Edwards v Litchfield Shire* [2019] FWC 6660 [103] (written evidence, summarized); *Fisher* (n 76) [36] (written statement, summarized/quoted); *Jarmain v Linfox Armaguard Pty Ltd* [2018] FWC 3255 [62] (Cambridge C) (verbal evidence, summarized).

[92] See, eg, *McCouaig* (n 85) [83] (verbal and written evidence, quoted and summarized); *Horan v Tren Trading Pty Ltd* [2019] FWC 3249 [22] (Sams DP) (verbal evidence, quoted); *Johns* (n 80) [195] (verbal evidence, summarized).

[93] *Snell v Bendigo and Adelaide Bank Ltd* [2019] FWC 8050 [11]–[12] (Gregory C) (written statement, summarized).

[94] *Horan* (n 92) [22] (verbal evidence, summarized).

[95] This sub-group comprised eight decisions; employer directions regarding confidentiality were quoted or summarized in twenty-nine decisions. See, eg, *Andrawos v MyBudget Pty Ltd* [2018] FWC 4288 [220] (Anderson DP) (written submissions, summarized); *Bird v BHP Coal Pty Ltd* [2019] FWC 7444 [91] (Ashbury DP) (written statement and evidence, summarized); *Chileshe v EnergyAustralia Pty Ltd* [2019] FWC 7622 [16] (Millhouse DP) (written statement and evidence, summarized). Some workers stated they were asked to sign confidentiality agreements, see, eg, *Groza v Toll Transport Pty Ltd* [2020] FWC 5838 [38] (Yilmaz C) (written submissions, summarized).

[96] See, eg, *Mazi v Arcare Pty Ltd* [2020] FWC 6172 [102] (Spencer C) (verbal evidence, summarized); *Chileshe* (n 95) [16] (written evidence, summarized).

[97] See, eg, *Jeffs v Qantas Ground Services Pty Ltd* [2019] FWC 7963 [125] (Beaumont DP) (verbal evidence, summarized); *Singh v Crown Melbourne Ltd* [2020] FWC 1927 [19] (Young DP) (written evidence, summarized); *Waite* (n 79) [38] (verbal evidence, summarized).

[98] *Jeffs* (n 97) [89], [127] (verbal evidence, summarized).

not communicate the reason for the direction with them.[99] For example, respondents noted that their employers had directed them not to perform work without specifying their duties or obligations while they were not at work,[100] or who they could speak to or contact during the investigation.[101] Other workers said that they were not sure whether they would be paid while they were directed not to perform work.[102]

There were respondents who also described the emotions that they felt because of the way their employer had directed them not to perform work during a workplace investigation.[103] Some said they felt distressed at how their managers communicated the direction.[104] For example, one respondent described the experience in the following way:

> I was humiliated . . . being escorted up to my floor and out of the building . . . when I tried to tell Kerry yesterday she shut me down . . . I was not even allowed to express my thoughts, my fears, my feelings.[105]

Another respondent stated that her manager had advised her that an investigation had commenced into a 'business account' she had worked on and had immediately escorted her from the premises in front of customers and clients. The respondent stated, '[t]his whole incident was highly distressing, unnecessary and humiliating for me'.[106]

B Conducting the investigation

Decisions in the study sample also provide insights regarding how respondents viewed and experienced: seeking information about the process; seeking information about the allegations; asking their employers for information about time frames and any delays that might arise; participating in an interview or other meetings with the employer; and facing obstacles that impeded their participation in the interview/meeting based on their needs and/or abilities.

(a) Communication about the process

Some respondents in the sample of decisions recounted that they struggled to access information from their employers about the process that the employer would follow during the workplace investigation and/or copies of applicable policies and procedures.

[99] This sub-group comprised twelve decisions.
[100] *Horan* (n 92) [16] (verbal witness evidence, summarized).
[101] *Andrawos* (n 95) [188] (verbal evidence, summarized).
[102] See, eg, *Paech v Hage Retail Group* [2019] FWC 6487 [14] (Platt C) (written evidence, summarized); *Steffens v Greenmountain Food Processing Pty Ltd* [2020] FWC 1281 [90] (written evidence, quoted).
[103] This sub-group comprised eleven decisions.
[104] *Snell* (n 93) [24] (written submissions, summarized).
[105] *Andrawos* (n 95) [81] (written statement, quoted).
[106] *Snell* (n 93) [9] (witness statement, summarized).

Information about the process

There were respondents who recounted poor communication by employers about the process of investigation.[107] Some respondents stated that their employers had provided them with unclear information,[108] and other respondents recounted that their employers had given them information that they later learned was incorrect,[109] or misleading.[110] For example, one respondent said her employer had not explained the import of the workplace investigation process or potential disciplinary consequences and so she did not to bring a support person to a meeting where the employer presented the findings of the investigation. She said, 'because I wasn't aware of what that meeting was for and nothing like that. I wasn't aware, because I've never, like, been fired before, that I was allowed to have a support person, like, by my choice. So therefore I didn't take anyone there.'[111]

Another respondent stated that her employer told her she would soon be 'contacted to verify her story'. The respondent relied on this information, but ultimately, she did not get the opportunity to tell her side of the story before the employer dismissed her for misconduct.[112]

Respondents in the sample recounted how they had felt uncertainty regarding the investigation process and how this had caused them to feel distress or concern.[113] There were respondents who said that it was the employer's approach to the process that had impacted them, as separate from the outcome.[114] For example, one respondent stated that the 'whole [investigation] process and the manner in which it was handled by [the employer] was unfair. At various times I felt ambushed by what was happening and by the changing parameters of what was, or was not, required of me.'[115] Respondents described feeling concerned or overwhelmed by processes that they regarded as inconsistent or unclear.[116]

[107] This sub-group comprised sixteen decisions.

[108] See, eg, *Bartlett v Ingleburn Bus Services Pty Ltd* [2020] FWC 2914 [6] (witness statements, summarized); *Perich v Hanson Construction Materials Pty Ltd* [2018] FWC 1336 [10] (Spencer C) (verbal submission, summarized); *Westlake v Illawarra Coal Holdings Pty Ltd* [2020] FWC 2504 [22] (Riordan C) (written evidence, summarized). In these decisions, respondents recounted that their employers did not properly or fully explain that an outcome of the investigation could be that they would be dismissed.

[109] See, eg, *Bajelis v Reserve Bank of Australia* [2020] FWC 3740 [31] (Cross DP) (verbal evidence, summarized).

[110] See, eg, *Okoye v SACARE Supported Accommodation and Care Services* [2020] FWC 704 [85] (Anderson DP) (verbal evidence, summarized); *Waite* (n 79) [87] (verbal evidence, summarized); *Facchin v Tasmanian Networks Pty Ltd* [2020] FWC 2796 [62] (Barclay DP) (verbal evidence, summarized).

[111] *Ford v Marlau Nominees Pty Ltd* [2019] FWC 4178 [29] (Wilson C) (verbal evidence, summarized and quoted). See, eg, *Johns* (n 80) [195] (verbal submissions, summarized and quoted); *McCouaig* (n 85) [82] (written submission and evidence, summarized).

[112] *Okoye* (n 110) [85] (verbal evidence, summarized).

[113] See, eg, *Hill v Cobham Aviation Services Pty Ltd* [2019] FWC 7875 [165] (Anderson DP) (witness statement, summarized and quoted); *Siminsky v Gunlake Concrete NSW Pty Ltd* [2019] FWC 2429 [40] (Bull DP) (verbal evidence, quoted).

[114] See, eg, *Siminsky* (n 113) [14], [40] (verbal evidence, quoted); *Perich* (n 108) [13] (written submissions, quoted); *Cahill v Sydney Trains* [2020] FWC 6064 [140] (McKenna C) (verbal evidence, summarized).

[115] *Weatherall v Elevate Education Pty Ltd* [2020] FWC 6143 [45] (Sams DP) (verbal evidence, summarized and quoted).

[116] *Andrawos* (n 95) [187]–[190] (written evidence, summarized).

Access to policies and procedures

Some respondents in the sample of decisions stated that they had asked their employers to give them copies of relevant policies or procedures about the investigation process but their employers did not do so, or only did so after a long delay.[117] Some respondents recounted that they made multiple requests to their employers,[118] or refused to respond to allegations until their employers had responded to the request.[119] There were respondents who stated that their employers did give them information about the policies and procedures after they had made repeated requests.[120]

Information about time frames

Respondents in the sample described poor communication by employers regarding time frames and the reason for delays, and some recounted that the poor communication added to feelings of stress and/or impacted on their ability to recall key events later on.[121] For example, one respondent stated that he felt stressed by the process and that the stress was worsened by his employer leading him to understand the investigation would take 'much less time' than it did.[122] Another respondent stated that she had lodged an internal grievance about delays in the workplace investigation process and 'a deficit in the communication that was provided to her' and her employer later provided an apology.[123] Despite the apology, the respondent stated that she could not recall details of key events, when asked at an interview, because of 'the passage of time'.[124]

Respondents who were directed by their employers not to perform work during the workplace investigation recounted further impacts arising from delays and poor communication about time frames. It was not always expressly stated in the decisions whether the respondents were paid when they were directed to stand down from performing work. Respondents stated that they experienced stress and distress because of the long and uncertain duration of their absence from the workplace. Respondents spoke about feeling 'stress[ed]' by the experience of months-long absences.[125] A respondent described the investigation as being 'strung out' and feeling that she was 'in limbo'.[126] Another respondent who had been directed by her employer not to perform

[117] This sub-group comprised six decisions. See, eg, *Bird* (n 95) [94] (verbal evidence, summarized and quoted); *Katrib* (n 81) [151]–[152] (written and verbal evidence, summarized); *Kandeena* (n 82) [52] (verbal evidence, summarized).

[118] See, eg, *Katrib* (n 81) [151]–[152] (written and verbal evidence, summarized).

[119] See, eg, *Law v Groote Eylandt Mining Company Pty Ltd* [2018] FWC 1824 [32] (Asbury DP) (verbal evidence, quoted summarized).

[120] Eg, *Katrib* (n 81) [152] (verbal evidence summarized).

[121] This sub-group comprised ten decisions. Eg, *Lecaude v Westpac Banking Corporation* [2018] FWC 1969 [48] (Williams C) (written witness statement, attachment, summarized); *Boyle v BHP Coal Pty Ltd* [2020] FWC 1080 [52] (Hunt C) (verbal evidence, summarized).

[122] *Gigney v Qantas Airways Ltd* [2018] FWC 1352 [180] (Bissett C) (verbal evidence, summarized).

[123] *Major v Resilience Solutions Pty Ltd* [2018] FWC 660 [27] (Beaumont DP) (written and verbal evidence, summarized).

[124] ibid [27] (written and verbal evidence, summarized).

[125] See, eg, *Gigney* (n 122) [180] (Johns C) (verbal evidence, summarized); *Beltrame v Essential Energy* [2019] FWC 2592 [8] (witness statement and evidence, summarized).

[126] *Hay v Ambulance Victoria* [2020] FWC 2193 [317] (Young DP) (verbal evidence, quoted).

work said the long duration of the investigation impacted on his recollection of key events, and he was placed under 'stress . . . as a consequence of the process adopted'.[127]

(b) Access to information about the allegations

Respondents in the sample of decisions recounted a range of experiences regarding responding to allegations of misconduct, either in writing or at an interview with an investigator. While some respondents recounted how their employers provided detailed information about allegations and available evidence, other respondents spoke about difficulties in obtaining details about the allegations or accessing evidence from their employers. Respondents also spoke about employers that provided them with inconsistent material about the allegations and/or changed the content or number of allegations during the investigation.

Details about the allegations

Some respondents stated that their employers provided them with vague, incomplete, or insufficient information about the allegations of misconduct and/or did not explain how alleged conduct contravened a policy, direction, or requirement of employment.[128] Respondents recounted that they had to ask their managers or HRM personnel for further details, supporting documents, or records in order to properly respond to allegations.[129] A few respondents who asked for more details said that their employers refused or ignored their requests.[130] For example, one worker said his manager had told him that he would get details about the allegations against him at a meeting, but when the respondent arrived at the meeting 'no further information was provided about the details of the allegations, or about the evidence relied upon to substantiate those claims'. Instead, his manager asked him to respond to a 'show cause notice'.[131] Other respondents stated that details were only provided at interviews and not beforehand, and they were required to immediately respond.[132]

Evidence that supports or refutes the allegations

Respondents in the sample recounted concerns or challenges associated with gaining access to evidence relevant to the allegations.[133] Some respondents said that their

[127] *Cowper v St Josephs Flexible Learning Centre* [2019] FWC 6630 [48] (Gregory C) (written and verbal evidence, summarized).

[128] This sub-group comprised twenty-eight decisions. See, eg, *Turland v Yass Valley Aged Care Ltd* [2020] FWC 843 [70] (Kovacic DP) (written submissions, summarized); *Stevens v ISS Property Services Pty Ltd* [2020] FWC 1340 [96] (Asbury DP) (written evidence, summarized).

[129] See, eg, *Kaur v Moorditch Gurlongga Assoc* [2019] FWC 5574 [36] (Williams C) (written submissions, summarized); *Lakew v MSS Security Pty Ltd* [2019] FWC 4462 [3] (Colman C) (verbal submissions, summarized).

[130] See, eg, *Cowper* (n 127) [23], [26] (written evidence, summarized); *Kapoor v Teleperformance Australia* [2018] FWC 4520 [13] (verbal evidence, summarized).

[131] *Cowper* (n 127) [23] (written evidence, summarized). A 'show cause notice' is a letter that sets out findings of misconduct and asks the employee to make submissions on why the employee should not be dismissed.

[132] *Emery v City of Stirling* [2018] FWC 6853 [203] (Bissett C) (written submissions, summarized).

[133] See, eg, *Cahill* (n 114) [27] (written evidence, quoted and summarized); *Edwards* (n 91) [31] (written submissions, summarized).

ability to access evidence was decided by employer discretion rather than a policy.[134] Respondents also spoke about employers who had refused or ignored their requests to access evidence or information,[135] such as witness statements,[136] incident reports,[137] or investigation reports.[138] For example, one respondent stated that he had repeatedly asked his employer for 'statements of witnesses, CCTV footage or any other evidence' that related to the allegations of misconduct against him, but his employer refused to provide any of these records to him. The investigator relied upon these records to make findings that the allegations were proven even though the respondent had not seen them.[139] Other respondents stated that their employers gave them extracts or summaries of documents to read, rather than access to whole documents or copies of them, but the extracts were hard to understand.[140]

Respondents in the decisions recounted that they did not know that their employers possessed more detailed, or additional, evidence in relation to the allegations until after the investigator had made findings.[141] Some respondents stated that they had responded to allegations based on the evidence their employer had given them, but at the hearing of their unfair dismissal claim, the employer had produced a broader body of evidence.[142] For example, one respondent stated that she 'responded as best she could in relation to the allegation' but that she remained unaware of its 'precise nature' because the records she had been provided were limited and unclear.[143] At the hearing, full records (CCTV footage and transaction records) were provided to the respondent and these enabled her to provide a more detailed response.[144]

The content and number of allegations

Some respondents in the sample also stated that their employers had set out allegations inconsistently between documents,[145] or had changed the content or number of allegations over time.[146] Some respondents stated that their employers added

[134] Terms of enterprise agreements or applicable policies and procedures can also affect or shape employers' approaches to providing access to evidence.

[135] See, eg, *Milad v Melbourne Health* [2020] FWC 1939 [36] (verbal and written evidence, summarized); *Ayres v City of Kingston* [2018] FWC 4291 [41] (verbal evidence, summarized).

[136] *Turland* (n 128) [21] (witness statement, summarized).

[137] *Boyle* (n 121) [223] (written submissions, summarized).

[138] *Nemcic v Australian Electoral Commission* [2018] FWC 5645 [312] (Anderson DP) (written submissions, summarized).

[139] *Thomas v Virgin Australia Airlines Pty Ltd* [2019] FWC 4464 [61] (Sams DP) (written submissions, summarized).

[140] See, eg, *Turland* (n 128) [21] (witness statement, summarized); *Vai v ALDI Stores* [2018] FWC 4118 [13] (Gregory C) (verbal evidence, summarized).

[141] See, eg, *Andrawos* (n 95) [210] (witness statement, summarized); *Pericich* (n 108) [13] (written submissions, summarized).

[142] See, eg, *Kezic v Brand Developers (Aus) Pty Ltd* [2019] FWC 7889 [13] (Gregory C) (verbal evidence, summarized); *Thomas v Virgin* (n 139) [61] (written and verbal submissions, summarized).

[143] *Edwards* (n 91) [31], [82] (verbal evidence, summarized).

[144] *Puth v Precision Valve Australia Pty Ltd* [2020] FWC 7027 [56] (Sams DP) (verbal evidence, quoted and summarized).

[145] See, eg, *Nemcic* (n 138) [296] (written submissions, summarized).

[146] This sub-group comprised eleven decisions. See, eg, *Lupson v Australian Pacific Airports (Melbourne) Pty Ltd* [2020] FWC 6721 [86] (Mansini DP) (verbal evidence, quoted); *Tainsh v Toyota Motor Corporation Australia Ltd* [2018] FWC 4192 [189], [190] (Harper-Greenwell C) (written evidence, summarized).

trivial and ancillary allegations to the list,[147] added historical complaints,[148] or raised additional allegations at the interview with the investigator.[149] For example, one respondent stated that he had been told about some allegations against him before a scheduled interview but was then 'ambushed' by a question that related to a new allegation when he attended the interview. He said this affected his ability to respond as it made him feel 'under pressure . . . to defend himself'.[150] Another respondent said he experienced 'distress and embarrassment' when an investigator unexpectedly raised a new allegation that he had been storing child pornography in emails on a work computer during an interview.[151] The respondent recounted that the allegation was presented unexpectedly, and 'the emails were quickly 'fanned' at [the worker and his support person] during the meeting and they were not given copies of the emails at that time'.[152]

(c) Planning for interview, interview process, and process in other meetings

Respondents in the sample of decisions recounted how they experienced planning for the interview with the investigator, the interview process with the investigator and the process in other meetings, and the accuracy of employers' records of interview.

Planning for the interview

Respondents in the sample of decisions provided various accounts regarding how their employers communicated plans for holding an interview to respond to allegations of misconduct.[153] Some respondents stated that managers and HRM personnel were inflexible regarding their requests to change or alter plans. For example, respondents stated that their employers had refused to accept a written response to allegations rather than a verbal response at an interview,[154] to allow a legal representative to attend the interview,[155] or to allow postponement of an interview, such as to allow more time for the worker to prepare.[156] Respondents also said that employers provided them with support persons, rather than allowing them to bring a support person or representative of their choice.[157]

[147] See, eg, *Finn v Gippsland & East Gippsland Aboriginal Co-Operative Ltd* [2019] FWC 1506 [34] (Hamilton DP) (written statement, quoted and summarized); *Lee v Alexandria Imex Pty Ltd* [2020] FWC 4837 [97] (Asbury DP) (written submissions, summarized).

[148] *Lupson* (n 146) [86] (written submissions, quoted and summarized); *Steffens* (n 102) [139] (Simpson C) (verbal evidence, summarized).

[149] See, eg, *Singh v Sydney Trains* [2019] FWC 182 [292] (Sams DP) (written submissions, summarized); *Bajelis* (n 109) [199] (evidence, quoted and summarized).

[150] *Kabidi v Metro Trains Melbourne Pty Ltd* [2020] FWC 6941 [71] (Young DP) (written submissions, quoted and summarized).

[151] *Lupson* (n 146) [60] (verbal evidence, summarized and quoted). See also *Horan* (n 92) [30] (written statement, summarized).

[152] *Lupson* (n 146) [60] (verbal evidence, summarized and quoted).

[153] This sub-group comprised seventeen decisions.

[154] *Akpey* (n 83) [11] (verbal witness evidence, summarized).

[155] *Mazi* (n 96) [33] (written witness statement, summarized).

[156] ibid (written witness statement, summarized); *Nash v Bacchus Marsh Coaches Pty Ltd* (2018) 347 FWC [39] (Colman DP) (written witness statement, summarized).

[157] *Jarmain* (n 91) [63] (verbal evidence, summarized).

The interview with the investigator

Some respondents recounted how they experienced the interview with an investigator or with their manager. There were respondents who described feelings of 'shock',[158] 'agitat[ion]',[159] 'confusion' and 'anxiety',[160] 'stress',[161] distress,[162] or of being 'in tears and highly emotional'[163] before, or during, interviews or other meetings during investigations.[164] Respondents stated that these feelings affected their ability to answer questions fully and accurately.[165] For example, one respondent stated that his response to questions was that of a person 'under pressure . . . and trying to defend himself . . . [it] was an automatic response of a person under stress . . . '[166] Another respondent stated that an investigator continued with an interview while they were upset and crying.[167]

Respondents also recounted participating in interviews or meetings during an investigation in which they viewed the conduct of investigators or managers as oppressive or unprofessional. Specifically, respondents spoke of investigators or managers who were 'aggressive',[168] 'discourteous',[169] 'unprofessional',[170] or 'intimidating'[171] during interviews. Respondents said they had become 'upset' or 'emotional' in response to an investigator's approach to asking questions.[172] One respondent stated that the investigator inferred that she had a hostile demeanour in a meeting but instead she had felt 'very concerned at the nature of the meeting'.[173] Another respondent recounted that the investigator had threatened him with dismissal if he 'refused to answer a question or left the interview early'.[174]

Record of interview

There were respondents in the sample of decisions who recounted that records that had been produced by their employer during workplace investigations were inaccurate, but

[158] *Cahill* (n 114) [159] (verbal evidence, summarized); *Okoye* (n 110) [33], [34] (verbal evidence, summarized).

[159] *McCouaig* (n 85) [88] (verbal evidence, summarized).

[160] *Pickering* (n 84) [22] (verbal evidence, quoted); *Plesiotis v Huhtamaki Australia Pty Ltd* [2020] FWC 120 [21] (Lee C) (witness statement, quoted).

[161] *Kabidi* (n 150) [71] (verbal evidence, summarized); *McCouaig* (n 85) [88] (verbal evidence, summarized); *Ryan v Orbitz Elevators Pty Ltd* [2019] FWC 8445 [85] (Simpson C) (verbal evidence, summarized).

[162] *Kezic* (n 142) [11] (Gregory C) (witness statement, summarized).

[163] *Snell* (n 93) [24] (witness statement, summarized). See also *Akpey* (n 83) [15] (written evidence, summarized); *Cahill* (n 114) [144] (verbal evidence, quoted and summarized).

[164] This sub-group comprised sixty-five decisions.

[165] See, eg, *Snell* (n 93) [107] (witness statement, summarized); *Williams v Viridian Glass Limited* [2020] FWC 250 [67] (verbal submissions, summarized).

[166] *Kabidi* (n 150) [71] (verbal evidence, summarized).

[167] *Nash* (n 156) [39] (written witness statement, summarized).

[168] *Lautaimi v Pabs Furniture Rentals Pty Ltd* [2020] FWC 3819 [12] (Sams DP) (verbal evidence, summarized and quoted).

[169] *Abarra* (n 17) [28] (witness statement, summarized).

[170] *Addo v Safe Places Community Services Ltd* [2020] FWC 3858 [35] (Spencer C) (witness statements, summarized).

[171] *Akpey* (n 83) [47] (verbal evidence, summarized and quoted); *Groza* (n 95) [10] (written submissions, summarized).

[172] *Yang v FCS Business Service Pty Ltd* [2020] FWC 4560 [19] (Cambridge C) (verbal evidence, summarized); *Nash* (n 156) [39] (witness statement, summarized).

[173] *Addo* (n 170) [20] (witness statements, summarized).

[174] *Abarra* (n 17) [28] (verbal evidence, summarized).

that they had been unable to correct the record at the time.[175] Respondents recounted concerns about the accuracy of documents including transcripts of interviews,[176] notes of interviews,[177] attributed quotes in summaries of findings,[178] and investigation reports,[179] as part of their unfair dismissal applications. For example, one respondent stated that her employer had finalized a 'record of interview' that set out a preamble, printed questions, and the investigator's handwritten notes of her answers that were inaccurate. The respondent said she had not been read the preamble at the interview and the questions, and her answers, provided at the interview had differed from those recorded. The respondent said that the investigator had not shown her the record (or asked her to confirm it was correct) at the conclusion of the interview or afterwards.[180] Other respondents described how employers had not provided them with the written records of interview for review or correction and, due to this, they could not correct errors.[181]

(d) Accommodation of respondents' needs

There were respondents who recounted situations where they did not think their employer accommodated their needs or abilities during a workplace investigation.[182] Some respondents in the sample of decisions stated that they struggled to answer questions and understand the documents provided to them when interviewed by investigators. In some decisions, respondents said that English was not the language they mainly spoke at home and that the investigator did not take this into account when conducting an interview, such as by providing an interpreter.[183] For example, one respondent submitted (via his representative) that 'the fact that English is not his first language caused some confusion in terms of the responses that he provided at different times during the investigation.'[184] Another respondent stated that he had been provided with notes of an interview that recorded that he 'struggle[d] to understand' questions and that the interviewer 'accepted that at least to a degree [the worker] has difficulties with the English language.'[185]

In other decisions, respondents referred to characteristics or circumstances that they experienced and that they asserted were not accommodated by employers and investigators. These included dyslexia,[186] illness,[187] autism spectrum disorder,[188]

[175] This sub-group comprised fifteen decisions. See, eg, *Cowper* (n 127) [23] (written evidence, summarized); *Kapoor* (n 130) [9] (verbal evidence, summarized).

[176] See, eg, *Clarke v Toll Transport Pty Ltd* [2019] FWC 606 [198] (Hunt C) (verbal evidence, quoted and summarized); *Cowper* (n 127) [23] (written evidence, summarized).

[177] See, eg, *Fernandopulle v Taylors Business Pty Ltd* [2018] FWC 3557 [37] (Wilson C) (verbal evidence, summarized); *Kapoor* (n 130) [8]–[9] (verbal evidence, summarized).

[178] *Cowper* (n 127) [22] (written statement, summarized and quoted).

[179] ibid [23], [53] (written statement, summarized and quoted).

[180] *Kapoor* (n 130) [13] (verbal evidence, summarized).

[181] See, eg, *Hatch v WesTrac Pty Ltd* [2020] FWC 5729 [41] (Saunders DP) (written evidence, summarized); *Kapoor* (n 130) [8] (verbal evidence, summarized).

[182] This sub-group comprised fourteen decisions.

[183] See, eg, *Kabidi* (n 150) [71] (Young DP) (written submissions, summarized); *Thein v Melbourne Health* [2020] FWC 3628 [52] (Wilson C) (verbal evidence, summarized).

[184] *Do v MSS Security Pty Ltd* [2019] FWC 8010 [92] (Gregory C) (verbal evidence summarized).

[185] *Thein* (n 183) [52] (verbal evidence, summarized).

[186] *Barber-Fleming* (n 74) [26]–[27] (verbal submissions, summarized).

[187] *Mammarella v Department of Parliamentary Services* [2019] FWC 6340 [65], [68] (Harper-Greenwell C) (verbal submissions, summarized).

[188] *Prosser v Ziegam Pty Ltd* [2019] FWC 676 [76] (Simpson C) (verbal evidence, summarized).

'family responsibilities',[189] and 'medical and compassionate issues'.[190] For example, one decision noted that a respondent with dyslexia described a meeting where his manager:

> did not provide [him] with an opportunity to take the document [listing credit card transactions] away and to consider it carefully but instead compelled [him] to make an immediate decision and provide answers about the identified transactions.[191]

In another decision, a respondent said that her employer had considered her history of being a victim of domestic violence (and related mental health) to be relevant to the investigation and subsequent findings, without putting her on notice about these matters.[192]

The decisions include accounts by respondents that they found the workplace investigation process stressful or challenging.[193] Few decisions specifically referred to how employers provided support for respondents' mental wellbeing during a workplace investigation. There were decisions that referred to offers for workers to access Employee Assistance Programs (EAPs) during workplace investigations,[194] but only two respondents in the sample of decisions expressly stated that they used one of these programs, although others may have done so but did not disclose it.[195]

C Making findings and decisions to discipline

Respondents in the sample provided a range of perspectives regarding the approach taken by the investigators to making findings. Respondents expressed concern about how investigators and managers made findings,[196] and some stated that the manager/investigator had not seemed interested in their responses to the allegations at the interview and already appeared to have decided the findings. For example, respondents described interviews where the outcome seemed predetermined,[197] the manager/investigator had already made findings,[198] the interview was very brief,[199]

[189] *Paech* (n 102) [11], [62] (written evidence, summarized).
[190] *Natoli* (n 78) [128] (written submissions, summarized).
[191] *Barber-Fleming* (n 74) [26]-[27] (written statement, summarized).
[192] *Murphy v ECEC Management Pty Ltd* [2019] FWC 3169 [43]–[44] (McKinnon C) (verbal evidence, summarized).
[193] This sub-group comprised twenty decisions.
[194] This sub-group comprised seventeen decisions.
[195] *Elliot v Australian Rail Track Corporation Ltd* [2019] FWC 3786, [37]; *Kordek v Marsh Pty Ltd* (2020) 6972 FWC [48].
[196] This sub-group comprised nineteen decisions.
[197] See, eg, *Kandeena* (n 82) [52] (verbal evidence, summarized); *Beltrame* (n 125) [21] (written submissions, summarized).
[198] See, eg, *Bartlett v Ingleburn* (n 108) [6] (written witness statement, summarized); *Kandeena* (n 82) [51]–[52] (verbal evidence, summarized).
[199] See, eg, *Milad* (n 135) [36] (verbal and written evidence, summarized); *Gomes v Gemela Pty Ltd* [2019] FWC 4222 [11] (Bissett C) (verbal evidence, summarized and quoted).

and the manager/investigator had been dismissive of the worker's responses.[200] One respondent stated that the employer had asked him to resign during the interview.[201] Another respondent recounted that she was in the process of responding to an allegation when findings were made and her employer dismissed her.[202]

There were respondents who described how they felt or responded when their employer told them of the decision to dismiss them based on the findings of the investigation. Some respondents stated that they felt upset or distressed because they did not understand that dismissal was a potential outcome of the investigation process.[203] Specifically, respondents recounted emotional reactions to being dismissed at the conclusion of workplace investigations where they had been initially told by their managers that dismissal was not a possible outcome, or not a likely outcome, of the process.[204] For example, the Member in one decision described the respondent's evidence as follows:

> The applicant did not . . . seriously envisage that he could be dismissed for what had occurred when he was on holidays . . . The applicant felt completely 'blindsided' by the advice he was given; the applicant was to describe in his evidence that this was like 'Pearl Harbour' to him in its element of surprise.[205]

Some respondents recounted how their employers combined their first interview with the investigator with a 'show cause' discussion and decision to dismiss.[206]

Respondents also told the FWC that their employer had decided to dismiss them based on findings about their behaviour and conduct during the workplace investigation, rather than because of the original allegations of misconduct.[207] Respondents described how employers relied on conduct such as breaches of directions to maintain confidentiality during the workplace investigation,[208] and unprofessional/disrespectful conduct during interviews with the investigator,[209] to justify dismissal. One respondent stated that he did not know that his employer had decided to dismiss him because it had found he was dishonest during the investigation, and he had not been given a chance to respond to this finding.[210]

[200] *Addo* (n 170) [35] (witness statements, summarized); *Betar v Cricks Sunshine Coast* [2019] FWC 6547 [42]–[43] (Spencer C) (written submissions, summarized).

[201] *Boyce v Ikon Administration Pty Ltd* [2019] FWC 4763 [41] (Wilson C) (verbal witness evidence, quote). See also *Moylan* (n 75) [43] (verbal submissions, summarized).

[202] *Lee* (n 147) [91] (written submissions, summarized).

[203] This sub-group comprised thirteen decisions.

[204] See, eg, *Westlake* (n 108) [22] (written evidence, summarized); *Cahill* (n 114) [140] (verbal evidence, summarized and quoted).

[205] *Cahill* (n 114) [140] (verbal evidence, summarized).

[206] *Bartlett v Ingleburn* (n 108) [6] (written witness statement, summarized).

[207] This sub-group comprised six decisions.

[208] *Mazi* (n 96) [55] (written witness statement, summarized).

[209] *Boyle* (n 121) [220] (written witness statement, summarized).

[210] *Duggan v Metropolitan Fire and Emergency Services Board* [2018] FWC 4945 [194] (Masson DP) (written submissions, summarized).

V Themes and Implications for Justice for Respondents in Workplace Investigations

I discuss below the four central themes drawn from the findings and consider their implications for justice for respondents in workplace investigations.

A Informational asymmetry

Various findings coalesce around the theme of informational asymmetry between employers and respondents, about the process of the workplace investigation and the substance of the inquiry. There were respondents in the sample of decisions who felt concerned or disadvantaged because their employers did not provide them with relevant and/or timely information when commencing an investigation, while investigating, and when making findings and decisions on discipline. The findings shed new light on the extent to which a respondent might experience disadvantage or distress because of deficient communication by an employer about the process of a workplace investigation. The disadvantages discernible from respondents' accounts included being unprepared to answer allegations, unsupported or unrepresented at meetings, and unprepared or unable to respond to the findings of an investigation.

As shown in chapter 2, conducting a workplace investigation can be complex and uncertain for employers, and this might understandably affect the extent to which an employer can provide a respondent with specific and accurate information about the process or substance of an inquiry. Yet the findings highlight accounts from respondents, in which they recount experiences of employers withholding basic information, such as that a workplace investigation has commenced, or that the inquiry being conducted could result in the respondent's dismissal.

The theme of informational asymmetry reveals the extent to which discretionary managerial power governs workplace investigations. The respondents' accounts indicate power is amplified because trade unions are rarely involved as support people or advisors to respondents, and crucial information is distributed between multiple managerial representatives of the employer (eg information about the process, the allegations, or the outcome). Some respondents who recounted that they took steps to address informational asymmetry were sanctioned (eg disciplinary action for not complying with directions during the workplace investigation) or their efforts were unsuccessful (eg raising an internal complaint that resulted in a late apology).

Informational asymmetry during a workplace investigation is inconsistent with at least six of the nine elements of justice for respondents in workplace investigations, as developed in chapter 3. Specifically, informational asymmetry undermines:

- good faith performance of the contract of employment by the employer, including because informational asymmetry that is the result of deliberate or arbitrary employer conduct 'lacks due care to avoid or minimise adverse consequences' to the respondent;[211]

- dignified treatment of the respondent, including because informational asymmetry undermines respectful treatment of the respondent and can cause them distress;[212]
- a procedurally and substantively fair process that could result in the respondent's dismissal, including because informational asymmetry can potentially lead to a respondent being denied adequate information, notice or time to prepare a response to allegations;[213]
- workplace democracy, augmented by the mediation of the process through nominated representatives, including to the extent that informational asymmetry might result in a respondent being denied an opportunity to involve a support person or representative of their choice;[214]
- the elimination of risk to worker health and safety to the extent that informational asymmetry to the disadvantage of a respondent might cause or exacerbate mental harm to that respondent;[215] and
- effective dispute resolution to the extent that respondents' requests and complaints remained unresolved or unanswered.[216]

B Denial/minimization of respondent voice

Key findings are also underpinned by a theme of denial or minimization of respondent voice by employers during workplace investigations. Respondents' accounts of situations where employers denied them the support person of their choice or refused to allow them to bring a legal representative to a meeting exemplify this theme. More broadly, this theme is reflected in accounts by respondents about how they felt unable to tell the employer their side of the story completely or accurately. The sample of decisions includes examples where respondents described oppressive or perfunctory interviews with investigators, and inaccurate and uncorrected records of interview. Respondents recounted how they struggled to correct records of interviews.

The findings also highlight tension between employer directions to respondents to maintain confidentiality and the capacity of respondents to collect information or evidence to support their responses to allegations and give them voice. This issue involves a complex balancing of competing interests for employers. Some respondents

[211] *Russell v the Trustees of the Roman Catholic Church For the Archdiocese of Sydney* [2007] NSWLR 104 [117] (Rothman J). See also Joellen Riley, 'Good Faith Performance' in Mordy Bromberg and Mark Irving (eds), *Australian Charter of Employment Rights* (Hardie Grant Books 2007) 9.

[212] Greg Bamber and Bob Russell, 'Work with Dignity' in Mordy Bromberg and Mark Irving (eds), *Australian Charter of Employment Rights* (Hardie Grant Books 2007) 19.

[213] Marilyn Pittard, 'Protection from Unfair Dismissal' in Mordy Bromberg and Mark Irving (eds), *Australian Charter of Employment Rights* (Hardie Grant Books 2007) 70–71.

[214] Anthony Forsyth, 'Workplace Democracy' in Mordy Bromberg and Mark Irving (eds), *Australian Charter of Employment Rights* (Hardie Grant Books 2007).

[215] Peter Rozen, 'A Safe and Healthy Workplace' in Mordy Bromberg and Mark Irving (eds), *Australian Charter of Employment Rights* (Hardie Grant Books 2007).

[216] Sean Reidy, 'Effective Dispute Resolution' in Mordy Bromberg and Mark Irving (eds), *Australian Charter of Employment Rights* (Hardie Grant Books 2007).

in the study recounted that they did not know how to proceed given their employer's direction that they ensure confidentiality. Directions by employers for respondents to maintain confidentiality can protect the interests of the employer, the respondents, and other persons who participate in the investigation or who are named in relevant documents. However, the findings reveal that employers might not reconcile these broad directions with specific information and support for respondents regarding how they can comply with the direction but nevertheless seek relevant information.

The individualistic character of workplace investigations and directions to respondents (and all employee parties) to ensure confidentiality is apparent from the respondents' accounts. These factors impede employees from speaking up, sharing accounts of these processes with each other, and, potentially, collectively asking for changes to these processes. As processes enabled by managerial prerogative and the individual contract of employment, workplace investigations minimize individual and collective employee voice.

Denial/minimization of respondent voice during a workplace investigation is inconsistent with at least five of the nine elements of justice in workplace investigations developed in chapter 3. Specifically, this issue undermines:

- good faith performance of the contract of employment by the employer, including because denial/minimization of respondent voice may lead to adverse consequences for respondents;[217]
- dignified treatment of the respondent, including because denying/minimizing a respondent's voice or representation is inconsistent with respectful treatment of the respondent;[218] and
- right to representation, and workplace democracy, augmented by the mediation of the process through nominated representatives to the extent that an employer's process might deny a respondent the opportunity to involve a support person or representative of their choice;[219]
- a procedurally and substantively fair process that could result in the respondent's dismissal including where an employer's direction to maintain confidentiality undermines a respondent's capacity to fully respond to allegations;[220] and
- the elimination of risk to a respondent's health and safety to the extent that deficient, insensitive, or unreasonable employer/investigator conduct might cause mental harm to the respondent.[221]

C Failure to consider or accommodate respondents' needs or attributes

Findings also point to a theme of employers failing to consider or accommodate respondents' needs or attributes during workplace investigations. Not all refusals by employers to accommodate respondents' needs or abilities will be unlawful. Employers

217 Riley (n 211) 9.
218 Bamber and Russell (n 212) 19.
219 Forsyth (n 214).
220 Pittard (n 213) 70–71.
221 Rozen (n 215).

may be legally required to provide reasonable accommodations to workers based on protected grounds, such as disability, during work.[222] However, accommodation based on other circumstances may be subject to employer discretion, such as a respondent's preference to answer questions in writing. An employer's unfair refusal to accommodate the needs of a respondent may diminish their ability to participate in workplace investigations fully and fairly.

This theme also reinforces the primacy of employer power in workplace investigations. The processes described in respondents' accounts were determined by the employer. Some respondents' accounts pointed to standardized and impersonal processes that manifest bureaucratic power. Other accounts indicated processes that were less systematic but impenetrable to respondents. Concerningly, respondents' accounts reveal how hard these behaviours by managers and investigators were for respondents to challenge or resist during their employment, even when they faced a potentially discriminatory detriment.

Conduct by employers that fails to consider or accommodate a respondent's needs or abilities is inconsistent with at least three of the nine elements of justice in workplace investigations developed in chapter 3. Specifically, this theme detracts from:

- good faith performance of the contract of employment by the employer, including because an employer's refusal to accommodate a respondent's needs or abilities is underpinned by conduct that 'lacks due care to avoid or minimise adverse consequences' to the respondent;[223]
- dignified treatment of the respondent including because the employer's behaviour undermines respectful treatment;[224] and
- potentially, freedom from discrimination,[225] which includes various rights to reasonable adjustments and accommodations for respondents.[226]

D Risk of harm to respondents' mental health

As shown in chapter 2, HRM texts highlight that participants including respondents are at risk of stress or mental injury during workplace investigations. The findings based on the sample of decisions also reveal a theme that the process of a workplace investigation impacts the mental health of respondents. Respondents' accounts in the sample include wide-ranging examples of stress and distress, from feeling 'ambushed' to experiencing isolation when the employer directed them not to perform their duties. Some respondents recounted that their feelings of stress and distress were amplified because of the process adopted by the employer. There were respondents who also described how poor/unprofessional behaviours by managers/investigators impacted their mental health.

[222] See chapter 5 IV.
[223] *Russell* (n 211) [117] (Rothman J). See also Riley (n 211) 9.
[224] Bamber and Russell (n 212) 19; Joanna Howe, 'Dignity at Work' in Clare Ozich (ed), *Employment Rights Now: Reflections on the Australian Charter of Employment Rights* (Hardie Grant Books 2015) 27.
[225] Carol Andrades, 'Freedom from Discrimination and Harassment' in Mordy Bromberg and Mark Irving (eds), *Australian Charter of Employment Rights* (Hardie Grant Books 2007).
[226] Anna Chapman, 'Freedom from Discrimination and Harassment' in Clare Ozich (ed), *Employment Rights Now: Reflections on the Australian Charter of Employment Rights* (Hardie Grant Books 2015) 35–36.

Respondents' accounts also illuminate how lack of support can impact their mental health. The findings highlight that some employers informed respondents about the availability of EAPs. However, respondents needed to proactively contact EAPs. Some respondents referred to the absence of support during time when their employer directed them not to perform work, and other respondents recounted that they were not able to bring their preferred support person to interviews. It is revealing that no respondents reported ways their employer took proactive steps to support their mental health during a workplace investigation.

Accounts by respondents of disrespectful or oppressive interviewing techniques by managers/investigators provide a troubling picture about how pronounced the disparity of power might be in the setting of an interview during workplace investigation, and how pressurized that setting can be for respondents.

The risk of mental harm to respondents during workplace investigations is inconsistent with at least three of the nine elements of justice in workplace investigations developed in chapter 3. Specifically, this risk of harm to respondents detracts from:

- good faith performance of the contract of employment by the employer because the performance is underpinned by conduct that lacks 'due care to avoid or minimise adverse consequences' to the respondent;[227]
- dignified treatment of the worker, including where the conduct of an employer is inconsistent with respectful treatment of the worker;[228] and
- elimination of risk to worker health and safety to the extent that an employer's conduct or the absence of adequate support might cause or exacerbate mental harm to the respondent.[229]

VI Conclusion

This chapter used qualitative content analysis to derive information from a sample of decisions of the FWC under pt 3-2 of the *FW Act* about how respondents viewed and experienced workplace investigations. I made findings from the sample of decisions and flagged four central themes relating to informational asymmetry, denial/minimization by their employers of respondents' voices and opportunities for advocacy, failure to consider respondents' needs or requests for accommodation, and harm to respondents' mental health.

This chapter mapped interactions between the themes and the framework of justice for respondents in workplace investigations developed in chapter 3 and identified how eight out of nine elements of justice were lacking in the accounts of employer conduct provided by respondents. The findings and themes expose the extent to which employer power governs workplace investigations, and are used to inform law reform proposals explored in chapter 7.

[227] *Russell* (n 211) [117] (Rothman J). See also Riley (n 211) 9.
[228] Bamber and Russell (n 212) 19.
[229] Rozen (n 215).

7
An Evaluation of the Legal Regulation of Employer Conduct During Workplace Investigations

I Introduction

Chapters 2 to 6 provided a legal, philosophical, and sociological account of employer conduct during workplace investigations with a focus on the respondent as the subject of the law. In chapters 4 and 5, I concluded that judge-made law and statute incompletely and unsystematically regulate workplace investigations. I identified gaps, inconsistencies, and uncertainties in the law and argued that these deficiencies mean that the legal regulation of employer conduct towards respondents in workplace investigations is inadequate.

This chapter positively and normatively analyses whether the legal regulation of workplace investigations promotes justice for respondents and draws on the findings of that analysis to propose an agenda of law reform. I apply the concept of justice that I developed in chapter 3, which builds on the *Charter*.[1] I argue that legal regulation is inadequate because it is fragmented, unsettled, and uncertain. As explored in this chapter, it is also deficient because it does not adequately promote justice for respondents. On this basis, I argue that work law should be reformed to include direct and targeted constraints on employer conduct towards respondents to apply during workplace investigations.

This chapter is divided into three main parts. In part II, I positively analyse the legal regulation of employer conduct towards respondents during workplace investigations to determine if it promotes justice for respondents by reference to the framework of justice for respondents in workplace investigations developed in chapter 3. In part III, I normatively examine how the law should promote justice for respondents in workplace investigations. In part IV, I develop a proposal for law reform that is informed by the preceding positive and normative analysis. The proposal is targeted and realistic; it is aimed at creating a clearly expressed minimum standard of employer conduct towards respondents under work statute that complements the existing law.

[1] Mordy Bromberg and Mark Irving (eds), *Australian Charter of Employment Rights* (Hardie Grant Books 2007).

Workplace Investigations. Adriana Orifici, Oxford University Press. © Adriana Orifici 2026.
DOI: 10.1093/9780198970019.003.0007

II The Limited Role Played by the Law in Promoting Justice for Respondents During Workplace Investigations

I examine whether the judge-made and statute law that applies to employer conduct during workplace investigations promotes justice for respondents below. I evaluate the law using the framework of justice in workplace investigations that I developed in chapter 3. This concept builds on and augments the rights set out in the *Charter* and has nine elements, which comprise:[2]

- good faith performance of the contract of employment by the parties;[3]
- dignified treatment of respondents;[4]
- freedom from discrimination and harassment;[5]
- elimination of risk to respondents' physical and psychiatric health and safety so far as reasonably practicable;[6]
- promotion of workplace democracy, augmented by consultation with nominated representatives and giving respondents access to information;[7]
- rights to representation for respondents;[8]
- a procedurally and substantively fair process where it could result in dismissal of the respondent;[9]
- fair and relevant minimum standards mandated by law;[10] and
- effective dispute resolution,[11] augmented by internal dispute resolution mechanisms mandated by law.

A Good faith performance of the contract of employment

The first element of the framework of justice for respondents in workplace investigations relates to parties performing their contractual obligations in good faith.[12]

[2] ibid.

[3] Joellen Riley, 'Good Faith Performance' in Mordy Bromberg and Mark Irving (eds), *Australian Charter of Employment Rights* (Hardie Grant Books 2007).

[4] Greg Bamber and Bob Russell, 'Work with Dignity' in Mordy Bromberg and Mark Irving (eds), *Australian Charter of Employment Rights* (Hardie Grant Books 2007).

[5] Carol Andrades, 'Freedom from Discrimination and Harassment' in Mordy Bromberg and Mark Irving (eds), *Australian Charter of Employment Rights* (Hardie Grant Books 2007).

[6] Peter Rozen, 'A Safe and Healthy Workplace' in Mordy Bromberg and Mark Irving (eds), *Australian Charter of Employment Rights* (Hardie Grant Books 2007).

[7] Anthony Forsyth, 'Workplace Democracy' in Mordy Bromberg and Mark Irving (eds), *Australian Charter of Employment Rights* (Hardie Grant Books 2007).

[8] Mark Irving, 'Union Membership and Representation' in Mordy Bromberg and Mark Irving (eds), *Australian Charter of Employment Rights* (Hardie Grant Books 2007).

[9] Marilyn Pittard, 'Protection from Unfair Dismissal' in Mordy Bromberg and Mark Irving (eds), *Australian Charter of Employment Rights* (Hardie Grant Books 2007).

[10] Paul Munro, David Peetz, and Barbara Pocock, 'Fair Minimum Standards' in Mordy Bromberg and Mark Irving (eds), *Australian Charter of Employment Rights* (Hardie Grant Books 2007).

[11] Sean Reidy, 'Effective Dispute Resolution' in Mordy Bromberg and Mark Irving (eds), *Australian Charter of Employment Rights* (Hardie Grant Books 2007).

[12] Bromberg and Irving (n 1) 9–18.

The HCA is yet to determine if an implied duty of good faith generally exists under Australian employment contracts and applies to employers and employees.[13]

In practical terms, an implied duty of good faith under employment contracts would require an employer and employee to act in a manner that would not defeat the purpose of the contract.[14] It would require employers and employees to perform their contractual duties honestly and reasonably, and not capriciously or arbitrarily,[15] so that the other party 'can enjoy the agreed benefits of the relationship'.[16]

A duty of good faith in contractual performance is supported by the concept of citizenship at work, because citizenship promotes a vision of freedom from arbitrary power and domination in the workplace.[17] This element is significant for respondents in workplace investigations because there is a broad scope for employers to exercise discretionary power during these processes and the law currently includes few constraints that prevent employers from exercising power arbitrarily or unfairly in this context.[18]

Chapter 4 included an examination of central judicial principles developed under contract that constrain certain types of unreasonable employer conduct towards respondents. Some of these principles are underpinned by requirements for employers to act honestly and reasonably and avoid capricious or arbitrary conduct. To that extent, these principles promote specific forms of good faith performance of contractual duties by employers during workplace investigation processes. For example, I identified that judge-made law has established principles in contract that require an employer to:

- act reasonably (to the *Wednesbury* standard),[19] and honestly (consistent with the principle in *Service Station Association*),[20] when exercising rights and powers under the express terms of an employment contract at least so far as its workplace investigation process goes, as distinct from the result;[21] and

[13] *Commonwealth Bank of Australia v Barker* (2014) 253 CLR 169. On the role of the court and current issues arising from implying terms by law into employment contracts see, eg, Gabrielle Golding, 'Rethinking the Rationale for Implying Terms by Law into Australian Employment Contracts' (2020) 39 University of Tasmania Law Review 1; Gabrielle Golding, 'Role of Judges in the Regulation of Australian Employment Contracts, The Special Section: The Future of Common Law in Employment Regulation' (2016) 32 International Journal of Comparative Labour Law and Industrial Relations 69. See chapter 4 IV.

[14] See, eg, Joellen Riley, 'Siblings But Not Twins: Making Sense of "Mutual Trust" and "Good Faith" in Employment Contracts' (2012) 36 Melbourne University Law Review 521.

[15] Susan Kiefel, 'Good Faith in Contractual Performance' (2020) 13 Judicial Review: Selected Conference Papers: Journal of the Judicial Commission of New South Wales 41.

[16] Joellen Riley, 'Good Faith and Bargaining Overview', *The Debate: Good Faith and the Employment Relationship* (Australian Institute of Employment Rights 2009) <https://www.aierights.com.au/wp-content/uploads/2011/05/The-Debate-Good-Faith-and-the-employment-relationship.pdf> accessed 20 August 2025.

[17] TH Marshall and Tom Bottomore, *Citizenship and Social Class* (Pluto Press 1987) 41; Harry W Arthurs, 'The New Economy and the New Legality: Industrial Citizenship and the Future of Labour Arbitration Commentary' (1999) 7 Canadian Labour & Employment Law Journal 45, 46.

[18] See chapter 2.

[19] See chapter 4 IV. *Bartlett v Australia & New Zealand Banking Group Ltd* (2016) 92 NSWLR 639, 651–52 (Macfarlan JA); *Associated Provincial Picture Houses Ltd v Wednesbury Corp* (1948) 1 KB 223 (Lord Greene MR, Somervell LJ, and Singleton J).

[20] *Service Station Association Ltd v Berg Bennett & Associates Pty Ltd* (1993) 45 FCR 84, 303–04 (Gummow J).

[21] *Avenia v Railway & Transport Health Fund Ltd* (2017) 272 IR 151, 203 [207]. See *Wednesbury* (n 19).

- comply with its internal policy about a workplace investigation where the policy is directive and predicated on mutual compliance.[22]

However, as shown in chapter 4, the extent of an employer's obligations under judge-made law to act honestly or reasonably during a workplace investigation pursuant to its contractual obligations is uncertain. For example, courts have not definitively resolved whether employers are required to:

- act reasonably or honestly when they exercise implied contractual powers during a workplace investigation process;[23] or
- initiate a workplace investigation for a bona fide purpose and in a manner that enables the respondent to fairly respond to allegations as part of the implied contractual duty of cooperation.[24]

The state of judge-made law regarding an employer's obligations to exercise contractual powers in good faith during workplace investigations is inadequate because it is underdeveloped, and this limits justice for respondents in workplace investigations.

No Australian statute sets out a duty that requires employers and employees to generally exercise powers under the employment contract in good faith.[25] Despite this, some statutory provisions apply during workplace investigations in ways that require employers to act honestly and reasonably. These provisions promote good faith conduct by employers. For example, employers that are bound by the *PS Act*, *CA*, and/or *PIDA* are obliged to afford forms of fair treatment to respondents during some workplace investigation processes.[26] However, the efficacy and scope of these provisions is confined, including because they only apply to certain employers and in particular circumstances, and because they comprise fragmented rules that lack coherence.

Overall, there are some judicial principles and statutory provisions that promote justice by imposing requirements that align with good faith performance of the employment contract by the parties. However, these legal obligations are fragmented and confined and, at times, uncertain. They do not promote a broad obligation for employers to ensure that they act in good faith when exercising contractual powers towards respondents during workplace investigations. In this way, the legal regulation of employer conduct during workplace investigations inadequately promotes this element of justice for respondents.

[22] *Romero v Farstad Shipping (Indian Pacific) Pty Ltd* (2014) 231 FCR 403, 420. See chapter 4 IV.

[23] See chapter 4 IV.

[24] The interrelationship between the implied duty of cooperation, and the concepts regarding good faith and reasonableness in the exercise of contractual powers, is yet to be clearly enunciated in case law regarding the contract of employment. This analysis discusses these obligations separately but recognizes that they are related.

[25] A statutory duty of this kind exists, for example, in New Zealand. See *Employment Relations Act 2000 (NZ) ss 4, 4A*. For an explanation of the development of this statutory duty, see further Gordon Anderson, 'Good Faith in the Individual Employment Relationship in New Zealand' (2011) 32 Comparative Labor Law & Policy Journal 685.

[26] See chapters 5 IV(D) and 5 IV(E).

B Dignified treatment of respondents

The second dimension of justice in workplace investigations entails employers ensuring dignified treatment of respondents.[27] As noted in chapter 3, scholars have broadly conceptualized dignity at work. For example, dignity at work is realized when employers treat workers with respect,[28] ensure that they are not subjected to bullying, harassment, or unreasonably intrusive conduct,[29] and when they exercise managerial discretion in a reasonable manner.[30] Scholars such as Hugh Collins have formulated contemporary visions of citizenship at work that recognize rights that promote dignity at work such as rights to fair treatment and freedom from discrimination.[31] The principle is significant to respondents in workplace investigations because, for example, employers can exercise power during these processes in a manner that causes workers to feel intimidated or humiliated.[32]

Principles under judge-made law and various statutory provisions provide certain protections that apply to respondents against disrespectful treatment, bullying, harassment, or unreasonably intrusive conduct during workplace investigations. For example:

- the duty of reasonable care under contract and/or tort requires an employer to provide a safe system of work that includes adequate support for a respondent in the workplace while a workplace investigation is ongoing, so as to avoid reasonably foreseeable psychiatric injury to the respondent;[33]
- judicial reasoning regarding the application of the privilege of self-incrimination under the *Evidence Act* indicates that respondents can claim the privilege to refuse to answer questions asked during an interview with an investigator;[34] and
- pts 3-1 and 6-4B of the *FW Act* respectively enable eligible respondents to take legal action if their employer engages in 'adverse action' or 'bullying' during a workplace investigation.[35]

However, there is no direct or explicit requirement that employers must ensure respondents are treated with dignity during workplace investigations under judge-made or statutory law. The application of some principles to workplace investigations depends on unsettled or nascent statutory interpretation,[36] and the legal rules are generally unsystematic. This means that there is little promotion of dignified treatment of respondents in workplace investigations through the law.

[27] Bromberg and Irving (n 1) 19.
[28] Hugh Collins, *Justice in Dismissal: The Law of Termination of Employment* (OUP 1992) 140.
[29] Bromberg and Irving (n 1) 19.
[30] Bamber and Russell (n 4) 22.
[31] Hugh Collins, *Employment Law* (2nd edn, OUP 2010) 25.
[32] See findings in chapters 6 IV(A) and 6 IV(B).
[33] *Hayes v Queensland* (2017) 1 Qd R 337 [6], [100], [123]–[125] (Dalton J, Mullins J agreeing at 371, [104]) (Court of Appeal).
[34] *Grant v BHP Coal Pty Ltd* [2017] FCR 295 [108]. On this matter, the Court cited *Police Service Board v Morris* (1985) 156 CLR 397, 397, 403, 408, and 411 (Gibbs CJ).
[35] See chapters 5 III(A) and 5 III(C).
[36] See, eg, discussion in chapter 5 III(C) regarding *Fair Work Act 2009 (Cth) pt 6-4B*.

C Freedom from discrimination and harassment

The third element of justice in workplace investigations requires respondents to have protection against discrimination and harassment based on a wide range of relevant grounds.[37] Scholarship has articulated that the realization of citizenship at work requires a right to freedom from discrimination.[38] The principle is significant for respondents in workplace investigations including because employers possibly conduct workplace investigations for discriminatory reasons[39] or might refuse a respondent's request for reasonable accommodations during a workplace investigation process.[40]

The *FW Act* and anti-discrimination laws set out a range of protections against discrimination that are relevant to respondents in workplace investigations. For example, the *FW Act* prohibits an employer from taking 'adverse action' against a respondent because of one or more protected grounds of discrimination.[41] Anti-discrimination laws also include requirements for employers to make reasonable adjustments or accommodations during workplace investigations because of disability.[42] Taken together, these provisions promote justice for affected workers who are respondents in workplace investigations by providing protections against discrimination.

However, there are limitations to the statutory protections against discrimination that are relevant in the context of a workplace investigation. As identified in chapter 6, there were respondents in the sample of decisions who recounted that their employers did not adjust the workplace investigation process to accommodate their English language proficiency.[43] It is unclear whether this type of conduct would constitute unlawful discrimination.

D A safe and healthy workplace

The fourth element of justice in workplace investigations entails the elimination of risk to respondents' health and safety so far as reasonably practicable.[44] This includes an obligation on employers to ensure that a worker's psychiatric health is protected in the workplace.[45] Scholars including Collins have identified WHS rights as a key part of a modern vision of citizenship rights at work.[46] As shown in chapter 2, this right is

[37] Andrades (n 5).
[38] Iain Ross, 'Commentary: Industrial Citizenship' in Joe Isaac and Russell Lansbury (eds), *Labour Market Deregulation: Rewriting the Rules* (The Federation Press 2005); Joe Isaac, 'Reforming Australian Industrial Relations?: The 21st Foenander Lecture, 28 August 2006' (2007) 49 Journal of Industrial Relations 410; Paul Munro, 'Changes to the Australian Industrial Relations System: Reforms or Shattered Icons? An Insider's Assessment of the Probable Impact on Employers, Employees and Unions' (2006) 29 University of New South Wales Law Journal 128.
[39] See chapter 5 IV(A).
[40] See chapter 6 IV(B).
[41] *FW Act s 351*. See chapter 5 III(A).
[42] See chapter 5 IV(B).
[43] See chapter 6 IV(B).
[44] Rozen (n 6) 39.
[45] ibid.
[46] Collins (n 31) 25.

significant in the context of workplace investigations because these processes potentially pose a risk to respondents' mental health.

In chapter 4, I examined the uncertain scope and content of the duty of reasonable care owed by an employer towards a respondent in contract and/or tort in the context of a workplace investigation under judge-made law. On the one hand, a court has determined that an employer must provide a safe system of work that includes reasonable support for respondents who were vulnerable to injury because they were working in a hostile workplace while their conduct was being investigated.[47] On the other hand, courts have declined to recognize that the duty of reasonable care extends to require an employer to provide a respondent with a safe system of:

- workplace investigation or decision-making so as to avoid reasonably foreseeable psychiatric injury;[48] or
- decision-making when directing a respondent not to perform work during a workplace investigation so as to avoid reasonably foreseeable psychiatric injury.[49]

These judicial principles raise complex questions including about:

- whether the ratio in *Paige* precludes a respondent from pursuing a claim for damages for psychiatric injury in contract or tort on the basis that the employer's conduct during a workplace investigation breached the implied duty of reasonable care in all circumstances;[50]
- public policy considerations that weigh the 'appreciable' risk of psychiatric injury to respondents raised by workplace investigations and the need to ensure that employers can effectively conduct workplace investigations into allegations of employee misconduct. These considerations were first discussed in *Paige* but were repeated in other decisions such as *Lloyd*;[51] and
- whether an employer has a duty to exercise contractual powers in a reasonable way so as to avoid psychiatric injury to a respondent during a workplace investigation, including when it does not lead to a dismissal.[52]

At present, the inadequate state of principles under judge-made law with respect to the implied duty of reasonable care substantially undermines a respondent's right to health and safety during a workplace investigation. It sends an unhelpful message to employers that there is no legal obligation to ensure a safe system of workplace investigation and decision-making specifically under judge-made law.

As I have argued in chapter 4, the public policy considerations first discussed in *Paige* are finely balanced. They were also developed in cases that pivoted on particular

[47] *Hayes* (n 33).

[48] *New South Wales v Paige* (2002) 60 NSWLR 371405 [182] (Spigelman CJ, Mason P agreeing at 416 [330], Giles JA agreeing at 419 [358]).

[49] *Potter v Gympie Regional Council* [2022] QCA 255 [36] (Flanagan JA, Mullins P agreeing at [1], Williams J agreeing at [83]) (Court of Appeal).

[50] *Elisha v Vision Australia Ltd* [2022] VSC 754 [492] (O'Meara J).

[51] *Lloyd v Healthscope Operations Pty Ltd* [2020] VCC 2032 [288] (Ginnane J).

[52] *Govier v Uniting Church in Australia Property Trust (Q)* [2018] HCATrans 65.

facts. The prioritization of the need for employers to conduct efficient workplace investigations over the risk of mental injury that these processes pose to respondents requires further scrutiny. In this way, these aspects of judge-made law do not promote this element of justice in workplace investigations for respondents.

In contrast, the *WHS Acts* include a primary duty that requires employers to ensure, so far as is reasonably practicable, the physical and mental health and safety of workers including during workplace investigations.[53] The *WHS Regulations* were amended in 2022 to expressly state that a PCBU such as an employer must manage 'psychosocial hazards',[54] and these amendments have legal effect in New South Wales, Queensland, Western Australia, Tasmania, and the Northern Territory. The *Psychosocial Hazards Code of Practice* provides practical guidance to employers about how to comply with the *WHS Acts* and *WHS Regulations*,[55] and it relevantly states that employers must eliminate or minimize any risks in their 'management process' including risks associated with 'poor organisational justice by ensuring [it applies] policies transparently and fairly'.[56] PCBUs risk prosecution and criminal sanctions if they fail to comply with the primary duty.[57] The primary duty under the *WHS Acts* is proactively oriented and promotes the elimination of risk to respondents' health and safety so far as reasonably practicable during workplace investigations.

Statutory provisions under pt 6-4B of the *FW Act* and workers' compensation laws also promote respondents' health and safety during workplace investigations. First, workers' compensation statutes provide respondents with compensation for injuries that they have sustained during workplace investigations. While these are 'no fault' schemes, they generally exclude from compensation mental injury that is wholly or partly caused by the employer's reasonable management action conducted in a reasonable manner.[58] Second, the FWC has interpreted pt 6-4B of the *FW Act* in a manner that includes unreasonable conduct by an employer during a workplace investigation within the definition of 'bullying'.[59] A respondent can rely on this interpretation to apply to the FWC for an order to stop 'bullying' by an employer during a workplace investigation that poses a risk to their health and safety.[60] These statutory mechanisms

[53] *Work Health and Safety Acts s 19(1)*. See chapter 5 IV(B).

[54] *Work Health and Safety Regulations 2011 (Cth)*. The *WHS Regulations* define a psychosocial hazard as a hazard that may cause a worker or other person psychological harm, which arises from or relates to the design or management of work, the working environment, the plant at a workplace, or workplace interactions or behaviours: ibid reg 55A. The *WHS Regulations* also define a 'psychosocial risk' as a risk to health and safety arising from a psychosocial hazard: ibid reg 55B.

[55] *WHS Acts s 274*. A code of practice is admissible as evidence in court proceedings under the *WHS Acts* and a court may rely on the code as evidence of what is known about a hazard, risk, or control method and may rely on the code to determine what is reasonably practicable in the circumstances to which the code relates: ibid s 275(2)–(3).

[56] Safe Work Australia, 'Managing Psychosocial Hazards at Work' (2022) Model Code of Practice 28 <https://www.safeworkaustralia.gov.au/doc/model-code-practice-managing-psychosocial-hazards-work> accessed 9 August 2025.

[57] *WHS Acts s 230*. For an examination of enforcement and compliance mechanisms under the *WHS Acts*, see Elizabeth Bluff and Richard Johnstone, 'Supporting and Enforcing Compliance with Australia's Harmonised WHS Laws' (2017) 30 Australian Journal of Labour Law 30.

[58] See chapter 5 IV(C).

[59] See chapter 5 III(C).

[60] *FW Act* s 789FD(1).

provide legal pathways for respondents to stop further employer conduct that could cause harm or to seek compensation for harm in some circumstances.

Judicial principles do not align with the primary duty under the *WHS Acts* in key ways. For example, judge-made law does not require employers to exercise implied contractual powers reasonably during a workplace investigation, and does not recognize that the duty of reasonable care in contract and tort includes a duty to ensure a safe system of workplace investigation and decision-making. The application of pt 6-4B of the *FW Act* is also uncertain because it relies on statutory interpretation of relevant provisions. The absence of coherence and certainty undermines health and safety in workplace investigations for respondents and amplifies the risk of psychiatric injury.

Elisha exemplified the magnitude of psychiatric injury that a respondent can suffer because of unreasonable and negligent conduct by an employer during an investigation and disciplinary process;[61] this decision reinforces this area needs attention and harmonization through a definitive decision of the HCA or legislative enactment to advance justice for respondents.

E Workplace democracy

The fifth element of justice in workplace investigations for respondents entails the promotion of workplace democracy, including through consultation with nominated representatives for respondents and giving respondents access to information.[62] This dimension of justice for respondents contemplates the role of collectivism in regulating employer conduct; it challenges the highly individualized turn in work law in Australia, and comparable jurisdictions such as the United Kingdom and Canada,[63] that is exemplified in how respondents are required to articulate their legal rights, and articulate claims, about unreasonable or negligent employer conduct.

Workplace democracy and citizenship at work envisage that employers will provide employees and their representatives with opportunities and information to ensure that they can consult about processes and decision-making that affects them.[64] These values also seem to require employers to consult with workers and their representatives about any decision to discipline a worker.[65] As discussed in chapter 3, workplace democracy is closely aligned with citizenship at work.[66] This element is significant for respondents in workplace investigations because they are affected by the process that an employer adopts and potentially face disciplinary action such as dismissal.

In chapter 6, I identified that a theme in the sample of decisions from the FWC under pt 3-2 of the *FW Act* was informational asymmetry between employers and respondents during workplace investigations. Employers may choose to set out a workplace investigation process in an internal policy or be bound by terms in an enterprise agreement that set out a workplace investigation process. However, neither

[61] *Elisha (First Instance)* (n 50); *Vision Australia Ltd v Elisha* (2023) 328 IR 299; *Elisha v Vision Australia Ltd* (2024) 421 ALR 184. See chapter 4 III.
[62] Forsyth (n 7).
[63] cf chapter 1.
[64] Forsyth (n 7) 44.
[65] For further analysis of workplace democracy and justice in dismissal, see Collins (n 28) 108–09.
[66] See chapter 3 V.

judge-made law nor statute requires an employer to provide information to respondents or their representatives about its workplace investigation process. As discussed in chapter 4, the decision of the HCA in *Elisha (HCA)* would seem to encourage employers to take steps to commit little of the disciplinary process to writing.

Legal regulation under judge-made law and statute does not include an explicit obligation for employers to consult with individual respondents or their representatives before deciding to discipline them following a workplace investigation or about the process that will be used for the investigation. A relevant criterion for assessing if a dismissal was 'harsh, unjust or unreasonable' under the protection against unfair dismissal under pt 3-2 of the *FW Act* is whether the employer gave the respondent 'an opportunity to respond to any reason related to the capacity or conduct of the person'.[67] However, it does not impose a positive obligation on an employer to consult with a respondent about its decision-making and only applies in cases of dismissal. The statutory law of evidence also provides employers with broad scope to make claims of legal professional privilege during workplace investigations, and it is costly and legally uncertain for respondents to challenge these claims of privilege.[68] Claims of legal professional privilege can amplify informational asymmetry between employers and respondents. As found in chapter 6, respondents in the sample of decisions referred to having little or no information about the process the employer would follow in a workplace investigation. In this way, the law is inadequate in terms of promoting workplace democracy for respondents during workplace investigations.

F Rights to representation for respondents

The sixth element of justice in workplace investigations relates to the rights of representation for respondents.[69] The right to union representation not only includes the right to join a union but also to have the union represent workers in matters that affect them.[70] This element is underpinned by the idea of citizenship at work that conceives of all workers as citizens who are members of the community of the workplace who are entitled to representation and voice.[71] This element is significant for respondents in workplace investigations. Respondents may ask to bring a representative of their choosing to meetings or interviews.[72] At the same time, employers are often legally represented or advised in these processes.[73]

Judge-made law and statute that apply to workplace investigations do not include an express entitlement for respondents to be represented by a union delegate or another person such as a legal practitioner.[74] It is not known whether employers regularly

[67] *FW Act s 387(c)*. See chapter 5 III(B).
[68] See chapters 2 III(C) and 5 IV(F).
[69] Forsyth (n 7) 53.
[70] ibid 60.
[71] Ronald C McCallum, 'Crafting a New Collective Labour Law for Australia' (1997) 39 Journal of Industrial Relations 405, 410. See also Isaac (n 38) 414.
[72] See chapter 6 IV(B).
[73] See chapter 2 III.
[74] Terms that provide respondents with a right to representation may be included in enterprise agreements made under the *FW Act* or in internal policies.

disallow respondents' representatives to attend interviews or meetings. However, the findings in chapter 6 included that some respondents recounted how their employer had not allowed them to bring a legal representative to a meeting.[75]

The legal position differs with respect to support persons. As noted in chapter 5, a criterion for assessing if a dismissal was 'harsh, unjust or unreasonable' under the protection against unfair dismissal under pt 3-2 of the *FW Act* is any unreasonable refusal by an employer to allow an employee to have a support person present to assist at any discussions relating to dismissal.[76] This criterion indirectly promotes the presence of support persons for respondents at interviews and meetings during workplace investigations. However, it does not impose a positive obligation on an employer to tell a respondent that they can bring a support person to an interview or meeting.

A support person is not an advocate or representative but is a person who can provide emotional support and, if qualified, advice to a respondent to enable them to respond to allegations of misconduct. This is reflected in comments set out in non-binding determinations of the FWC.[77] The lack of an express entitlement under legal regulation to bring a representative to a meeting or interview undermines this element of justice in workplace investigations.

G A fair workplace investigation

The seventh dimension requires that employers ensure a procedurally and substantively fair workplace investigation where it could result in dismissal of a respondent.[78] As explained in chapter 2, procedural fairness is legally defined in the field of administrative law in Australia and consists of two basic rules, which are the 'hearing rule' and the 'bias rule'.[79] Substantive fairness is not legally defined in administrative law in Australia, but it requires the ultimate decision to be fair on its merits.[80] In the context of dismissal, Collins has observed that substantive unfairness will arise unless an employer can justify the dismissal by demonstrating fault by the respondent.[81]

The idea of citizenship at work conceives of workers as having a right to their job, which an employer may revoke if the worker acts in a manner that forfeits their entitlement to be a member of the community.[82] It also envisages that workers will have an opportunity for consultation and to express their views before the employer makes a decision to dismiss them.[83] As a rights-based framework, the idea recognizes that workers and employers can have divergent interests in these matters and the law plays

[75] See chapter 6 IV(B).

[76] Chapter 5 III(B). See *FW Act s 387(d).*

[77] See, eg, *Victorian Association for the Teaching of English Inc v De Laps* [2014] IR 1. See also Nicholas Kelly, 'Support Persons for Employees and the Fair Work Act' (2018) 24 Employment Law Bulletin 47, 47; Lindy Richardson and Mathew Gashi, 'Bracing for the Worst: The Role of Support Persons in Workplace Investigations' 22 Employment Law Bulletin284.

[78] See also Pittard (n 9) 62.

[79] See chapter 2 III(B).

[80] Matthew Groves, 'Substantive Legitimate Expectations in Australian Administrative Law' (2008) 32 Melbourne University Law Review 470, 479.

[81] Collins (n 28) 70. See also Pittard (n 9) 70.

[82] Marshall and Bottomore (n 17) 6.

[83] Collins (n 28) 108.

a role in mediating these conflicting interests.[84] This element is significant for respondents because they could potentially be dismissed following a workplace investigation.

Judge-made law in contract and/or tort does not impose a clear obligation for employers to ensure a workplace investigation process that leads to dismissal is procedurally or substantively fair.[85] As noted, some principles have emerged that are arguably underpinned by requirements for employers to act honestly and reasonably. To that extent, they promote fair workplace investigation processes but are inadequate in terms of promoting justice for respondents.

Statutory work law does not include a uniform obligation for employers to ensure a workplace investigation process is procedurally or substantively fair. In chapter 5, I noted that the protection against unfair dismissal indirectly applies to employer conduct during workplace investigations.[86] An employer might be incentivized to ensure its workplace investigation procedure is consistent with the factors under s 387 to minimize the possibility that a respondent who is dismissed and is eligible to make an application under pt 3-2 would succeed in remedial orders.[87] These criteria articulate concepts of substantive and procedural fairness but they are unsatisfactory because they are indirect and conceive of these concepts quite narrowly.[88]

As noted above, statutory provisions under the *CA* and/or *PIDA* require employers to afford forms of fair treatment to respondents during workplace investigations in certain circumstances.[89] These obligations are also underpinned by concepts of substantive and procedural fairness and apply in circumstances where workplace investigations can lead to dismissal. Statutory obligations that require applicable employers in the public sector to establish written procedures and ensure procedural fairness (as defined by statute) also impose important constraints on employer conduct towards respondents. However, these concepts of procedural fairness are fragmented, and their application is confined. There is a lack of parity between the legal rights of respondents to a procedurally and substantively fair workplace investigation, depending on whether they are employed in the public or private sectors, and the circumstances of the workplace investigation.

There is also an absence of coherence and consistency in legal standards of substantive and procedural fairness in workplace investigations that can lead to dismissal and this arguably undermines justice for respondents.

H Fair and relevant minimum standards

The eighth element of justice in workplace investigations requires fair and relevant minimum standards to be mandated by the law of work. In the Australian system of statutory work regulation, minimum standards are primarily set out in the NES under

[84] ibid 82.
[85] cf Philippa Collins and Gabrielle Golding, 'An Implied Term of Procedural Fairness During Disciplinary Processes: Into Contracts of Employment and Beyond?' (2024) 53 Industrial Law Journal 125; Douglas Brodie, 'Disavowing an Implied Term of Fairness' (2024) 53 Industrial Law Journal 157.
[86] See chapter 5 III(B).
[87] See chapter 2.
[88] *FW Act s 387(a)–(d).*
[89] See chapters 5 IV(D) and 5 IV(E).

the *FW Act*,[90] and through a system of modern awards that are given legislative force by the *FW Act*.[91] However, it is posited that they can also be developed via the common law. As discussed in chapter 3, experts have identified that minimum standards for citizens at work should include entitlements to fair treatment and fair dealing, WHS, and representation in individual grievances.[92] This element is relevant to respondents in workplace investigations because it promotes certainty regarding the standard of conduct that applies to employers during these processes.

In chapter 5, I explored how work statute lacks direct and explicit provisions that regulate employer conduct towards respondents during workplace investigations. Modern awards do not include terms about workplace investigations. There are no minimum standards for workplace investigations that are established under the *FW Act*, and this undermines justice for respondents. The common law has been slow to develop principles with respect to workplace investigations. As explored in chapter 4, some principles exist that limit unreasonable employer conduct during workplace investigations, but these rights are not certain or comprehensive.

I Effective dispute resolution

The ninth element of justice for respondents in workplace investigations entails effective dispute resolution, augmented by mandatory procedures and internal dispute resolution mechanisms.[93] Sean Reidy has noted that there are two types of disputes involving workers that require effective mechanisms for dispute resolution.[94] First, there are interests disputes at workplace level, such as individual grievances.[95] Second, there are rights disputes that involve complaints and claims by workers to external bodies such as tribunals and courts to secure compliance by employers with work laws.[96]

Citizenship at work envisages effective resolution of work disputes at workplace level and through external bodies.[97] This element is important for respondents in workplace investigations because an absence of mechanisms for resolving disputes (well before any dismissal) amplifies the vulnerability of respondents to harm and injury during these processes where there are few explicit constraints on employer power under the law.

There are some specific circumstances where an employer is legally obliged to resolve interests disputes about workplace investigations. First, an employer may be required to do so pursuant to terms of a contract of employment. Second, employees who are covered by relevant terms in enterprise agreements may invoke dispute resolution

[90] *FW Act* pt 2-2.
[91] ibid pt 2-3. *FW Act*.
[92] Ross (n 38); Isaac (n 38); Munro (n 38). See also Collins (n 31) 25.
[93] Reidy (n 11).
[94] ibid 109–10.
[95] ibid 105–06.
[96] ibid.
[97] Ronald C McCallum, 'Citizenship at Work: An Australian Perspective' (2011) Sydney Law School Research Paper No 11/17 10 <https://papers.ssrn.com/abstract=1769271> accessed 28 July 2025.

mechanisms under those agreements to resolve a dispute about an employer's conduct during a workplace investigation.[98] These terms ordinarily require that the parties attempt to resolve the dispute at workplace level before the parties seek resolution from the FWC or a relevant court. Third, employees of Commonwealth, state, and territory governments may be entitled to seek a review of actions with respect to action that relates to a workplace investigation and/or a decision that is based on the findings of a workplace investigation.[99] One avenue is for a review of actions to be conducted internally.[100] These legal mechanisms promote justice for eligible respondents through ensuring that they can seek the resolution of interests disputes during workplace investigations but they are fragmented and only apply to particular employees and in certain circumstances.

As also noted by Reidy, once a workplace dispute becomes the subject of a claim about an employer's compliance with legal obligations, it becomes a rights dispute. Chapters 4 and 5 refer to a range of rights disputes about employer conduct during workplace investigations. These disputes rely on various legal mechanisms that indirectly apply during workplace investigations and arise under different areas of law. There are no provisions under statute law that set out explicit mechanisms for enabling workers to pursue rights disputes about workplace investigations.

Some statutory mechanisms allow eligible respondents to pursue rights disputes during workplace investigations, but these are fragmented, and their application is uncertain at times. For example, an eligible respondent can potentially apply to the FWC for an order to stop employer conduct that meets the definition of 'bullying' under pt 6-4B of the *FW Act*.[101] In addition, a respondent who is covered by an enterprise agreement that sets out a term about a workplace investigation process can potentially apply to the FWC for an order that interprets the employer's obligations under the term and requires the employer to comply with that term or to reasonably or fairly exercise rights or powers under that term.[102] However, the availability of both of these mechanisms is contingent; the first relies on statutory interpretation of relevant provisions by the FWC and the second mechanism depends on the existence of relevant terms under an enterprise agreement that applies to an employee.

Rights disputes about workplace investigations can involve respondents who make claims in contract and/or tort that they have sustained a foreseeable psychiatric injury because of an employer's negligent conduct during a workplace investigation and seek damages. As I have explored in chapter 4, *Elisha (HCA)* established that damages may be available to a respondent for psychiatric injury caused by an employer's breach of an express contractual term as relevant to dismissal. However, the availability of damages for psychiatric injury to a respondent caused by an employer's breach of the implied duty of reasonable care under contract or tort is uncertain.[103] No statutory mechanism completely addresses this uncertainty, and this diminishes justice in workplace investigations for respondents.

98 See chapter 5 III(D).
99 See chapter 5 IV(D).
100 *Public Service Act 1999 (Cth) s 33; Public Service Regulations 2023 (Cth) regs 36–38, 41.*
101 See chapter 5 III(C).
102 See chapter 5 III(D).
103 See chapter 4 III(D).

J Does legal regulation ensure justice for workers who are respondents in workplace investigations?

I have examined whether the legal regulation of employer conduct during workplace investigations ensures justice for workers who are respondents, and I have adopted the theoretical lens of citizenship at work and evaluated the legal framework against the nine elements of justice for respondents in workplace investigations developed in chapter 3.

I have identified judicial principles and statutory rules that promote dimensions of justice for respondents in workplace investigations. I have also discerned ways that work law is currently unsatisfactory in terms of promoting justice for respondents in workplace investigations. There are gaps and deficiencies in, and tensions between, judge-made law and statute when considered through the lens of each of the nine elements that comprise the framework of justice in workplace investigations.

There is no direct or comprehensive statutory code under work law that governs the area and judge-made law sets out few unequivocal principles that constrain employer power towards respondents. There are also various gaps in the legal regulation of workplace investigations, and these amplify injustice for respondents. The most pressing gaps from the perspective of justice for respondents seem to be that:

- courts have declined to recognise that the duty of reasonable care in contract and/or tort extends to require an employer to provide a respondent with a safe system of workplace investigation and decision-making;
- there is no legal obligation for employers to proactively advise a respondent that they may nominate a support person or to allow a respondent to nominate a legal or union representative;
- an employer is not statutorily required to establish or abide by a fair or consistent process for workplace investigations or consult with respondents or their representatives about the process unless the employer is a Commonwealth, state and territory government;[104] and
- neither judge-made law nor statute mandates the basic content of a fair workplace investigation, except for Commonwealth, state and territory government employers and in whistleblowing investigations.

These gaps undermine respondents' attainment of elements of justice in workplace investigations including with respect to WHS, workplace democracy, union representation, good faith performance, and work with dignity.

The development of the law that applies to workplace investigations is fragmented, unsettled, and unduly complex. Key aspects of statute and judge-made law also pull in different directions. This is exemplified through comparison of the judicial principles regarding an employer's duty of reasonable care during workplace investigations,[105]

[104] The exceptions are if the employer is a government department or agency, is bound by a relevant term of an enterprise agreement that includes these requirements, or is conducting a workplace investigation that must comply with whistleblowing laws.

[105] See chapter 4 III.

and the expansive scope of the proactively-oriented primary duty owed by employers under the *WHS Acts* during workplace investigations.[106] The absence of clarity and coherence potentially makes it difficult for respondents to discern their legal rights and seek improvements through individual and collective action, and for employers to understand their obligations. This means that justice eludes respondents in workplace investigations.

III The Case for Reforming the Law to Ensure Justice for Respondents in Workplace Investigations

The positive examination of work law that applies to employer conduct during workplace investigations has shown that justice for respondents is lacking. It illuminates that the legal regulation of employer conduct towards respondents during workplace investigations is not only inadequate because it is fragmented and often unclear and uncertain, but also because it falls short in terms of promoting justice for respondents. This invites critical consideration of how legal regulation should be improved to promote justice for respondents in workplace investigations.

In chapters 1 and 2, I identified that respondents in workplace investigations are often overlooked as subjects of the law. Work laws lack specific rules that are directed towards protecting them during the process of a workplace investigation irrespective of its findings or outcome. Yet, respondents are arguably a category of workers who require specific protections during the process of a workplace investigation.

It might be presumed that the primary risk to a respondent that arises from a workplace investigation is the possibility that they will be dismissed at its conclusion and that work law responds to this risk through statutory protections against unfair dismissal. However, in chapters 2–6, I have identified how workplace investigations are shaped by employer power and how respondents are vulnerable to a range of potential injuries and detriments during these processes.

In chapter 4, I examined key decisions that related to disputes pursued by respondents who claimed that they experienced serious and permanent mental injuries or work-related detriments during workplace investigations.[107] In *Govier* and *Hayes*, the respondents emphasized in their claims that their mental injuries were caused by their employer's workplace investigation process.[108] In these cases, courts accepted evidence that employers had acted unreasonably during workplace investigations.[109]

I also discerned themes about respondents' views and experiences of workplace investigations that arose from qualitative content analysis of a sample of decisions made under pt 3-2 of the *FW Act*.[110] These themes relate to informational asymmetry between employers and respondents, denial/minimization by employers of respondents' voices and opportunities for advocacy, denial by employers of respondents'

[106] See chapter 5 IV(B).
[107] See, eg, *Paige* (n 48); *Govier v Uniting Church in Australia Property Trust (Q)* [2017] QCA 12; *Elisha (HCA)* (n 61).
[108] *Govier* (n 107). See also *Hayes* (n 33) [121] (Dalton J).
[109] *Govier* (n 107). See also *Hayes* (n 33).
[110] See chapter 6 V.

requests for accommodation, and harm to respondents' mental health. These themes point to a broad spectrum of risks and detriments for respondents during a workplace investigation.

As shown in chapter 3, scholarship reinforces that a central rationale of work law continues to be protecting workers from the unfair impact of the unequal power that underpins work contracts.[111] The philosophical literature recognizes that work law is a mechanism that can be used to impose reasonable limits on employer power to ensure worker protection. This indicates that work law should include direct and targeted protections that address the significant risks and detriments that are posed to respondents during workplace investigations and encompass individual and collective dimensions.

As I identified in chapter 3, the concept of citizenship at work has shaped the narrative of work law in Australia.[112] This concept also supports reforming work law to ensure it furthers the protection of respondents during internal employer processes. The value of citizenship conceives of all workers as citizens at work who are holders of equivalent rights at work and is underpinned by principles of equality and egalitarianism. It also supports reforming work law to include protections for respondents as a category of workers in need of specific protections and recognition under the law.

IV A More Prominent Role for Statute in the Legal Regulation of Workplace Investigations

In this part, I consider how work law could be reformed to promote justice for respondents in workplace investigations. First, I consider whether the reforms are best achieved through judge-made law, legislation, or a hybrid model proposed by Gabrielle Golding that recognizes the potential for interaction between judicial and statutory development of the law pertaining to the contract of employment.[113] I argue that the hybrid model provides an optimal approach for reforming the law. Second, I set out an agenda of law reform that includes a Proposed NES on workplace investigations in the *FW Act* and an amendment to pt 6-4B of the *FW Act*.

The proposed reforms are targeted and achievable. I recognize that the analysis of law in this monograph identifies many ways in which the law is inadequate in terms of promoting justice for respondents. The reforms are intended to comprise a cogent starting point for directly regulating employer conduct towards respondents under work law that addresses the most pressing issues of justice for respondents in workplace investigations.

The reforms respond to key gaps and deficiencies in the law that applies to employer conduct towards respondents in workplace investigations identified in this study. They codify principles that directly regulate workplace investigations, limit managerial discretion, and allow for incremental development of the law through judicial decision-making and additions to the *FW Regulations*.[114]

[111] See chapter 3 A(II).
[112] See chapter 3 VI.
[113] Golding, 'Role of Judges' (n 13) 86–89.
[114] *Fair Work Regulations 2009 (Cth).*

A Can justice for respondents be promoted through developments under judge-made law?

In chapter 4, I argued that key judicial principles under contract and tort that apply to employer conduct towards respondents during workplace investigations are underdeveloped and unclear. I have concluded that several important principles nevertheless emerge from judgments, and these arguably promote aspects of justice for respondents.

The judicial development of these principles can be seen as a promising start towards promoting justice for respondents. However, as identified in chapter 4, crucial aspects of the judicial reasoning require attention. For example, uncertainty exists regarding an employer's duty to avoid reasonably foreseeable mental injury to workers during workplace investigations (including where the inquiry does not result in dismissal) and regarding employers' obligations to exercise discretionary contractual powers reasonably. These matters require clarification by superior courts to promote justice for respondents in workplace investigations.

The decision of the HCA in *Elisha* represents a significant development. However, the joint judgement of the HCA, as well as the judgments of Jagot J and Steward J, afforded primacy to the express terms of the contract of employment as a representation of the will and agreement of the parties. This approach could be internalized by employer practices. So, employers may seek to limit or exclude obligations developed under judge-made law through express contractual terms.

It is also unlikely that underdeveloped or uncertain principles will be addressed promptly through determinations of a superior court. The evolution of reasoning about *Paige* over more than two decades illustrates this issue. The HCA must be presented with a suitable factual dispute in future to determine these matters. Even if a suitable case arises, superior courts have generally demonstrated reluctance to develop the law of contract and/or tort to recognize novel implied terms in the context of the law relating to termination under a contract of employment.

In *Paige*, Spigelman J also reasoned that the statutory framework regulating termination of employment seemed to cover the field and indicated that it should be left to the legislature to decide if it was necessary to develop or adjust the obligations of employers.[115] In *Barker*, the unanimous decision of the HCA exhibited similar reticence in terms of developing implied terms in the contract of employment.[116] The dissenting judgment of Steward J in *Elisha (HCA)* reflected a similar approach.[117] These attitudes indicate that it is unlikely that a superior court would develop the law to recognize new obligations on employers during workplace investigations under contract and/or tort considering that these processes play a significant role in dismissals.

Legal principles regarding employers' obligations during workplace investigations need prompt clarification and clear enunciation. For this to happen efficiently and effectively, it is helpful to turn to the legislature.

[115] *Paige* (n 48). See chapter 4 III(B).
[116] *Barker* (n 13). See chapter 4 III(C).
[117] *Elisha (HCA)* (n 61).

B Can justice for respondents be promoted through developments under statute?

In chapter 5, I identified key dimensions of the statutory regulation that apply to employer conduct during workplace investigations across seven areas of law. I argued that the application of statutory rules to employer conduct during workplace investigations is unsatisfactory, and that the Australian Parliament should consider reforming the law. I identified that the *FW Act* does not include any provisions that directly and completely regulate employer conduct towards respondents during workplace investigations.

No Commonwealth, state, or territory Parliament has made express policy choices regarding whether or how it should regulate the conduct of employers during workplace investigations in the private sector. It is possible that the existence of a statutory protection against unfair dismissal under the *FW Act* has led policymakers to overlook the significance of employer practices during workplace investigations that precede disciplinary action. Employer conduct during workplace investigations is a suitable subject for regulation under statute. As a matter that relates to workplaces and workers, it seems apposite for the direct legislative regulation of workplace investigations to be situated within the *FW Act* as the principal statute that regulates employment.

As I have examined in chapter 5, statute law inadequately regulates employer conduct towards respondents during workplace investigations because it is fragmented and, at times, incoherent and unduly complex. There is also disharmony between statute law and the development of judicial principles. For example:

- key statutory provisions only apply to employer conduct in specific circumstances and jurisdictions, and this results in undue legal complexity and inconsistency. This is exemplified in key differences between *WHS Regulations* in different states and territories; and
- there is no consistent articulation or standard of fair treatment of respondents under statute law, but at least three statutes require employers to ensure some form of fairness/fair treatment towards respondents in prescribed circumstances;[118] and
- there is no consistent obligation under statute for employers to establish an internal policy that explains how they will conduct a workplace investigation, but some employers must establish internal policies in accordance with statutes such as the *PS Act*, *CA* or *PIDA*.

As also identified in chapter 5, the way that some statutory provisions apply to employer conduct during workplace investigations depends on statutory interpretation, and this means that the application of the law to the subject is indirect and uncertain. For example, this affects how pt 6-4B of the *FW Act* and the *Evidence Act* apply in this

[118] These statutes are the: *FW Act pt 3-1, 6-4B; Public Service Act 1999 (Cth); Corporations Act 2001 (Cth); Public Interest Disclosure Act 2013 (Cth).*

context. The absence of clear and direct regulation of workplace investigations has led to uncertainty that can be addressed through statutory reform.

Overall, the analysis in chapters 4 and 5 reveals three key reasons why statutory work law should be amended to directly regulate the conduct of workplace investigations. First, it would remove the uncertainty and unpredictability that characterize the development of key principles under judge-made law in this area. Second, it would send a clear message to employers about the scope of their obligations to employees during workplace investigations and the potential for liability. Third, it would overcome tension between judge-made law and statute regarding whether the duty of reasonable care requires employers to ensure a safe system of workplace investigation and decision-making. Legislative amendment to the *FW Act* can be used to harmonize and achieve consistency on these matters and contribute to justice for respondents.

C Options for a hybrid model

Golding has evaluated the relative merits of entrusting the development of the law relating to the contract of employment to the judiciary as compared to statutory intervention as part of considering the development of Australian judge-made law regarding the implication of a term of good faith in the contract of employment.[119] Golding has examined factors that support courts engaging in judicial lawmaking,[120] such as flexibility, coherence, and predictability.

Golding has also identified factors that support the development of the law through statutory intervention alone such as democratic legitimacy, efficiency, and the reinforcement of judicial independence.[121] Golding has ultimately proposed a hybrid model, which recognizes the potential for interaction between statutory and judicial development of the law pertaining to the contract of employment. The proposal, in effect, envisages that the Australian Parliament would determine a model set of default terms to apply to employment contracts, which would be interpreted and applied in individual cases by the courts.[122]

Golding's proposal has a range of merits in terms of proposing a model for reforming the legal regulation of employer conduct towards respondents during workplace investigations. It can be adapted to envisage the development of a framework of central statutory principles about workplace investigations that courts would develop through the determination of specific disputes and that would evolve through incremental developments under regulations that support the *FW Act*. Statutory prescription need not be rigid or specific, and this provides latitude for diverse employer practices in workplace investigations. The proposal strikes a balance between efficiency and flexibility.

The hybrid model suggested by Golding inspires a model of law reform that includes direct statutory regulation of employer conduct during workplace investigations

[119] Golding, 'Role of Judges' (n 13) 79–86.
[120] ibid 80–82.
[121] ibid 82–84.
[122] ibid 86–89.

that imposes minimum standards that apply to the broadest range of employers and employees.

As I have identified in chapter 2, employees at all salary levels can be respondents in workplace investigations. A concern regarding the current legal regulation of workplace investigations that has emerged in this study is the lack of parity of legal protections that can exist between respondents. It is fitting to include minimum standards about employer conduct during workplace investigations in pt 2-2 of the *FW Act*, which sets out the NES. The NES apply to all 'national system' employers and employees,[123] which comprises most employers and employees in Australian workplaces. An employer must not contravene the NES, and all provisions of the NES are civil remedy provisions.[124]

This is more suitable than seeking to insert minimum standards within parts of the *FW Act* that set out individual statutory protections that only apply to eligible employees.[125] Minimum terms under modern awards similarly only apply to specified employees and generally exclude persons such as senior managers.[126] Situating proposed amendments in the NES ensures that they apply to the broadest range of employees and does not add further complexity to other parts of the *FW Act* that deal with different, although linked, workplace issues such as the protection against unfair dismissal under pt 3-2.

D A law reform proposal to promote justice for respondents in workplace investigations

I propose a new NES that directly and explicitly regulates employer conduct towards respondents during workplace investigations. The Proposed NES would comprise a new pt 2-2 div 13. It would comprise a framework of minimum standards to address key deficiencies and gaps in the legal regulation of workplace investigations under judge-made law and statute. The Proposed NES would require:

- an employer to establish a policy for conducting workplace investigations into allegations of worker misconduct that sets out core procedural requirements (as articulated in the *FW Regulations*), or to alternatively adopt the model policy, and (in either case) make that policy available to persons within the organisation;[127]
- the *FW Regulations* to set out:
  - the core procedural requirements for a fair workplace investigation process;
  - how the employer will address internal complaints by employees about the workplace investigations process;
  - the model policy;

[123] *FW Act* ss 13, 14, 60, 61.

[124] ibid s 44. On civil remedy provisions, see: ibid pt 4-1.

[125] For example, under the unfair dismissal protection in pt 3-2, a person must have completed the 'minimum employment period', earn less than the 'high income threshold', and must be covered by a modern award or enterprise agreement to make an application: *FW Act* ss 382–84.

[126] ibid s 143(2).

[127] Noting the discussion in chapter 1, it would be necessary to define a workplace investigation for the purposes of the Proposed NES.

- an employer to exercise any power or right under the policy in a reasonable way so as to avoid reasonably foreseeable psychiatric injury to an employee under investigation, a non-exhaustive list of factors for determining 'reasonableness', and any delimitation of liability and penalties as considered necessary and appropriate;
- an employer to advise an employee at the commencement of a workplace investigation that they are permitted to nominate a representative such as a union delegate and/or a support person;
- an employer to consult with an employee and their nominated representative about the process of the investigation when it commences, and allow the employee to nominate witnesses and sources of information; and
- an employer to recognise an employee's right to refuse to answer questions during a workplace investigation where the employee holds a reasonable belief that the answer could incriminate them in actual or anticipated civil or criminal proceedings and notifies the employer of that belief; and
- an employer to provide an employee with a fair workplace investigation information statement upon commencement of employment.

Like each NES, the Proposed NES would comprise a civil penalty provision. The FCA or the Federal Circuit and Family Court of Australia may make any order that the court considers appropriate if satisfied that there has been a contravention of a civil remedy provision.[128] This includes making an order awarding compensation for loss that a person has suffered because of the contravention.[129]

The Proposed NES would augment and complement existing statutory provisions of the *FW Act* that apply to employers during workplace investigations. It would ensure that a clear and targeted minimum code of employer conduct applies during workplace investigations under the work statute. The central elements of the Proposed NES are intended to promote justice in workplace investigations for respondents having regard to the framework that I developed in chapter 3 and its nine elements.

The core procedural requirements to be set out in the *FW Regulations* could draw from or build on key requirements in the *APSC Directions* that apply to Australian Public Service employers.[130] This would ensure greater parity and consistency between the rights of employees within the public and private sectors during workplace investigations. It is not proposed, however, that the policy include a requirement for employers to ensure 'procedural fairness' as defined under administrative law. The legal concept of 'procedural fairness' is nuanced and would be challenging for employers, and even lawyers who do not practice in the field of administrative law, to apply.[131]

The Proposed NES also contemplates that employers and workers could continue to negotiate enterprise-specific terms about workplace investigations in enterprise

[128] *FW Act* s 545(1).
[129] ibid s 545(2)(b).
[130] See chapter 5 IV(D).
[131] This point is sensibly made by James Mattson and Mark Paul, 'Workplace Investigations: Time to Reform Our Thinking?' (Australian Labour Law Association Conference, Melbourne, Australia, 4 November 2016) 9.

agreements, provided they are consistent with or are an improvement on the model provisions.

The Proposed NES includes a requirement for an employer to exercise any power or right under its policy or the model policy (as applicable) in a reasonable way so as to avoid reasonably foreseeable psychiatric injury to an employee under investigation. This responds to the uncertain state of judge-made law about the scope of an employer's duty of reasonable care under contract and/or tort towards a respondent in a workplace investigation.[132]

In chapter 4, I identified that respondents may be entitled to damages in relation to psychiatric harm caused by an employer's breach of an express contractual term by conduct during a workplace investigation. However, the availability of damages depends on factors including the construction of contractual terms, and the respondent demonstrating the employer's conduct during a workplace investigation breached a contractual term, and demonstrating that the damage was not too remote. In chapter 5, I also identified that state and territory workers' compensation regimes differ in terms of regulating claims that relate to unreasonable management conduct carried out in an unreasonable way in the context of workplace investigations.

The Proposed NES seeks to provide a remedial pathway for all national system employees that is consistent and coherent with respect to unreasonable or negligent employer conduct that leads to reasonably foreseeable psychiatric injury to a respondent.[133] The framework is intended to operate compatibly with the protections under pts 3-1 and 3-2 of the *FW Act* with respect to adverse action and unfair dismissal, including the remedies available.[134] It could also be integrated into the framework of provisions that address and limit multiple actions under the *FW Act*.[135]

The Proposed NES aligns with obligations on employers to manage psychosocial hazards during workplace investigations under *WHS Acts*.[136] It does not conflict with the statutory rights to compensation that exist under workers' compensation legislation that are available to employees with respect to psychiatric injuries caused by unreasonable management action conducted in an unreasonable way. Most importantly, it sends a clear and coherent message to employers that they must exercise powers reasonably and with care during a workplace investigation process so as to avoid psychiatric injury to respondents. A clear message is lacking in judge-made law in tort that follows from the decisions including *Paige* and *Elisha*.[137] The proposed framework promotes a key aspect of justice for respondents in workplace investigations.

An additional matter arises from the analysis in chapter 7 II, which calls for a statutory response to address a key gap and promote justice for workers under investigation. This matter relates to the prevention of psychiatric injury to workers during workplace investigations. It is apparent from cases such as *Paige*, *Govier*, and *Elisha* that there can be lifelong impacts of psychiatric injury on respondents. This

[132] See chapter 4 III.
[133] See chapter 5 IV(C).
[134] See in particular *FW Act s 392(4)*.
[135] ibid pt 6-1 div 3.
[136] See chapter 5 IV(B).
[137] *Paige* (n 48); *Elisha (HCA)* (n 61).

illuminates that justice for respondents in workplace investigations should promote the prevention of psychiatric injury. Statutory work law is silent on this matter.

On this basis, I suggest an additional amendment that supports the Proposed NES. I recommend changing the definition of when a worker is 'bullied at work' under s 789FD. The amendment would make it explicit that bullying can constitute unreasonable conduct by an employer during a workplace investigation that creates a risk to a respondent's psychiatric health. The amendment could be set out as a new s 789FD(2A).

There are at least two reasons why this additional amendment should be included in the *FW Act*. The first reason is that there is a small body of cases where workers have sought orders under the stop bullying jurisdiction of the *FW Act* to prevent further unreasonable employer conduct during a workplace investigation. These applications require a worker to establish that the employer's conduct comprises 'bullying at work', as currently defined in the *FW Act*. The availability of this right of redress is currently dependent on how Members of the FWC have interpreted the definition of 'bullying at work' under s 789FD.

There is no other statutory mechanism that is specifically available to respondents to obtain orders that prevent psychologically hazardous conduct during workplace investigations. For example, workers cannot individually enforce the obligations under the *WHS Acts* on employers and others to manage psychosocial hazards.[138] The proposed amendment would provide a straightforward mechanism that permits the FWC to make orders (in a timely manner) that stop employer conduct that poses a risk to mental health during a workplace investigation. It sends a clear message to employers and a direct (and relatively quick) avenue of redress for affected workers.

The second reason is that this proposed amendment does not raise concerns about enlivening a separate pathway for workers to seek monetary remedies for unreasonable or negligent conduct, as pt 6-4B excludes pecuniary orders. This is because pt 6-4B is concerned with the prevention of a continuation of bullying. It complements the Proposed NES.

Together, the Proposed NES and proposed reform of pt 6-4B would provide basic certainties to employers and respondents. This includes certainty that employers will prepare a basic policy on workplace investigations, apply it consistently, and give that policy to employees. The inclusion of an obligation for employers to ensure they reasonably exercise powers under the policy so as to avoid reasonably foreseeable psychiatric injury to respondents clarifies ambiguity between judge-made and statute law and complements the prioritization given to eliminating hazards to mental health that underpins the *Psychosocial Hazards Code of Practice*.[139]

The recommendation comprises a simple framework of targeted and clear regulation of employer conduct during workplace investigations under work law that responds to significant uncertainties and gaps in current legal regulation and is based on findings and conclusions set out in chapters 2–6 of this monograph. It promotes many of the elements of justice in workplace investigations set out in the framework,

[138] Options are available to other parties to address risks in a workplace such as Health and Safety Representatives. See chapter 5 IV(B).

[139] Safe Work Australia (n 56).

from dignified treatment of respondents to fair and relevant minimum standards and effective dispute resolution. It also provides employers with scope to tailor their processes to the workplace.

V Conclusion

In this chapter, I have conducted a positive examination of whether the law that regulates employer conduct during workplace investigations ensures justice for respondents. I have also examined the normative question of whether legal regulation should ensure justice for respondents and, if so, how the law might be reformed. I have argued that there are many aspects of the legal regulation of workplace investigations that are lacking when viewed through the theoretical framework of justice for respondents developed in chapter 3. The existing legal rules are fragmented and unduly complex. Gaps and deficiencies in current legal regulation amplify dimensions of injustice for respondents.

I have proposed a model of legal reform to work law that relies on legislative intervention to establish minimum standards and contemplates the further development of principles over time through judicial reasoning and amendments to the *FW Regulations*. The model sets out basic rules to apply to employers during workplace investigations and features:

- a Proposed NES that refers to a basic code of fair process in workplace investigations that is situated in the *FW Regulations*; and
- an explicit provision to allow workers to apply to the FWC to stop unreasonable conduct by an employer that constitutes 'bullying' during a workplace investigation.

The model of legal reform consolidates the legal, philosophical, and sociological analysis of workplace investigations in this monograph and contemplates direct and targeted statutory regulation of workplace investigations directed towards promoting justice for respondents. The model responds to key legal gaps and uncertainties. It does not displace or conflict with existing legal regulation but comprises a code that is directed at constraining management power during workplace investigations through work law that explicitly contemplates respondents as subjects of the law.

8

Conclusion

A Call for Justice for Respondents in Workplace Investigations

I Introduction

For work law to promote justice, it must address how an employer's use of power impacts on the rights of all employees. The value of citizenship at work encourages scholars to scrutinize whether work law endows all employees with adequate protection.

Respondents in workplace investigations are citizens at work who are vulnerable to a distinct range of detriments or injuries. While respondents may have engaged in conduct that warrants disciplinary action, they depend on employers to conduct a workplace investigation into allegations of misconduct competently and in good faith.

The broad scope for employers to exercise discretionary power during internal processes deserves sustained and in-depth scrutiny by legal scholars. It is crucial to consider how employer conduct towards respondents is legally regulated and give attention to respondents as subjects of the law.

In this volume, I have drawn on interdisciplinary literature and used sociological research methods to better understand how employers conduct workplace investigations and respondents experience them. I have interrogated how employer conduct during workplace investigations towards respondents is legally regulated in Australia, and how the law should be reformed to promote justice for respondents in workplace investigations.

Chapters 4 and 5 examined how workplace investigations are legally regulated in Australia and focused on respondents as subjects of the law. Chapters 2, 3, 6, and 7 engaged in legal, philosophical, and sociological analyses of workplace investigations and interrogated how the law should be reformed to promote justice for respondents in workplace investigations. In chapter 7, I consolidated these analyses and set out a proposal for legal change.

II Major Findings and Conclusions

Chapter 2 problematized the concept of a workplace investigation from a legal perspective. I consolidated and critically examined a broad body of HRM literature to identify common employer practices and central conflicts and controversies between parties during workplace investigations. I argued that workplace investigations are often described as impartial processes in HRM texts, but the position of the employer

Workplace Investigations. Adriana Orifici, Oxford University Press. © Adriana Orifici 2026.
DOI: 10.1093/9780198970019.003.0008

is inherently conflicted. The HRM texts reveal that employer practices vary greatly, and there is wide scope for employers to exercise discretionary power during workplace investigations. The HRM texts describe workplace investigations as often confronting and stressful processes that can harm workers including respondents and reveals the inherently conflicted role of the employer as a party that conducts the process but also an entity that experiences risk and has a partisan interest in the process and its findings.

In chapter 3, I developed a theory of justice in workplace investigations. While philosophical texts about workplace democracy and citizenship as sources of justice at work have mainly focused on case studies from jurisdictions beyond Australia,[1] the analysis in chapter 3 examined how these ideas have evolved in the Australian context. I argued that the importance of workplace investigations as a tool of HRM, the fragmented state of the law, and the lack of academic attention within law to the topic increases the potential vulnerability of respondents. I identified that a central aim of the field of work law remains the protection of workers, and that citizenship at work is a key value that can be promoted through law to achieve justice. I argued that citizenship at work is apposite to considering respondents in workplace investigations because they are less often conceptualized as requiring protection against employer power. By translating and adapting the template of rights in the *Charter*,[2] which is underpinned by the concept of citizenship at work, I established a framework of justice in workplace investigations for respondents with nine elements.

In chapters 4 and 5, I examined the legal regulation of employer conduct during workplace investigations with a focus on respondents as the subjects of the law. I identified that superior and appellate courts in Australia have developed some helpful judicial principles that regulate aspects of employer conduct towards respondents during workplace investigations. However, I identified that central principles are underdeveloped and unclear and that judge-made law inadequately regulates employer conduct towards respondents in workplace investigations. I scrutinized decisions and identified how courts have been reluctant to develop principles in ways that further constrain employer conduct in deference to statutory regulation of the law of dismissal. Notably, courts have not recognized:

- the duty of care owed by employers in contract and/or tort to include a safe system of workplace investigation and decision-making; or
- an obligation under the employment contract for employers to exercise discretionary powers reasonably or honestly so far as their workplace investigation process goes.

I noted that courts provide various explanations for not developing principles. One central reason is that courts consider that the decision to develop principles that intersect with the law regarding termination of employment should be made by the

[1] See, eg, Ruth Dukes and Wolfgang Streeck, 'Labour Law After Neoliberalism?' (2023) 50 Journal of Law and Society 165, 182.

[2] Mordy Bromberg and Mark Irving (eds), *Australian Charter of Employment Rights* (Hardie Grant Books 2007).

Australian Parliament and achieved through legislative amendment. I identified that the development of judge-made law has the potential to produce inconsistent outcomes for respondents who suffer similar psychiatric injuries because of employer conduct during workplace investigations, depending on the express terms of their contracts of employment.

I also argued that it is surprising that there is no overarching or comprehensive statutory code that governs workplace investigations given their importance as a tool of HRM. I identified that statutory work law does not directly or uniformly regulate employer conduct towards respondents during workplace investigations. I critically examined how employer conduct towards respondents during workplace investigations is governed by key provisions of the *FW Act*, anti-discrimination laws, WHS laws, and workers' compensation laws. I also explored how workplace investigations may also be governed by statutes about public sector employment, whistleblowing, and evidence.

I concluded that this framework of statutory regulation is a collection of disparate rules that are fragmented, unnecessarily complex, and unsystematic. I argued that legislation incompletely regulates workplace investigations, that there are inconsistencies between key rules, and that the law is therefore inadequate and in need of reform.

In chapter 6, I used qualitative content analysis in a novel way to examine a sample of decisions of the FWC under pt 3-2 of the *FW Act* to better understand how the respondents in the decisions viewed and experienced workplace investigations. I argued that legal scholarship and HRM texts lack insights about the views and experiences of respondents during these processes, and that it is necessary to understand respondents' experiences to ensure proposals for law reform have regard to them. I identified four central themes regarding how respondents in the sample of decisions experienced workplace investigations. Their recounted experiences revealed informational asymmetry between themselves and their employers, denial/minimization by their employers of their voices and opportunities for advocacy, denial by their employers of requests for accommodation, and harm to their psychological health. I argued that these themes reflected respondents' accounts of how they experienced dimensions of workplace investigations and that these themes could be used to inform law reform proposals.

Chapter 7 consolidated the legal, philosophical, and sociological strands of analysis of workplace investigations. I argued that the law that applies to employer conduct towards respondents is not only inadequate because it is fragmented, unsettled, and unduly complex. It is also inadequate because it does not promote justice for respondents in workplace investigations.

I posited that direct and targeted statutory regulation of workplace investigations was needed to promote justice for respondents. I suggested that the pathway of law reform was best achieved through statutory amendment, with scope for the development of the principles through judicial decision-making. I proposed a specific and achievable agenda of reform to the *FW Act* that featured:

- a new NES on workplace investigations (Proposed NES). I recommended that the Proposed NES include requirements for an employer to:
  - establish a policy for conducting workplace investigations into allegations of worker misconduct that sets out core procedural requirements (as articulated

in the *FW Regulations*)[3], or to alternatively adopt the model policy, and (in either case) make that policy available to persons within the organizations; and

- exercise any power or right under the policy in a reasonable way so as to avoid reasonably foreseeable mental injury to an employee under investigation, and set out a non-exhaustive list of factors for determining 'reasonableness' and any delimitation of liability and penalties as considered necessary and appropriate; and

- an explicit provision to allow workers to apply to the FWC to stop unreasonable conduct by an employer that constitutes 'bullying' during a workplace investigation.

The recommendations respond to central gaps in the legal regulation of employer conduct towards respondents during workplace investigations. As revealed in chapter 7, these gaps not only arise because the law is uncertain and fragmented, but also because it does not adequately promote justice for respondents, having regard to the framework of justice developed in chapter 3, and its nine elements.

The reforms that I have proposed do not displace existing legal regulation and are directed at constraining employer power towards respondents during workplace investigations through work law and setting consistent standards of employer conduct. The proposal responds to and fills key gaps in the law and promotes the framework of justice for respondents in workplace investigations, as developed in chapter 3. It builds on the findings about how employers conduct workplace investigations in chapter 2 and is informed by the recounted experiences of respondents as revealed in chapter 6.

The law reform proposal is also informed by the conditions that have led to the rise in workplace investigations as a prevalent HRM tool in workplaces in Australia and beyond. The central shift from collectivism towards individualism is reflected in the history of legal disputes about workplace investigations under contract and tort before Australian courts. Workplace investigations exemplify the atomization of workplace governance to individualized processes that precipitate individualized grievances. The proposal seeks to implement a consistent basic standard for workplace investigations processes, and a mechanism that enables consultation about the process with the respondent and any nominated industrial representative. It recognizes the role of collectivism and representation in promoting justice for respondents, and the scope for parties in enterprise bargaining to tailor the basic standard to the enterprise in accordance with the *FW Act*.

III A Call to Change the Law to Promote Justice for Respondents in Workplace Investigations

In *Elisha (First Instance)*, O'Meara J observed that the employer's workplace investigation process was 'nothing short of a sham and a disgrace',[4] and that this conduct

[3] *Fair Work Regulations 2009 (Cth).*

[4] *Elisha v Vision Australia Ltd* [2022] VSC 754 [236]. A Full Court of the Supreme Court of Victoria and the HCA left this finding undisturbed on appeal. See further references to this case in chapter 5.

ultimately led the plaintiff, who was the respondent in a workplace investigation, to suffer a very severe and permanent psychiatric injury.[5] O'Meara J held that this injury left the respondent permanently incapacitated but that the employer had no duty to provide a safe system of workplace investigation under contract and/or tort and had not breached its duty of reasonable care under Australian law. At a minimum, the law needs to consistently respond to situations such as these where an employer's deficient investigation process risks profoundly injuring a respondent.

It is time for the Australian Parliament to regulate workplace investigations directly and proactively through statutory work law. Statutory regulation of workplace investigations needs to be underpinned by a policy objective to constrain employer power and limit the risk of harm or injury to respondents. This objective aligns with theoretical scholarship that recognizes that a purpose of work law is protection of workers. It is also consistent with the idea of citizenship at work as a source of justice.

The proposed legal reforms included in chapter 7 are informed by doctrinal, philosophical, and sociological research and are practical and achievable. They augment rather than repeal or displace existing regulation. They seek to ensure basic procedural aspects of workplace investigations are standardized and understood by all parties. They also provide respondents with mechanisms to improve procedural transparency, promote respondent voice, ensure employers contemplate and accommodate respondents' needs and circumstances, and stop unreasonable conduct by an employer that poses a risk to a respondent's mental health.[6]

The conclusions in this study are relevant to employers, employees, unions, lawyers, and academia as well as governments and lawmakers. In this monograph, I have challenged the perception of workplace investigations as neutral processes that precede managerial decision-making and problematized this HRM phenomenon from a legal perspective as a tool of employer power. Comprehensive and clear legal regulation of workplace investigations promotes efficiency and certainty for employers and provides clarity to respondents and their representatives about legal rights and potential remedies. Workplace investigations require recognition in legal scholarship because there is so much at stake for all parties; the subject warrants continued academic attention.

The exploration of philosophical themes about justice, citizenship, employer discretion, and employer power in internalized organizational processes in this volume invites reflection on the normative rationale of legal protections that apply at work. Work law should clearly and comprehensively codify the obligations of employers towards respondents during workplace investigations to promote justice for these workers as subjects of the law. The prevalence of workplace investigations in Australian workplaces means that the time to petition for law reform is now.

5 ibid [629].
6 See chapter 6 V.

APPENDIX 1

Chapter 6—Codebook First Cycle Coding

Respondents' Reported Experiences and Perceptions of Three Stages of Workplace Investigation Process First Stage Codes

COMMENCING THE INVESTIGATION	
PARENT CODE: Notifying the respondent of the investigation (employer)	
CHILD CODE	DESCRIPTION[1]
Not notifying employee of decision to investigate	Employer commenced an investigation into allegations of misconduct against respondent employee but did not notify him/her that it had done so[2]
Providing little/no information on process to employee at outset	Employer provided the employee respondent with little or no information about the process/ procedure that would be followed in the investigation[3]
Arranging a 'meeting' without explaining it is an investigation interview/commencement of investigation	Employer/investigator told the employee respondent that they needed to attend a meeting and only told him/her that the meeting was an interview as part of an investigation for allegations of misconduct against him/her at the start of the meeting[4]
Directing employee respondent to attend an interview with little/no notice	Employer directed employee respondent to attend interview with little/no notice (eg, 'unprepared', 'blindsided')[5]
Combining another inquiry with a workplace investigation	Employer started a preliminary inquiry/ 'information gathering' or safety inquiry that became an investigation into allegations of misconduct[6]

[1] An example decision was identified to annotate the description.

[2] *Eagland v BMW Melbourne Pty Ltd* [2018] FWC 649 [54] (Harper-Greenwel C) (written witness statement, summarized).

[3] *Horan v Tren Trading Pty Ltd* [2019] FWC 3249 [25] (Harper-Greenwel C) (written witness statement, summarized).

[4] *Allen v Kandeena Pty Ltd* [2020] FWC 761 [51] (Hunt C) (verbal witness evidence, summarized).

[5] *Cahill v Sydney Trains* [2020] FWC 6064 [140] (McKenna C) (verbal witness evidence, quoted/ summarized).

[6] *Fisher v Cabra-Vale Ex-Active Servicemen's Club Ltd* [2020] FWC 5703 [73] (Riordan C) (written witness statement, summarized).

PARENT CODE: Directing the respondent to maintain confidentiality during the investigation (employer)	
CHILD CODE	DESCRIPTION
Directing employee to maintain confidentiality without explaining how to access information/evidence	Employer directed employee respondent to maintain confidentiality over the investigation but did not explain how they could access information, documents, witnesses, etc that they needed to respond to allegations[7]
Directing the employee to sign confidentiality agreement	Employer directed employee respondent to sign a confidentiality agreement relating to the investigation/investigation process[8]
PARENT CODE: Suspending the respondent (employer)	
CHILD CODE	DESCRIPTION
'Singling out' employee for suspension	Employee respondent believed they were investigated but not other employees who may have engaged in similar misconduct[9]
Suspending employee without explaining rules/requirements	Employer suspended the employee respondent and did not explain to him/her what obligations/ rules and/or requirements applied to them while suspended and/or whether the suspension was with pay/no pay[10]
Suspending employee without explaining allegations	Employer suspended the employee respondent and did not provide details about the allegations to them[11]
Suspending employee in front of others	Employer suspended the employee respondent publicly and/or in front of other staff[12]
CONDUCTING THE INVESTIGATION (INCLUDING INFORMATION GATHERING AND INTERVIEWING)	
PARENT CODE: Managing the investigation process (employer)	
CHILD CODE	DESCRIPTION
Skipping steps/rushing through	Perception/experience of employer skipping steps and/or rushing through steps prescribed in the employer's policy/procedure[13]

[7] *Bajelis v Reserve Bank of Australia* [2020] FWC 3740 [28] (Cross DP) (written witness statement, summarized).

[8] *Groza v Toll Transport Pty Ltd* [2020] FWC 5838 [38] (Yilmaz C) (verbal witness evidence, summarized).

[9] *Ali v Choban Pty Ltd i* [2019] FWC 4406 [53] (McKinnon C) (verbal witness evidence, summarized).

[10] *Horan* (n 3) [16] (verbal witness evidence, summarized).

[11] ibid.

[12] *Snell v Bendigo and Adelaide Bank Ltd* [2019] FWC 8050 [109] (Gregory C) (written witness statement, summarized).

[13] *Clarke v Toll Transport Pty Ltd* [2019] FWC 606 [58] (Hunt C) (written witness statement, attachment, quoted).

Circulating information unnecessarily	Information was circulated about the workplace investigation or allegations to colleagues within the employer's organization that were not involved in the matter by a manager or other employee involved in the investigation[14]
Following process/procedure 'in form' only	Employer followed the steps prescribed in the employer's investigation policy/procedure in form only[15]
Using a legalistic/formalized/heavy-handed process	Employer conducted an investigation in a heavy-handed manner (eg, 'overkill', excessive)[16]
Delaying/prolonging next steps without explanation	Employer conducted an investigation with many delays and did not explain to the employee respondent the reason for the delays[17]
Providing little/no updates on next steps/progress	Employer only explained the initial steps in the investigation process to the employee in writing/verbally but did not give subsequent information about next steps or progress[18]
Providing incorrect/misleading information on process	Employer gave employee respondent incorrect or misleading information about investigation process[19]
Providing information on process only after request/complaint	Employer gave employee respondent information about process but only after a request from the employee[20]
Providing no information on process after request	Employer did not respond to request for information about process from respondent information and/or did not provide access to policies/procedures[21]
Providing information on process but delayed	Employer gave employee respondent information about process but after a long delay[22]

[14] *Betar v Cricks Sunshine Coast* [2019] FWC 6547 [165] (Spencer C) (written witness statement, quoted).

[15] *Andrawos v MyBudget Pty Ltd* [2018] FWC 4288 [227] (Anderson DP) (written witness statement, summarized).

[16] *Plesiotis v Huhtamaki Australia Pty Ltd* [2020] FWC 120 [21] (Lee C) (verbal witness evidence, quoted).

[17] *Maxitanis v Department of Justice and Community Safety* [2020] FWCFB 4529 [87] (Hatcher VP, Sams DP, Spencer C) (verbal witness evidence, quoted).

[18] *Lecaude v Westpac Banking Corporation* [2018] FWC 1969 [48] (Williams C) (written witness statement, attachment, summarized).

[19] *Waite v Serco Australia Pty Ltd* [2018] FWC 3113 [87] (Asbury DP) (verbal witness evidence, summarized).

[20] *Major v Resilience Solutions Pty Ltd* [2018] FWC 660 [27] (Beaumont DP) (verbal witness evidence, summarized).

[21] *Drake v BHP Coal Pty Ltd* [2019] FWC 7444 [94] (Asbury DP) (verbal witness evidence, summarized).

[22] *Boyle v BHP Coal Pty Ltd* [2020] FWC 1080 [52] (Hunt C) (verbal witness evidence, summarized).

PARENT CODE: **Suspending the respondent (employer)**	
CHILD CODE	DESCRIPTION
Providing suspended employee respondent with little/no updates/long delay	Employer suspended the employee respondent and then provided them with little or no information on the progress of the investigation or with long delays between communications (eg, feeling left in the dark)[23]
PARENT CODE: **Providing allegations (and/or particulars and/or supporting documents) to the respondent (employer)**	
CHILD CODE	DESCRIPTION
Not providing allegations before interview	Employer did not provide employee respondent with any allegations before conducting the interview but told them they were under investigation[24]
Providing vague, broad or brief allegations	Employer provided the employee respondent with written allegations that were vague, broad or brief[25]
Providing written allegations but no details/supporting documents	Employer provided the employee respondent with written allegations but no particulars and/or supporting documents[26]
Adding to allegations over time	Employer added more allegations to the list over time[27]
Modifying allegations over time	Employer modified the allegations that had been provided to the employee respondent in subsequent correspondence/documentation[28]
Refusing to provide more detail about allegations/only after long delay	Employer refused request by employee respondent to provide more detail about allegations/particulars or only provided after long delay[29]
PARENT CODE: **Gathering evidence (respondent)**	
CHILD CODE	DESCRIPTION
Refusing access to documents/other information	Employer did not give employee access to documents/other information relevant to allegations when they requested it[30]

[23] *Akpey v Perth Re Pty Ltd* [2018] FWC 5699 [16] (Beaumont DP) (written witness statement, attachment, summarized).

[24] *Bartlett v Ingleburn Bus Services Pty Ltd* [2020] FWC 2914 [6] (Boyce DP) (written witness statement, summarized).

[25] *Snell* (n 12) [11] (written witness statement, summarized).

[26] *Cowper v St Josephs Flexible Learning Centre* [2019] FWC 6630 [23] (Gregory C) (written witness statement, summarized).

[27] *Tainsh v Toyota Motor Corporation Australia Ltd* [2018] FWC 4192 [189] (Harper-Greenwell C) (verbal witness evidence, summarized).

[28] *Cahill* (n 5) [156] (written witness statement, summarized).

[29] *Kapoor v Teleperformance Australia* [2018] FWC 4520 [13] (Gregory C) (verbal witness evidence, summarized).

[30] *Turland v Yass Valley Aged Care Ltd* [2020] FWC 843 [21] (Kovacic DP) (written witness statement, summarized).

Withholding documents/other information	Employer did not give employee access to documents/other information relevant to allegations and they realized at hearing when they were produced[31]
PARENT CODE: **Interviewing the respondent (employer)**	
CHILD CODE	DESCRIPTION
Asking humiliating/embarrassing questions at interview	Employee respondent reported feeling humiliated/embarrassed by employer/investigator during interview (eg, due to personal questions, etc)[32]
Asking intimidating questions at interview	Employee respondent reported feeling intimidated by employer/investigator during interview (eg, due to 'yelling', 'aggressive', 'threatening', etc)[33]
Not listening to responses from employee respondent at interview	Employee respondent reported employer/investigator was dismissive/disinterested in his/her responses during interview[34]
Introducing new allegations at interview	Employer/investigator introduced new allegations during the interview that the employee respondent had not previously been told about[35]
Proceeding with interview when employee respondent was upset or crying	Employee respondent reported participating in interview while feeling upset (eg, 'crying', feeling 'stressed', 'upset', 'concerned', etc)[36]
Producing witness statement/record of interview that is incomplete/with errors	Employer prepared a record of interview or witness statement for employee respondent at/after interview that contained errors and they refused to confirm or sign it but it was relied on[37]
Preparing a witness statement with errors and no chance of correction	Employer prepared a witness statement for employee respondent at/after interview that contained errors but did not ask him/her to read over or confirm contents[38]

[31] *Puth v Precision Valve Australia Pty Ltd* [2020] FWC 7027 [56] (Sams DP) (verbal witness evidence, summarized).
[32] *Lupson v Australian Pacific Airports (Melbourne) Pty Ltd* [2020] FWC 6721 [60] (Mansini DP) (verbal witness evidence, quoted/summarized).
[33] *Abarra v Toyota Motor Corporation Australia Ltd* [2018] FWC 3761 [28] (Harper-Greenwell C) (written witness statement, summarized).
[34] *Betar* (n 14) [42]–[43] (written submissions, summarized).
[35] *Kabidi v Metro Trains Melbourne Pty Ltd* [2020] FWC 6941 [71] (Young DP) (written submissions, summarized).
[36] *Nash v Bacchus Marsh Coaches Pty Ltd* [2018] FWC 347 [39] (Colman DP) (written witness statement, summarized).
[37] *Fernandopulle v Taylors Business Pty Ltd* [2018] FWC 3557 [37] (Wilson C) (verbal witness evidence, summarized).
[38] *Cowper* (n 26) [23] (written witness statement, summarized).

Refusing to accept written rather than verbal response	Employer/investigator put allegations to employee respondent at interview and refused to allow him/her to provide response in writing[39]
PARENT CODE: Requesting support or representation (respondent)	
CHILD CODE	DESCRIPTION
Refusing request for postponement of interview	Employer declined request by employee respondent for postponement of an interview so that chosen support person could attend with them[40]
Refusing request for legal representation at interview	Employer refused request by employee respondent to be legally represented at an interview[41]
Denying employee respondent chance to ask for support/representation	Employer did not tell the employee respondent about the purpose of the meeting (ie, that it was an interview relating to allegations of misconduct) and they reported that this denied them the chance to bring a support person/representative[42]
PARENT CODE: Modifying/not modifying the process to accommodate request for support or assistance by the respondent (employer)	
CHILD CODE	DESCRIPTION
Modifying/not modifying process for English capacity	Employee respondent asked for assistance with interview and/or responding to allegations in writing because of written or verbal English language skills and employer accommodated/declined to accommodate[43]
Modifying/not modifying process because of disability, impairment, or other impediment	Employee respondent asked for assistance with interview and/or responding to allegations in writing because of disability, impairment, or other impediment and employer accommodated/declined to accommodate[44]

39 *Akpey* (n 23) [11] (verbal witness evidence, summarized).
40 *Mazi v Arcare Pty Ltd* [2020] FWC 6172 [33] (Spencer C) (written witness statement, summarized).
41 ibid [33] (written witness statement, summarized).
42 *Cahill* (n 5) [147] (verbal witness evidence, quoted/summarized).
43 *Thein v Melbourne Health* [2020] FWC 3628 [52] (Wilson C) (written submissions, quoted/summarized).
44 *Barber-Fleming v Billi Australia Pty Ltd* [2020] FWC 6029 [26] (Cambridge C) (verbal submissions, quoted/summarized).

MAKING FINDINGS AND DECISIONS TO DISCIPLINE	
PARENT CODE: **Putting findings about the allegations to the respondent (employer)**	
CHILD CODE	DESCRIPTION
Making findings about unheard allegations	Employer/investigator put findings to the employee respondent about allegation/s that they had not previously been told about and asked for response/show cause[45]
PARENT CODE: **Making findings about the allegations (employer)**	
CHILD CODE	DESCRIPTION
Making findings at interview and dismissing employee respondent	Employer asked employee respondent to respond to allegations, made findings, and dismissed him/her at the same interview meeting[46]
Denying access to investigation report	Employer did not give employee respondent access to investigation report and/or preliminary findings and/or witness statements and/or incident reports or other documents when they requested it in order to provide response or only after repeated requests/delay[47]
Asking employee to resign during interview	Employer/investigator asked employee respondent if they wished to resign during interview[48]
PARENT CODE: **Disciplining the respondent due to conduct in investigation (employer)**	
CHILD CODE	DESCRIPTION
Disciplining employee respondent for conduct during investigation	Employer made findings about the conduct of the employee respondent during the investigation and disciplined them on the basis of that conduct (eg, unprofessional conduct, raising voice, misleading answers, aggression, etc)[49]
Disciplining employee for breaching confidentiality direction	Employee respondent did not follow direction to maintain confidentiality to access information, documents, and/or speak to witnesses to respond to allegations and on this basis was disciplined by employer[50]

[45] *Mazi* (n 40) [36] (written witness statement, summarized).
[46] *Bartlett* (n 24) [6] (written witness statement, summarized).
[47] *Boyle* (n 22) [223] (verbal witness evidence, summarized).
[48] *Boyce v IKON Administration Pty Ltd* [2019] FWC 4763[41] (Wilson C) (verbal witness evidence, quoted).
[49] *Boyle* (n 22) [220] (written witness statement, summarized).
[50] *Mazi* (n 40) [55] (written witness statement, summarized).

APPENDIX 2

Chapter 6—Codebook Second Cycle Concepts and Categories

RESPONDENT VIEW OR EXPERIENCE—CONCEPT	RESPONDENT VIEW OR EXPERIENCE—CATEGORY
Not knowing they are a respondent	Informational asymmetry
Not knowing the subject/details of allegations	Informational asymmetry
Not given information, policies, explanation about process that would apply	Informational asymmetry
Not given chance to participate in all steps in process	Denial/ minimization of worker voice
Not given chance to explain	Denial/ minimization of worker voice
Not able to discuss investigation with others or ask for information from others because of confidentiality obligations	Denial/ minimization of worker voice Informational asymmetry
Lacking English language, legal, other support during interview or meeting	Denial of accommodation of workers' needs and abilities
Not given a requested adjournment or extension so could not attend or attended without support/representation	Denial/ minimization of worker voice
Not given relevant information or updates during investigation	Informational asymmetry
Not given relevant evidence or documents	Informational asymmetry
Denied respect or dignity in interview or meeting	Risk of harm to workers' psychological health
Concerned by investigation timeframe or uncertainty about timeframe	Risk of harm to workers' psychological health
Not given support or information while directed not to attend work	Risk of harm to workers' psychological health Informational asymmetry

APPENDIX 3

Chapter 6—Decisions Analyzed

1. *Abarra v Toyota Motor Corporation Australia Ltd* [2018] FWC 3761
2. *Addo v Safe Places Community Services Ltd* [2020] FWC 3858
3. *Ahmadyar v Visy Board Pty Ltd* [2019] FWC 6083
4. *Akpey v Perth Re Pty Ltd* [2018] FWC 5699
5. *Ali v Chobani Pty Ltd* [2019] FWC 4406
6. *Allen v Kandeena Pty Ltd* [2020] FWC 761
7. *Amba v HCL Australia Services Pty Ltd* [2018] FWC 5786
8. *Andrawos v MyBudget Pty Ltd* [2018] FWC 4288
9. *Anson v Western District Health Service* [2018] FWC 2132
10. *Atherton v Airmaster Australia Pty Ltd* [2018] FWC 3109
11. *Ayres v City of Kingston* [2018] FWC 4291
12. *Bajelis v Reserve Bank of Australia* [2020] FWC 3740
13. *Barber-Fleming v Billi Australia Pty Ltd* [2020] FWC 6029
14. *Barnes v BHP Coal Pty Ltd* [2019] FWC 6569
15. *Bartlett v Ingleburn Bus Services Pty Ltd* [2020] FWC 2914
16. *Belan v National Union of Workers (NSW Branch)* [2017] FWC 5027; *Belan v National Union of Workers (NSW Branch)* [2018] FWCFB 94
17. *Beltrame v Essential Energy* [2019] FWC 2592
18. *Betar v Cricks Sunshine Coast* [2019] FWC 6547
19. *Bird v BHP Coal Pty Ltd* [2019] FWC 7444
20. *Bond v Wynbob Pty Ltd* [2018] FWC 1337
21. *Boris v Metcash Trading Ltd* [2019] FWC 3993
22. *Boyce v IKON Administration Pty Ltd* [2019] FWC 4763
23. *Boyle v BHP Coal Pty Ltd* [2020] FWC 1080
24. *Cachia v Scobel Pty Ltd* [2018] FWC 2648
25. *Cahill v Sydney Trains* [2020] FWC 6064
26. *Carmody v ISS Integrated Services* [2019] FWC 6070
27. *Chandan v Language Smart Pty Ltd* [2020] FWC 1057
28. *Chileshe v EnergyAustralia Pty Ltd* [2019] FWC 7622
29. *Clarke v Toll Transport Pty Ltd* [2019] FWC 606
30. *Colwell v Sydney International Container Terminals Pty Ltd* [2018] FWC 174
31. *Coombs v Sydney Water Corporation* [2019] FWC 7940
32. *Cowper v St Josephs Flexible Learning Centre* [2019] FWC 6630
33. *D'Ortenzio v Charles Parletta Real Estate Pty Ltd* [2018] FWC 1002
34. *Devine v Enagic Australia Pty Ltd* [2020] FWC 4825
35. *Dias v Commonwealth Bank* [2019] FWC 5479
36. *Do v MSS Security Pty Ltd* [2019] FWC 8010
37. *Duggan v Metropolitan Fire and Emergency Services Board* [2018] FWC 4945

38. *Dyson v Centennial Myuna Pty Ltd* [2020] FWC 5486
39. *Eagland v BMW Melbourne Pty Ltd* [2018] FWC 649
40. *Edwards v Litchfield Council* [2019] FWC 6660
41. *Elliot v Australian Rail Track Corporation Ltd* [2019] FWC 3786
42. *Emery v City of Stirling* [2018] FWC 6853
43. *Facchin v Tasmanian Networks Pty Ltd* [2020] FWC 2796
44. *Fernandopulle v Taylors Business Pty Ltd* [2018] FWC 3557
45. *Finn v Gippsland & East Gippsland Aboriginal Co-Operative Ltd* [2019] FWC 1506
46. *Fisher v Cabra-Vale Ex-Active Servicemen's Club Ltd* [2020] FWC 5703
47. *Ford v Marlau Nominees Pty Ltd* [2019] FWC 4178
48. *Fussell v Transport for NSW* [2019] FWC 1182
49. *Gelagotis v Esso Australia Pty Ltd* [2018] FWC 2398
50. *Gigney v Qantas Airways Ltd* [2018] FWC 1352
51. *Gilani v GNZ Enterprises Pty Ltd* [2018] FWC 1719
52. *Gomes v Gemela Pty Ltd* [2019] FWC 4222
53. *Groza v Toll Transport Pty Ltd* [2020] FWC 5838
54. *Hajder v Agnew Gold Mining Company Pty Ltd* [2020] FWC 4547
55. *Hatch v WesTrac Pty Ltd* [2020] FWC 5729
56. *Hay v Ambulance Victoria* [2020] FWC 2193
57. *Hey v Pacific Golf Club* [2020] FWC 3496
58. *Hill v Cobham Aviation Services Pty Ltd* [2019] FWC 7875
59. *Hodgson v Bendigo Kangan Institute* [2018] FWC 69
60. *Horan v Tren Trading Pty Ltd* [2019] FWC 3249
61. *Hutton v ACFS Port Logistics Pty Ltd* [2020] FWC 4693
62. *Innes v Heathcote Dairy* [2019] FWC 6812
63. *Jarmain v Linfox Armaguard Pty Ltd* [2018] FWC 3255
64. *Jeffs v Qantas Ground Services Pty Ltd* [2019] FWC 7963
65. *Johns v Zone RV Pty Ltd* [2020] FWC 5049
66. *Kabidi v Metro Trains Melbourne Pty Ltd* [2020] FWC 6941
67. *Kapoor v Teleperformance Australia* [2018] FWC 4520
68. *Katrib v Commonwealth Insurance Limited* [2020] FWC 6872
69. *Kaur v Moorditch Gurlongga Assoc* [2019] FWC 5574
70. *Kelly v The Hills Christian Community School Inc* [2018] FWC 4134
71. *Kezic v Brand Developers (Aus) Pty Ltd* [2019] FWC 7889
72. *Khan v Who Bathroom Warehouse Pty Ltd* [2018] FWC 3440
73. *Khoshaba v Woolstar Pty Ltd* [2020] FWC 6596
74. *Kordek v Marsh Pty Ltd* [2020] FWC 6972
75. *Kuskey v Clarke* [2020] FWC 5901
76. *Lakew v MSS Security Pty Ltd* [2019] FWC 4462
77. *Lamacq v Smerff Electrical* [2019] FWC 181
78. *Lautaimi v Pabs Furniture Rentals Pty Ltd* [2020] FWC 3819
79. *Law v Groote Eylandt Mining Company Pty Ltd* [2018] FWC 1824
80. *Lear v BHP WAIO Pty Ltd* [2020] FWC 4949
81. *Lecaude v Westpac Banking Corporation* [2018] FWC 1969
82. *Lee v Alexandria Imex Pty Ltd* [2020] FWC 4837

83. *Lewis v SGA (1994) Pty Ltd* [2019] FWC 8552
84. *Liistro v Services of Top Cut Foods (Vic) Pty Ltd* [2020] FWC 70
85. *Lim v Aeonic Group Pty Ltd* [2020] FWC 4692
86. *Lupson v Australian Pacific Airports (Melbourne) Pty Ltd* [2020] FWC 6721
87. *Lynd-Stevenson v Flinders University* [2018] FWC 5722
88. *Mabil v Rew Bros Pty Ltd* [2018] FWC 1379
89. *Mackay v Woolworths Group Ltd* [2019] FWC 5584
90. *Maguire v BHP Billiton Iron Ore Pty Ltd* [2019] FWC 8046
91. *Major v Resilience Solutions Pty Ltd* [2018] FWC 660
92. *Mallia v Toll Transport Pty Ltd* [2018] FWC 1713
93. *Mammarella v Department of Parliamentary Services* [2019] FWC 6340
94. *Maxitanis v Department of Justice and Community Safety* [2020] FWCFB 4529
95. *Mazi v Arcare Pty Ltd* [2020] FWC 6172
96. *McAuley v Northern Territory Government* [2018] FWC 330
97. *McCouaig v Colliers International (SA) Pty Ltd* [2019] FWC 1517
98. *Mcillwain v Northern Territory Water Ski Association* [2019] FWC 8606
99. *McLean v Nyrstar Hobart Pty Ltd* [2020] FWC 6457
100. *Mellios v Qantas Airways Ltd* [2020] FWCFB 5885
101. *Meredith v Chad Group Australia Pty Ltd* [2020] FWC 1467
102. *Milad v Melbourne Health* [2020] FWC 1939
103. *Misovic v Linfox Australia Pty Ltd* [2019] FWC 7771
104. *Monaghan v Greyhound Racing Control Board* [2018] FWC 4933
105. *Meaney v Monash University* [2018] FWC 5796
106. *Montgomery v Essential Energy* [2020] FWC 3684
107. *Morgan v Serco Australia Pty Ltd* [2018] FWC 5835
108. *Moylan v Gosnells Golf Club Inc* [2020] FWC 3130
109. *Murphy v ECEC Management Pty Ltd* [2019] FWC 3169; *Murphy v ECEC Management Pty Ltd* [2019] FWCFB 6914
110. *Mwango v WesTrac Pty Ltd* [2018] FWC 3135
111. *Nash v Bacchus Marsh Coaches Pty Ltd* [2018] FWC 347
112. *Natoli v Envision Employment Services* [2018] FWC 4034
113. *Nemcic v Australian Electoral Commission* [2018] FWC 5645
114. *Neville v Lake Fox Ltd* [2020] FWC 5809
115. *Newton v Toll Transport Pty Ltd* [2020] FWC 5960
116. *Ninon v Metropolitan Taxi Club Inc* [2018] FWC 3293
117. *Okoye v SACARE Supported Accommodation and Care Services* [2020] FWC 704
118. *Paech v Hage Retail Group* [2019] FWC 6487
119. *Palmer v USG Boral Building Products Pty Ltd* [2017] FWC 147; *Palmer v USG Boral Building Products Pty Ltd* [2018] FWC 654.
120. *Pavlovic v Alcoa of Australia Ltd* [2020] FWC 3919
121. *Pecoski v Alpha Flight Services* [2018] FWC 356
122. *Pericich v Hanson Construction Materials Pty Ltd* [2018] FWC 1336
123. *Petz v Jamieson Sales and Service Pty Ltd* [2020] FWC 4451
124. *Pickering v Linfox Australia Pty Ltd* [2020] FWC 6595
125. *Plesiotis v Huhtamaki Australia Pty Ltd* [2020] FWC 120

126. *Prasad v Cordina Chicken Farms Pty Ltd* [2019] FWC 7075
127. *Prosser v Ziegam Pty Ltd* [2019] FWC 676
128. *Puth v Precision Valve Australia Pty Ltd* [2020] FWC 7027
129. *Reihana v GEO Group Australia Pty Ltd* [2018] FWC 994
130. *Robinson v Emprja Pty Ltd* [2020] FWC 6525
131. *Roche v Trustees of the Roman Catholic Church for the Diocese of Wagga Wagga* [2018] FWC 3933
132. *Rojas v Beacon Products Pty Ltd* [2018] FWC 4317
133. *Ryan v Orbitz Elevators Pty Ltd* [2019] FWC 8445
134. *Puszka v Ryan Wilks Pty Ltd* [2019] FWC 1132
135. *Sclater v Transdev Harbour City Ferries Pty Ltd* [2019] FWC 7968
136. *Scoffern v Griffin Coal Mining Company Pty Ltd* [2020] FWC 3201
137. *Scott v Latrobe Regional Hospital* [2019] FWC 5680
138. *Shamoon v Cabin Services Australia* [2019] FWC 2260
139. *Sikalias v Qantas Airways Ltd* [2020] FWC 1830
140. *Siminsky v Gunlake Concrete NSW Pty Ltd* [2019] FWC 2429
141. *Singh v Crown Melbourne Ltd* [2020] FWC 1927
142. *Singh v Sydney Trains* [2019] FWC 182
143. *Smith v SafeRad SE Asia Pty Ltd* [2018] FWC 2104
144. *Snell v Bendigo and Adelaide Bank Ltd* [2019] FWC 8050
145. *Steel v Hitachi Power Tools Australia Pty Ltd* [2019] FWC 1195
146. *Steffens v Greenmountain Food Processing Pty Ltd* [2020] FWC 1281
147. *Stevens v ISS Property Services Pty Ltd* [2020] FWC 1340
148. *Straschko v Casino Canberra Ltd* [2020] FWC 1991
149. *Sully v CBMG North Pty Ltd* [2020] FWC 3509
150. *Sydney Trains v Hilder* [2020] FWCFB 1373
151. *Symes v Linfox Armaguard Pty Ltd* [2018] FWC 7142
152. *Tainsh v Toyota Motor Corporation Australia Ltd* [2018] FWC 4192
153. *Tamwoy v Northern Peninsula Area Justice Services Aboriginal and Torres Strait Islander Corporation* [2020] FWC 3718
154. *Tang v National Australia Bank Ltd* [2019] FWC 1950
155. *Taylor v StarTrack Express* [2018] FWC 3909
156. *Thein v Melbourne Health* [2020] FWC 3628
157. *Thomas v KDR Victoria Pty Ltd* [2018] FWC 2698
158. *Thomas v Serco Immigration Detention Centre* [2020] FWC 3738
159. *Thomas v Virgin Australia Airlines Pty Ltd* [2019] FWC 4464
160. *Tracey v BP Refinery (Kwinana) Pty Ltd* [2020] FWCFB 820
161. *Troiano v BlueScope Steel (AIS) Pty Ltd* [2018] FWC 439
162. *Turland v Yass Valley Aged Care Ltd* [2020] FWC 843
163. *Urso v QF Cabin Crew Australia Pty Ltd* [2018] FWC 4436
164. *Vai v ALDI Stores* [2018] FWC 4118
165. *Vennix v Mayfield Childcare Ltd* [2019] FWC 8283
166. *von Erkel v Solar Station Alpha Pty Ltd* [2018] FWC 2473
167. *Wait v Tenterfield Care Centre Limited* [2018] FWC 2472
168. *Waite v Serco Australia Pty Ltd* [2018] FWC 3113
169. *Ward v Great Southern Rail Pty Ltd* [2019] FWC 5064

170. *Ward v TRG Administration Pty Ltd* [2018] FWC 1475
171. *Warr v Qantas Airways Ltd* [2019] FWC 2182
172. *Waters v Mt Arthur Coal Pty Ltd* [2018] FWC 3285
173. *Weatherall v Elevate Education Pty Ltd* [2020] FWC 6143
174. *Weekley v Essential Energy* [2018] FWC 1448
175. *Westlake v Illawarra Coal Holdings Pty Ltd* [2020] FWC 2504
176. *Wilkins v Green Gables Express Pty Ltd* [2019] FWC 2892
177. *Williams v Viridian Glass Ltd* [2020] FWC 250
178. *Williamson v Path Transit* [2019] FWC 6153
179. *Willigen v AHG Services (VIC) Pty Ltd* [2020] FWC 3770
180. *Wood v Mingara Recreation Club Ltd* [2020] FWC 686
181. *Yadav v Maddingley Montessori Centre Pty Ltd* [2018] FWC 2883
182. *Yang v FCS Business Service Pty Ltd* [2020] FWC 4560
183. *Yazgan v Australian Pharmaceutical Industries Ltd* [2018] FWC 3973

Bibliography

Adams Z, *Labour and the Wage: A Critical Perspective* (OUP 2020)

AHRC, 'Respect@Work: Sexual Harassment National Inquiry Report' (Final Report 2020)

AIER, 'The Australian Charter of Employment Rights' <https://www.aierights.com.au/charter/> accessed 29 July 2025

Albin E and Mantouvalou V, 'Active Industrial Citizenship of Domestic Workers: Lessons Learned from Unionizing Attempts in Israel and the United Kingdom' (2016) 17 Theoretical Inquiries in Law 321

Allen D, 'Reducing the Burden of Proving Discrimination in Australia' (2009) 31 Sydney Law Review 579

Allen D and Blackham A, 'Under Wraps: Secrecy, Confidentiality and the Enforcement of Equality Law in Australia and the United Kingdom' (2019) 43 Melbourne University Law Review 384

Anderson G, 'Employment Rights in an Era of Individualised Employment' (2007) 38 Victoria University of Wellington Law Review 417

Anderson G, 'Grasping the Moment: Some Cross-Tasman Thoughts on Australian Labour Law Reform' (2008) 18 Economic and Labour Relations Review 113

Anderson G, 'Good Faith in the Individual Employment Relationship in New Zealand' (2011) 32 Comparative Labor Law & Policy Journal 685.

Anderson G, Brodie D and Riley J, 'Development and Character of the Contract of Employment: A Comparative Study' in Gordon J Anderson, Douglas Brodie and Joellen Riley (eds), *The Common Law Employment Relationship: A Comparative Study* (Edward Elgar 2017)

Andrades C, 'Freedom from Discrimination and Harassment' in Mordy Bromberg and Mark Irving (eds), *Australian Charter of Employment Rights* (Hardie Grant Books 2007)

Andrades C, 'When Worlds Collide—Intersections between Anti-Discrimination Law and Workers' Compensation Law—The Decision in "Friend v Comcare"' (2021) 26 Employment Law Bulletin 82

Arthurs H, 'Labour Law After Labour' in Guy Davidov and Brian A Langille (eds), *The Idea of Labour Law* (OUP 2011)

Arthurs H, 'Can Davidov's Legal Slingshot Slay the Goliath of Political Economy? On Guy Davidov's *A Purposive Approach to Labour Law*' (2017) 16 Jerusalem Review of Legal Studies 1

Arthurs H, 'Foreword: Mining the Philosophers' Stone: Sixteen Tons and What Do You Get? Another Day Older and Deeper in Doubt' in Hugh Collins, Gillian Lester and Virginia Mantouvalou (eds), *Philosophical Foundations of Labour Law* (OUP 2018)

Arthurs HW, 'The New Economy and the New Legality: Industrial Citizenship and the Future of Labour Arbitration Commentary' (1999) 7 Canadian Labour & Employment Law Journal 45

Arup C and others (eds), *Labour Law and Labour Market Regulation: Essays on the Construction, Constitution and Regulation of Labour Markets and Work Relationships* (The Federation Press 2006)

ASIC, 'Regulatory Guide 270 Whistleblower Policies' (2019) 270 <https://download.asic.gov.au/media/5702691/rg270-published-13-november-2019-20200727.pdf> accessed 20 August 2025

Association of Workplace Investigators, 'AWI Publications—Guiding Principles, AWI Weekly and AWI Journal' <https://www.awi.org/page/publications> accessed 7 July 2025

Bagguley P, 'Industrial Citizenship: A Re-conceptualisation and Case Study of the UK' (2013) 33 International Journal of Sociology and Social Policy 265

Baker J, 'Investigating Fraud and Bribery by Staff' (2017) 4 Public Finance 46

Baker J and Jaspan C, 'Nine Investigates Complaints as Staff Voice Anger at Response to Workplace Report' *The Age* (18 October 2024) <https://www.theage.com.au/national/nine-staff-furious-at-response-to-gut-wrenching-devastating-report-20241018-p5kjgk.html> accessed 9 July 2025

Baldwin M and Lewin C, 'High Court to Determine Employer's Duties during Workplace Investigations' (2017) 21 Inhouse Counsel 222

Ballard A, 'In the Shadow of the Law: The Silence of Workplace Abuse' (PhD Thesis, University of Canberra 2019)

Ballard A and Easteal P, 'Procedural Fairness in Workplace Investigations: Potential Flaws and Proposals for Change' (2018) 43 Alternative Law Journal 177

Bamber G and Russell B, 'Work with Dignity' in Mordy Bromberg and Mark Irving (eds), *Australian Charter of Employment Rights* (Hardie Grant Books 2007)

Barker K and others, *The Law of Torts in Australia* (5th edn, OUP 2012)

Barmes L, 'The Continuing Conceptual Crisis in the Common Law of the Contract of Employment' (2004) 67 Modern Law Review 435

Barmes L, *Bullying and Behavioural Conflict at Work: The Duality of Individual Rights* (OUP 2016)

Barmes L, 'Silencing at Work: Sexual Harassment, Workplace Misconduct and NDAs' (2023) 52 Industrial Law Journal 68

Beard G and Bryant-Smith R, 'Delay Workplace Investigations at Your Peril' (2008) 82 Law Institute Journal 40

Beck J, 'Importance of Fair Workplace Investigations' (2012) 50 Law Society Journal 46

Bell S and Keating M, *Fair Share: Competing Claims and Australia's Economic Future* (Melbourne University Publishing 2018)

Berelson B, *Content Analysis in Communication Research* (Hafner 1971)

Betteridge J, 'Useful Cases for Investigators to Achieve Practical Justice' (Conference Paper, Australasian Association of Workplace Investigators Conference, Melbourne 2017)

Bhat PI, *Idea and Methods of Legal Research* (1st edn, OUP 2020)

Blackham A, 'Interrogating the "Dignity" Argument for Mandatory Retirement: An Undignified Development?' (2019) 48 Industrial Law Journal 377

Blackham A, 'Why Do Employment Age Discrimination Cases Fail? An Analysis of Australian Case Law' (2020) 42 Sydney Law Review 1

Bluff E and Johnstone R, 'Supporting and Enforcing Compliance with Australia's Harmonised WHS Laws' (2017) 30 Australian Journal of Labour Law 30

Bogg A, *The Democratic Aspects of Trade Union Recognition* (Bloomsbury 2009)

Bogg A, '"Individualism" and "Collectivism" in Collective Labour Law' (2017) 46 Industrial Law Journal 72

Bogg A, 'Employment Status in the Social Democratic Constitution: Law and Politics' in Alan Bogg, Jacob Rowbottom and Alison Young (eds), *The Constitution of Social Democracy: Essays in Honour of Keith Ewing* (Hart Publishing 2020)

Bogg A, 'Can We Trust the Courts in Labour Law? Stranded Between Frivolity and Despair' (2022) 38 International Journal of Comparative Labour Law and Industrial Relations 103

Bogg A and Estlund C, 'The Right to Strike and Contestatory Citizenship' in Hugh Collins, Gillian Lester and Virginia Mantouvalou (eds), *Philosophical Foundations of Labour Law* (OUP 2018)

Bonny P, Goode S and Lacey D, 'Revisiting Employee Fraud: Gender, Investigation Outcomes and Offender Motivation' (2015) 22 Journal of Financial Crime 447

Bornstein J, 'HR Is Not Always Here to Help' *The Age* (15 October 2015) <https://www.theage.com.au/business/workplace/hr-are-not-always-here-to-help-20151013-gk8d9k.html> accessed 31 July 2025

Boucaut L and Kavanagh T, 'A Limitation on Employer Power to Direct Employees to Attend an Interview' *Allens* (30 June 2021) <https://www.allens.com.au/insights-news/insights/2021/06/a-limitation-on-employer-power-to-direct-employees-to-attend-an-interview/> accessed 27 July 2025

Branigan KS and others, 'Conducting Effective Independent Workplace Investigations In A Post-#Metoo Era' (2019) 74 Dispute Resolution Journal 85

Brodie D, 'The Irrepressible Common Law: The Economic Torts and the Right to Strike' in Alan Bogg, Jacob Rowbottom and Alison Young (eds), *The Constitution of Social Democracy: Essays in Honour of Keith Ewing* (Hart 2020)

Brodie D, 'Disavowing an Implied Term of Fairness' (2024) 53 Industrial Law Journal 157

Brodie D and Riley J, 'A Duty of Good Management? Protected Interests and the Employment Contract' (2019) 50 Victoria University of Wellington Law Review 303

Bromberg M, 'Introduction' in Mordy Bromberg and Mark Irving (eds), *Australian Charter of Employment Rights* (Hardie Grant Books 2007)
Bromberg M and Irving M (eds), *Australian Charter of Employment Rights* (Hardie Grant Books 2007)
Bromberg M and Irving M (eds), 'The Scope of the Charter' in Mordy Bromberg and Mark Irving (eds), *Australian Charter of Employment Rights* (Hardie Grant Books 2007)
Burke T, 'Delivering Secure Jobs, Better Pay and a Fairer System' (*Ministers' Media Centre*, 27 October 2022) <https://ministers.dewr.gov.au/burke/delivering-secure-jobs-better-pay-and-fairer-system> accessed 29 July 2025
Burns K and Hutchinson T, 'The Impact of "Empirical Facts" on Legal Scholarship and Legal Research Training' (2009) 43 The Law Teacher 153
Burr C and Wyatt A, 'Investigation of Workplace Bullying and Harassment Complaints' in Premilla D'Cruz and others (eds), *Dignity and Inclusion at Work* (Springer 2021)
Butler TL, 'The FCRA and Workplace Investigations' (2020) 15 The Labour Lawyer 391
Byrnes M and Arndt J, 'Major Court and Tribunal Decisions in Australia in 2013' (2014) 56 Journal of Industrial Relations 365
Carey A, 'No Water, No Loo for Yarra Trams Staff Grilled over Napoleon Poster, Court Hears' *The Age* (10 May 2016) <http://www.theage.com.au/victoria/no-water-no-loo-for-yarra-trams-staff-grilled-over-napoleon-poster-court-hears-20160510-gorspx.html> accessed 9 July 2025
Carnie S, 'How to Cull Misconduct Allegations to Those That Really Matter- a Preliminary Assessment Approach' *Worklogic* (21 July 2021) <https://www.worklogic.com.au/workplace-investigations/how-to-cull-misconduct-allegations-to-those-that-really-matter-a-preliminary-assessment-approach/> accessed 31 July 2025
Carolan J and others, 'Charter of Workers' Rights' (Draft for Consultation, Institute of Employment Rights 2019) <https://strathprints.strath.ac.uk/67615/1/Carolan_etal_IER_2019_A_Charter_of_Workers_Rights_for_Scotland.pdf>
Carroll B, 'New Rules To Protect Workers' Mental Health' (21 February 2025) <https://www.premier.vic.gov.au/new-rules-protect-workers-mental-health> accessed 4 August 2025
Catanzariti J and Birch D, 'A Cautionary Tale on Workplace Bullying and Its Investigation: Wood v Rainbow Coast Neighbourhood Centre Inc' (2012) 18 Employment Law Bulletin 82
Chapman A, 'Unfair Dismissal Law and Work Choices: From Safety Net Standard to Legal Privilege' (2006) 16 The Economic and Labour Relations Review 237
Chapman A, 'Protections in Relation to Dismissal: From the *Workplace Relations Act* to the *Fair Work Act*' (2009) 32 University of New South Wales Law Journal 746
Chapman A, 'Unfair Dismissal Law and Work Choices: From Safety Net Standard to Legal Privilege' (2020) 16 The Economic and Labour Relations Review 237
Chapman A, Love K and Gaze B, 'The Reverse Onus of Proof Then and Now: The Barclay Case and the History of the Fair Work Act's Union Victimisation and Freedom of Association' (2014) 37 University of New South Wales Law Journal 471
Cholbi M, 'The Duty to Work' (2018) 21 Ethical Theory and Moral Practice 1119
Cirkovic T, 'Avoiding Practical Injustice - Observations from the Bench' (Melbourne, 20 October 2017) Conference Paper, Australasian Association of Workplace Investigators Conference
Collins H, 'Market Power, Bureaucratic Power, and the Contract of Employment' (1986) 15 Industrial Law Journal 1
Collins H, 'Labour Law as a Vocation' (1989) 105 Law Quarterly Review 468
Collins H, *Justice in Dismissal: The Law of Termination of Employment* (OUP 1992)
Collins H, *Employment Law* (2nd edn, OUP 2010)
Collins H, 'Theories of Rights as Justifications for Labour Law' in Guy Davidov and Brian Langille (eds), *The Idea of Labour Law* (OUP 2011)
Collins H, 'Constructive Dismissal and the West Lothian Question: Aberdeen City Council v McNeill' (2011) 40 Industrial Law Journal 439
Collins H, 'Justice at Work' (2020) 1 Judiciary Forum Review 59
Collins H, 'Relational and Associational Justice in Work' (2023) 24 Theoretical Inquiries in Law 26
Collins H, Lester G and Mantouvalou V (eds), *Philosophical Foundations of Labour Law* (OUP 2019)

Collins P, 'The Role of Human Rights in Labour Law' in Philippa Collins (ed), *Putting Human Rights to Work: Labour Law, The ECHR, and The Employment Relation* (OUP 2022)
Collins P and Golding G, 'An Implied Term of Procedural Fairness During Disciplinary Processes: Into Contracts of Employment and Beyond?' (2024) 53 Industrial Law Journal 125
Colquitt JA and others, 'Justice at the Millennium: A Meta-Analytic Review of 25 Years of Organizational Justice Research' (2001) 86 Journal of Applied Psychology 425
Cook H and Jacks T, 'La Trobe University Could Face Legal Action over Suspension of Safe Schools Co-Founder Roz Ward' *The Age* (2 June 2016) <https://www.theage.com.au/national/victoria/lawyers-academics-condemn-la-trobe-universitys-suspension-of-safe-schools-cofounder-roz-ward-20160602-gp9nmz.html> accessed 31 July 2025
Copley B and Forder S, 'Sexual Harassment Investigations' in Paula Hoctor and Kerryn Tredwell (eds), *Workplace Investigations: Principles and Practice* (2nd edn, LexisNexis Butterworths 2023)
Corbin J and Strauss A, *Basics of Qualitative Research: Techniques and Procedures for Developing Grounded Theory* (3rd edn, SAGE Publications 2008)
Cornes R, 'Drafting Allegations' in Paula Hoctor and Kerryn Tredwell (eds), *Workplace Investigations: Principles and Practice* (2nd edn, LexisNexis Butterworths 2023)
Cornes R, 'Procedural Fairness in Workplace Investigations' in Paula Hoctor and Kerryn Tredwell (eds), *Workplace Investigations: Principles and Practice* (2nd edn, LexisNexis Butterworths 2023)
Coutu M and Murray G, 'Towards Citizenship at Work? An Introduction' (2005) 60 Relations Industrielles 617
Crockett A, Armao I and Sammut J, 'Piercing the Secrecy Veil and Restricting NDA Use in Sexual Harassment Claims in Australia: Victoria Leads the Way' (2022) 27 Employment Law Bulletin 78
Cropanzano RS and Ambrose ML, 'Organizational Justice: Where We Have Been and Where We Are Going' in Russell S Cropanzano and Maureen L Ambrose (eds), *The Oxford Handbook of Justice in the Workplace* (OUP 2015)
Crowther M, 'Wrigleys' Essential Employment Guide - The Disciplinary Process' (*Wrigleys Solicitors LLP*, 18 November 2021) <https://www.wrigleys.co.uk/news/employment-hr/wrigleys-essential-employment-guide-the-disciplinary process/> accessed 27 July 2025
Dabscheck B, 'Book Review: *Australian Charter of Employment Rights*' (2020) 18 The Economic and Labour Relations Review 155
Davidov G, 'Collective Bargaining Laws: Purpose and Scope' (2004) 20 International Journal of Comparative Labour Law and Industrial Relations 81
Davidov G, 'Re-Matching Labour Laws with Their Purpose' in Guy Davidov and Brian Langille (eds), *The Idea of Labour Law* (OUP 2011)
Davidov G, *A Purposive Approach to Labour Law* (OUP 2016)
Davidov G, 'Distributive Justice and Labour Law' in Hugh Collins, Gillian Lester and Virginia Mantouvalou (eds), *Philosophical Foundations of Labour Law* (OUP 2018)
Davidov G and Langille B (eds), *Boundaries and Frontiers of Labour Law: Goals and Means in the Regulation of Work* (Bloomsbury 2006)
Davidov G and Langille BA (eds), *The Idea of Labour Law* (OUP 2011)
Davies A, 'Identifying "Exploitative Compromises": The Role of Labour Law in Resolving Disputes Between Workers' (2012) 65 Current Legal Problems 269
Davies P and Freedland M, 'The Complexities of the Employing Enterprise' in Guy Davidov and Brian A Langille (eds), *Boundaries and Frontiers of Labour Law: Goals and Means in the Regulation of Work* (Bloomsbury 2006)
Deakin S, 'The Comparative Evolution of the Employment Relationship' in Guy Davidov and Brian Langille (eds), *Boundaries and Frontiers of Labour Law: Goals and Means in the Regulation of Work* (Hart 2006)
Deakin S, 'Labor Law: The Pragmatist's Guide—Comments on *A Purposive Approach to Labor Law*' (2017) 16 Jerusalem Review of Legal Studies 28
Dent C and Kenyon AT, 'Defamation Law's Chilling Effect: A Comparative Content Analysis of Australian And US Newspapers' (2004) 9 Media & Arts Law Review 89
Department of Employment and Workplace Relations, 'Trends in Federal Enterprise Bargaining – March Quarter 2025' (2025) <https://www.dewr.gov.au/enterprise-agreements-data/resources/trends-federal-enterprise-bargaining-march-quarter-2025> accessed 1 August 2025

Djurkovic N and others, 'The Role of Human Resource Professionals (HRPs) in Managing Workplace Bullying: Perspectives from HRPs and Employee Representatives in Australia' (2021) 50 Personnel Review 1599
Drisko JW and Maschi T, *Content Analysis* (OUP 2015)
Dukes R, 'Identifying the Purposes of Labor Law: Discussion of Guy Davidov's *A Purposive Approach to Labour Law*' (2017) 16 Jerusalem Review of Legal Studies 52
Dukes R and Streeck W, 'From Industrial Citizenship to Private Ordering? Contract, Status, and the Question of Consent' (MPIfG Discussion Paper 20/13, Max Planck Institute for the Study of Societies, 18 November 2020) <http://hdl.handle.net/21.11116/0000-0007-6AAA-3> accessed 29 July 2025
Dukes R and Streeck W, *Democracy at Work: Contract, Status and Post-Industrial Justice* (Polity Press 2023)
Dukes R and Streeck W, 'Labour Law after Neoliberalism?' (2023) 50 Journal of Law and Society 165
Dunckley M, 'Westpac Worker Subjected to Five Hour "Star Chamber" Wins Back Job' *The Age* (2 December 2018) <https://www.theage.com.au/business/banking-and-finance/westpac-worker-subjected-to-five-hour-star-chamber-wins-back-job-20181202-p50jpg.html> accessed 9 July 2025
Dunlop C and Hanson R, 'Don't Touch My Stuff: Client Legal Privilege in Employment Law' (2016) 22 Employment Law Bulletin 278
Dwoskin LB and Squire MB, 'Best Practices in Conducting Internal Workplace Investigations of Discrimination and Harassment Complaints' (2018) 44 Employee Relations Law Journal 20
Eastwood A and Smyth M, 'Internal Investigations and Privilege: A Response to Recent Challenges' (2018) 33 Australian Journal of Corporate Law 3
Eccleston D and Goschen K, *The Manager's Guide to Discipline* (Taylor & Francis Group 2008)
Edelman LB, 'Legal Environments and Organizational Governance: The Expansion of Due Process in the American Workplace' (1990) 95 American Journal of Sociology 1401
Edelman LB, 'Legal Ambiguity and Symbolic Structures: Organizational Mediation of Civil Rights Law' (1992) 97 American Journal of Sociology 1531
Edelman LB, 'Law at Work: The Endogenous Construction of Civil Rights' in Laura Beth Nielsen and Robert L Nelson (eds), *Handbook of Employment Discrimination Research: Rights and Realities* (Springer 2005)
Edelman LB, *Working Law: Courts, Corporations, and Symbolic Civil Rights* (University of Chicago Press 2016)
Edelman LB, 'Organizations, Institutions, and Law: The Sociological Significance of Philip Selznick's Law, Society, and Industrial Justice' in Paul van Seters (ed), *The Anthem Companion to Philip Selznick* (Cambridge University Press 2021)
Edelman LB and Suchman MC, 'The Legal Environments of Organizations' (1997) 23 Annual Review of Sociology 479
Edelman LB, Uggen C and Erlanger HS, 'The Endogeneity of Legal Regulation: Grievance Procedures as Rational Myth' (1999) 105 American Journal of Sociology 406
Eichenbaum S, 'Employment Policy and Breach of Contract: The Conundrum Continues' (2015) 21 Employment Law Bulletin 14
Ellery N and others, 'Mental Health and Workplace Investigations: What Are Your Obligations?' (2018) 70 Governance Directions 82
Elliot E, 'Within "Spitting Distance" of a Fair Investigation?' (*WISE Workplace Training*, 7 December 2016) <https://www.wiseworkplacetraining.com.au/2016/12/07/within-spitting-distance-of-a-fair-investigation/> accessed 31 July 2025
Elliot T, 'Under Investigation' (2016) Employers' Law 18
Ellis J and John R, 'Protecting Privilege during Internal Investigations: Is Lawyer Work Product at Risk?' (2017) 33 Law Society of NSW Journal 88
Elster J, 'Is There (or Should There Be) a Right to Work?' in Amy Gutmann (ed), *Democracy and the Welfare State* (Princeton University Press 1988)
Epstein RA, 'A Common Law for Labor Relations: A Critique of the New Deal Labor Legislation' (1983) 92 The Yale Law Journal 1357
Estlund C, 'Rebuilding the Law of the Workplace in an Era of Self-Regulation' (2005) 105 Columbia Law Review 319

Estlund C, 'Just the Facts: The Case for Workplace Transparency' (2011) 63 Stanford Law Review 351

Ewing K, 'Democratic Socialism and Labour Law' (1995) 24 Industrial Law Journal 103

Ewing K, 'Australian and British Labour Law: Differences of Form or Substance?' (1998) 11 Australian Journal of Labour Law 44

Ewing KD, Hendy J and Jones C, 'Rolling out the Manifesto for Labour Law' (Institute of Employment Rights 2018) <https://www.ier.org.uk/wp-content/uploads/RollingOutTheManifestoForLabourLaw.pdf>

Fair Work Ombudsman, 'Workplace Investigations' <https://www.fairwork.gov.au/about-us/compliance-and-enforcement/workplace-investigations> accessed 25 July 2025

Ferraro EF, *Investigations in the Workplace* (2nd edn, Taylor & Francis 2012)

Fine J, 'A Marriage Made in Heaven? Mismatches and Misunderstandings between Worker Centres and Unions' (2007) 45 British Journal of Industrial Relations 335

Fleming J (ed), *A New Work Relations Architecture: The AIER Model for the Future of Work* (Hardie Grant Books 2022)

Fleming J (ed), 'Introduction' in James Fleming (ed), *A New Work Relations Architecture: The AIER Model for the Future of Work* (Hardie Grant Books 2022)

Floyd L and others, *Employment, Labour and Industrial Law in Australia* (Cambridge University Press 2018)

Ford S, 'At Last, a Workplace Investigations Manual' (2019) 39 The Proctor 40

Forsyth A, 'Workplace Democracy' in Mordy Bromberg and Mark Irving (eds), *Australian Charter of Employment Rights* (Hardie Grant Books 2007)

Forsyth A, *The Future of Unions and Worker Representation: The Digital Picket Line* (Hart 2022)

Forsyth A, 'Closing the Labour Hire Loophole: Legislative Enshrinement of the "Same Job, Same Pay" Principle for Australian Labour Hire Workers' (2024) 37 Australian Journal of Labour Law 135

Fox C, 'Union Democracy and Collective Bargaining: Public Policy in Transition' (1999) 41 Journal of Industrial Relations 393

Fox J, 'Four Tips for Conducting Trauma Informed Investigation Interviews' *Worklogic* (16 November 2021) <https://www.worklogic.com.au/workplace-investigations/four-tips-in-conducting-trauma-informed-investigations/> accessed 31 July 2025

Fox J, *Workplace Investigations* (3rd edn, CCH Australia 2020)

Fox J, *Workplace Investigations* (4th edn, Wolters Kluwer 2023)

Frazer A, 'Reconceiving Labour Law: The Labour Market Regulation Project' (2008) 8 Macquarie Law Journal 21

Freckelton I, 'Foreword' in Paula Hoctor and Michael Robertson (eds), *Workplace Investigations: Principles and Practice* (1st edn, LexisNexis Butterworths 2018)

Freedland M, *The Personal Employment Contract* (OUP 2005)

French B, 'Australian Charter of Employment Rights' (2008) 16 International Journal of Employment Studies 131

Fudge J, 'After Industrial Citizenship: Market Citizenship or Citizenship at Work?' (2006) 60 Relations Industrielles 631

Fudge J, 'Fragmenting Work and Fragmenting Organizations: The Contract of Employment and the Scope of Labour Regulation' (2006) 44 Osgoode Hall Law Journal 609

Fudge J, 'The New Discourse of Labor Rights: From Social to Fundamental Rights' (2007) 29 Comparative Labor Law & Policy Journal 29

Fudge J, 'Blurring Legal Boundaries: Regulating for Decent Work' in Judy Fudge, Shae McCrystal and Kamala Sankaran (eds), *Challenging the Legal Boundaries of Work Regulation* (Bloomsbury 2012)

FWC, 'Annual Report 2018–19' (2019) 27 <https://www.fwc.gov.au/documents/reporting/fwc-annual-report-2018-19.pdf> accessed 28 July 2025

FWC, 'Fair Work Commission Annual Report 2022–23' (2023) 21 https://www.fwc.gov.au/documents/reporting/fwc-annual-report-2022-23.pdf accessed 28 July 2025

FWC, 'Find Decisions and Orders' (2025) <https://www.fwc.gov.au/hearings-decisions/find-decisions-and-orders> accessed 31 July 2025

FWC, 'Hearings and Decisions'(2023) <https://www.fwc.gov.au/hearings-and-decisions> accessed 26 July 2023

FWC, 'Practice Note: Unfair Dismissal Proceedings' (2014) para [54] <https://www.fwc.gov.au/hearings-decisions/practice-notes/practice-note-unfair-dismissal-proceedings> accessed 2 August 2025

FWC, 'Unfair Dismissals Benchbook' (2025) <https://www.fwc.gov.au/benchbook/unfair-dismissals-benchbook> accessed 15 July 2025

FWC, 'What Is Conciliation?' (2025) <https://www.fwc.gov.au/job-loss-or-dismissal/unfair-dismissal/conciliation-unfair-dismissal/what-conciliation> accessed 2 August 2025.

Gageler S, 'Evidence and Truth' (2017) 13 Judicial Review 1

Gardiner K and Acaro E, 'Overview of Workplace Investigations in Australia' (2021) 164 Precedent 22

Gaze B and Smith B, *Equality and Discrimination Law in Australia: An Introduction* (Cambridge University Press 2017)

General Conference of the International Labour Organisation, 'Declaration Concerning the Aims and Purposes of the International Labour Organization' annex l(a) to the *Constitution of the International Labour Organisation and Standing Orders of the International Labour Conference, 1994* (adopted at Philadelphia 10 May 1994)

Genn H, Partington M and Wheeler S, 'Law in the Real World: Improving Our Understanding of How Law Works' (Nuffield Foundation 2006)

Ghaleigh NS, 'Just Transitions for Workers: When Climate Change Met Labour Justice' in Alan Bogg, Jacob Rowbottom and Alison Young (eds), *The Constitution of Social Democracy: Essays in Honour of Keith Ewing* (Hart 2020)

Gilabert P, 'Dignity at Work' in Hugh Collins, Gillian Lester and Virginia Mantouvalou (eds), *Philosophical Foundations of Labour Law* (OUP 2018)

Goldberg CB, Rawski SL and Perry EL, 'The Direct and Indirect Effects of Organizational Tolerance for Sexual Harassment on the Effectiveness of Sexual Harassment Investigation Training for HR Managers' (2019) 30 Human Resource Development Quarterly 81

Goldin A, 'Social Justice for an Ongoing Theoretical Reconfiguration of Labour Law' in Brian Langille and Anne Trebilcock (eds), *Social Justice and the World of Work: Possible Global Futures* (Hart 2023)

Golding G, 'Rethinking the Rationale for Implying Terms by Law into Australian Employment Contracts' (2020) 39 University of Tasmania Law Review 1

Golding G, 'Role of Judges in the Regulation of Australian Employment Contracts, The Special Section: The Future of Common Law in Employment Regulation' (2016) 32 International Journal of Comparative Labour Law and Industrial Relations 69

Goldman B, 'Organizational Justice and Legal Justice: How Are They Related?' in Russell S Cropanzano and Maureen L Ambrose (eds), *The Oxford Handbook of Justice in the Workplace* (OUP 2015)

Gray PRA, 'Fearless or Fraught - The Investigator's Approach' (Australasian Association of Workplace Investigators Conference, Melbourne Australia, 20 October 2017)

Green L, 'The Who, What and How of Workplace Investigations' (2018) Australasian Law Management Journal 1

Greenberg J, 'A Taxonomy of Organizational Justice Theories' (1987) 12 Academy of Management Review 9

Grieve C, 'Lawyers for Former AMP Employee Demand Documents Ahead of Harassment Report Release' *The Sydney Morning Herald* (19 August 2020) <https://www.smh.com.au/business/banking-and-finance/amp-to-release-sexual-harassment-report-stands-by-execs-20200819-p55n3q.html> accessed 26 July 2025

Grieve C, 'AMP's Behaviour "unacceptable" Says Lawyer for Former Employee' *The Sydney Morning Herald* (21 August 2020) <https://www.smh.com.au/business/banking-and-finance/amp-s-behaviour-unacceptable-says-lawyer-for-former-employee-20200821-p55nzz.html> accessed 31 July 2025

Grieve C, 'AMP Reels from Scandal amid Calls for Scrutiny of Workplace Investigations' *The Age* (25 August 2020) <https://www.theage.com.au/business/banking-and-finance/amp-reels-from-scandal-amid-calls-for-scrutiny-of-workplace-investigations-20200825-p55p6d.html> accessed 9 July 2025

Groves M, 'Substantive Legitimate Expectations in Australian Administrative Law' (2008) 32 Melbourne University Law Review 470, 479
Guerin L, *The Essential Guide To Workplace Investigations* (6th edn, Nolo 2022)
Hall MA and Wright RF, 'Systematic Content Analysis of Judicial Opinions' (2008) 96 California Law Review 63
Hanley GM and O'Rourke A, 'The Race without a Finishing Line: Legislative Means for Confronting Bullying in the Australian Workplace' (2016) 54 Asia Pacific Journal of Human Resources 352
Harris K, 'Thorny Issues for Workplace Investigation Processes' *Worklogic* (27 March 2018) <https://www.worklogic.com.au/review-of-actions/thorny-issues-for-workplace-investigation-processes/> accessed 31 July 2025
Hart C, *Doing a Literature Review: Releasing the Social Science Research Imagination* (SAGE 2002)
Hayek FA, *1980s Unemployment and the Unions: Essays on the Impotent Price Structure of Britain and Monopoly in the Labour Market* (Institute of Economic Affairs 1980)
Heissner S, *Managing Business Integrity: Prevent, Detect, and Investigate White-Collar Crime and Corruption* (Springer 2015)
Hempel S, *Conducting Your Literature Review* (American Psychological Association 2020)
Hepple B, 'Four Approaches to the Modernisation of Individual Employment Rights' in Roger Blanpain and Manfred Weiss (eds), *Changing Industrial Relations and Modernisation of Labour Law: Liber Amicorum in Honour of Professor Marco Biagi* (Kluwer Law International 2003)
Hoctor P, 'Legal Professional Privilege' in Paula Hoctor and Kerryn Tredwell (eds), *Workplace Investigations: Principles and Practice* (2nd edn, LexisNexis Butterworths 2023)
Hoctor P, 'Workplace Investigations and the Emergence of an Australian Profession' in Paula Hoctor and Kerryn Tredwell (eds), *Workplace Investigations: Principles and Practice* (2nd edn, LexisNexis Butterworths 2023)
Hoctor P, Robertson M and Tredwell K, 'Workplace Investigation Overview' in Paula Hoctor and Kerryn Tredwell (eds), *Workplace Investigations: Principles and Practice* (2nd edn, LexisNexis Butterworths 2023)
Hoctor P and Tredwell K (eds), *Workplace Investigations: Principles and Practice* (2nd edn, LexisNexis Butterworths 2023)
Hoel H and Einarsen SV, 'Investigating Complaints of Bullying and Harassment' in Ståle Valvatne Einarsen and others (eds), *Bullying and Harassment in the Workplace* (2nd edn, Taylor & Francis Group 2010)
Holland P, 'Drug Testing in the Australian Workplace: Still a Contested Terrain' (2016) 58 Journal of Industrial Relations 688
Hopt KJ, 'Internal Investigations, Whistleblowing and External Monitoring, Comparative Experiences, Economic Insights, Findings from Corporate Practice' (2021) Law Working Paper N° 574/2021 <https://www.ssrn.com/abstract=3812497> accessed 9 July 2025
House of Representatives Standing Committee on Education and Employment, Parliament of Australia, 'Workplace Bullying: We Just Want It to Stop' (Final Report 2012)
Howe J, *Rethinking Job Security: A Comparative Analysis of Unfair Dismissal Law in the UK, Australia and the USA* (Routledge 2017)
Hutchinson T, 'Doctrinal Research: Researching the Jury' in Dawn Watkins and Mandy Burton (eds), *Research Methods in Law* (2nd edn, Routledge 2017)
ILO, 'Decent Work Indicators: Guidelines for the Producers and Users of Statistical and Legal Framework Indicators' (ILO Manual 2nd edn, 2013)
Irving M, 'Union Membership and Representation' in Mordy Bromberg and Mark Irving (eds), *Australian Charter of Employment Rights* (Hardie Grant Books 2007)
Irving M, *The Contract of Employment* (2nd edn, LexisNexis Butterworths 2019)
Isaac J, 'Reforming Australian Industrial Relations?: The 21st Foenander Lecture, 28 August 2006' (2007) 49 Journal of Industrial Relations 410
Jenkins M, Winefield H and Sarris A, 'Consequences of Being Accused of Workplace Bullying: An Exploratory Study' (2011) 4 International Journal of Workplace Health Management 33
Jensen K and Kleiner BH, 'How to Determine Proper Corrective Action Following Sexual Harassment Investigations' (1999) 18 Equal Opportunities International 23

Jesson J, Matheson L and Lacey FM, *Doing Your Literature Review: Traditional and Systematic Techniques* (SAGE 2011)
Kahn-Freund O, *Labour and the Law* (Stevens for the Hamlyn Trust 1972)
Kaine S and Josserand E, 'The Organisation and Experience of Work in the Gig Economy' (2019) 61 Journal of Industrial Relations 479
Kelly N, 'Support Persons for Employees and the Fair Work Act' (2018) 24 Employment Law Bulletin 47, 47
Kiefel S, 'Good Faith in Contractual Performance' (2020) 13 Judicial Review: Selected Conference Papers: Journal of the Judicial Commission of New South Wales 41
King M, 'Out of Obscurity: The Contemporary Private Investigator in Australia' (2020) 22 International Journal of Police Science & Management 285
King M, 'What Makes a Successful Corporate Investigator: An Exploration of Private Investigators Attributes' (2020) 27 Journal of Financial Crime 701
King M, 'Financial Fraud Investigative Interviewing – Corporate Investigators' Beliefs and Practices: A Qualitative Inquiry' (2021) 28 Journal of Financial Crime 345
King M, 'Pathways and Partnerships: A Study of Private Policing Economic Crime in Australia' (PhD Thesis, Queensland University of Technology 2021)
Kirby M, 'Human Rights and Industrial Relations' (2002) 44 Journal of Industrial Relations 562
Kirby M, 'Securing a "Fair Go"–ILO, Australia and the World' (International Industrial Relations Association, 15th World Congress, Sydney, 2009) <https://www.michaelkirby.com.au/images/stories/speeches/2000s/2009%2B/2391.Speech_-_Iira_-_Darling_Harbour%2C_26_August_2009.pdf> accessed 29 July 2025
Kirkham R and O'Loughlin E, 'A Content Analysis of Judicial Decision-Making' in Naomi Creutzfeldt, Marc Mason and Kirsten McConnachie (eds), *Routledge Handbook of Socio-Legal Theory and Methods* (Routledge 2020)
Korpi W, 'The Iceberg of Power below the Surface: A Preface to Power Resources Theory' in Julia S O'Connor and Gregg M Olsen (eds), *Power Resource Theory and the Welfare State: A Critical Approach* (University of Toronto Press 1998)
Krippendorff K, *Content Analysis: An Introduction to Its Methodology* (4th edn, SAGE 2019)
Kuehne G, 'Implied Obligations of Good Faith and Reasonableness in the Performance of Contracts: Old Wine in New Bottles?' (2006) 33 University of Western Australia Law Review 63
Kuldova TØ and Nordrik B, 'Workplace Investigations, the Epistemic Power of Managerialism and the Hollowing out of the Norwegian Model of Co-Determination' (2023) 48 Capital & Class 463
Lander and Rogers, 'Difficult People in Workplace Investigations' (April 2018) <https://www.landers.com.au/legal-insights-news/how-to-deal-with-difficult-people-in-a-workplace-investigation> accessed 31 July 2025
Langille B, 'Labour Law's Back Pages' in Guy Davidov and Brian Langille (eds), *Boundaries and Frontiers of Labour Law: Goals and Means in the Regulation of Work* (Hart 2006)
Langille B, 'What Is International Labor Law For? Labor Rights in the Era of Globalization' (2009) 3 Law & Ethics of Human Rights 48
Langille B, 'Labour Law's Theory of Justice' in Guy Davidov and Brian Langille (eds), *The Idea of Labour Law* (OUP 2011)
Langille B, 'Human Development: A Way out of Labour Law's Fly Bottle' in Hugh Collins, Gillian Lester and Virginia Mantouvalou (eds), *Philosophical Foundations of Labour Law* (OUP 2018)
Lansbury RD, 'Workplace Democracy and the Global Financial Crisis' (2009) 51 Journal of Industrial Relations 599
Lee E, 'Globalization and Labour Standards: A Review of Issues' (1997) 136 International Labour Review 173
Lester G, 'Beyond Collective Bargaining: Modern Unions as Agents of Solidarity' in Guy Davidov and Brian A Langille (eds), *The Idea of Labour Law* (OUP 2011)
Lieber LD, 'HR and the "High-Level" Workplace Investigation' (2012) 39 Employment Relations Today 85
Love K, 'Union Victimisation, the Reverse Onus and the Causal Link: The Development of Principles Prior to the Fair Work Act' (2014) Melbourne Law School Working Paper 52 <https://labourlawr

esearch.net/union-victimisation-the-reverse-onus-and-the-causal-link-the-development-of-principles-prior-to-the-fair-work-act/> accessed 10 August 2025

MacDermott T, 'Managing Individual Workplace Grievances and Disciplinary Procedures' (2002) Australian Centre for Industrial Relations Research and Training Working Paper 80 <https://ses.library.usyd.edu.au/bitstream/handle/2123/13411/WP80.pdf?sequence=1&isAllowed=y> accessed 31 July 2025

Maher C and others, 'Ensuring Rigor in Qualitative Data Analysis: A Design Research Approach to Coding Combining NVivo With Traditional Material Methods' (2018) 17 International Journal of Qualitative Methods 1

Mantouvalou V, 'Human Rights and Unfair Dismissal: Private Acts in Public Spaces' (2008) 71 The Modern Law Review 912

Marshall TH and Bottomore T, *Citizenship and Social Class* (Pluto Press 1987)

Mattson J, 'Workplace Scandals: Some Lessons for Employers' (*Bartier Perry Lawyers*, 29 March 2018) <https://www.bartier.com.au/insights/articles/workplace-scandals-some-lessons-for-employers> accessed 31 July 2025

Mattson J and Paul M, 'Workplace Investigations: Time to Reform Our Thinking?' (Australian Labour Law Association Conference, Melbourne, Australia, 4 November 2016)

Mawdsley H and Thirlwall A, 'Third-Party Interventions in Workplace Bullying: A Neoliberal Agenda?' (2019) 41 Employee Relations: The International Journal 506

McAuliffe J and Murphy J, '"Exemplary" Investigation Process Still Results in Successful Workers Compensation Claim' (*Piper Alderman*, 18 August 2021) <https://piperalderman.com.au/insight/exemplary-investigation-process-still-results-in-successful-workers-compensation-claim/> accessed 31 July 2025

McCallum RC, 'The New Millennium and the Higgins Heritage: Industrial Relations in the 21st Century' (1996) 38 Journal of Industrial Relations 294

McCallum RC, 'Crafting a New Collective Labour Law for Australia' (1997) 39 Journal of Industrial Relations 405

McCallum RC, 'Collective Labour Law, Citizenship and the Future' (1998) 22 Melbourne University Law Review 42

McCallum RC, 'The Australian Constitution and the Shaping of Our Federal and State Labour Laws' (2005) 10 Deakin Law Review 460

McCallum RC, 'Justice at Work: Industrial Citizenship and the Corporatization of Australian Labour Law' (2006) 48 Journal of Industrial Relations 131

McCallum RC, 'Australian Labour Law after the Work Choices Avalanche: Developing an Employment Law for Our Children' (2007) 49 Journal of Industrial Relations 436

McCallum RC, 'Australian Labour Law and the Rudd Vision: Some Observations' (2008) 18 Economic and Labour Relations Review 23

McCallum RC, 'Citizenship at Work: An Australian Perspective' (2011) Sydney Law School Research Paper No 11/17 <https://papers.ssrn.com/abstract=1769271> accessed 28 July 2025

McCallum RC and Martin HM, 'A Forgotten Cohort: Citizenship through Work and Persons with Disabilities' (2016) 41 Queen's Law Journal 317

McCrudden C, 'Labour Law as Human Rights Law: A Critique of the Use of "Dignity" by Freedland and Kountouris' in Alan Bogg, Cathryn Costello and ACL Davies (eds), *The Autonomy of Labour Law* (Bloomsbury 2015)

McDonald P, Backstrom S and Dear K, 'Reporting Sexual Harassment: Claims and Remedies' (2008) 46 Asia Pacific Journal of Human Resources 173

McGee C, 'Being a Workplace Investigator Is No Job for a "Wilting Flower"' *Gilshenan & Luton* (3 August 2020) <https://www.gnl.com.au/articles/2020/august/workplace-investigations-objectivity/> accessed 31 July 2025

McNally L, 'Random Drug Tests Spark Claims of Homophobic Bullying at Newtown Police Station' *ABC News* (9 October 2016) <http://www.abc.net.au/news/2016-10-09/allegations-of-homophobic-bullying-at-newtown-police-station/7916186> accessed 25 July 2025

Mitchell R, 'Where Are We Going in Labour Law? Some Thoughts on a Field of Scholarship and Policy in Process of Change' (2011) 24 Australian Journal of Labour Law 45

Mitchell R and Fetter J, 'Human Resource Management and Individualisation in Australian Labour Law' (2003) 45 Journal of Industrial Relations 292

Moir M, 'Discretion, Good Faith and Employer Control Over Executive Remuneration' (2011) 24 Australian Journal of Labour Law 121

Molnar C, 'Apprehended Conflicts of Interest in Employment Investigations and Decision-Making' (2015) 21 Employment Law Bulletin 91

Moorhouse P, 'When Does Dishonesty Provide a Valid Reason for Dismissal?' (2021) 80 Law Society Journal 86

Motro B and Murphy J, 'The Do's and Dont's of Workplace Investigations' *Piper Alderman* (13 August 2021) <https://piperalderman.com.au/insight/the-dos-and-donts-of-workplace-investigations/> accessed 31 July 2025

Mundlak G, 'Industrial Citizenship, Social Citizenship, Corporate Citizenship: I Just Want My Wages' (2007) 8 Theoretical Inquiries in Law 719

Mundlak G, 'The Third Function of Labour Law: Distributing Labour Market Opportunities among Workers' in Guy Davidov and Brian A Langille (eds), *The Idea of Labour Law* (OUP 2011)

Mundlak G, 'The Power of Purpose: Comments on *A Purposive Approach to Labour Law*' (2017) 16 Jerusalem Review of Legal Studies 40

Munro P, 'Changes to the Australian Industrial Relations System: Reforms or Shattered Icons? An Insider's Assessment of the Probable Impact on Employers, Employees and Unions' (2006) 29 University of New South Wales Law Journal 128

Munro P, Peetz D and Pocock B, 'Fair Minimum Standards' in Mordy Bromberg and Mark Irving (eds), *Australian Charter of Employment Rights* (Hardie Grant Books 2007)

Munton JR, 'Executive Employment Grievances Brought under the *Fair Work Act*: A New Challenge to Orthodox Contract Law?' (2021) 37 Journal of Contract Law 105

Murphy J, 'Alternatives to Workplace Investigations' *Worklogic* (13 October 2021) <https://www.worklogic.com.au/workplace-investigations/alternatives-to-workplace-investigations/> accessed 31 July 2025

Naughton R, 'Termination of Employment and Workplace Investigations' (2016) 22 Employment Law Bulletin 186

Nel P and others, *Human Resource Management in Australia* (2nd edn, OUP 2016)

Nethercote JR, 'The Australian Public Service: Statutory, Doctrinal and Institutional Arrangements for Its Governance' in Marilyn Pittard and Phillipa Weeks (eds), *Public Sector Employment in the Twenty-First Century* (ANU Press 2007)

Nickels L and Hennessy K, 'Stop Bully! How the New Anti-Bullying Measures in the Fair Work Act Operate' 18 Inhouse Counsel 19

Odgers S, *Uniform Evidence Law* (15th edn, Thomson Reuters 2020)

O'Neil M and White S, 'Trade Unions and Political Equality' in Hugh Collins, Gillian Lester and Virginia Mantouvalou (eds), *Philosophical Foundations of Labour Law* (OUP 2018)

Oppenheimer A, 'Workplace Harassment Investigations Worldwide' (2019) 10 Association of Workplace Investigators Journal 1

Oppenheimer A and Pratt C, *Investigating Workplace Harassment: How to Be Fair, Thorough, and Legal* (Society for Human Resource Management 2008)

Orifici A, 'Reframing Addis: A Clarification of the Law of Damages for Psychiatric Injury in Dismissal in Elisha v Vision Australia Ltd' (2025) 38(3) Australian Journal of Labour Law 1

Orifici A, 'Unsystematic and Unsettled: A Map of the Legal Dimensions of Workplace Investigations in Australia' (2019) 42 University of New South Wales Law Journal 1075

Ozich C (ed), *Employment Rights Now: Reflections on the Australian Charter of Employment Rights* (Hardie Grant Books 2015)

Paret M, 'Citizenship and Work in Global Capitalism: From Domination to Aspiration' (2018) 12 Sociology Compass e12602

Peters A, 'Planning the Investigation' in Paula Hoctor and Kerryn Tredwell (eds), *Workplace Investigations: Principles and Practice* (2nd edn, LexisNexis Butterworths 2023)

Pickering M, 'Qualitative Content Analysis' in Michael S Lewis-Beck, Alan Bryman, and Tim F Liao (eds), *The SAGE Encyclopedia of Social Science Research Methods* (SAGE 2004)

Pittard M, 'Protection from Unfair Dismissal' in Mordy Bromberg and Mark Irving (eds), *Australian Charter of Employment Rights* (Hardie Grant Books 2007)

Pittard M and Weeks P (eds), *Public Sector Employment in the Twenty-First Century* (ANU Press 2007)

Plosker E, 'Employers Can Factor into a Disciplinary Investigation Prior Incidents Even If They Went Unpunished at the Time' (*BDBF LLP*, 1 February 2018) <https://www.bdbf.co.uk/employers-can-factor-disciplinary-investigation-prior-incidents-even-went-unpunished-time/> accessed 27 July 2025

Prassl J, *Humans As a Service: The Promise and Perils of Work in the Gig Economy* (OUP 2018)

Prior L, 'Content Analysis' in Patricia Leavy (ed), *The Oxford Handbook of Qualitative Research* (2nd edn, OUP 2020)

Productivity Commission, 'Workplace Relations Framework (Inquiry Report No. 76)' (2015)

Rawling M, 'Regulating beyond the Employment Relationship to Protect Road Transport and "Gig" Workers: The Regulated Worker Provisions' (2024) 37 Australian Journal of Labour Law 178

Rawls J, *John Rawls, A Theory of Justice* (Otfried Höffe ed, Joost den Haan tr, Brill 2013)

Read R, 'A Loophole Big Enough to Walk a Stolen Horse Through: Delegates' Rights and the Precarity of Workplace Activism under the Fair Work Act' (2024) 37 Australian Journal of Labour Law 157

Rees N, Rice S and Allen D, *Australian Anti-Discrimination and Equal Opportunity Law* (3rd edn, The Federation Press 2018)

Reidy S, 'Effective Dispute Resolution' in Mordy Bromberg and Mark Irving (eds), *Australian Charter of Employment Rights* (Hardie Grant Books 2007)

Remedios M, 'Ten Tips for Successful Workplace Investigations' (2017) 69 Governance Directions 234

Reynolds DB and Kleiner BH, 'Understanding and Managing Sexual Harassment in Organisations' (1995) 14 Equal Opportunities International 37

Richardson L and Gashi M, 'Bracing for the Worst: The Role of Support Persons in Workplace Investigations' 22 Employment Law Bulletin 284.

Riley J, 'Good Faith Performance' in Mordy Bromberg and Mark Irving (eds), *Australian Charter of Employment Rights* (Hardie Grant Books 2007)

Riley J, 'Good Faith and Bargaining Overview', *The Debate: Good Faith and the Employment Relationship* (Australian Institute of Employment Rights 2009) <https://www.aierights.com.au/wp-content/uploads/2011/05/The-Debate-Good-Faith-and-the-employment-relationship.pdf> accessed 20 August 2025

Riley J, 'Siblings But Not Twins: Making Sense of "Mutual Trust" and "Good Faith" in Employment Contracts' (2012) 36 Melbourne University Law Review 521

Riley Munton J, 'Preface' in James Fleming (ed), *A New Work Relations Architecture: The AIER Model for the Future of Work* (Hardie Grant Books 2022)

Robertson M, 'Workplace Investigator Ethics' in Paula Hoctor and Kerryn Tredwell (eds), *Workplace Investigations: Principles and Practice* (2nd edn, LexisNexis Butterworths 2023)

Robinson M (ed), *Judicial Review: The Laws of Australia* (Thomson Reuters 2014)

Rollinson M, 'Call in the Experts' *The Sydney Morning Herald* (27 September 2018) <https://www.smh.com.au/business/workplace/call-in-the-experts-20180927-p506hp.html> accessed 9 July 2025

Roos C, Bostock M and Forder S, 'Management of a Successful Workplace Investigation' in Paula Hoctor and Kerryn Tredwell (eds), *Workplace Investigations: Principles and Practice* (2nd edn, LexisNexis Butterworths 2023)

Roos C and Tredwell K, 'Perils in the Pursuit of Procedural Fairness' (Australasian Association of Workplace Investigators Conference, Sydney 2019)

Rose S, 'Workplace Investigations Series – Getting It Right (Part 1)' (*Moores*, 5 July 2019) <https://www.moores.com.au/news/workplace-investigations-series-getting-it-right-part-1/> accessed 25 July 2025

Rose S, 'Workplace Investigations Series–Navigating the "Human" Element in HR Investigations (Part 2)' (*Moores*, 17 September 2019) <https://www.moores.com.au/news/workplace-investigations-series-navigating-the-human-element-in-hr-investigations-part-2/> accessed 31 July 2025

Ross I, 'Commentary: Industrial Citizenship' in Joe Isaac and Russell Lansbury (eds), *Labour Market Deregulation: Rewriting the Rules* (The Federation Press 2005)

Rozen P, 'A Safe and Healthy Workplace' in Mordy Bromberg and Mark Irving (eds), *Australian Charter of Employment Rights* (Hardie Grant Books 2007)

Ruskin N, 'Role of Lawyers in Workplace Investigations' (2014) 18 Inhouse Counsel 62

Safe Work Australia, 'Comparison of Workers' Compensation Arrangements in Australia and New Zealand' (2021) 28th edn <https://www.safeworkaustralia.gov.au/doc/comparison-workers-compensation-arrangements-australia-and-new-zealand-2021> accessed 20 August 2025

Safe Work Australia, 'Managing Psychosocial Hazards at Work' (2022) Model Code of Practice <https://www.safeworkaustralia.gov.au/doc/model-code-practice-managing-psychosocial-hazards-work> accessed 9 August 2023

Safe Work Australia, 'Australian Work Health and Safety Strategy 2023–2033' (2023) Strategy Paper <https://www.safeworkaustralia.gov.au/awhs-strategy_23-33> accessed 24 August 2025

Saldaña J, 'Qualitative Data Analysis Strategies' in Patricia Leavy (ed), *The Oxford Handbook of Qualitative Research* (2nd edn, OUP 2020)

Saldaña J, *The Coding Manual for Qualitative Researchers* (4th edn, Thousand Oaks 2021)

Sams PJ, 'Workplace Investigations – The Good, the Bad and the Ugly' (Conference Paper, Australasian Association of Workplace Investigators Conference, 25 October 2019)

Sappideen C, O'Grady P and Riley J, *Macken's Law of Employment* (9th edn, Thomson Reuters 2022)

Scopelliti V, 'Document Examiners: When to Make Use of Them' (*WISE Workplace*, 13 September 2017) <https://www.wiseworkplace.com.au/2017/09/document-examiners-when-to-make-use-of-them/> accessed 31 July 2025

Scopelliti V, 'How to Deal with an Uncooperative Respondent' (*WISE Workplace*, 29 May 2019) <https://www.wiseworkplace.com.au/2019/05/how-to-deal-with-an-uncooperative-respondent/> accessed 31 July 2025

Scopelliti V, 'Interview Techniques for Workplace Investigations' (*WISE Workplace*, 24 July 2019) <https://www.wiseworkplace.com.au/2019/07/interview-techniques-for-workplace-investigations/> accessed 31 July 2025

Scopelliti V, 'Outsourcing or In-House Investigations?' (*WISE Workplace*, 3 October 2019) <https://www.wiseworkplace.com.au/2019/10/outsourcing-or-in-house-investigations/> accessed 31 July 2025

Scopelliti V, 'When a Pre-Determined View Leads to an Unfair Investigation' (*WISE Workplace*, 10 October 2019) <https://www.wiseworkplace.com.au/2019/10/when-a-pre-determined-view-leads-to-an-unfair-investigation/> accessed 31 July 2025

Scopelliti V, 'Supporting Stakeholder Wellbeing during an Investigation' (*WISE Workplace*, 26 March 2021) <https://www.wiseworkplace.com.au/2021/03/supporting-stakeholder-wellbeing-during-an-investigation/> accessed 31 July 2025

See A, Barry M and Peetz D, 'The Australian Unfair Dismissal Regime: Exploring How Applications for Unfair Dismissal Remedy Resolve' (2022) 35 Australian Journal of Labour Law 27, 41–42

Selznick P, *Law, Society, and Industrial Justice* (Russell Sage Foundation 1969)

Sen A, *Development as Freedom* (OUP 2001)

Sharp A, 'Workplace Bullying: Are Stop Bullying Orders Really the Answer?' (2014) 1 Law Society Journal 82

Sivaraman G, 'Poor Workplace Investigations Can Leave Path of Destruction' *Brisbane Times* (7 February 2017) <https://www.brisbanetimes.com.au/business/workplace/poor-workplace-investigations-can-leave-path-of-destruction-20170207-gu7kmo.html> accessed 9 July 2025

Spry M, 'Natural Justice and Public Sector Misconduct Investigations' (2007) 54 Australian Institute of Administrative Law Forum 117

Stacey H and Page A, *Investigative Interviewing: A Guide for Workplace Investigators* (WISE Workplace 2012)

Standing G, 'The Australian Charter of Employment Rights: The Missing Dimensions' (2008) 50 Journal of Industrial Relations 355

Standing G, *Work after Globalization: Building Occupational Citizenship* (Edward Elgar 2009)

Starkey E, 'What Does Practical Justice Look Like for Complainants and Respondents?' (Conference Paper, Australasian Association of Workplace Investigators Conference, Melbourne 2017)

Stewart A and others, 'The (Omni)Bus That Broke Down: Changes to Casual Employment and the Remnants of the Coalition's Industrial Relations Agenda' (2021) 34 Australian Journal of Labour Law 132

Stewart A, Forsyth A and Irving M, *Creighton and Stewart's Labour Law* (7th ed, The Federation Press 2025)

Stredwick J, *An Introduction to Human Resource Management* (3rd edn, Taylor & Francis Group 2013)

Streeck W, 'Industrial Citizenship under Regime Competition: The Case of the European Works Councils' (1997) 4 Journal of European Public Policy 643

Sutherland C, 'Making the "BOOT" Fit: Reforms to Agreement-Making from Work Choices to Fair Work' in Anthony Forsyth and Andrew Stewart (eds), *Fair Work: The New Workplace Laws and the Work Choices Legacy* (The Federation Press 2009)

Sweatman K and Ruskin N, 'Gone Fishing: When and How to Conduct Workplace Investigations' (2012) 15 Inhouse Counsel 282

Sweeney A and Cornes R, 'Gathering Evidence' in Paula Hoctor and Kerryn Tredwell (eds), *Workplace Investigations: Principles and Practice* (LexisNexis Butterworths 2023)

Taylor A, 'Disability Discrimination, the Duty to Make Adjustments and the Problem of Persistent Misreading' (2019) 45 MonashULawRw 461

Thawley T, 'Adversarial and Inquisitorial Procedures in the Administrative Appeals Tribunal' (1997) 4 Australian Journal of Administrative Law 61

Thomas BJ and Harris S, 'A New, Established Approach to Managing Misbehavior: System Justification Theory' (2021) 50 Personnel Review 1582

Thomlinson C and Rubin J, *Human Resources Guide to Workplace Investigations* (2nd edn, Thomson Reuters 2018)

Thomson A, '"It Was Hell": Former Sydney Hospital Doctor Speaks Out' *The Sydney Morning Herald* (5 July 2023) <https://www.smh.com.au/national/nsw/it-was-hell-former-sydney-hospital-doctor-speaks-out-20230704-p5dll4.html> accessed 9 July 2025

Thomson P, 'Public Servant's Joke Gone Wrong: Code of Conduct Investigation after Staff Member Pulls a Knife' *The Age* (26 February 2016) <https://www.theage.com.au/public-service/public-servants-joke-gone-wrong-code-of-conduct-investigation-after-staff-member-pulls-a-knife-20160223-gn1cjl.html> accessed 9 July 2025

Thornton E, Sivaraman G and James M, 'EILS Seminar: Workplace Investigations' (16 June 2016) <http://www.slideshare.net/mauriceblackburn/eils-seminar-workplace-investigations-june-2016> accessed 31 July 2025

Tidley S, 'Workplace Investigations, Australian Style' (2013) 4 Association of Workplace Investigators Journal 17

Tobin A and Garnett A, 'Misconduct Investigations: Our Top Tips' (2015) 67 Governance Directions 306

Tomasello F, 'From Industrial to Digital Citizenship: Rethinking Social Rights in Cyberspace' (2023) 52 Theory and Society 463

Tredwell K, 'Making Findings and Writing the Investigation Report' in Paula Hoctor and Kerryn Tredwell (eds), *Workplace Investigations: Principles and Practice* (2nd edn, LexisNexis Butterworths 2023)

Tredwell K and Donovan H, 'Categories and Sufficiency of Evidence' in Paula Hoctor and Kerryn Tredwell (eds), *Workplace Investigations: Principles and Practice* (2nd edn, LexisNexis Butterworths 2023)

Turnbull J, 'Participants in a Workplace Investigation–The Untouchables?' (*Seyfarth: Workplace Law & Strategy*, 27 March 2015) <https://www.workplacelawandstrategy.com.au/2015/03/participants-in-a-workplace-investigation-the-untouchables/> accessed 31 July 2025

Turnbull J, 'Initial Considerations' in Paula Hoctor and Kerryn Tredwell (eds), *Workplace Investigations: Principles and Practice* (2nd edn, LexisNexis Butterworths 2023)

Turner P, 'Workplace Investigations: Being the Respondent in a Workplace Complaint' (*Maurice Blackburn*) <https://www.mauriceblackburn.com.au/blog/employment-issues/being-respondent-in-a-workplace-complaint/> accessed 9 July 2025

United Nations, 'Transforming Our World: The 2030 Agenda for Sustainable Development (Adopted 25 September 2015, Entered into Force 1 January 2016)' GA Res 70/1, UN GAOR, 70th sess, 4th plen mtg, Agenda Items 15 and 116, UN Doc A/RES/70/1 <https://sdgs.un.org/2030agenda> accessed 28 July 2025

United Nations, 'Universal Declaration of Human Rights (Adopted 10 December 1948)' UNGA Res 217 (III), UN GAOR, UN Doc A/810 <https://www.un.org/sites/un2.un.org/files/2021/03/udhr.pdf> accessed 28 July 2025

Visser J, 'Trade Unions in the Balance' (2019) ILO/ACTRAV Working Paper <https://www.ilo.org/wcmsp5/groups/public/---ed_dialogue/---actrav/documents/publication/wcms_722482.pdf> accessed 28 July 2025

Waldron J, 'Law, Dignity and Self-Control' in Jeremy Waldron and Meir Dan-Cohen (eds), *Dignity, Rank, and Rights* (OUP 2012)

Walker V, 'Confidentiality: The Personnel Dilemma' (1992) 4 Employee Counselling Today 15

Walter M, *Social Research Methods* (4th edn, OUP 2019)

Webber A, 'Duty of Care and the Employee Accused of Wrongdoing' (*Personnel Today*, 31 July 2019) <https://www.personneltoday.com/hr/dismissed-worker-duty-of-care/> accessed 27 July 2025

Webley L, 'Qualitative Approaches to Empirical Legal Research' in Peter Crane and Herbert M Kritzer (eds), *The Oxford Handbook of Empirical Legal Research* (OUP 2010)

Weeks P, 'The Reshaping of Australian Public Service Employment Law' in Phillipa Weeks and Marilyn Pittard (eds), *Public Sector Employment in the Twenty-First Century* (ANU Press 2007)

Weil D, *The Fissured Workplace: Why Work Became So Bad for So Many and What Can Be Done to Improve It* (Harvard University Press 2014)

Weiss M, 'Re-Inventing Labour Law?' in Guy Davidov and Brian A Langille (eds), *The Idea of Labour Law* (OUP 2011)

Williams G, 'The Constitution and a National Industrial Relations Regime' (2005) 10 Deakin Law Review 498

Williams N, '*Bartlett v Australia & New Zealand Banking Group Ltd* [2016] NSWCA 30 (7 March 2016)' (2016) 37 Adelaide Law Review 571

Williamson BC, 'Disciplinary Investigations: The Need To Be Both Effective And Fair' (14 February 2019) <http://brianwilliamson.com.au/Docs/Investigations%20-%20BCW%20-%20140219.pdf> accessed 25 July 2025

Wilson J, 'Dodging Quagmires in Disciplinary Investigations' *The Age* (31 March 2014) <https://www.theage.com.au/public-service/dodging-quagmires-in-disciplinary-investigations-20140330-35rh5.html> accessed 25 July 2025

Wilson J, 'Investigating Bullying or Bullying by Investigation?' *The Sydney Morning Herald* (28 April 2017) <https://www.smh.com.au/public-service/investigating-bullying-or-bullying-by-investigation-20170428-gvv4mx.html> accessed 25 July 2025

Wilson J, 'The Most Common Workplace Issues That Never Reach the Courts' (*The Mandarin*, 21 August 2017) <https://www.themandarin.com.au/82592-common-workplace-issues-never-reach-courts/> accessed 31 July 2025

Wilson J and Pender K, 'Searching for an Elusive Truth: Briginshaw in the Workplace' (2021) 259 Ethos: Law Society of the ACT Journal 36

Woodrow C and Guest DE, 'When Good HR Gets Bad Results: Exploring the Challenge of HR Implementation in the Case of Workplace Bullying: Implementation of Workplace Bullying Policy' (2014) 24 Human Resource Management Journal 38

Workplace Express, 'Bullying Jurisdiction to Put Spotlight on Unregulated Workplace Investigators: Lawyer' *Workplace Express* (9 April 2014)

Wyborn J and others, 'Workplace Investigations Refresher 01: Where to Begin' (*Clayton Utz*, 4 February 2021) <https://www.claytonutz.com/insights/2021/february/workplace-investigations-refresher-part-1-where-to-begin> accessed 31 July 2025

Wyborn J, Discipio A and Beasley C, 'Workplace Investigations Refresher Part 11: Weighing Evidence' *Clayton Utz* (23 December 2021) <https://www.claytonutz.com/insights/2021/december/workplace-investigations-refresher-part-11-weighing-evidence> accessed 31 July 2025

Wyborn J, Matthews C and Beasley C, 'Workplace Investigations Refresher Part 3: Legal Professional Privilege and Workplace Investigation Reports' (*Clayton Utz*, 1 April 2021) <https://www.claytonutz.com/knowledge/2021/april/workplace-investigations-refresher-part-3-legal-professional-privilege-and-workplace-investigation-reports> accessed 25 July 2025

Zetlin D and Whitehouse G, 'Gendering Industrial Citizenship' (2003) 41 British Journal of Industrial Relations 773

Index

For the benefit of digital users, indexed terms that span two pages (e.g., 52–53) may, on occasion, appear on only one of those pages.